The Nuclear Borderlands

1 The Enlightened Earth

The Enlightenment has always aimed at liberating men from fear and establishing their sovereignty. Yet the fully enlightened earth radiates disaster triumphant.
—Horkheimer and Adorno, *The Dialectic of Enlightenment*

The nuclear age began in earnest in New Mexico.[1] Los Alamos scientists created much more than simply a new technology with the invention of a military atomic device in 1945; they engendered new forms of consciousness, new means of being in the world distinct from those that came before. For over a half century now, the psychosocial spaces of American modernity have been shaped by the most prominent legacies of Los Alamos: a utopian belief in the possibility of an unending technological progress, and an everyday life structured around the technological infrastructures of human extinction. The Manhattan Project not only marks the beginning of American big science and a new kind of international order; the invention of the atomic bomb transformed everyday life, catching individuals within a new articulation of the global and the local, and producing social imaginaries drawn taut by the contradictory impulses of the technologically celebratory and the nationally insurgent, as well as the communally marginalized and the individually abject.

Looking back across the temporal surface of the Cold War, the purple fireball and glassified green earth created in the deserts of New Mexico at exactly 5:29:45 a.m. on July 16, 1945, can only be narrated as a moment of historical rupture and transformation (see Figure 1.1).[2] For the detonation of the first atomic bomb marked the end of one kind of time, and the apotheosis of another, an uncanny modernity that continually exceeds the language of "national security," "mutual assured destruction," the "Cold War," or even "terror." For this reason alone, we might profitably return to the northern Rio Grande to assess the legacy and implications of one of the twentieth century's most enigmatic, yet lasting, achievements. For with the flash of the explosion known as Trinity, certain contradictions in modern life—involving the linkages

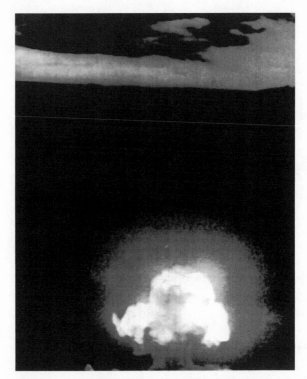

1.1. The Trinity Test, July 16, 1945, 5:29:45 a.m.
(U.S. Department of Energy photograph)

between secrecy, security, technoscience, and national identity—become increasingly extreme in the United States, and much of this book is an exploration of the anxieties and ambivalences in American power made visible by the end of the Cold War in New Mexico.

Attention to the local effects of the nuclear age, however, also promises a different vantage point on the phantasmagoria of nuclear conflict promulgated during the Cold War, both disturbing its familiarity and challenging its social purpose. Since Hiroshima and Nagasaki, nuclear war has repeatedly been marked in American culture as "the unthinkable," an official declaration that no government would willingly engage in actions that could potentially end life on earth.[3] But today, in the absence of the Soviet-U.S. global polarism and during an expanding "war on terror," we might interrogate the "unthinkability" of the nuclear age anew, and ask: What kind of cultural work is performed in the act of making something "unthinkable"? How has the social regulation of the imagination—in this case, of nuclear war—been instrumental in American life since World War II? What are the legacies of this social project after the Cold War, in a world once again negotiating "nuclear terror"? For to make something "unthinkable" is to place it outside of language, to deny its comprehensibility and elevate it into the realm of the sublime. The incomprehensibility of the bomb is therefore an enormous national-cultural project, one whose effects constantly exceed the modernist logics required to build the nuclear complex in the first place. But what then encompasses the cultural spaces left behind when a national project of the size and scope of the nuclear complex is excised from political discourse? What happens when the submerged cultural legacies of nuclear nationalism come flooding back into the public sphere, as they did for communities in and around Los Alamos upon the end of the Cold War in 1991 or for a broader American public after the terrorist attacks on New York and Washington on September 11, 2001?

In a post–Cold War world, then, we might usefully interrogate the cultural work performed by a nation-state in managing so explicit an image of its own end, of controlling the terms whereby citizens are confronted with their own, impossibly sudden, nonexistence. For if it is reasonable, as Benedict Anderson has argued, to "begin a consideration of the cultural roots of nationalism with death" (1991: 10), then the nuclear complex remains a particularly potent national project, informing one way in which citizens imagine both their collective lives and deaths. The unthinkability of the nuclear age has from this vantage point been perhaps *the* American nation-building project since World War II. The cultural logic of ensuring the "immortality" of the nation, which Anderson has shown is characteristic of the modern nation-state, is also, however, immediately compromised by the reality of nuclear weapons. The contradiction nuclear arsenals evoke is that as more national-cultural energy is put into generating "security" through improved weapons systems, the vulnerability of the nation to new military technology is ever further revealed; indeed, as the U.S.-Soviet arms race demonstrated, it is worked out in ever-exacting detail. The pursuit of "security" through ever-greater technological means of destruction thus troubles the nation's internal coherence by constantly forwarding the everyday possibility of the ultimate national absence. Indeed, what Paul Edwards (1996) has called the "closed world" system of American Cold War technology—the ideological commitment to encompassing the globe with perfect technologies of command, control, surveillance, and military nuclear power—ultimately offered nuclear superpowers a perverse new form of immortality, one drawn from the recognition that a nuclear war might well be the last significant *national* act on earth.

The "unthinkability" of the nuclear age has right from the beginning, then, produced its rhetorical opposite; namely, a proliferation of discourses about vulnerability and insecurity.[4] This is easiest to see in the periods of heightened international tensions of the early 1950s, 1960s, 1980s, and 2000s, when the unthinkability of nuclear war, in fact, made it impossible for many in the United States to think about anything else. But even in periods of relative international calm, Cold War nuclear discourse retained a specific trajectory in the United States, one that inevitably focused attention on the imagined end of the nation, and thus of life itself. Given that a nuclear war has not yet occurred, this apocalypticism remains at the level of a national imaginary. Nevertheless, an imagined end to the nation, or the human species, energized the argumentative core of (post) Cold War nuclear discourse and continues to this day to enable social movements both for and against the construction of the U.S. nuclear complex.[5] In other words, the nuclear politics of the Cold War, the steady discourse and counterdiscourse of nuclear/antinuclear commitments, has promoted a specific apocalyptic vision in the United States, one that has made it difficult to see how the nuclear age has already impacted everyday lives.

With the end of that multigenerational project known as the Cold War, we might now interrogate the repressed spaces within nuclear modernism; that is, the social logics, technoscientific practices, and institutional effects that were rendered invisible by this national fixation on extinction. We can now examine how more than a half century of international work to construct a global nuclear economy has affected everyday lives on a local level, paying attention to the regional and cultural complexities and specificities of life in the nuclear age. For while we all still live in a world quite capable of nuclear war, the cumulative effects of the nuclear complex are already both more subtle and more ever-present than (post) Cold War culture has allowed, affecting some lives more than others, and impacting local ecologies and cultural cosmologies in ways that we have yet to recognize fully. To approach nuclear technologies from the quotidian perspectives of tactile experience, focusing on how people experience an orientation in time and space, and an individual relationship with a national-cultural infrastructure, is to fundamentally rewrite the history of the nuclear age. Indeed, attention to the local effects of the nuclear complex makes strange the invisibility of the U.S. arsenal in everyday American life, and allows us to interrogate the national-cultural work performed in the act of making so enormous a national project reside in the "unthinkable." Consequently, it may be more useful to approach nuclear war as a phantasmagoria, a spectral fascination that distracts attention from the ongoing daily machinations of the U.S. nuclear complex. Indeed, the constant end game articulation of nuclear discourse has, I think, enabled two of the most profound cultural achievements of the nuclear age: the near erasure of the nuclear economy from public view, and the banalization of the *U.S.* nuclear weapons in everyday

American life. The consequence of this historical structure is that the U.S. nuclear complex is primarily visible today only in moments of crisis, when the stakes of nuclear policy are framed by heightened anxiety, and thus, subject, not to reassessment and investigation, but to increased fortification. The material and cultural effects of U.S. nuclear weapons— involving local, national, and global structures—are more deeply embedded in everyday life than is visible in moments of national crisis, making a contemporary analysis of the regional effects of the Manhattan Project simultaneously an ethnographic study of a specific technoscientific project, a sociocultural investigation into American Cold War culture, and an anthropology of American power in the twenty-first century.

THE NUCLEAR STATE OF EMERGENCY

From the invention of the cross-bow in the 12th century, to gunpowder in the Middle Ages, to Alfred Nobel's invention of high explosives, man has had but few restraints on having learned how to kill more effectively. Our ability to destroy each other reached new heights early this century with the invention of mustard and nerve gases, and airplanes and submarines deployed in war. By World War II, mankind had escalated its ability to kill 55 million people in one war. The atomic bomb changed all of this . . . Over 80 million of the 100 million war related deaths so far this century occurred in its first half. I believe the devastation and the psychological impact of Hiroshima and Nagasaki combined with the realization of even greater destructive power of modern nuclear arsenals, drove deterrence diplomacy and bought us time. It appears that for the first time in human history mankind has paused and not used the latest technological innovation in warfare . . . However, the resulting "peace" was an uneasy one at best as the Soviet Union and the United States built nuclear arsenals totaling the destructive power of millions of Hiroshimas. —Sig Hecker (director, Los Alamos National Laboratory), *Reflections on Hiroshima and Nagasaki*

The tradition of the oppressed teaches us that the "state of emergency" in which we live is not the exception but the rule. We must attain to a conception of history that is in keeping with this insight. Then we shall clearly realize that it is our task to bring about a real state of emergency, and this will improve our position in the struggle against Fascism. One reason why Fascism has a chance is that in the name of progress its opponents treat it as a historical norm. The current amazement that the things we are experiencing are "still" possible in the twentieth century is not philosophical. This amazement is not the beginning of knowledge—unless it is the knowledge that the view of history which gives rise to it is untenable.

—Walter Benjamin, *Theses on the Philosophy of History*

Sig Hecker's statement offers a compelling modernist history of the nuclear age, a Cold War narrative of nuclear technology "buying time" for humanity even as the stakes of national conflict grow ever higher. As director of Los Alamos National Laboratory (LANL) (1985–97), Hecker's primary job was to certify the viability of the nuclear arsenal, to ensure that the United States maintain the ability to inflict "overwhelming power" against any would-be aggressor. His genealogy of the bomb—moving from the crossbow to the thermonuclear warhead—forwards weapons science as an inseparable component of historical progress. Published in LANL's *Newsbulletin* on the occasion of the fiftieth anniversary of the atomic bombing of Hiroshima and Nagasaki in 1995, Hecker's essay reiterates the necessity of nuclear weapons as a means of deterring both nuclear and conventional war. He ends with a call for Los Alamos employees to "keep the horrid images of Hiroshima and Nagasaki in front of us as a stark reminder of what we must avoid" and to focus attention "on dealing with the current nuclear dangers to the benefit of mankind so that at the 100th anniversary people can look back and say the Manhattan Project turned out all right."

What is remarkable in this statement is not simply the brute calculation of life attributed to the U.S. nuclear arsenal—80 million killed in twentieth-century wars before the bomb, 20 million after—or the taken-for-granted assumption that the existence of nuclear weapons prevented a third World War in this century; it is that Hecker seems to suggest that the bomb's primary power is cultural not technological: nuclear weapons affect how people think. But while the cultural work of the bomb may have postponed a nuclear war with the Soviet Union, it did not slow the commitment to developing technologies of mass destruction. Between August 6, 1945, and August 6, 1995, the power of nuclear weapons, as Hecker notes, increased many thousandfold, and technologies were invented to deliver U.S. nuclear weapons to any part of the world in less than thirty minutes. Hecker's notion of the cultural work of the bomb is, then, quite specific, one based on separating the social effects of the bomb from the reality of the bomb itself. For implicit within the cosmology of weapons scientists is an understanding that nuclear technologies are now forever part of the world system, and consequently, the need for a state-of-the-art nuclear arsenal, as a deterrent, is a near-permanent feature of modern life. Thus, the Manhattan Project can never really end. It can, however, "turn out all right" in Hecker's view, if a national commitment to new technologies enables renewed investment in nuclear power, a global system for tracking plutonium, environmental cleanup of contaminated sites, safe storage of nuclear waste, and ongoing investments to maintain a state-of-the-art nuclear arsenal. Within this philosophy of history, the end of the Cold War offers merely a moment of pause, a chance to readjust the trajectory of the Manhattan Project, but it does not significantly reduce (indeed, in some ways it reenergizes) the technostrategic worldview that enabled the U.S. nuclear complex to become ubiquitous in the first place.

Walter Benjamin's, like Hecker's, theory of progress is grounded in the terrifying reality of World War. But whereas Hecker looks to technology to provide solutions to nationalist violence, Benjamin looks for answers in the vulnerability of the human body to modern technology. Benjamin wrote the "Theses on the Philosophy of History" while trying to escape an advancing Nazi army in 1940. It has often been evoked by contemporary Euro-American scholars as a prescient critique of the anesthesia-effect of modern life, the increasing sense of isolation and insulation from experience brought about by the combined effect of the swift pace of new industrial technologies and a flood of new urban forms (see Buck-Morss 1991). Benjamin believed this overstimulation of the body after World War I forced individuals to retreat inward, to take psychological refuge from the new dangers of an increasingly industrialized world by cutting themselves off from sensory experience, by anesthetizing themselves in everyday life.[6] By drawing together contemporary social forms and their recently outmoded predecessors to create a "dialectical image," Benjamin sought to produce a "shock" effect, one that revealed the constantly reconstructed sameness of modern life, enabling people to break through the trancelike state produced by a sea of changing commodities and technologies, and envision an emancipatory social movement. In this way, he sought to create "a real state of emergency" that would disrupt the historical possibility of fascism by changing the terms of "progress" to emphasize not the machine, but the quality of everyday life and the fragility of the human body.

Though Benjamin did not live to enter the nuclear age, his critique of modernity in the 1930s remains relevant to any investigation into how nuclear technologies have affected everyday life since the bombing of Hiroshima and Nagasaki. For Benjamin saw not only the liberatory potential of technology but also how the aestheticizing effects of technology could enable new kinds of mass control, making industrial warfare even seem beautiful, and therefore, seductive (1969b: 241).[7] In his most celebrated essay, "The Work of Art in the Age of Mechanical Reproduction," largely remembered for its embrace of technology as a form of social revolution, Benjamin also warned that "all efforts to render politics aesthetic culminate in one thing: war" (1969b: 240–41; see also Buck-Morss 1992). The aestheticizing of nuclear technology by nation-states during the Cold War would elevate Benjamin's question about the social consequences of industrial technology into the realm of planetary survival. Indeed, America's initial response to fascism was profoundly modernist: it consisted of a radical break with history achieved through a new industrial technology, the atomic bomb. The Manhattan Project, quite subversively, produced the kind of "shock" effect Benjamin had hoped to achieve—a new experience of everyday life grounded in the vulnerability of the human body. In the brief window between the bombings of Hiroshima and Nagasaki and the start of the Cold War, many in the United States, including some of the primary figures at Los Alamos, believed that the achievement of the atomic bomb made war obsolete as a means of solving conflict and initiated a global movement for the control of nuclear technologies.[8] America's explosive entry into the nuclear age, thus, produced a flash of insight enabling some in the United States to imagine a fundamental restructuring of (inter)national order. This detonation in political consciousness was on the order of what Benjamin hoped to achieve through his critical work, as national violence was now irrevocably tied to the possibility of human extinction, a reality that seemed to demand imaginative new possibilities for organizing social life.

Nuclear weapons, however, quickly became not merely a "historical norm," they became the preeminent national fetish in the United States. With the official start of the Cold War after the Soviets' first nuclear test on August 29, 1949, nuclear weapons became the one true sign of "superpower" status and the ultimate arbiter of "national security." Constant technological improvements in the scope and versatility of nuclear weapons and missile systems ultimately enabled a global achievement of "mutual assured destruction" (or MAD)—a technoscientific belief system that promised immediate retaliatory nuclear strikes for any nuclear aggression. During the Cold War, the logics behind MAD led to a constantly shrinking window of warning for an incoming nuclear strike. In other words, technological advances within the nuclear complex were paralleled by a global contraction in time and space, creating a "closed world" of American and Soviet technology, which, by the early 1960s, was always less than thirty minutes away from a global firestorm. At the beginning of the twenty-first century these technological systems remain firmly in place: the United States and Russia each maintain over ten thousand nuclear weapons in their arsenals and continue to have nuclear submarines on constant alert, positioned to launch immediate and overwhelming nuclear (counter)strikes. Thus, the technological infrastructure of the Cold War lives on, as do the cultural and environmental effects of our first half century in the nuclear age.

By tracing the transformation of nuclear weapons from a technology producing cultural critique to a technonational fetish, we can see a counterhistory to Hecker's story of technological progress. Following Benjamin, we can trace the cultural reception of preceding "catastrophic" technologies like gunpowder in the sixteenth century or dynamite in the nineteenth century, looking for the human relations rendered invisible by the power of these technologies and noting their tactile effect on experiences of everyday life. For each of these military technologies produced psychological shocks manifested in a new awareness of the fragility of the human body, and therefore produced the possibility for new understandings about the consequences of (nationalist) violence. Each new means of destruction, however, also required a greater level of social anesthesia to normalize its impact on everyday life. For Benjamin, this dulling of the senses to violence was accomplished through a fundamental reorganization of the human sensorium under modern industrial life. The industrial revolution restructured everyday life around repetition (the factory assembly line), speed (city life), and technologically mediated violence (industrial accidents and mechanized war). The repetitive shocks to the body as sensory organ produced by these new social forms required a new means of processing stimuli, a system based not on engaging one's environment but on insulating and protecting the sensorium from it. As Susan Buck-Morss explains it (1992: 18), Benjamin believed that:

> being "cheated out of experience" has become the general state, as the synaesthetic system is marshaled to parry technological stimuli in order to protect both the body from the trauma of accident and the psyche from the trauma of perceptual shock. As a result, the system reverses its role. Its goal is to numb the organism, to deaden the senses, to repress memory: the cognitive system of synaesthetics has become, rather, one of anaesthetics.

That is, the traumatic experience of rapid technological change has produced a reversal of the polarity of the human senses, which increasingly work not to engage the world but to insulate individuals from it.[9]

We can see this new type of modernity expressed in how the U.S. military responded to one of the immediate physiological limitations of the nuclear age: flashblindness. The visual intensity of a nuclear explosion, which reaches the brilliance of thousand midday suns, readily blinds; without eye protection the observing retina can burn, resulting in lesions on the eye and permanent blindness. In the early days of the Cold War, nuclear war planners set out to assess how the blast effects of a nuclear bomb would impact soldiers (and pilots in particular, as they would be responsible for delivering nuclear bombs in an era before intercontinental missiles). A series of flashblindness experiments were conducted at the Nevada Test Site in the 1950s that illustrates the new cognitive and anesthetic order of the nuclear age. During Operation Upshot-Knothole in 1953, twelve army volunteers were placed in a light-tight trailer with their right eyes covered. A shuttered lens was placed over their left eyes and synch-calibrated to the flash of a nuclear explosion. Five nuclear devices, ranging from seven to fourteen miles in distance from the trailer, were detonated. Each nuclear flash blinded the volunteers, allowing scientists to measure exactly how long it took their vision to return. A number of protective lenses were tested in the experiments, and the final report concludes:

> reasonably good central vision (20/40) under reduced illumination (1.57 HIT) returned in approximately 154 sec[onds] . . . Peripheral vision returned in an average of 160 seconds under 0.001 HIT luminance (approximately that of a moonless night sky) and in an average of 249 seconds under 0.00001 HIT of luminances (slightly less than moonless night sky with overcast). It is concluded that the filter of the type used protects almost all individuals from retinal burns under the conditions of the experiment and allows performance of typical visual tasks required of a pilot flying the aircraft within 20 to 60 sec[onds] following the flash of the atomic detonation.[10]

The filter protects almost all individuals from retinal burns. Here we have a demonstration of a new anesthetic system at work. These flashblindness experiments explore exactly how a new technology, the atomic bomb, traumatizes the human body, and record in minute detail the damaged body's effort (in intervals of 154, 160, and 249 seconds) to recover.[11] Flashblindness is a literal impairment of sensibility. The shock of the nuclear flash traumatizes the visual sense organ, and the process of recovery requires blindness, a deadening of the senses. Here, the technological reality of a "nuclear age" is located in the ability of the human body to recover from the trauma of a nuclear flash that is literally seared onto the surface of the observing retina. The senses that are vulnerable to the exploding bomb, however, are also transformed via the experiments, producing a new sensorium tuned to the nuclear age. Within the culture of the Cold War, the intent of these experiments was not to eliminate or avoid the trauma but to find a prosthetic device, some form of visual protection, to enable the body to be insulated from repeated nuclear flashes. Such protection would allow the body to survive repeated nuclear shocks, but at a cost of being ever further anesthetized from a tactile experience of the world. These flashblindness experiments reveal a Cold War anesthetic system already ascendant in 1953, one enabling twelve people to volunteer for an experiment in which they were calmly strapped in a chair and, quite meticulously, blinded.

The historical process that registers each new "catastrophic technology" as the end of warfare, the innovation that makes the prospect of war "unthinkable," is ultimately through this anestheticizing process absorbed as simply another fact of modern life, one more shock to the bodily system from which the psyche requires insulation. From this perspective, the Manhattan Project represents a link in a certain modernist chain of being, one that has consistently relied on technology to solve problems of the social, and where the human sensorium evolves by deadening itself in order to normalize the ever-accelerating changes in the technological possibilities of everyday life. For Benjamin, increasing levels of social anesthesia demand new kinds of shock therapy, new means of reorienting individuals to the emancipatory possibilities in everyday life. The end of the Cold War provides a rare moment of pause in the technological advancement of a nuclear, militarized American modernity, and thus offers an opportunity to assess from a new vantage point the effects of the bomb.

In this light, the nuclear bomb is literally an explosive and an explosive cosmological practice, a world-making enterprise that can reorganize how people experience everyday life. In fact, if we locate the Manhattan Project within a genealogy not only of technological progress, but also of an ongoing "state of emergency," what is unique about the bomb is drawn less from its destructiveness than from the acceleration of time and contraction of space it produces. Paul Virilio concurs, arguing in *War and Cinema* that "weapons are tools not just of destruction but also of perception—that is to say, stimulants that make themselves felt through chemical, neurological processes in the sense organs and the central nervous system, affecting human reactions and even the perceptual identification and differentiation of objects" (1989: 6). As a means of reorganizing a tactile engagement with the everyday, nuclear technologies therefore have profound effects regardless of nuclear warfare. The instantaneous destructive power of nuclear weapons and the long-term dangers posed by nuclear materials—*the dangers of the millisecond and the multimillennium*—require a postnational, transhuman view of the future. Indeed, the reliance on nuclear materials that remain deadly for hundreds of thousands of years immediately troubles a national-cultural perspective, as these dangers long exceed any reasonable assumption about the lifetime of the nation-state. Nuclear materials not only disrupt the experience of nation-time (confounding notions of both the present and the future), they also upset the concept of nation-space, in that they demonstrate the permeability, even irrelevance, of national borders to nuclear technologies (to intercontinental missiles and radioactive fallout, for example). The first thing that nuclear technologies explode, then, are experiences of time, undermining the logics of the nation-state by simultaneously enabling both the absolute end of time and the exponential proliferation of a toxic future.

Though caught in the interstitial space between present and future, while exceeding both the global and the local, nuclear weapons nonetheless have very exacting physical and cultural effects. A close analysis of where nuclear projects are situated and how they are executed ultimately reveals a hidden aspect of the nuclear age, namely, the nuclear state's equation of citizenship. For the entire production cycle for a nuclear weapon—from uranium mining, to plutonium production, to weapons testing, to nuclear waste storage—produces human and environmental costs that are borne by particular bodies in particular places. The social contexts informing nuclear projects therefore necessarily evoke questions about historical presence and identity, often of race and rights, always of citizenship and sacrifice. How individuals engage the nuclear complex puts them in a tactile experience not only with the technology of the bomb but also with the nation-state that controls it, making the interrelationship between the human body and nuclear technologies a powerful site of intersection in which to explore questions of national belonging, justice, and everyday life.

We might now ask: What does it mean when the "state of emergency" has *so explicitly* become the rule, when in order to prevent an apocalypse the governmental apparatus has prepared so meticulously to achieve it? What are the cross-cultural effects of living in an age when "mutual assured destruction" is a normalized, all but invisible, fact of life, a technological fix to the proliferation of nuclear weapons that makes the everyday intricately caught up in the negotiation of an imagined, and possibly real, end? How have tactile experiences of the world evolved cross-culturally in response to the growth of the nuclear complex, the spread of nuclear materials, and the cognitive remapping of time and space? What might be the social consequences of living in a world where the everyday has been so thoroughly colonized by the possibility of annihilation that, for most, it has become simply banal? Finally, if in fact people can be so anesthetized by the possibility of extinction that it no longer seems to register, how do we now regain our senses in order to even begin to answer such questions?

If we were to forward a specific historical moment in which nuclear weapons first showed signs of becoming normalized in the American imagination, we might choose Operation Crossroads in 1946. Operation Crossroads was a series of nuclear tests performed by Los Alamos Science Laboratory at Bikini Island in the Marshall Islands. Newsreels from the time show Los Alamos scientists preparing for the detonation, which was designed both to sink the collected remnants of the German, Japanese, and American navies and to explore the effects of a nuclear explosion on everything from animals (goats, pigs, mice, guinea pigs—5,664 in all), to ships (nearly 100), to the ocean itself in order to further understand how to use nuclear weapons in war (Weisgall 1994: 120). In the black-and-white film footage that remains, Vice Admiral Blandy, who directed the tests, takes time to calm public fears: *No, the bomb will not start a chain reaction in the water converting it all to gas and letting all the ships on all the oceans drop down to the bottom. No, the bomb will not blow out the bottom of the sea letting all the water run down the hole. No, the bomb will not destroy gravity.*[12] Here, we see how the first non-wartime public encounter with the bomb provoked a monstrous imagination, a new kind of apocalyptic sensibility. Scientists at Los Alamos preparing for the Trinity test had negotiated a similar imaginary, wondering for a time if a nuclear explosion might not ignite the atmosphere, rendering the earth lifeless, a burnt cinder (Rhodes 1986; Szasz 1984). At Bikini, the first bomb was dropped off-target, leaving many of the ships intact. The second bomb was detonated underwater, destroying the armada and coating the region with dangerous levels of radioactivity.[13] But in many ways the awesomeness of the bomb failed the awesomeness of the American imagination in these highly publicized tests, allowing the first step toward the normalization of the nuclear age—for the world did not come to an end, the ocean and gravity endured. Soon to be recaptured by an elaborate system of government secrecy, the public debate that followed Operation Crossroads was quickly subverted by the start of the Cold War, beginning an oscillation in an American national culture between imagining the nuclear arsenal as the ultimate terror (simultaneously referencing America's vulnerability and its global insurgency) or dismissing it as an utterly banal fact of life, one not worth considering.

In this light, Gertude Stein's (1947) statement on the bomb foreshadows one powerful strand of American thought:

> They asked me what I thought of the atomic bomb. I said I had not been able to take any interest in it . . . What is the use, if they are really as destructive as all that there is nothing left . . . If they are not as destructive as all that then they are just a little more or less destructive than other things . . . I never could take any interest in the atomic bomb, I just couldn't any more than in everybody's secret weapon. That it has to be secret makes it dull and

meaningless. Sure it will destroy a lot and kill a lot, but it's the living that are interesting not the way of killing them, because if there were not a lot left living how could there be any interest in destruction . . . There is so much to be scared of so what is the use of bothering to be scared, and if you are not scared the atomic bomb is not interesting. Everybody gets so much information all day long that they lose their common sense. They listen so much that they forget to be natural. This is a nice story.

If you are not scared the atomic bomb is not interesting. Here, Stein seizes on the apocalypticism of the bomb not to mobilize for or against the nuclear complex but simply to banalize it. Because the bomb is caught up in an imagined end, it becomes simply irrelevant for Stein, one among too many dangerous things to worry about in everyday life. We can see in her explanation the constellation of positions (the dismissal of national security rhetoric, the expected psychic release of an apocalyptic end, and the problematic negotiation of risk in modern life) that enables the bomb to be irrelevant to her, even as others came to feel utterly colonized by it. The power of Stein's statement is that it seems to reveal the failure of the national-security state to control the national imaginary. For Stein, nuclear war is not the "unthinkable," and thus embedded in the nuclear sublime, it is simply irrelevant, a bore.

But if, as Stein argues, the bomb is banal, how did it come to be so? For surely, a national project that has required so enormous a scientific, industrial, and economic sacrifice, and that is intricately involved in defining "security" for every citizen should evoke some feeling of belonging or at least of engagement. What Stein reveals is that public discourse about the bomb is always doubled: simultaneously terrifying and banal. Consequently, it prevents thought through either an anesthesia effect or overstimulation. Both of these attitudes reveal the cognitive impossibility of thinking past the remainderless event, of thinking through the nuclear apocalypse (see Derrida 1984). The notion of technological progress enabling the nuclear complex participates in a modernity that systematically denies this cognitive effect. This type of modernism encourages people to approach the invention of new technology as an inevitable part of an evolving natural world, and not as a cultural product that requires everyday decisions and infrastructural support and that produces profound cultural contradictions at the level of everyday life. In other words, nuclear modernism transforms a cultural invention into an unchanging aspect of a world system, making the other worlds that might still be invented inaccessible and installing a limit to thought at the center of the national security project. In this regard, Stein is more deeply embedded in the nuclear age than she allows. For her statement simply inverts the dominant logic of the U.S. nuclear complex, reducing the bomb to irrelevance while others elevate it into the sublime. The banality of the bomb becomes merely one counterdiscursive effect of an institutional structure that is always preparing for the "unthinkable."

Nevertheless, the utopian potential and traumatic effects of the nuclear project continue to shape American imaginations. The phantasmagoria of nuclear war leads some to find anesthetic-comfort in a privatized everyday space, while encouraging others to find it, not through a psychic withdrawal and disinvestment, but through the flooding of the senses offered by participation in an all-or-nothing cosmology. The term *phantasmagoria* derives from an early-nineteenth-century optical illusion in which magic lanterns were used to project spectral forms and ephemeral beings in parlors and theaters for the amusement of a new middle class.[14] Benjamin found the phantasmagoria to be a powerful illustration of the new technosocial context of modern life, in which a fascination with artificial environments was making access to the real problematic. Here, Susan Buck- Morss identifies the political import of the phantasmagoria as an expansive new social form:

Phantasmagorias are a technoaesthetics. The perceptions they provide are "real" enough—their impact upon the senses and nerves is still "natural" from a neurophysical point of view. But their social function is in each case compensatory. The goal is manipulation of the synaesthetic system by control of environmental stimuli. It has the effect of anaesthetizing the organism, not through numbing, but through flooding the senses. These simulated sensoria alter consciousness, much like a drug, but they do so through sensory distraction rather than chemical alteration, and—most significantly—their effects are experienced collectively rather than individually. Everyone sees the same altered world, experiences the same total environment. As a result, unlike with drugs, the phantasmagoria assumes the position of objective fact. Whereas drug addicts confront a society that challenges the reality of their altered perception, the intoxication of phantasmagoria itself becomes the social norm. Sensory addiction to a compensatory reality become a means of social control. (1992: 22–23)

Approaching nuclear war as a national phantasmagoria allows us to see its social effects without reducing its claim on the real. As Buck-Morss notes, the bodily effects of a phantasmagoria are as real as anything else—they engage the nervous system through tactile stimuli—but as a kind of mass hallucination, they also enable new kinds of social control. Thus, nuclear weapons do not have to be detonated to have profound cultural effects. Indeed, one illustration of the social control enabled by the phantasmagoria of nuclear war is a general inability to see the effects of the nuclear complex itself on everyday life. The hypnotic focus on nuclear annihilation during the Cold War provided a sensory distraction in the

United States, one that displaced the everyday consequences of life within a nuclear economy.

For Cold Warriors, the phantasmagoria of nuclear conflict provoked an imagination that was prolific, resolutely conjuring up, and then institutionally preparing for, the very worst: here one might point to the constant overestimation of the nature of the Soviet nuclear threat by U.S. government officials (i.e., the "bomber gaps" of the 1950s and the "missile gaps" of the 1960s and 1980s; see York 1970). In an imaginative economy of terror, the hyperstimulation of the psyche offered by the possibility of annihilation can only be maintained by expanding the degree of threat; hence, the constant acceleration and improvement in the means of destruction far beyond what was useful for a nuclear deterrent. This can also be seen in American Cold War projects that were less central but perhaps more clearly reveal the totalizing scope of the national security mind-set. Take, for instance, the twenty-four-year, multimillion-dollar CIA investigation into the military uses of psychics, an energetic response to signs of Soviet interest in the paranormal.[15] Here, the imaginative economy of the Cold War is revealed to operate not only at the level of military-industrial technology but also in, perhaps, its truer register, the technology of the mind itself. For just as psychics purport to know the future and to make manifest their desires directly through mental prowess, so too did the apocalyptic mirror-imaging between national security states enable Cold Warriors on each side to see their own worst fears manifested in the other, allowing a constant escalation and acceleration of risk. We begin to see here how a global circuit of imaginative exchange supported the Cold War nuclear economy, a psychically charged space of desire and expectation allowing Cold Warriors in the United States and the Soviet Union to "identify" a world of constantly expanding technological terror—a *nuclear phantasmagoria*—and then set about making that world manifest through a process of international mirror-imaging, misrecognition, and technophilia.

While the nuclear phantasmagoria was undoubtedly instrumental in consolidating certain national projects in the United States during the Cold War,[16] one unexpected development is the ease with which citizens now turn an apocalyptic imagination on the government itself, engendering in the post–Cold War period what some have called a "paranoid public sphere," where a kind of "ambient fear" and conspiratorial subtext seems to inform much of public life.[17] The Manhattan Project, in fact, now exists for many citizens as a prototype for a kind of secretive governmentality taken to be axiomatic of modern life, one in which world-changing national projects are only visible in their permanent effects. A suspicion that a secret master-narrative is operating beneath the surface of everyday life is an important Cold War after-image in the

United States, one that now informs how many citizens engage (or disengage from) their government. For the post–Cold War period has brought forth a series of revelations about the kinds of national sacrifices that U.S. citizens were unwittingly subjected to in the name of "national security" during the Cold War. Revelations about environmental contamination of an unprecedented magnitude, of secret plutonium experiments on citizens, of atmospheric releases of nuclear materials to test fallout patterns over the United States, have all problemitized the purity of the Cold War narrative about the "security" enabled by the nuclear complex. We might now interrogate how the overstimulation of the body produced by an all-or-nothing Cold War cosmology, in which the world was always only minutes away from total annihilation, has mutated; how an addiction to the drama of everyday life in the Cold War—the flooding of the senses enabled by the nuclear phantasmagoria—could be unmoored, transforming into something else, in which the government as readily plays the villain. In any case, the U.S. nuclear complex can only appear to be banal because an enormous national-cultural project has worked to make it so, transforming human senses while deflecting attention away from the multitudinous effects of a nuclear economy on everyday lives. These effects have nothing to do with geopolitical strategy as traditionally conceived, or necessarily with a global apocalypse, but have everything to do with how individuals experience a national and a global sphere, in the context of a lived, localized existence.

Thus, contra Stein, the bomb is not interesting merely because it can be destructive, even if cataclysmically so. It is interesting because it is a *national fetish*, indeed perhaps *the* national fetish of our time. The bomb is not important simply because it offers the possibility of global destruction, but because it requires a nuclear economy to build it, one that has created new experiences of time and space, and that has produced cultural and environmental effects we have yet to account for. The apocalypticism and government secrecy supporting the bomb during the Cold War made it difficult to see the bomb as a social institution, with wide-ranging cultural, environmental, and psychosocial, as well as geostrategic effects. In the post–Cold War period, and really for the first time, we can examine the material and cultural effects of living within a nuclear economy, recognizing both its global impact and its local specificities. But to do so, we need to approach the nuclear complex as a material cosmological statement, in whose nature we can read a constellation of issues concerning technoscience, militarism, and security to be sure, but in which we can also see the terms of national belonging articulated and explore how individuals experience the tactile nature of everyday life. As American reactions to the terrorist attacks on September 11, 2001, clearly demonstrate, the unthinkability of the nuclear age as a discursive practice works to keep a cultural space open, one available for oppositional nation-building through a mobile production of threat. As we shall see, however, "danger" now circulates within a national-cultural space that is also highly mutable, allowing the production of new articulations of "security" and "risk" to readily challenge those produced by the state. The task that remains is to identify the circuits of exchange produced by the U.S. nuclear economy, circuits that engage new articulations of the global and the local but that also expose the tense relationships between regional and national cultures within a sphere of both imagined and material risk.

RADIOACTIVE NATION-BUILDING

At the start of the Manhattan Project, physicist Niels Bohr quipped that it would take turning America into a factory to make enough plutonium to create a nuclear bomb (quoted in DOE 1995c: 2). A half century later America not only proved him right, it turned a project-specific nuclear economy in 1943 into a major national infrastructure (see Figure 1.2). Nuclear weapons remain to this day the preeminent *national* product of the twentieth century, and one of America's leading industries. Between 1940 and 1996 the United States spent over $5.8 trillion to construct seventy thousand nuclear weapons, making the U.S. nuclear arsenal one of the largest industrial enterprises in history (Schwartz 1998). During this time, the United States conducted a total of 1,149 nuclear detonations, the majority of them—942 to be precise—within the continental United States.[18] U.S. nuclear programs now inhabit a total landmass of over 36,000 square miles, larger than the combined states of Massachusetts, New Hampshire, Vermont, Maryland, and the District of Columbia (ibid.). The environmental contamination produced by the Cold War nuclear complex will take a financial and scientific commitment exceeding that of the original Manhattan Project to clean up those sites that can be cleaned up and to stabilize those that are already recognized as national sacrifice zones.[19] The nuclear waste and environmental contamination left from the Cold War, in fact, pose a new kind of threat to the nation, one that will continue generating danger for the hundreds of thousands of years it will take for radioactive materials to decay into less volatile forms. This is one illustration of the new global-local dynamic evoked by the nuclear arsenal—a trade-off between the security offered by a nuclear deterrent in a world of competing nation-states, the domestic consequences of environmental contamination, and the global effects of a nuclear economy dependent on foreign others to maintain its internal stability.

The U. S. Nuclear Weapons Complex

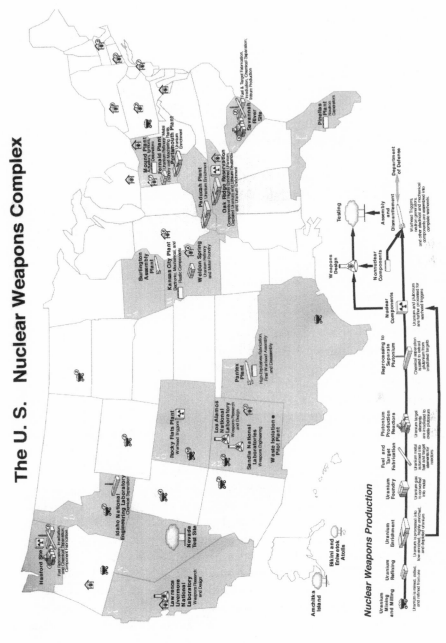

1.2. Map of the U.S. Nuclear Complex. (U.S. Department of Energy illustration)

Still, if one were to ignore the social and environmental consequences associated with the Cold War nuclear complex, then the U.S. nuclear economy might be a highly efficient means for distributing resources throughout American society. Americans from all races, classes, genders, and regions of the country have participated in the production of the U.S. nuclear arsenal. Even in a post–Cold War world, after the United States has provisionally supported a Comprehensive Test Ban Treaty (signed by President Clinton in 1996 but voted down by the Senate in 2000), begun dismantling thousands of weapons, and closed down some of its nuclear production complex, the United States continues to spend over $6 billion a year at the three national laboratories on nuclear weapons science.[20] This $6 billion is actually greater than what Los Alamos, Sandia, and Livermore National Laboratories averaged for nuclear weapons programs during the Cold War (about $3.7 billion; see Schwartz 1998). This money is devoted, however, not to designing, building, and testing new weapons, as it was from 1943 to 1992, but to maintaining nuclear expertise, upgrading the nuclear arsenal, and watching (through an array of new, state-of-the-art technologies) Cold War-era bombs age.[21]

To describe nuclear weapons as the national fetish par excellence is not to be facetious. For over fifty years, the United States has privileged nuclear weapons above all other federal programs, declaring the nuclear arsenal to be of "supreme national interest."[22] When the Berlin Wall came down in 1989, the United States had over 22,000 nuclear weapons deployed around the world; the Soviet Union had over 40,000.[23] Given that the simultaneous detonation of a few thousand weapons might produce a "nuclear winter" effect, severely changing the global climate and potentially bringing on a radioactive ice age, the extravagance of the nuclear arsenal begs a number of questions that have nothing to do with nuclear deterrence.[24] If we approach the nuclear arsenal as a tool for mobilizing a national-cultural imaginary, then we begin to see how the nuclear complex has become a cultural as well as industrial infrastructure. The mobilization of the phantasmagoria of nuclear war as a means of building up a military-industrial infrastructure (from the hydrogen bomb to President Reagan's Strategic Defense Initiative) is well documented, and need not be revisited here (e.g., see FitzGerald 2000; Rhodes 1995; Broad 1992; York 1970). From a cultural point of view, however, an equally important moment in the development of the bomb as national fetish is found in the career trajectory of Robert Oppenheimer, the physicist who directed Los Alamos during the Manhattan Project and who helped define America's immediate postwar nuclear policy. In the American culture of the late 1940s and 1950s, Oppenheimer was perhaps the most prominent public authority on nuclear weapons, serving as a veritable symbol of the "nuclear age" itself. His resistance to building the hydrogen bomb led the Atomic Energy Commission (AEC) to censure him publicly in 1954, resulting in the loss of his security clearance and his expulsion from the arena of nuclear strategists (see Herken 2002). The Oppenheimer trial reinforced a split inherent in the initial organization of the Manhattan Project between a professional nuclear culture of scientists and strategists and the larger American public sphere; the trial provided a national spectacle, demonstrating to all that the Cold War nuclear complex was not only going to be rigorously protected from public debate, but that even those who inhabited its highest levels would be readily sacrificed to the bomb as national fetish (see AEC 1971, as well as Rhodes 1995: 530–59).

But what does it mean to say that nuclear weapons are a "national fetish"? As material objects nuclear weapons occupy a peculiar position in the world system. In his discussion of commodity fetishism, Marx describes the commodity as a "social hieroglyphic" in which a "definite social relation between men . . . assumes, in their eyes, the fantastic form of a relation between things" (1967: 77). I have been arguing thus far that the phantasmagoria of nuclear war allowed an apocalyptic focus on weapons to preempt attention to the everyday social and material effects of the U.S. nuclear production complex. One can also certainly see in the Cold War logics of nuclear deterrence a fetishizing of nuclear technology: Los Alamos and Livermore designed over sixty-five different nuclear weapons systems during the Cold War, each to perform a specific military purpose, and the weapons laboratories in the Soviet Union produced a similarly versatile arsenal. In fact, both countries invested in a technological mirror imaging of each other through nuclear weapons, as each new weapons system was met by a corresponding new technological development on the other side. Thus, we might say that, during the Cold War, the technofetishistic appeal of nuclear weapons enabled a social relation between nations to be mystified as a strategic orientation between machines.

However, before pushing Marx's insight too far, we must ask: Are nuclear weapons actually commodities? A commodity is, in Marx's view, an object in which use value and labor value are erased by social investment in a system of exchange value; that is, all commodities can be converted into their "equivalent worth" in terms of money. While it has taken a multitrillion-dollar economy to produce the U.S. nuclear arsenal, in which nearly every component of the bomb—from microchips to underground nuclear test cables to surveillance satellites—is commodified to some degree, the bomb itself had only one consumer in the twentieth century, the nation-state. Moreover, the bomb as object has never been convertible into a cash relation to other commodities, and it does not circulate among other commodities. Nuclear weapons are national projects in which the normal rules of economic exchange are suspended under the sign of "national security." Since 1945, the United States has determined what its nuclear needs are independent of market logics and regardless of economic expenditure. But if labor value is erased in the bomb as national fetish, and it does not circulate as a commodity among other commodities, what then of its use value? Nuclear weapons are, paradoxically, designed never to be used. Their "use value" is as a deterrent to international conflict, not as weapons to be used in a war that remains "unthinkable." Nuclear weapons are therefore a technoaesthetic whose primary importance in the global order is one of appearance. In other words, while it is important for other nation-states to believe the U.S. nuclear arsenal is viable, it need not actually be so to provide a military deterrent. Thus, nuclear weapons present a bizarre and hyperfetishized material logic, one that confounds the standard logic of commodities, and suggests the arrival of a new social form.

But if the bomb is not a commodity, in the traditional sense, then what is it? I say it is a *national fetish* because it takes a nation-state to build and maintain it, and because the international hierarchy of nation-states is mediated through possession of the bomb. Nuclear weapons therefore maintain a magical hold on people's thinking, and in doing so, energize very specific national-cultural imaginaries. As Ann McClintock (1995: 184) explains it, the fetish:

> stands at the crossroads of psychoanalysis and social history, inhabiting the threshold of both personal and historical memory. The fetish marks a crisis in social meaning as the embodiment of an impossible irresolution. The contradiction is displaced onto and embodied in the fetish objects, which is thus destined to recur with compulsive repetition. Hence the apparent power of the fetish to enchant the fetishists. By displacing power onto the fetish, then manipulating the fetish, the individual gains symbolic control over what might otherwise be terrifying ambiguities. For this reason, the fetish can be called an impassioned object.

Nuclear weapons, as "impassioned objects," are not only the material products of complicated linkages between government, military, and scientific communities but are also national-cultural sites of fetishistic projection. Positioned as the "supreme" object of national power and fascination since 1945, nuclear weapons are imbued with all the contradictions of the nation itself. Each nuclear weapon in the U.S. arsenal presents a site of national cultural fascination/contradiction because it carries displaced historic ambivalences about violence, alterity, and power in a democracy. As industrial infrastructure and national fetish, the bomb links all domains of American society and provides powerful modes of circulation. Indeed, the bomb presents a strange new articulation of what Marcel Mauss (1990) called a "total prestation," an object of exchange that engages all social institutions—economic, political, religious, and sociocultural. For example, building the U.S. nuclear arsenal required unprecedented coordination between military, industrial, academic, and legislative sectors of American society. LANL is part of the Department of Energy (DOE) but managed by the University of California, and maintains a complex set of relations with each branch of the U.S. military as well as corporations and industrial suppliers. A map of the institutions involved in the production of any U.S. nuclear device is a map of the significant political, industrial, academic, and scientific relationships in American society.

During the Cold War, nuclear weapons also participated in a perverse international gift economy, in which the development of a new nuclear device was an invitation for greater and greater military expenditures on each side. Take, for example, the sixteen-month period between September 1961 and December 1962, when the United States and the Soviet Union engaged in an entirely new type of global exchange—detonating well over two hundred nuclear bombs in rapid succession at their respective test sites (averaging three a week).[25] Here the earth itself was used to convey the gift, as the tectonic impacts of each nuclear detonation carried the message of national prowess through the earth's crust to the hundreds of seismic monitoring outposts each country had set up around the world for just such a purpose.[26] Within the circuits of international exchange supporting the Cold War, each detonation required a response. The proliferation of testing during this period (which included the building of the Berlin Wall and the Cuban Missile Crisis) was not merely the rush to verify new weapons designs before an above-ground test moratorium took effect, it was also calculated to display nuclear surplus at a time of heightened Cold War tension, as each side detonated dozens of bombs to send the simple message that they could afford to.

The *intimate* power of this Cold War nuclear gift economy is not often recognized, which is another effect of the bomb as national fetish. It does, however, reveal itself in one of the first acts of the post–Cold War era in Los Alamos; namely, an energetic effort by LANL weapons scientists to meet with their counterparts in Arzamas-16, the Russian nuclear weapons laboratory (see Figure 1.3; and also LANL 1996a). Here, the forty-odd-year struggle between Cold War weapons scientists quickly dissolved into a proliferation of concern by Los Alamos weapon scientists for the fate of their Russian counterparts in a rapidly disintegrating political situation. This unprecedented dialogue generated new joint research projects, a sharing of technology on how to monitor the nuclear arsenal in Russia, as well as cash support for Russian weapons scientists all but abandoned by the Russian state. These conversations revealed that,

1.3. Directors of the U.S. and Russian nuclear weapons laboratories meet in Cheyabinsk-70, Russia, in 1992. (Courtesy of Los Alamos National Laboratory)

while absolutely separated by national affiliation, the American and Russian weapons designers were perhaps more closely linked in techno-scientific culture and worldview than any two such communities on earth. If this seems at odds with the Cold War presumption that each had been devoted to devising ever more powerful and elegant means of destroying the other, it is because we have yet to acknowledge the psychological intimacy of the U.S.-Soviet relationship during the Cold War. By 1995, however, Los Alamos residents who had spent two generations "at war" with the Soviets were investing in clothing, food, and medicine drives for the citizens of their new official "sister city"—Arzamas-16 (now restored to its pre-Soviet name, Sarov).

The strange new intimacy of life in the nuclear age is often overlooked. Partly this is drawn from the ways in which nuclear technologies come to restructure how people experience the world, their positioning in time and space. But it is also drawn from how ubiquitous the nuclear complex has become, from how many unacknowledged aspects of everyday life are connected in some way to the national fetish. The industrial base needed to create plutonium, to design and test bombs, and to monitor the earth for signs of nuclear proliferation has produced an array of new technologies now seamlessly interwoven into everyday life. The interstate highway system, for example, was created by President Eisenhower in 1956 explicitly as a means of evacuating cities in the case of a nuclear war (Winkler 1993: 117). The Federal Emergency Management Agency (FEMA), now deployed predominantly to advise citizens during natural disasters, originated in Cold War nuclear civil defense planning, when the sirens signaled not hurricanes and floods but Soviet missiles and bombers. These are but the most apparent everyday nuclear infrastructures because they are linked directly to civil defense. However, technological advances in supercomputing, lasers, and satellite telecommunications are also directly tied to, on the one hand, the scientific need to understand what happens in a nuclear explosion, and on the other, the need to maintain communications in the midst of a nuclear war. Microelectronics, plastics, new technologies of global surveillance (seismic, atmospheric, and geo-orbital), computer memory, modems, color photographic film, as well as the Internet all have lineages deriving from the nuclear weapons programs. As Paul Edwards (1996) has powerfully argued, the minute-to-minute threat of nuclear war produced a totalizing vision of American technology during the Cold War, a "closed world" of early warning systems and military technology linked by always-on computers, encompassing the earth in an always expanding technoscientific form of American power. As the central American project of the twentieth century, the technological infrastructures supporting the nuclear arsenal have come to define everyday American life in ways both subtle and far reaching: put simply, America in the twenty-first century remains a society built around, and to a large extent, through the bomb.

The unprecedented national resources devoted to the bomb, its infrastructural role in everyday life, and the cross-section of American society working within the nuclear complex make the bomb an example of what I call *radioactive nation-building*. I mean this to operate in both a literal and a figurative register. For the huge national security projects of the nuclear age created new technologies for everyday life, just as the new apocalyptic possibilities that energized them colonized national imaginaries and changed relationships between citizens and the state. Nation-building projects that pursue the public good through means that are simultaneously corrosive of the social contract are, in a sense, always "radioactive," because they contaminate the public sphere, invading bodies and disrupting cosmologies in ways that promise to mutate over time. In this sense, the nuclear age has always been culturally toxic, but it is only after the Cold War that the long-term effects are becoming visible. With each new revelation of covert human plutonium experiments, public misinformation campaigns, or environmental contamination, the state's ability to define security in a meaningful way is further compromised, engendering a paranoid public sphere. Radioactive nation-building involves, therefore, not only the past practices of the U.S. nuclear complex performed in the name of Cold War national security, but also the collective, future-oriented national cultures it engenders.

Indeed, the legacies of a half century of radioactive nation-building are not only in our technological infrastructure and our social institutions—they are in our bodies. Every person on the planet now receives a certain amount of radiation each day produced by the cumulative effects of above-ground nuclear weapons tests and radioactive releases from within the global nuclear complex. Most of us have some level of radioactive toxins in our bodies directly derived from the U.S. nuclear complex. As the cumulative radioactive fallout trajectories from the era of above-ground nuclear tests in the United States testify, none have been immune (see Figure 1.4). The National Cancer Institute (NCI) now estimates that if you were alive in the United States between 1945 and 1963 you received at least two rads of iodine-131 (a radioactive isotope that can produce thyroid cancer) from U.S. nuclear testing.[27] If you were a child living in the western states who liked to drink milk you quite likely received more, perhaps eight times as much (as proximity to the Nevada Test Site, combined with tendency of iodine-131 to concentrate in animals that graze, put children at greatest risk). The NCI estimates that between ten thousand and seventy thousand people (most of whom were children at the time of above-ground testing) will develop thyroid cancer over the course of their lifetime as a result of nuclear testing. It should be underscored here that iodine-131 is but one of a number of radioactive toxins distributed by atmospheric fallout—including plutonium-239, strontium-90, and cesium-137—that can produce dangerous or deadly health effects (see IPPNW and IEER 1991).

Thus, all Americans participate in the nuclear complex, whether they realize it or not. In this sense, the Manhattan Project inaugurated what Ulrich Beck (1972) would call a "risk society," a new modernity in which dangers produced by the nation-state can no longer be controlled by it or be contained within its borders. The nuclear fallout from the 1986 Chernobyl accident in the Ukraine, for example, not only severely irradiated northern Europe and Greece but also was found in the water supply of Portland, Oregon—halfway around the world. This kind of transnational risk obliterates the possibility of a specifically "national" security, and places what Adriana Petryna (2002) has called "partial knowledge" at the center of a new social contract between citizens and the state over the terms of health, scientific knowledge, and governmentality. The

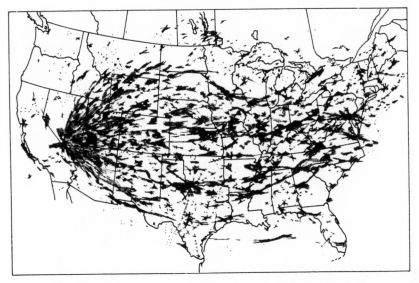

1.4. Cumulative U.S. fallout trajectory map. (*Source: Under the Cloud: The Decades of Nuclear Testing,* Courtesy of Richard L. Miller)

international nuclear complex is estimated to have already produced over four hundred thousand cancer deaths worldwide simply from the dispersion of radioactive materials into the environment (IPPNW and IEER 1991). It also has consistently targeted minority communities for the most dangerous nuclear projects, creating a new form of global environmental discrimination some have called "radioactive colonialism" (Churchill 1997; see also Kuletz 1998). Put differently, even as the sole remaining superpower, the United States is also the most nuclear-bombed country in world, having detonated nearly one thousand nuclear devices within its own territorial borders. The social anesthesia required to insulate the public from the combined social and biological effects of the nuclear complex adds a new dimension to our previous discussion of the "nuclear state of emergency" and illustrates once again the ferocious investment in the nuclear arsenal as American fetish. Now, however, it is important to look more closely at how radioactive nation-building over the past half century has engendered new tactile experiences of everyday life in the United States, and with them, new psychosocial realities.

THE NUCLEAR UNCANNY

The nuclear age has witnessed the apotheosis of the uncanny. During the Cold War this was most obviously manifested in the psychic anxieties produced by knowledge that less than thirty minutes were all that separated the quotidian from annihilation, from living within a temporal space in which the missiles may have always already been launched. Fear of radioactive contamination has also colonized psychic spaces and profoundly shaped individual perceptions of the everyday from the start of the nuclear age, leaving people to wonder if invisible, life-threatening forces intrude upon daily life, bringing cancer, mutation, or death. The dislocation and anxiety produced by these moments of tense recognition is what I call the *nuclear uncanny*. The nuclear uncanny exists in the material effects, psychic tension, and sensory confusion produced by nuclear weapons and radioactive materials. It is a perceptual space caught between apocalyptic expectation and sensory fulfillment, a psychic effect produced, on the one hand, by living within the temporal ellipsis separating a nuclear attack and the actual end of the world, and on the other, by inhabiting an environmental space threatened by military-industrial radiation. We can see the nuclear uncanny manifested today in a variety of new forms, from new biological beings created by the effect of radiation on living cells, to new social formations brought together by the joint experience of risk and/or fear of contamination.[28] It is in the arena of the nuclear uncanny that the concept of "national security" becomes most disjointed, as citizens find themselves increasingly separated from their own senses and distrusting of their own surroundings due to an engagement with nuclear technologies. This "theft" of sensibility is a complicated phenomenon, enabled not only by the space/time contraction of thermonuclear missile technology, but also by the unique physical properties of nuclear materials, and in particular, the phenomenon of radiation.

In a now famous essay, Freud defined the uncanny (*das Unheimliche*— literally, the unhomely) as a psychic process whereby sensory experience becomes haunted and untrustworthy, a return of the repressed that reveals a secret desire to return "home." For Freud the uncanny consists of (1) a sudden loss (or distrust) of one's senses (often represented as a fear of being blinded), and (2) the psychic ambiguity produced by inanimate objects that appear to be alive. Describing the uncanny as a slippage whereby "the distinction between reality and the imagination is effaced," Freud identifies the uncanny in a number of social forms: automatons, ghosts, dead bodies, and doppelgangers. For him, the uncanny is that which blurs the distinction between the living and the dead, the hallucinatory and the real, and which, in essence, makes sensory experience untrustworthy and strange. This psychic slippage is, for Freud, always a return of something repressed, a repetition that ultimately is tied to castration anxiety and the urge to return to that ultimate experience of "home"—the womb. However, what makes the uncanny weird is that it is often informed by outmoded cultural forms, beliefs that are supposed to have fallen away in the age of industrial modernism. The supernatural aspects of the uncanny are ultimately for Freud moments of cultural as well as psychic slippage, episodes where animistic beliefs colonize the modernist everyday, points of confusion where an industrial society wonders if ghosts might, in fact, still exist. The uncanny evokes fear, then, because it is an instant when modernist psychic and cultural structures become momentarily undone or out of joint, thus revealing the dangerous vulnerability of the human sensorium to an uncertain and uncertainly haunted universe.

Some moments of the nuclear age now resonate with all the accoutrements of the Victorian horror stories Freud based his reading of the uncanny on. Take, for example, Project Sunshine, a series of experiments conducted by the AEC in 1953. Run out of the University of Chicago, Columbia University, and the New York offices of the AEC, Project Sunshine was publicly marketed as an investigation into naturally occurring radiation, in which radiation doses to people were measured in "sunshine units" (a ploy to counter widespread public fear of radiation).[29] Project Sunshine was in reality, however, a classified project to find out how much strontium-90 had been introduced into the global environment as a result of above-ground nuclear explosions.[30] Its goal was to assess the genetic impact of atmospheric nuclear testing on individuals, to discover exactly how many nuclear explosions it might take to pose a threat to the genetic stability of the human species. To do so, scientists sought a worldwide sample of human teeth and bones to test for levels of strontium-90. The bones of infants were particularly desired, as children are more susceptible to nuclear materials (making young bones a better measure of strontium-90 distribution). "Sunshine" scientists therefore initiated a secretive global search for baby bones and entered into discussions about "bodysnatching" as a means of getting their samples. Then AEC commissioner Willard Libby, in a classified meeting on Project Sunshine in 1953, concluded: "So human samples are of prime importance and if anybody knows how to do a good job of body snatching they will really be serving their country."[31] *Bodysnatching, baby bones, genetic mutations, sunshine units*—these are the terms of a new American modernity based not only on technoscience but on managing the appearance of the bomb.

Project Sunshine can be read as an official articulation of nuclear fear, a tacit recognition that a new tactile experience of the world was being created by the distribution of nuclear materials into the environment. Like the early nuclear flashblindness experiments, however, it was intended not to prevent the introduction of nuclear materials into the world—to stop the trauma of potential genetic mutation—but rather to measure the effects of nuclear technologies on the human body in a world already committed to a nuclear arms race. A decade later, when the Atmospheric Test Ban Treaty was signed (1963), the earth was explicitly incorporated into the nuclear complex as a means of insulating people from the effects of fallout.[32] The submersion of bomb testing produced a number of psychic effects world-wide: on the one hand, contributing to the banalization of a bomb that no longer had dramatically visible effects (the mushroom cloud), but on the other, allowing nuclear fear to become more mobile as the invisibility of nuclear contamination engaged new psychic and cultural registers in a global, Cold War nuclear complex. I want now to examine two specific aspects of the nuclear uncanny. The first has to do with the cognitive effects produced by nuclear materials; that is, how a tactile engagement with the world can be effected by the sensory-disorientation produced by the phenomenon of radiation. The second has to do with a special type of repression located in the nuclear uncanny, one that, because it is drawn from an engagement with the national fetish, necessarily involves national-cultural as well as psychosocial registers.

Nuclear materials are sources of invisible power. Radiation is colorless and odorless, yet capable of affecting living beings at the genetic level. In this sense, nuclear materials produce the uncanny effect of blurring the distinction between the animate and the inanimate, and between the natural and the supernatural. For example, the plutonium pit that fuels a nuclear weapon might feel warm to the touch but such warmth is completely at odds with the enormous power it represents (see Figure 1.5). It took only one gram of a sphere of plutonium-239 to produce enough energy to destroy the city of Nagasaki in 1945 (McPhee 1974: 163). Plutonium is as uncanny a material as can be imagined: from a molecular perspective, it has six different crystalline structures existing at ambient pressures; this allows it to change radically in density with the slightest shift in its unstable atomic structure. Heat plutonium in some of its phases and it shrinks; in others, it can ignite on contact with oxygen. Discovered in 1941, plutonium is all but nonexistent in nature, yet it now can be found in trace amounts everywhere on the planet as a result of atmospheric nuclear testing; and with a life span of 240,000 years, it is, from a human perspective, virtually eternal. Plutonium's value has always been its molecular instability, useful for fueling the atomic chain reaction that ignites a nuclear bomb, but highly problematic in its millennial essence. Not unlike a strange new life form, plutonium is always evolving, changing in appearance, threatening to explode. Here is how two senior weapons scientists at Los Alamos (Hecker and Martz 2000: 238) describe the problem presented by managing Cold War plutonium:

Like other reactive materials, plutonium ages with time. In moist air, it "rusts" much more profusely than iron, and when exposed to other atmospheric

1.5. Weapons-grade plutonium button. (U.S. Department of Energy photograph)

environments, it will react to form several surface-corrosion products. In other words, plutonium ages from the outside in. What makes plutonium really special, however, is that is also ages from the inside out. As a result of its radioactive nature, it relentlessly undergoes self-irradiation damage throughout its volume. Consequently, nature's most unusual element becomes even more complex as it ages. In the past, we were resigned to keeping plutonium from self-destructing—at least for two or three decades. Today, we are intensely interested in extending its storage life for many more decades, preferably as much as a century.

Plutonium becomes more complex as it ages. As such, plutonium's mutability parallels its varied effects on American society and the environment; its uncontainable, and already global, presence promises unknown biosocial effects on a 240,000-year time frame. While the prosthetic devices that populate nuclear physics laboratories enable scientists to enter the subatomic realm and measure the material effects of plutonium and other radionuclides, most people in the nuclear age remain literally senseless to radiation, dependent in everyday life on biological, not machinic, insights. Consequently, the invisible dangers posed by millennial materials that can incite cancer or induce genetic change have added a critical new dimension to everyday life—a nonlocalizable threat of contamination, mutation, and possible death.

Nuclear materials can produce powerful psychic resonances because radiation fundamentally distorts how people experience an orientation in time and space. Consider for a moment how radiation affects the human body.[33] First, radioactive contamination is cumulative, measured over the course of an entire life, not in individual doses. This means that radiation sickness or cancer is temporally separated from the moment of exposure: those exposed to iodine-131 from atmospheric fallout in the late 1950s, for example, may have experienced the first signs of thyroid cancer only in the 1980s. Exposure to radiation affects the molecular structure of living cells, potentially leading to cancers while putting future generations at risk as well. If reproductive cells are irradiated, genetic damage can result, leading to the possibility of mutation, deformation, or disease in developing embryos. This temporal ellipsis between radiation exposure and radiation effect is a specific aspect of the nuclear uncanny, one that can generate a proliferating psychic anxiety as potentially exposed individuals realize their inability to evaluate risk in everyday life. Second, if radiation powerfully affects how people experience their own bodies over time, it also affects how people experience an orientation in space.

For radiation traverses space in ways that can make the air, earth, and water seem suspect, even dangerous, though no sensory evidence is at hand. Thus, for those living near nuclear facilities, radiation often becomes a means of explaining all manner of illness and misfortune—its very invisibility allowing its proliferation in the realm of the imagination. In this way radiation disrupts the ability of individuals to differentiate their bodies from their environment, producing paranoia. The nuclear uncanny is, therefore, a rupture in one of the basic cognitive frames of orientation to the world. The inability to disarticulate a traumatized self from the local environment is one experience of the nuclear uncanny. It inevitably produces paranoia because it involves assimilation to a radioactive space (real or imagined); thus, one becomes possessed by a space that certainly disorients but may also actually maim or kill, and may do so now or somewhere in a multigenerational future. This is perhaps the most profound effect of the nuclear age, as individuals either numb themselves to the everyday threat, or are conditioned to separate themselves from their own senses, losing themselves in a space that is simultaneously real and imagined, both paranoid and technoscientific reality. For radioactive materials now execute their own uncanny form of manifest destiny, traveling an unpredictable course through ecosystems and bodies, creating new social and biological beings, and with them, new tactile experiences of everyday life.

Today, in Los Alamos, for example, in a place called Bayo Canyon, can be found a special creature of the nuclear age (see Figure 1.6). From all appearances it is a shrub like any other inhabiting the arid Southwest,

1.6. Radioactive chamisa, Bayo Canyon, Los Alamos County. (Photograph by Joseph Masco)

phylum *Chrysothamnus nauseosus*. Yet this chamisa plant is a postnuclear aberration. Scientists at LANL have discovered within its circulatory system a quantity of strontium-90 in excess of three hundred thousand times that of a normal shrub. Indistinguishable from other shrubs without a Geiger counter, this chamisa confounds belief in the containability of the nuclear age. Rooted on top of a nuclear waste treatment area, which was closed in 1963, covered with earth, and thought to be safely out of reach, this shrub illustrates the futility of simply pushing nuclear dangers out of sight, of burying the threat. Sending tap-roots fourteen feet into the earth, the chamisa mistakes strontium-90 for calcium, sucking it into its circulatory system and returning it back to the earth's surface to reenter the food chain almost as quickly as people bury it. What is startling about this shrub is not that it is radioactive, but that it appears to be thriving. This is one example of the strange duality of the nuclear age, that contamination, and the possibility of mutation, can travel hand in hand with visible signs of health and prosperity.

One psychosocial effect of nuclear materials is to render everyday life strange, to shift how individuals experience a tactile relationship to their immediate environment. This gets at the root definition of the uncanny as *Umheimliche*, or the unhomely, for the invisibility of radiation can make any space seem otherworldly, strange, and even dangerous. Indeed, what could be more "unhomely" than the introduction of nuclear materials into one's everyday environment or body? Thus, if one experience of the nuclear uncanny is a disorientation of self and environment, then we also need to acknowledge that experiences of self and environment are culturally specific. Consequently, I offer the *nuclear uncanny* here not simply as a figurative device, but as an ethnographic category, a subject eminently worthy of cross-cultural research. For if the everyday has been transformed by nuclear technologies, then such transformations must find unique expression within distinct concepts of the everyday. Much of this book is consequently an effort to chart ethnographically the diversity of responses to the Manhattan Project to be found just in the communities working in and neighboring LANL. As we shall see, Cold War discourses of national security, which assumed a unified national subject, worked to occlude the variety of national-cultural experiences informing the nuclear age, even among those living within the territorial boundaries of the United States.

Within the U.S. nuclear complex, a common refrain is that "you can't put the nuclear genie back in the bottle," a statement providing a moment of animistic self-reflection where nuclear technology is assumed to have taken on a life of its own, now defining its own destiny, charting an inevitable, if uncanny, course. The genie metaphor is carefully chosen, as it represents both the possibility of wondrous gifts (unlimited energy, national security, international prestige) and the potential for treacherous acts (terrorism, species mutation, nuclear war). The uncanny, as we know from Freud, always involves a return of the repressed. In the case of the nuclear uncanny, this necessarily involves issues of nation-building, citizenship, the legitimate uses of violence, and the possibility of genocide. Perhaps the least recognized aspect of the nuclear age is that it has put some communities more at risk than others, and created a new form of toxic politics directly tied to race and class. Indeed, we can see in the logistics of the nuclear complex not only a peculiar evaluation of risk and security in the name of an imagined national culture, but also a powerful display of the state's evaluation of citizenship. Los Alamos, for example, is immediately surrounded by Pueblo nations and Nuevomexicano villagers who trace national genealogies back prior to the founding of the United States, making New Mexico a powerful site to examine the national logics and environmental effects of the nuclear age. Indeed, the very existence of multicultural (even multinational) New Mexico offers an imminent critique of U.S. national identity. In this sense, New Mexico is both deconstructive and reflective of America's national security project; it is a region that not only produced the U.S. nuclear arsenal, and with it a global system of military technoscience, but also the nuclear uncanny and proliferating forms of post–Cold War anxiety.

"A MULTIDIMENSIONAL, NONLINEAR, COMPLEX SYSTEM"

The remainder of this book is a study of everyday life in the nuclear age, focusing on post–Cold War security debates around Los Alamos National Laboratory. It is an ethnographic study that explores the long-term national-cultural, technoscientific, and environmental effects of the U.S. nuclear weapons project in Los Alamos, interrogating how "security" is lived for those most directly involved in producing the U.S. nuclear arsenal. As such, it is also a study of complexity, an effort to recognize not only military science but also the multiple regimes of knowledge that continue to engage the Manhattan Project in New Mexico. LANL is, in this regard, the most complex U.S. nuclear facility: it maintains the most expansive nuclear and non-nuclear technoscientific mission, occupies the most rugged territorial space (forty-three square miles of mountainous terrain), and is surrounded by the most diverse regional populations in the U.S. Department of Energy (DOE) nuclear complex, including multiple sovereign Pueblo nations, four hundred-year-old Nuevomexicano villages, as well as a vibrant post–Cold War antinuclear movement. The immediate challenge of this project is thus to capture the multiple investments in place and U.S. technoscience in northern New Mexico, recognizing that the northern Rio Grande valley remains one of the most internally contested cultural spaces in North America. From an ethnographic point of view, there can even be a surreal quality to the overlapping claims in contemporary New Mexico, a region that is simultaneously foreign and domestic, a combination of the preindustrial and the technoscientific future, a cultural space that is Native American, Catholic, New Age, and military-industrial, an arena that deconstructs U.S. national security as readily as it creates it, a political sphere that is dominated by secret societies yet exploding with discourse, a home to both the hyperwealthy and the poorest of the poor, one that is simultaneously sacred space, U.S. experimental laboratory, tourist fantasyland, and national sacrifice zone.

New Mexico is not only where the atomic bomb was invented, it remains the center of the U.S. nuclear complex in the post–Cold War era. Five of the eight nuclear weapons in the post–Cold War U.S. nuclear arsenal are Los Alamos designs, making Los Alamos the essential U.S. nuclear facility for the foreseeable future. LANL weapons scientists entered the post–Cold War period describing their responsibilities this way:

> Los Alamos efforts to provide scientific and engineering leadership in support of the U.S. nuclear deterrent has focused on two areas: the application of physics, computational modeling, engineering, and materials science to the entire "cradle-to-grave" lifetime of a nuclear weapon and the use of nuclear weapons science and technology in support of national objectives in arms

control, nonproliferation, intelligence assessment, emergency response in the event of nuclear incidents, production and disposition of nuclear materials, manufacture and dismantlement of nuclear weapons, environmental restoration, and management of waste resulting from the Cold War. (1994a: 10)

The entire "cradle-to-grave" lifetime of a nuclear weapon. The laboratory thus promises lifetime support for each of its nuclear weapons designs, maintaining the full spectrum of technoscientific projects necessary to support that mission. New Mexico is also, not coincidentally, the only U.S. state supporting the entire "cradle-to-grave" U.S. nuclear economy: this involves uranium mining, nuclear weapons design and testing (at two of the three national weapons laboratories—Los Alamos and Sandia), missile testing (at The White Sands Missile Range), as well as the largest single arsenal of U.S. nuclear weapons (at Kirtland Air Force Base), and nuclear waste storage (at the Waste Isolation Pilot Plant [WIPP], which is currently the only permanent depository for U.S. military-industrial nuclear waste).

Thus, at the start of the twenty-first century, New Mexico, the perennial frontier space in many North American imaginations, remains most prominently on America's nuclear frontier; it is where the atomic bomb was invented and where the post–Cold War U.S. nuclear weapons complex is being slowly consolidated, and where the legacies of the bomb will be negotiated for generations to come. It is important to recognize that the Manhattan Project produced not only a transformation in scientific and international affairs; it initiated a conversion of northern New Mexico from a primarily rural, agrarian economy to a military-industrial state. Moreover, while U.S. military planners sought out a marginal space on America's periphery in 1943 to try to build an atomic bomb, they colonized the geographical center of Pueblo and Nuevomexicano territories, engaging cosmological orders that identify the northern Rio Grande valley as quite literally the center of the universe. The security logics of the Cold War state did not recognize these claims or provide a forum for expressing regional concerns about the laboratory. The end of the Cold War consequently produced an eruption of discourse in northern New Mexico about the (economic, environmental, cultural, and political) legacies of the bomb, as well as about the continued consolidation of New Mexico as a U.S. national security space. This book is also, then, an analysis of the first public sphere devoted to the long-term consequences of the Manhattan Project in New Mexico.

When I described this research project to one Los Alamos weapons scientist as an effort to engage the complexity of the nuclear revolution in northern New Mexico, he responded by asking, "How do you model a multidimensional, nonlinear, complex system?" Indeed, from one vantage point, his question objectifies economically the cultural complexity of northern New Mexico, a region with multiple tribal governments, subaltern political formations, competing nongovernmental organizations (NGOs), as well as state and federal agencies that are all deeply invested in LANL. However, he also reveals the immediate problem of the post–Cold War period in Los Alamos. Having focused their careers on the technoscientific challenge of producing U.S. national security in a world of competing states (providing the military technologies enabling deterrence and containment), the end of the Cold War forced laboratory managers to attend to local communities with radically different forms of government, contrary political agendas, disparate forms of scientific knowledge, and a unifying distrust of the U.S. nuclear security state. His desire for a "model" of northern New Mexico was thus a practical effort to find the equation-of-state that could transform the intensity of local political processes into something predictable and manageable for the laboratory. Approaching nuclear politics in northern New Mexico as a multidimensional, nonlinear, complex system underscores its complexity; however, it does not capture the intense, lived reality of these politics.

In the pages that follow, I offer not a model but a series of ethnographic perspectives on post–Cold War politics in northern New Mexico. One argument of the book is that there is no single text, model, or process that can capture all of the local investments in power, place, and identity in northern New Mexico, and that a recognition of this reality challenges the terms of a "U.S. national security" discourse that assumes a stable and homogeneous national subject. The complexity of cultural politics, the alternative modes of knowing, and the divergent experiences of citizenship that inform life in and around LANL is precisely what the Cold War state project rendered invisible, making the immediate challenge of the twenty-first century the transformation of "national security" discourse from an empty signifier to a lived experience for all U.S. citizens. The structure of this book emphasizes this point, presenting a series of different vantage points on the U.S. nuclear project in the first decade of the post–Cold War period. Those expecting a linear narrative will be disappointed. The text that follows pursues a multisited approach to the Manhattan Project, one that necessarily produces moments of contradiction, repetition, and temporal flux. For how could one approach a project on the scale of the U.S. nuclear complex without recognizing complexity, if not contradiction, at each turn?

In the early post–Cold War period, laboratory managers expressed concerns to me about the closure of nuclear material production plants at Hanford and Rocky Flats; they worried about how the bomb could be maintained over the long term without new U.S. inventories of pluto-nium. While some weapons scientists contemplated the end of plutonium production, which helped launch the Manhattan Project in 1943, com-munities in northern New Mexico began to realize, many for the first time, that plutonium was a saturating and permanent presence in their lives. Indeed, as weapons scientists explored a new sensory relationship to the bomb via a new experimental test regime, residents throughout northern New Mexico experienced a range of new fears about radiation, fundamentally changing the quality of their lived spaces. The 24,100-year half-life of plutonium became in the post–Cold War period a point of mutual recognition and mobilization for diverse citizens in northern New Mexico, providing a shared point of reference for engaging the U.S. nuclear project. Plutonium, in other words, became not only the key material enabling U.S. national security, it became a new kind of lingua franca enabling cross-cultural conversation about the Cold War nuclear project at Los Alamos and the terms of the nuclear future (see Siegel 1997). As the core material enabling the bomb, plutonium now operates as a complex ecological and social agent in northern New Mexico, mak-ing it a cross-cultural signifier capable of revealing the diversity of regional experience.

Consequently, the first section of this book investigates what I call the "plutonium economy" in northern New Mexico. The plutonium econ-omy exceeds the logics of military-industrial production, linking different regimes of knowledge through concerns about biological, ecological, and social futures. The Manhattan Project is now best thought of as an econ-omy because, like plutonium itself, the effects of the bomb are highly mobile and are the basis for exchanges across all communities, offering one important vantage point on everyday life in the nuclear age. Put sim-ply, an analysis of everyday life within the plutonium economy provides an ethnographic portrait of radioactive nation-building in New Mexico, tracking not only the institutions, expertise, and financial commitments supporting the bomb, but also the competing forms of knowledge, expertise, and cross-cultural anxiety informing life within the U.S. nuclear complex. In four chapters, devoted to how weapons scientists, neighboring Pueblo nations, Nuevomexicano communities, and antinu-clear activists alternatively engage the plutonium economy, I demon-strate that the Manhattan Project is not simply a technoscientific project in New Mexico. The bomb is now a multigenerational, national-cultural, economic, and environmental mutation, one that has already colonized a deep future. Indeed, by exploring different cultural experiences of the nuclear uncanny we soon discover that the plutonium economy not only provides the technological basis of American power globally, it defines how citizens engage their government and understand their long-term biological, ecological, and cultural security in New Mexico.

In part 2, "National Insecurities," I then explore the two events of the post–Cold War period that made national news, transforming Los Alamos from a nearly invisible U.S. laboratory into a location of intense national fear and insecurity. In fact, by the end of the 1990s, insecurity at LANL became a new kind of national resource, used to reenergize both the national fetish and the security state. Chapter 6 investigates the espionage allegations at LANL in 1999, focusing on how the perception of insecurity at Los Alamos was mobilized into a major reorganization of the U.S. nuclear project under heightened government secrecy. The new "hypersecurity" measures instituted in post–Cold War Los Alamos prefigured the U.S. responses to the terrorist attacks on New York and Washington, D.C., in 2001, and reveal efforts within the security state to mobilize nuclear fear to produce a more aggressive and secretive form of American power in the twenty-first century. Chapter 7 then begins by exploring reactions to the Cerro Grande fire, which burned Los Alamos County in 2000, closing the laboratory and displacing some 25,000 people. Tracing anxieties about mutation from the height of the Cold War in the 1950s to this post–Cold War moment in New Mexico, I demonstrate that a nuclear subtext now informs everyday life in northern New Mexico. The long-term effects of the Manhattan Project are now the basis not only for cross-cultural experiences of the nuclear uncanny but also for an ongoing transformation in both the nature of the nation-state and the state of nature.

As we shall see, an ethnographic investigation into the effects of the Manhattan Project in northern New Mexico challenges the assumed logic that the United States "won" the Cold War. Indeed, the legacies of the bomb—in terms of our global order, our political and scientific institutions, our democratic process, our notions of ecological and biological integrity—amount to a fundamental mutation in American life, leaving New Mexicans at the start of the twenty-first century as merely the most prominent residents of the nuclear borderlands.

Part I
Everyday Life in the Plutonium Economy

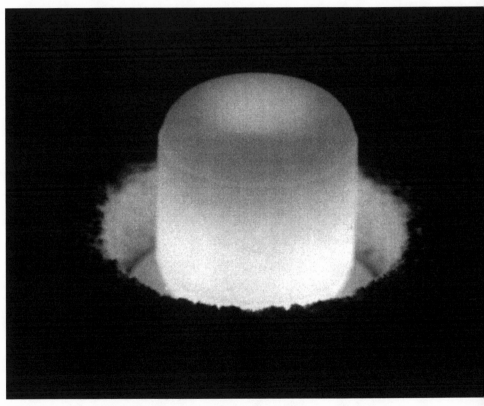

I.1 Light emitted by Plutonium-238 ingot (U.S. Department of Energy photograph)

2 Nuclear Technoaesthetics
The Sensory Politics of the Bomb in Los Alamos

A striking feature of nuclear weapons science—as a science—is that its experimental form would seem to have been most powerfully determined by nonscientists.[1] From the 1963 Atmospheric Test Ban Treaty through the 1992 Underground Test Moratorium, the experimental regimes open to nuclear weapons scientists have been predominately defined by international treaties and U.S. nuclear policy, rather than by experts within the laboratory. In the post–Cold War period, this means that U.S. nuclear weapons scientists cannot conduct what would appear to be the most basic experiment in their profession: namely, detonating a nuclear device.[2] Nuclear weapons science is further complicated in the United States by being a highly classified and compartmentalized enterprise, in which scientists are not able to engage freely even other weapons scientists on the technical nature of their work within the national laboratories. Moreover, the stated goal of post–Cold War nuclear weapons science is not to produce an explosive technology per se but rather to provide the technological infrastructure for a nuclear deterrent—a means of preventing a particular species of war. Thus, Los Alamos scientists today self-consciously devote their careers to engineering the bomb so that it will never actually be used *as a bomb*. Caught between the competing demands of a shifting experimental foundation, state secrecy, and the increasingly symbolic role nuclear weapons have come to play in (inter)national politics, the reality of the bomb as both a machine and a weapon of mass destruction for all but its most direct victims has become difficult to locate in post–Cold War America. Outside the national laboratories, U.S. nuclear weapons have come to exist primarily as political constructs, and are rarely considered as technologies subject to the usual scientific challenges of what Peter Galison (1997) has called theorization, instrumentalization, and experimentation.[3]

In Los Alamos, the post–Cold War order has consequently presented a unique set of technoscientific challenges, requiring nothing less than a reinvention of nuclear weapons science. Since weapons scientists trained after the 1992 test moratorium may never actually conduct or witness a nuclear detonation, it is important to ask: What constitutes the continuing intellectual appeal of nuclear weapons science *as a science?* To answer this question I suggest that we need to engage critically the technoaesthetics of the bomb, by which I mean the evaluative aesthetic categories embedded in the expert practices of weapons scientists.[4] I am interested here in how weapons scientists have negotiated the bomb at the level of sensory experience since 1945, and argue that technoaesthetics largely determine the politics of the enterprise within the epistemic cultures of the laboratory. Technoaesthetics are also important because they are the non-classified everyday modes of interacting with nuclear technologies, forms of perception, and practice that unify divergent groups of physicists, chemists, engineers, and computer specialists as nuclear weapons scientists. In Los Alamos, I would argue, it is in the realm of technoaesthetics that both the meaning of the bomb, and the pleasures of conducting nuclear weapons science, are constituted and expressed.[5]

In post–Cold War Los Alamos, for example, the technoaesthetic production of the U.S. nuclear arsenal is internally structured by a complicated dual deployment of time and the human body. Consider the following critique, spontaneously offered to me by a senior weapons scientist concerning public ideas about nuclear weapons. Nonweapons scientists usually describe nuclear weapons as "apocalyptic"—as the end of time, he said. But if you look at the damage produced by a one-megaton warhead detonated at maximum yield height over New York City it would incinerate everything within a one-mile radius on the island and severely damage a much larger area, but parts of Queens, Brooklyn, and New Jersey would still be there; thus, he said, it would be devastating but decidedly not apocalyptic. Moreover, he noted that a full-scale nuclear war would not be the end of everything. Instead, he offered an image of nuclear war as a kind of time travel, stating that a full-scale nuclear exchange would return the United States to "roughly the year 1860." "You'd lose the power grid," he offered, "but there would still be blacksmithing technology for making horse shoes and the like." In this presentation, all human achievement is collapsed through the bomb into a specific notion of temporal-technological progress. Consequently, after a nuclear war, techno-time would simply start over again at the 1860 level and the United States would build itself out of the ashes by producing new machines. In fact, within this concept, time might actually be speeded up after a nuclear war because this would be the second time around for the industrial revolution.

In this case, destruction is not ignored—indeed, it is precisely measured—but it is defined in terms of the presence or absence of technology. The effect of radioactive fallout on people, animals, or the environment is understated, which allows the primary evaluative meaning of nuclear war to be fixed in the realm of a specific notion of temporal technological progress (i.e., through a focus on the horseshoes and not the horse).

The deployment of time here performs a dual evacuation: first of the quotidian and then of the human body. The black humor in this narrative, characteristic of Los Alamos weapons science, is complicated in that it not only measures the destructive radius of the bomb on a U.S. city but also mobilizes an implicit image of an invulnerable scientific body, one that would be left to rebuild New York after the blast. Derrida (1984) has insightfully argued that nuclear war is "fabulously textual" because until it happens it only exists in the imagination. Nuclear war, he argues, is also the only "remainderless" event, marking the potential end of the human archive and thus of thought itself. The fabulous quality of the nuclear—its conceptual power—draws explicitly then on the future, creating a virtual world of possibility in the imagination that threatens to supplant the experiential reality of the technology. But if, as we have just seen, the bomb can be interpreted as enabling a form of time travel, illustrating a complicated understanding of where bodies and military nuclear technologies interact, this weapons scientists' story also points to a cognitive rupture experienced at Los Alamos by the end of the Cold War. For if time itself is measured in terms of a specific narrative of technomilitary progress within the laboratory, the breakup of the Soviet Union in 1991 and the accompanying U.S. moratorium on underground nuclear testing in 1992 would seem to have denied weapons scientists the possibility of a nuclear future on these very terms. The end of the Cold War thus challenged the cosmology supporting nuclear weapons science at Los Alamos, while fundamentally changing its experimental form.

This chapter explores how the reconfigured experimental regime of the post–Cold War period has altered how Los Alamos scientists experience the bomb as a technology, thereby changing the terms of our collective nuclear future. By examining the epistemic spaces where scientific bodies and nuclear devices actually interact—through pleasure—I believe we can see past the regimented statements of nuclear policy makers to engage the complicated world of nuclear weapons science as both an ideological and a technoscientific practice.[6] I argue that the shifting experimental regimes open to Los Alamos weapons scientists have, over time, worked to position the U.S. nuclear arsenal within the laboratory as an increasingly aesthetic-intellectual project, one that is both normalized and depoliticized.

I begin by tracing the internal narrative of weapons scientists about the political necessity of their work, noting a dramatically expanding time horizon on the nuclear future from 1945 to today. I then turn from the explicit ideology of weapons science to an analysis of the technoaesthetic production of the bomb within the laboratory itself, identifying three distinct experimental regimes. First, I examine how weapons scientists experienced the bomb—at the level of sense perception—during the era of above-ground nuclear testing (1945–62). Second, I then examine how the move to underground nuclear testing (1963–92) reconfigured sensory access to the exploding bomb, both abstracting its destructive potential and encouraging an intellectual engagement with complexity. Finally, I examine how the post–Cold War experimental program known as "Science-Based Stockpile Stewardship" (1995–2010), which relies on an increasingly virtual bomb, systematically confuses bodies and machines in such a way as to transform the experience of nuclear science from a military reality to one of potentially infinite technoaesthetic pleasure. The structural achievement of post–Cold War nuclear science in Los Alamos, I ultimately argue, is to have reinvented the bomb—at precisely the moment when America's nuclear project and the laboratory's future seemed most uncertain—as an unending technonational project that is simultaneously fragile, essential, and beautiful.

THE BOMB'S FUTURE

Time—in terms of both endings and possible futures—has been a defining concern within the U.S. nuclear complex from the start of the Manhattan Project; time is also a primary domain for the expression of the technoaesthetics, and thus the meaning, of nuclear weapons science. Indeed, an intellectual genealogy of Los Alamos weapons science reveals an ongoing conceptual fixation on the futurology of the bomb. On October 16, 1945, his last day as director of what was known during World War II simply as "Site Y," J. Robert Oppenheimer gave a farewell speech to his Los Alamos colleagues in which he troubled the apparent success of the Manhattan Project, telling the first generation of nuclear weapons scientists:

> If atomic bombs are to be added as new weapons to the arsenals of a warring world, or to the arsenals of nations preparing for war, then the time will come when mankind will curse the names of Los Alamos and Hiroshima. The peoples of this world must unite or they will perish. This war that has ravaged so much of the earth, has written these words. The atomic bomb has spelled them out for all men to understand. Other men have spoken them, in other times, of other wars, of other weapons. They have not prevailed. There are some, misled by a false sense of human history, who would that they will not prevail today. It is not for us to believe that. By our works we are committed, committed to a world united, before this common peril, in law, and in humanity. (Quoted in Hawkins 1983: 260–61)

The time will come when mankind will curse the name of Los Alamos and Hiroshima.   In this presentation, time has all but run out for America, and the very availability of a future hinges on a new kind of international order devoted to controlling atomic weaponry. Though the United States is the only nuclear power on the planet in October 1945, and Oppenheimer has devoted the past three years to a feverish effort to develop the bomb, the nuclear crisis for him is immediate and absolute. The new military "atomic age" invented under his leadership in Los Alamos is presented here not as a technoscientific achievement but rather as a desperate situation, one that must be resolved quickly before time itself ends in the form of a nuclear cataclysm. The strange tenses in his statement—awkwardly recognizing past technological innovations that were also imagined to be so terrible as to make war unthinkable, the reality of subsequent World Wars, and the exponentially higher explosive power of the bomb—marks a temporal uneasiness about the new age of atomic physics. For what Oppenheimer proposes here is nothing less than a race against a future arms race, as he attempts to mobilize nuclear fear to energize a new kind of international order.

Oppenheimer's depiction of a nuclear state of emergency is more attenuated but still a defining logic in the official statements of Norris Bradbury, who was the second director of "Los Alamos Scientific Laboratory" from 1945 to 1970. Looking back on his tenure as director in a 1970 talk entitled "Los Alamos—the First 25 Years," Bradbury reviewed the history of Los Alamos while presenting a slightly longer view of the nuclear future:

> No one makes nuclear weapons or bombs of any sort with any desire to use them. There is no pleasure in using them. In fact, one makes them with a profound desire never to have to use them, never to want to use them, never to find a need to use them. The whole project of the nuclear weapons business has been to put itself out of business. Strange business to be in but it's a fact. And yet, if you asked me in 1945, would we still be making bombs 25 years later, I would have said I don't think so. By that time the major powers would have seen some common sense. But we're still at it. And we have lots of partners in the race. What do you want to give me? Another 25 years, 50 years, 100 years, a thousand years, will we still be making atomic bombs? I simply don't know. I must admit to some personal discouragement; I didn't think it would last this long, but it has. (Bradbury 1980: 164–65)

The whole project of the nuclear weapons business has been to put itself out of business.   Here, the job of Los Alamos weapons scientists has become to put themselves out of business by building ever better nuclear weapons, so perfectly destructive as to ensure that warfare is simply removed as an international option for solving conflict. Nuclear weapons are presented as merely a temporary solution to international fear, an unpleasant one that has already gone on too long, contaminating the present with its longevity. Bradbury's denial of pleasure here is deceptive, for he ultimately attempts to separate "the bomb"—the weapon of mass destruction— from the intellectual challenges of nuclear science, which have proven to be fascinating for generations of Los Alamos scientists. Nevertheless, for both Oppenheimer and Bradbury the stated goal for weapons scientists is to end the military nuclear age they worked so tirelessly to create, ultimately to deny a future to nuclear weapons science in order to produce a more stable world. For Bradbury, as Oppenheimer, the problem remains one of international order, and specifically, the lack of a political alternative to the nuclear standoff with the Soviet Union. Bradbury's depiction of the nuclear arms race as a temporary solution to the international crisis was an important conceptual statement in Cold War Los Alamos, one that encouraged scientists to invest in weapons of mass destruction as a means of achieving peace in the short term. It ultimately enabled scientists intellectually to mobilize the destructive power of the hydrogen bomb as a peaceful, even nonviolent project.[7] This notion of "buying time" for politicians to diffuse potential conflicts through nuclear deterrence was the dominant ideology at the laboratory throughout the Cold War and remains an often evoked, core understanding among weapons scientists at Los Alamos to this day.

Los Alamos nuclear weapons scientists, however, "bought time" in ever-smaller units from 1945 to 1992, as the technological improvements in the weapons systems they designed reduced the temporal frame of nuclear war from weeks and days to hours and ultimately to mere minutes. The nuclear attacks on Hiroshima and Nagasaki took weeks to plan and days to execute by American forces, but by the mid-1960s the nuclear triad of always on-alert bombers, intercontinental missiles, and nuclear submarines (all carrying warheads designed at Los Alamos) meant that nuclear war could begin with less than a fifteen-minute window of warning, and could exceed the total explosive power of World War II in less than one hour of actual nuclear conflict. Thus, if securing "time" was the objective of the Cold War weapons program, Los Alamos weapons scientists pursued this goal through a complicated logic of technological determinism, in which the future was increasingly foreshortened in the name of producing a present-oriented space for political action. As explicitly a temporal project, the technoscience of nuclear deterrence simultaneously collapsed global space so efficiently during the Cold War that living on the brink of nuclear conflict quickly became naturalized as the very foundation of national security.

Studies by the Strategic Air Command in 1960, for example, concluded that with a ten-minute warning of Soviet attack only 14 percent of U.S. nuclear-equipped planes could be airborne but with a fourteen-minute warning 66 percent of U.S. bombers would be in the air (Richelson 1999: 20). Four minutes, thus, separated the possibility of a successful Soviet first strike against the United States from the establishment of a U.S. nuclear deterrent.[8] This global competition to control the first few minutes of a nuclear war through military technoscience placed Los Alamos scientists at the center of a broad-based military-industrial complex emphasizing production. In the U.S.-Soviet contest an "advantage" was increasingly recognized (after the development of the hydrogen bomb) not as a degree of destructive power but as a question of speed and accuracy of attack, making time the coordinating factor in a global system of nuclear deterrence. Put differently, this institutional investment in a particular kind of nuclear time (characterized by the speed of nuclear production as well as of warhead delivery systems) not only supported the entire U.S. nuclear project as an arms *race*, it was a cognitive structure in which weapons scientists understood that only the most sophisticated and cutting-edge nuclear weapons and delivery systems could deter war. Nuclear weapons were thus at the center of a nationalist cosmology in which Los Alamos scientists sought to regulate a world of minute-to-minute threat through military technologies. The evolution of nuclear weapons science in Los Alamos also constantly refined the immediacy of that threat. By steadily improving the size, weight, explosive power, and versatility of nuclear devices throughout the Cold War, Los Alamos scientists were not merely advancing a technical understanding of nuclear explosives but were intimately involved in a technologically mediated form of international relations. Seconds and minutes were not just the temporal horizon before the start of a nuclear war; they were the conceptual space of a new global economy of risk and communication, in which multiply redundant nuclear weapons systems (of bombers, missiles, and submarines) were deployed and constantly refined in hopes of producing a degree of certainty in international affairs.

After a half century of accelerated development in nuclear weapons technologies on these terms, new design work formally stopped at Los Alamos at 3:04 p.m. on September 23, 1992, with Divider, a twenty-kiloton device that was the last U.S. underground nuclear test of the 1990s. With the dissolution of the Soviet Union in 1991 and the subsequent U.S. moratorium on nuclear testing in 1992, one might imagine that nuclear time had simply run out, that the stopgap logics of U.S. nuclear weapons science had reached a logical end point, Oppenheimer and Bradbury's goal of a peacefully achieved postnuclear future realized. However, rather than producing a feeling of institutional achievement in Los Alamos, the end of the Cold War produced confusion and anxiety among weapons scientists now worried, among other things, about their own institutional future. While some weapons scientists worked on identifying new nuclear threats in the early 1990s—from "rogue states" to killer asteroids that might need to be destroyed in outer space with nuclear weapons—others contemplated new

Nuclear Posture Review

Force Structure Paths:

Protecting Options in an Uncertain World. . .

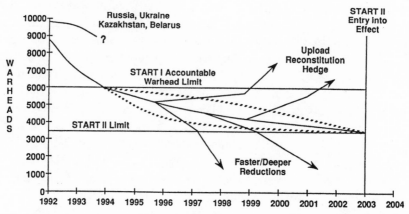

2.1. *Nuclear Posture Review,* futures chart. (*Source:* 1994 U.S. *Nuclear Posture Review*)

possible missions for the laboratory. One senior weapons scientist told me in 1994 that the laboratory should undertake a "new Manhattan Project to end world poverty" while another scientist stated in 1995 that perfecting airport security would be a profound contribution to the nation. Official laboratory statements in the immediate post–Cold War period privileged the opportunity for new corporate partnerships, and promoted the idea (of Manhattan Project-like) crash programs devoted to civilian needs (e.g., an environmentally clean "green car") or an expanded role in non-nuclear defense projects (Hecker 1993). This search for a new public image for the laboratory helped convince many employees that the end of the U.S. nuclear project was at hand: between 1991 and 1994, over one-third of Los Alamos weapons scientists retired.[9]

The 1994 U.S. Nuclear Posture Review, the first formal review of U.S. nuclear policy in the post–Cold War period, only magnified the uncertainty in Los Alamos. As Figure 2.1 shows, in the aftermath of the Cold War, U.S. policy makers considered everything from pursuing deep cuts in the U.S. nuclear arsenal to a return to full-scale nuclear production, with each line on the graph offering Los Alamos weapons scientists a radically different future mission (DOD 1994). The linguistically tortured "upload reconstitution hedge" option, a decision to dismantle rather than destroy nuclear weapons and to stockpile the components for future cold, and hot, wars,

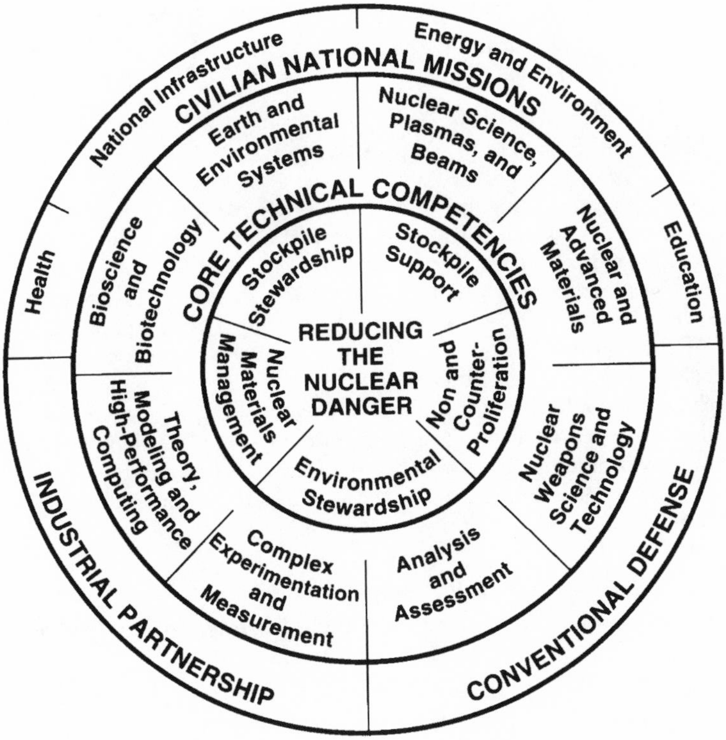
CIVILIAN NATIONAL MISSIONS
National Infrastructure
Energy and Environment
Health
Education
Earth and Environmental Systems
Nuclear Science, Plasmas, and Beams
CORE TECHNICAL COMPETENCIES
Bioscience and Biotechnology
Nuclear and Advanced Materials
Stockpile Stewardship
Stockpile Support
REDUCING THE NUCLEAR DANGER
Nuclear Materials Management
Non and Counter-Proliferation
Environmental Stewardship
Theory, Modeling and High-Performance Computing
Nuclear Weapons Science and Technology
Complex Experimentation and Measurement
Analysis and Assessment
INDUSTRIAL PARTNERSHIP
CONVENTIONAL DEFENSE

2.2. LANL post–Cold War mission diagram. (*Source*: 1995 *LANL Annual Report*)

won out in the Clinton administration's deliberations (see Nolan 1999). This "hedge" was total: President Clinton sought a global Comprehensive Test Ban Treaty while also simultaneously ordering the national laboratories to maintain the ability to design nuclear weapons and return to nuclear production. In this paradoxical policy environment (in which scientists were to maintain nuclear expertise but not their experimental regime), Los Alamos managers wrote their first post–Cold War mission statement. Devoting the laboratory to "reducing the global nuclear danger," this new mission statement reiterated a nuclear state of emergency by expanding the definition of "nuclear danger." The new post–Cold War mission chart for the laboratory presented these logics in the schematic form of a nuclear implosion device (see Figure 2.2). Mirroring the design of a plutonium pit, weapons science is surrounded in the diagram by non-nuclear research areas, presenting a imploding/exploding image of classified and nonclassified areas of research. In addition to the problems posed by foreign weapons programs, Los Alamos scientists were now to dedicate themselves to monitoring nuclear materials around the world, as well as solving questions about what to do with nuclear waste and how to clean up the environmental contamination from Cold War nuclear production sites.

In a special issue of *Los Alamos Science* commemorating the fiftieth anniversary of the laboratory, the fifth director of Los Alamos National Laboratory (LANL), Sig Hecker (1985–97), paid implicit homage to Bradbury's 1970 talk, with a contribution entitled "Los Alamos: Beginning the Second Fifty Years." Hecker wrote:

Just a few years ago, the superpowers had 75,000 weapons out there ensuring the peace. I contend that it was a rather uneasy peace. Now we will be dismantling tens of thousands of weapons, so all of us can sleep better. But nuclear weapons are still with us, and we at Los Alamos can't rest until each and every weapon that we have designed is actually retired and dismantled. We need to revamp the nuclear-weapons program to meet a dramatically changed situation, which I should emphasize, requires much more than an oil change and a lube job! It requires science. Although the country is not terribly interested in nuclear weapons, our responsibilities have not gone away. It will be up to us to provide the intellectual challenges needed to retain the best people and to maintain their experience and judgment. The latter goal is our highest priority. (1993: 230)

Los Alamos can't rest until each of its weapons is dismantled—it will be up to us. Here, the goal of eliminating nuclear weapons is forwarded as a proprietary responsibility: until there are no more Los Alamos–designed weapons on the planet Los Alamos scientists must take responsibility for tending to them. My conversations with weapons scientists in the mid-1990s frequently returned to this nuclear caretaker role for the laboratory, referencing an expectation that the U.S. nuclear complex would slowly collapse back into New Mexico, with Los Alamos staff responsible for an expanding notion of nuclear security after the Cold War.[10] Hecker makes sure to identify the future of the laboratory as a scientific institution, not as a production facility or merely a garage for ailing U.S. nuclear devices, arguing that it is state-of-the-art science that ultimately makes Los Alamos a national resource capable of dealing with the global nuclear danger. The project of the immediate post–Cold War period is thus to articulate those scientific challenges in terms that can garner economic support at the national level as well as enthusiasm within the laboratory.

The goal for Los Alamos weapons scientists is, thus, still to find a way out of the global nuclear weapons economy, but the scale and terms of that enterprise are being redefined for a post-Soviet world order. On the fiftieth anniversaries of the atomic bombing of Hiroshima and Nagasaki, Hecker addressed the nuclear future of the laboratory for employees, writing in the internal *LANL Newsbulletin* (1995):

In spite of grave political differences, nuclear weapons deterred the superpowers from global war. Over 80 million of the 100 million war-related deaths of this century occurred in its first half. I believe the devastation and the psychological impact of Hiroshima and Nagasaki, combined with the realization of the even greater destructive power of modern nuclear arsenals, drove deterrence diplomacy and bought us time ... Let's keep the horrid images of Hiroshima and Nagasaki in front of us as a stark reminder of what we must learn to avoid. Let's turn our attention to dealing with the current nuclear dangers to the benefit of all of mankind so that at the 100th anniversary people can look back and say that the Manhattan Project turned out all right.

So that people can say the Manhattan Project turned out all right. Here the military nuclear age is no longer explicitly marked as a regrettable or temporary situation but has become a positively valued achievement, one enabled by a remarkable accounting maneuver: by tallying up the wartime dead before and after the invention of the atomic bomb, Hecker argues that Los Alamos weapons scientists have saved literally millions of lives, having purchased a series of short-term futures (through the logics of deterrence) with each new Los Alamos–designed weapons system. Following Bradbury, nuclear weapons for Hecker are still "buying time" but the kind of time weapons scientists buy through their work has changed. Nuclear weapons are no longer just a short-term fix to the international crisis—with a focus on minutes and hours—but are a longer-term structure in the world system. Indeed, nuclear weapons now explicitly have a future for the first time, as Hecker imagines Los Alamos celebrating its hundredth birthday in 2043 still devoted to ending the global nuclear danger (first manifested with Los Alamos technology over Hiroshima and Nagasaki in 1945). The next half century of the atomic age, for Hecker, requires a Los Alamos commitment to making sure the Manhattan Project turns out "all right," a project that was already on Oppenheimer's mind in 1945 and on Bradbury's in 1970.

By separating the nuclear future from an arms race that the United States has already won, weapons scientists are redefining how they talk about nuclear weapons in the post–Cold War period. In an influential June 2000 essay, entitled "Nuclear Weapons in the Twenty-First Century," Stephen Younger (then the associate director of Nuclear Weapons Programs at LANL) argued for a fundamental rethinking of the use value of nuclear weapons for the new century. Identifying nuclear weapons as the "ultimate" defense of the nation, Younger asks what kind of nuclear forces the United States will need in the year 2020. He notes that advances in precision-guided weapons could reduce the U.S. reliance on some nuclear weapons while underscoring that the threat of "national annihilation" remains the supreme deterrent against all kinds of state aggression. Concluding that "it is almost impossible to conceive of technological and political developments that would enable the United States to meet its defense needs in 2020 without nuclear weapons," Younger articulates a number of new uses for nuclear weapons, from "mini-nukes" (explosives under one kiloton), to "earth-penetrator" weapons (for attacking buried structures), to a new type of robust warhead (based on the Hiroshima bomb) that could be built and deployed without underground nuclear testing, thus maintaining technical support for the Comprehensive Test Ban Treaty (Younger 2000). Rather than reducing the U.S. reliance on nuclear weapons in a post–Cold War world, Younger works here to reenergize the official nuclear imaginary, offering new targets, new technologies, and an updated but still foundational U.S. reliance on weapons of mass destruction. Unlike Oppenheimer, Bradbury, and Hecker, Younger presents the nuclear future here not as an unfortunate necessity whose time will eventually come, but rather as an expanding technoscientific project and a fundamental aspect of American power. When asked about the future mission of LANL by the *Albuquerque Journal*, Younger offered this appraisal of the twenty-first century project in Los Alamos:

> What we are is a nuclear-weapons laboratory. And I think we will continue to be . . . [Because] when is art done? When is medicine done? Or literature? It is never done. You are always learning more. (Hoffman 1999a)

When is art done? Here, nuclear weapons are finally freed of their negative connotations altogether, and the nuclear future is opened up in a new way, no longer caught in the image of a fiery apocalyptic end but rather energized by the intellectual possibilities of conducting nuclear weapons science on its own terms. From Younger's perspective, Los Alamos weapons scientists are no longer working to put themselves out of business, but should see themselves as proprietors of a permanent part of an American world system, one that requires continuing investments and innovation—because, after all, when is "art" done, or we might add, "U.S. security" complete? Here the state-of-the-art in nuclear weapons design has been reproduced literally as an art of the state, an aesthetic project as well as a military necessity.

If the nuclear future is not what it used to be in Los Alamos, the programmatic statements by laboratory management nonetheless demonstrate how claims on the future have been an essential aspect of conducting nuclear weapons science in the United States. The transition from Oppenheimer's "nuclear state of emergency" to Younger's "endless art form," however, marks not only a shift in the rhetorical debate about our collective nuclear future, it also signals more fundamental changes in how nuclear weapons science is conducted in the post–Cold War order. For if the epistemic cultures of the Cold War nuclear program provided a cognitive orientation for weapons scientists—a cosmology linking military technoscience and global politics—the end of the Soviet Union and of underground nuclear testing eliminated two central elements in that conceptual circuit: the arms race and its accompanying experimental regimes.[11] How weapons scientists negotiated the resulting technological and ideological changes in post–Cold War Los Alamos is not an esoteric question of the reproduction of expert knowledge; it is rather to interrogate the conceptual basis for America's commitment to nuclear weapons in the twenty-first century, and to do so at the very center of that enterprise. The remainder of this chapter interrogates the cognitive and experimental processes that transformed the bomb from a weapon into an art form. For if the temporal discourse of the bomb has shifted in fundamental ways since the end of the Cold War, so too has the tactile experience of nuclear weapons work for scientists. Paying attention to the technoaesthetics of nuclear weapons work allows insight into how the "bomb-ness" of the bomb—its conceptual meaning—is understood by those responsible for maintaining the U.S. arsenal, and how it has changed over time. As we shall see, an increasing abstraction of the bomb within the experimental regimes of U.S. weapons science makes it difficult for Los Alamos scientists to ever experience the explosive totality of the nuclear weapons they have designed and now maintain. As we shall see, the bomb is becoming increasingly beautiful in Los Alamos, not because it explodes but because it can be rendered in ways that are aesthetically pleasing to weapons scientists and that articulate an expanding view of the nuclear future.

ABOVE-GROUND TESTING (1945–1962): TACTILITY AND THE NUCLEAR SUBLIME

At the deepest level, the existence of atomic weapons has undermined the possibility of the sublime relationship to both natural and technological objects . . . Who identifies with the bomb?

—David E. Nye, *American Technological Sublime*

I firmly believe that if every five years the world's major political leaders were required to witness the in-air detonation of a multi-megaton warhead, progress on meaningful arms control measures would be speeded up appreciably.

—Harold Agnew, "Vintage Agnew," *Los Alamos Science*

In his study of American spectacular technologies, David Nye (1994) argues that nuclear weapons are so terrifying that they cannot be experienced through an aesthetic of the sublime. For Nye, the visual power of the Brooklyn Bridge or the *Apollo 11* Moon Mission fuses an experience of the sublime with a national consciousness for all spectators, creating a feeling of pride in American technology and a collective notion of uplift. The bomb, on the other hand, has no such positive dimension for him, as "to anyone who contemplates them, nuclear weapons can only be a permanent, invisible terror that offers no moral enlightenment" (Nye 1994: 253). Los Alamos scientists, however, have banked their careers on a diametrically opposed proposition; namely, that nuclear weapons are so powerful that they fundamentally reshape human consciousness in ways that can enable global security and peace. Harold Agnew, director of Los Alamos Scientific Laboratory from 1970 to 1979, for example, has argued that the visual power of a multimegaton explosion is transformative for all viewers (1983). In calling for regular public demonstrations of the power of the thermonuclear bomb, Agnew explicitly deploys a notion of the nuclear sublime to foster international enlightenment in the form of disarmament. But if human consciousness can be so thoroughly transformed by a physical experience of the exploding bomb, as Agnew argues, this also identifies a basic cognitive problem produced by the move to underground nuclear testing during the Cold War. Put simply, since no American has witnessed an atomic explosion without the use of prosthetic senses (computer screens and seismic monitors) since the signing of the 1963 Atmospheric Test Ban Treaty, who now has full cognitive access to the technology? And if, as Agnew suggests, the conceptual power of a nuclear weapon is fundamentally linked to a direct human sensory experience of the explosion, how has the shifting experimental regime of nuclear weapons science transformed the meaning of the technology within the laboratory?

In the Kantian formulation, the sublime is evoked by a natural object or process whose massive form produces a combination of awe and fear. Kant (1986) offers two species of the sublime that inform nuclear weapons science: the dynamic sublime, which is provoked by the terror of seeing a tornado or erupting volcano from a safe distance, and the mathematical sublime, which begins with the inability to comprehend the scale and vastness of a mountain or river. Both forms of the sublime are deeply disturbing because, in demonstrating the limits of human cognition, the confrontation with an infinitely powerful or infinitely complex form threatens to obliterate the self. As a sensory experience, the profundity of the sublime is inexpressible, placing it outside of language. The traumatized psyche recovers from this realization by naming the thing that is so disquieting, thereby containing the infinite within a conceptual category: importantly, the sublime does not end in comprehension but rather in an intellectual compensation. The pleasure of the sublime, for Kant, derives not from understanding the tidal wave or mountain but by internally managing an overwhelming sensory experience; the sublime is ultimately resolved via a false sense of intellectual control.

While for Kant the sublime is always tied to a natural form, the *nuclear* sublime is a more complex phenomenon in that the bomb is an invented technosocial form.[12] For weapons scientists, there is consequently an inherent tension between the reality of the bomb as a device built to certain specifications and detonated at precise moments (and thus under human control) and the experience of the nuclear explosion itself, which is a destructive force that is cognitively overwhelming and a direct threat to the human body. But if the conceptual force of the sublime is directly proportional to the danger involved in the experiential event, as Kant seems to argue, then nuclear weapons offer access to a uniquely powerful manifestation of sublimity. In Los Alamos, the pleasures of nuclear production—of experimental success—have always been mediated by the military context of nuclear explosions, requiring a complicated internal negotiation of the meaning of the technology. Consequently, an experience of the nuclear sublime for weapons scientists, I would argue, is always an eminently political thing. By historicizing expressions of the nuclear sublime within the Los Alamos weapons science community, we can see how the shifting experimental regimes open to weapons research since 1945 have worked to strip the exploding bomb of its visceral threat to the body of the scientist. The result has been a diminished access to the nuclear sublime, allowing the bomb to be experienced not through a circuit of terror/pleasure within the laboratory, but increasingly as simply an aesthetic-intellectual form.

For the first Los Alamos scientists, however, the first nuclear detonation on July 16, 1945, was not merely an intellectual accomplishment but an overwhelming physical event (see Figure 2.3). I. I. Rabi, for example, recoiled from the power of the flash, describing it as "the brightest light I have ever seen or that I think anyone has ever seen. It blasted; it pounced; it bored its way right through you. It was a vision which was seen with more than the eye. It was seen to last forever" (quoted in Rhodes 1986: 672). Experiencing the first nuclear explosion as something that "pounced" and "bored" through the human body, for Rabi the millisecond ushering in a new world of nuclear physics was terrifying. Emilio Segre was similarly moved:

> We saw the whole sky flash with unbelievable brightness in spite of the very dark glasses we wore . . . I believe that for a moment I thought the explosion might set fire to the atmosphere and thus finish the earth, even though I knew that this was not possible. (Quoted in ibid.: 673)

Here, an experimental success produces a new kind of terror that proliferates in Segre's mind to encompass the entire planet, as Segre experiences a split between what he knows to be true (that the atmosphere will

2.3. Trinity explosion at 0.016, 10, and 12 seconds. (Courtesy of Los Alamos National Laboratory)

not ignite) and what he feels to be true (that the world is on fire). Philip Morrison, also wearing welding glasses to protect his eyes from the flash, was moved more by "the blinding heat of a bright day on your face in the cold desert morning. It was like opening a hot oven with the sun coming out like a sunrise" (ibid.). The unprecedented heat of the explosion scared Morrison with its strange form, arriving with a velocity and a temperature exceeding that of several midday suns. For Otto Frisch, it was not the light or heat, but the sound of the explosion that terrified, and decades later he claimed he could still hear it (Szasz 1984: 88). In these descriptions the sight, the sound, and the heat of the first nuclear explosion—all part of the objective of the experiment—nonetheless still terrify, making the weapons scientist's body the most important register of the power of the bomb. Though protected by goggles, barriers, and miles of buffer zone, the Trinity explosion not only overwhelmed senses but also physically assaulted scientists: George Kistiakowsky was knocked off his feet by the shock wave, Enrico Fermi was so physically shaken by the Trinity explosion that he was unable to drive his car afterward, and Robert Serber, who looked directly at the blast without eye protection, was flashblinded for thirty seconds. In this first nuclear explosion, the weapons scientist's body was the primary register of the explosion, the physicality of blast effects—light, sound, shockwave, and heat—all assaulting human senses and demonstrating the fragility of the human body when confronted by the power of the bomb.

Witnesses to the first atomic blast later evoked the sublime to capture its meaning, in many cases mediating the physical pain and intellectual pleasure of their technoscientific achievement through a deployment of religious imagery. Oppenheimer described his experience of the Trinity test this way:

> We waited until the blast had passed, walked out of the shelter and then it was extremely solemn. We knew the world would not be the same. A few people laughed, a few people cried. Most people were silent. I remembered the line from the Hindu scripture, the Bhagavad-Gita: Vishnu is trying to persuade the prince that he should do his duty and to impress him he takes on his multiarmed form and says, "Now I am become Death, the Destroyer of worlds." I suppose we all thought that, one way or another. (Quoted in Rhodes 1986: 676)

Now I am become Death, the destroyer of worlds. Here the arrival of a new world of nuclear physics is immediately positioned along-side the end of a world—as creation and destruction are fused in a moment of borrowed religiosity. The dramatic quality of Oppenheimer's statement—its theatrical character—elevates the technical achievement of Trinity while mediating its proliferating form through a linguistic containment. William Laurence, the only reporter allowed to witness the Trinity test, also sought to ground the meaning of the explosion for the American public in mythology:

> It was a sunrise such as the world had never seen, a great green super-sun climbing in a fraction of a second to a height of more than eight thousand feet, rising ever higher until it touched the clouds, lighting up earth and sky all around with a dazzling luminosity. Up it went, a great ball of fire about a mile in diameter, changing colors as it kept shooting upward, from deep purple to orange, expanding, growing bigger, rising as it expanded, an elemental force freed from its bonds after being chained for billions of years. For a fleeting instant the color was unearthly green, such as one sees only in the corona of the sun during a total eclipse. It was as though the earth had opened and the skies had split. One felt as though one were present at

the moment of creation when God said: "let there be light" . . . In that infinitesimal fraction of time, inconceivable and immeasurable, during which the first atomic bomb converted a small part of its matter into the greatest burst of energy released on earth up to that time, Prometheus had broken his bonds and brought a new fire down to earth, a fire three million times more powerful than the original fire he snatched from the gods for the benefit of man some five hundred thousand years ago. (1946: 10–13)

Let there be light. Evoking God, gods, and Prometheus, Laurence provides the American public with an image of the bomb as beautific form, minimizing the physical effects of the explosion in favor of the conceptual power of a "new age." The terror of the nuclear sublime is subsumed here through an implicit religious discourse of Manifest Destiny, as Los Alamos scientists have reinvented both the physical world and international order from the deserts of central New Mexico. Laurence deploys the nuclear sublime to position the bomb as an intellectual project that stimulates the imagination, rather than one that threatens the body.

Nonetheless, the physical effects of a nuclear explosion—the flash, radiation, firestorm, blast wave, and fallout—threaten all witnesses, limiting the ability of scientists to experience the bomb as a purely aesthetic or intellectual form. From September 1945 to August 1963, U.S. weapons scientists would pursue an expansive above-ground testing program involving 210 atmospheric and five underwater detonations (turning much of the planet into an American nuclear test complex and producing nuclear victims on a equally large scale). The initial test series in the Pacific were conducted as giant military campaigns, involving tens of thousands of workers, followed by the establishment of a permanent test area in Nevada in 1951. A brief glance at the test program reveals an expansive development not only in military explosives (leading to multiply redundant systems of nuclear bombs, warheads, torpedoes, artillery shells, depth charges, and tactical field weapons) but also in the scope of America's nuclear imagination, as nuclear detonations were conducted on land, underwater, at various elevations, and in the upper atmosphere. Nuclear devices were exploded on towers, dropped from planes, suspended from balloons, floated on barges, placed in craters, buried in shafts and tunnels, launched from submarines, shot from cannons, and loaded into increasingly powerful missiles.

Consider, for example, how Los Alamos weapons scientist Ted Taylor describes seeing his first atomic explosion in the spring of 1951 on Enewetak Atoll during Operation Greenhouse (see Figure 2.4):

It was all extremely exciting, including many hours of floating in the lagoon with snorkel and face mask, watching countless numbers and varieties of

2.4. George Shot, Operation Greenhouse, Enewetak Atoll, May 1951. (U.S. Department of Energy photograph)

tropical fish so close that one often touched them. The explosion was every bit as awesome as I had expected—roughly five times as big as the one that destroyed Hiroshima. There was much pre-dawn activity on Perry Island, where the "scientific" (as opposed to military) headquarters and accommodations were, so there was plenty of time to get comfortably settled on the beach, straining with binoculars to see the shot tower about 15 miles away across much of the lagoon. The countdown started close to dawn . . . 1 minute . . . thirty seconds (put on your dark goggles) . . . fifteen . . . four, three, two, one: instant light, almost blinding through the goggles, and the heat that persisted for a time that seemed interminable. I was sure I was getting instant sunburn, and the back of my neck felt hot from the heat reflected off the beach house behind us. Goggles came off after a few seconds. The fireball was still glowing like a setting sun over a clear horizon, a purple and brown cloud rising so fast that in less than a minute we had to crane our necks to see the top. I had forgotten about the shock wave, a surprisingly sharp, loud crack that broke several martini glasses on the shelf on the beach house bar. The sight was beautiful at first, in an awesome way, then turned ugly and seemed threatening as the gray-brown cloud spread and began drifting towards us. I tried hard to shake off the feelings of exhilaration, and think about the deeper meanings of all this, without success. It was just plain thrilling.[13]

It was just plain thrilling. Here the pattern of pleasure is constantly interrupted by the threat of the bomb—the instant sunburn that disrupts the visual display, the shockwave that travels fifteen miles to break glasses—but still ends in aesthetic pleasure. After the detonation, Taylor remembers lying down on the beach to relax and ponder the event, but his contemplative moment was interrupted once again, this time by a peculiar cloud overhead raining down bits and pieces of metal:

a few minutes later we were shocked to know that our hair, up close, was reading about 10 R per hour. In the next half hour or so we took four or five showers, with vigorous shampooing, dropping the level several-fold each time. None of us were wearing film badges for recording our exposure to radiation. I have no idea how much total radiation we got.

As the cloud from the explosion rained down radioactive bits of the steel tower that had once held the nuclear device some fifteen miles away, the eighty-one-kiloton nuclear event was revealed to be not simply the flash of light and the mushroom cloud, but also the atmospheric fallout.

The circuit of pleasure here (the beach, the fish, the beauty of the mushroom cloud, the intellectual achievement of the blast) is constantly interrupted by physical danger (the flash, the shockwave, the radioactive fallout), underscoring that during the era of above-ground testing the bomb was not a technology that was ultimately "controllable." Scientists could determine when and where the blast occurred, but then were at the mercy of weather patterns and their protective gear. The weapons scientist's body was ultimately exposed to the reality of the bomb as an explosive device and to radioactive fallout as an airborne threat. The internal mediation of the event for Taylor is thus marked in the register of the nuclear sublime, as the awesomeness and terror of the event requires an intellectual compensation. As nuclear testing expanded in the 1950s, the scientific negotiation of the nuclear sublime took on a more calculated form. At Los Alamos, Taylor became fascinated by the possible scale of nuclear explosions; he would design both the smallest U.S. nuclear device of the 1950s (an atomic artillery shell) and the largest fission device ever detonated, before renouncing nuclear weapons work in the 1960s and committing himself to disarmament (Hansen 1988; McPhee 1974). Only one year after being simultaneously "thrilled" and "terrified" by witnessing his first nuclear detonation on Enewetak Atoll during Operation Greenhouse, Taylor orchestrated a new experience of the nuclear sublime at the recently created Nevada Proving Grounds. Prior to the test of his new design (which produced a key breakthrough in warhead miniaturization), Taylor positioned himself so that with the help of a parabolic mirror the flash from the twenty-kiloton nuclear detonation would light a cigarette (McPhee 1974: 93–95; Miller 1986: 154). This experiment was reproduced three years later on Operation Teapot and recorded on film (see Figure 2.5). Here the exploding bomb is used to produce a moment of technoaesthetic reverie, where the massive destructive power of the atomic age is marshaled to accomplish that most mundane—and purely sensual act—of smoking. Only seven years and twenty-five nuclear tests after the destruction of Hiroshima and Nagasaki, the technoaesthetic production of the bomb has already taken on a newly domesticated form: for Taylor, the exploding bomb produces, not mass destruction, but rather a unique dual opportunity for intellectual and physical stimulation, as he converts a successful experiment into pure tactile pleasure.

Discussing his commitment to the first atomic bomb, Oppenheimer told the Personnel Security Board in 1954 that "it is my judgment in these things that when you see something that is technically sweet, you go ahead and do it and you argue about what to do about it only after you have had your technical success" (AEC 1971: 81). But if the aesthetic power of the "technically sweet" could overwhelm the nascent political reality of nuclear explosives in July 1945, by the 1950s, Los Alamos scientists (post-Hiroshima and Nagasaki and in the midst of a Cold War arms race) were directly confronted with the military implications of their experiments. Consider the Apple II shot on May 5, 1955, which was part of Operation Teapot conducted at the Nevada Test Site. For Los Alamos scientists the primary task of the Teapot series was to work on miniaturizing nuclear warheads while simultaneously enhancing the explosive yield—to extract more destructive energy from a smaller machine. But while their research was focused on how to "boost" the nuclear yield by introducing a mixture of deuterium-tritium gas into the hollow core of a plutonium sphere during the implosion process, the Apple II detonation was also the center of a U.S. nuclear war fighting program; it was also part of a massive civil defense exercise televised live for a national audience.

In addition to designing the Apple II nuclear device, Los Alamos scientists conducted an elaborate set of experiments to test the radiation and blast

2.5. Lighting a cigarette with an atomic bomb
in Nevada 1955. (Stills from the DOD film,
Operation Teapot: Military Effects Studies)

effects of the explosion on machines, on human mannequins distributed
around the test area, and on animals. They deployed air force planes to collect atmospheric samples from within the mushroom cloud, track its fallout
pattern over Nevada, and study how the shockwave would hit a plane in
flight. Simultaneously, the U.S. military conducted Exercise Desert Rock VI
(see Figure 2.6), intended to acclimatize troops to an atomic battlefield and
develop nuclear war fighting tactics. One thousand troops, eighty-nine
armored vehicles, and nineteen helicopters participated in the exercise,
which constituted an armored assault on ground zero (DOD 1955). While
the troops marched into the swirling radioactive dust storm created by the
explosion, helicopters swooped in to evacuate soldiers who had been

2.6. Operation Desert Rock, U.S. Army troops at the Nevada Proving Grounds, 1950s. (U.S. National Archives)

designated in advance as "casualties" while other personnel fired cannons and machine guns loaded with blanks at this invading army to make the war game seem "real." After the assault, soldiers covered with the dust produced by the nuclear explosion were "decontaminated" with brooms.[14]

The Apple II detonation was also the centerpiece of Operation Cue, a civil defense exercise designed to measure how a "typical" American community would look after a nuclear attack.[15] An elaborately rendered town was built on the test site, consisting of a fire station, a school, a radio station, a library, and a dozen homes in the current building styles. These buildings were carefully constructed, furnished with the latest consumer items (appliances, furniture, televisions, carpets, and linens), and stocked with food that had been specially flown in from Chicago and

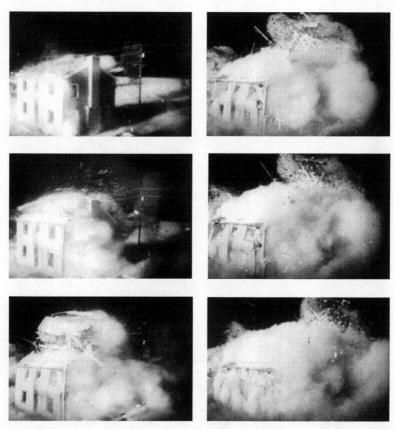

2.7. Stills from film of blast wave hitting brick house, Operation Cue, May 5, 1955. (U.S. National Archives)

San Francisco. Residences were populated with mannequins dressed in brand-new clothing and posed with domestic theatricality—at the dinner table, cowering in the basement, or watching television (like the national television audience). Over two thousand civil defense workers and media representatives participated in Operation Cue, an effort to visualize what would happen to an idealized American community (rendered down to the last detail of consumer desire) if bombed (see Figure 2.7). After the Apple II detonation, the television crews offered tips on surviving an atomic attack, while the civil defense teams practiced mass feeding—cooking the food (carefully recovered from trenches, refrigerators, and pantries) that had survived the explosion. As ritual sacrifice, Operation Cue made visible for an American audience the terror of a nuclear assault, while attempting to demonstrate the possibility of survival.

The Apple II device was, thus, at the center of a schizophrenic space, in which the same Los Alamos physics experiment was simultaneously a U.S.

nuclear strike against an imagined enemy and a U.S. nuclear attack on an American suburb. Los Alamos scientists were not simply working to perfect the bomb through new design work; they were also engaged in nuclear war fighting and civil defense all at the same moment, confusing the simulated and the real. The bullets in army machine guns may have been blanks, but the bomb detonated with a force of twenty-nine kilotons (twice that which destroyed Hiroshima); and while mannequins were used to simulate the effects of the explosion on human beings, the troops, pilots, civilian observers, and neighboring communities were all subjects of a real radiological experiment in the form of exposure to atmospheric fallout that was recorded as far away as Paris, Missouri (Miller 1986: 237; see also Gallager 1993; Hacker 1994: 164–69). As physics experiment, nuclear attack, civil defense exercise, national spectacle, and theatrical display of resolve for the Soviets, the Apple II explosion cannot be reduced to simply the goal of producing either a nuclear deterrent or a specific nuclear device: Los Alamos technology was used here to enact a nuclear event in which Americans were conceived simultaneously as military aggressors and victims. The complexity of this kind of national spectacle grounded the experimental work of weapons scientists in both Cold War politics and nuclear fear. In other words, the above-ground testing regime was devoted not only to the basic science of producing atomic, and then thermonuclear, explosions, but also to researching precisely how nuclear explosions traumatize the material structures of everyday life as well as the human body.[16]

Consequently, the dangers of the nuclear age were viscerally dramatized with each above-ground nuclear test. Critics pointed out that the twenty-nine-kiloton Apple II device was dwarfed in size by the multimegaton thermonuclear weapons—a thousand times more powerful—that both the United States and Soviet Union were stockpiling at the time. Thus, state spectacles, like Operation Cue, which were staged explicitly to illustrate the possibility of survival, also worked to undermine American beliefs in the possibility of civil defense from a Soviet nuclear attack. By the late 1950s, public concern about the global health effects of atmospheric fallout was directly competing with the official "national security" discourse supporting the bomb.[17] Nobel Prize–winning chemist Linus Pauling won a second Nobel Peace Prize for his efforts to publicize the accumulating environmental effects of atmospheric nuclear detonations. Pauling portrayed each above-ground nuclear detonation not as a sign of American technology and military strength but rather as a large-scale genetic experimentation on the human species, already involving tens of thousands of victims (Pauling 1963; see also Wang 1999). The scientific critique of atmospheric fallout expanded the definition of nuclear disaster from war—a thing that could be deferred into the future—to an everyday life already contaminated with the cumulative global effects of nuclear explosions. In response, a U.S.-Soviet test moratorium from 1958 to 1961 led to the Partial Test Ban Treaty in 1963, which banned all nuclear explosions in the atmosphere, underwater, and in outer space. Today, Los Alamos scientists remember the Partial Test Ban Treaty—the first international effort to restrain weapons science—as both a public health measure and a means of shielding nuclear tests from Soviet observation. However, the move to underground testing contained more than simply the nuclear device, it also redefined how Los Alamos scientists could experience the power of a nuclear explosion, fundamentally changing the technoaesthetic potential, and thus the politics, of the bomb.

UNDERGROUND TESTING (1963–1992): EMBRACING COMPLEXITY, FETISHIZING PRODUCTION

The consolidation of nuclear testing at the Nevada Test Site after 1963 regularized nuclear weapons science, replacing the military campaign structure of the above-ground testing regime (which required massive labor to simply equip remote test areas in the Pacific and in Nevada) with a more stable experimental form. National spectacles, like Operation Cue, were also eliminated by the underground test regime, which was configured to regularize nuclear production. During the underground test regime, seven formal stages in the development of a new weapon—conception, feasibility, design, development, manufacturing, deployment, and retirement—were institutionalized, placing Los Alamos weapons scientists on a carefully modulated calendar and at the center of a vast industrial machine (see Figure 2.8; DOE 1984). Los Alamos weapons scientists trained during the underground test regime consequently experienced the Cold War as a relentless series of nuclear warhead design and test deadlines (cf. Gusterson 1996a). It took roughly ten years to bring a new warhead or bomb from design conception to deployment. Multiple weapons systems were under production simultaneously, and were designed with the understanding that they would be replaced by a next-generation system within fifteen to twenty years. The resulting pace of U.S. nuclear weapons research was impressive: the United States conducted 1,149 nuclear detonations from July 1945 to September 1992 (including the thirty-five detonations of the plowshares program, and twenty-four joint U.S.-British nuclear tests).[18] This averages out to roughly two nuclear tests per month over the forty-six years between the first nuclear explosion, Trinity (July 16, 1945), and the last, Divider (September 23, 1992) (NRDC 1998).[19]

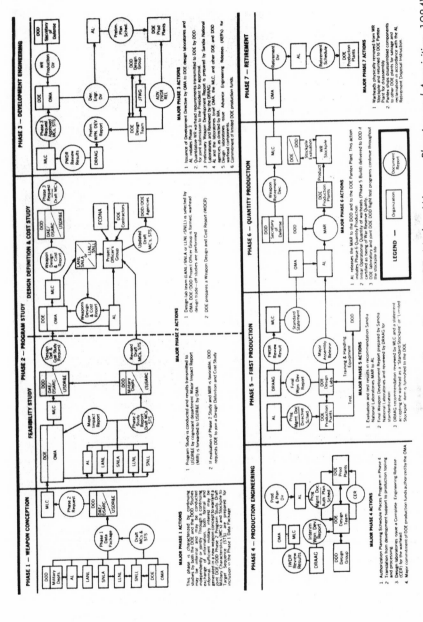

2.8. 1984 U.S. Nuclear Weapons Production Chart. (Source: DOE, *Nuclear Weapons Planning and Acquisition, 1984*)

Given that each nuclear test was a multimillion-dollar experiment under-scored by a national security imperative, the formal structures of U.S. nuclear production encouraged scientists to understand Cold War time along strictly technological terms. For Los Alamos scientists the nuclear age remains perfectly tangible—visible in machine form—with each nuclear test part of a technological genealogy of design concepts dating back to the first nuclear explosion on July 16, 1945.[20]

From a scientific point of view, the challenge of underground testing was how to both contain the explosion and make it visible to machine sensors, to extract technical data safely from an underground space in the midst of the most extreme pressures and temperatures imaginable (see OTA 1989). As one Los Alamos weapons scientist trained during the underground regime described it:

> A weapon is at a temperature and a density, and is over so fast, that you can't really get in there and look and see how it is doing. You can only guess from the results, how it actually behaved. In that sense, it is very complex. It is possibly like astrophysics. It is in a regime that is inaccessible to you: high temperature, high density. You can't put [detectors] in the [device] because it will affect the performance. You learn something from radio-chemistry because of the neutrons that come out of it; you put radiochem-ical detectors in the ground after the shot—and they were in where the action was—and that's the nearest you get to seeing how it actually behaves. So the difficulty [of underground testing] comes from the inaccessibility of the regime, for all those reasons.

The difficulty comes from the inaccessibility of the regime. Here we see the change in experimental regimes registered at the level of sen-sory perception. For the challenge of underground testing is revealed to be, not the effort to protect the human body from the effects of the explosion, but rather to make the exploding bomb visible to human senses. However, the "visibility" of the exploding bomb has fundamen-tally changed. No longer is a primary aspect of weapons science to inves-tigate the effects of the bomb on everyday objects, methodically subjecting cars, houses, plants, animals, and people to the blast, thermal radiation, and electromagnetic pulse effects of a nuclear explosion—an experimental project that made each above-ground test also explicitly a nuclear war fighting exercise. Instead, underground testing as an experi-mental regime limited the ability to test blast and radiation effects, leav-ing weapons scientists to work on the internal complexities of the nuclear explosion itself; that is, Los Alamos scientists became more narrowly focused on the physics of the detonation and the robustness of the machine, rather than on the effects of the bomb, substantially con-solidating the experimental project.[21]

The shift from above-ground to underground testing not only regularized nuclear production, disciplining the bodies of weapons scientists to meet a constant series of deadlines (underscored by the Cold War state of emergency; see Gusterson 1996a), it also fundamentally changed the technoaesthetic experience of conducting weapons science. Witnesses to a nuclear test might now feel an earthquake or see a great mass of earth heave upward at the moment of detonation (see Wolff 1984). But the most visibly dramatic aspect of the underground test came after the event itself, in the form of a large, perfectly symmetrical crater (see Figure 2.9). Underground testing replaced a full sensory experience of the exploding bomb (producing fear and awe in the mode of the dynamic sublime) with a more limited form, closer to what Kant called the "mathematical sublime" (Kant 1986). For Kant, the mathematical sublime involved a flooding of the senses with overwhelming scale and complexity, rather than physical fear. Underground testing rendered the exploding bomb all but invisible, also eliminating the immediate threat to the body of the scientist. Weapons science consequently became focused less on blast effects and more on the scale, temporal sequence, and nuclear progression of the event at the atomic level. In other words, when Los Alamos weapons scientists trained during the underground test regime talk about nuclear weapons they tend not to forward their own sensory experience of the explosion (as did the previous generation of weapons scientists), but rather the intellectual complexity of the detonation as a set of physical processes. For this generation, the intellectual pleasures of weapons science derive from investigating events that take place at millions and billions of degrees of heat, at millions of pounds of pressure, which release incredible energy in billionths of a second.

Indeed, the energy regimes at which nuclear weapons operate are unique; the closest approximation is what happens in the center of a star, which operates on a vastly different time scale. Consequently, many weapons scientists have been recruited out of astrophysics programs, and continue to think about their weapons research in relation to stars (LANL 1993: 11–12). This tracking back and forth between macro- and microcosmic regimes of scale not only produces a proliferating sense of space (a perfect register of the mathematical sublime) but also is underscored by a unique sense of time. Nuclear explosions happen in billionths of a second, requiring weapons scientists to develop their own languages for dividing microseconds into understandable units. Since World War II, Los Alamos weapons scientists have examined nuclear explosions in units called "shakes" (for "faster than the shake of a lamb's tail"): one shake equals 1/100,000,000th of a second, which is the time it takes one uranium atom to fission (Hansen 1988: 11). A hydrogen bomb explosion, the most devastating military force on the

2.9. Sedan Crater, Nevada Test Site. (U.S. National Archives)

planet, occurs in about hundred shakes, or a millionth of a second. The internal complexity of a nuclear explosion can consequently be approached as a potentially endless universe of processes, interactions, pressures, and flows all happening in a split second. Put differently, if we were to add up the 2,053 nuclear detonations conducted in human history—a force thousands of times the total destructive power unleashed during World War II—collectively these explosions would still not constitute a single second of time.[22]

To engage the scale and complexity of a nuclear explosion as simply an intellectual-aesthetic project, however, requires insulating the body from the physical and cognitive assaults of the explosion. During above-ground testing, part of the cognitive understanding of the "test" was the sheer visceral power of the explosion, which necessitated goggles, protective barriers, escape routes, and miles of distance to protect scientists from the results of their experiments. The restriction of weapons science to underground testing at the Nevada Test Site after 1963 allowed permanent control rooms to be established in which weapons scientists no longer watched the detonation itself, but rather data presented on video screens and seismic monitors for confirmation of a successful test (see Figure 2.10). The explosion became almost totally mediated by technology. New

2.10. Nuclear test control room, Nevada Test Site. (U.S. Department of Energy photograph)

prosthetic senses provided ever more precise and immediate information about the implosion as an experiment, while insulating scientists from a direct physical perception of the blast and radiation effects. Consequently, a sensory appreciation of the power of the exploding bomb was increasingly displaced in favor of mechanical measurement. Some weapons scientists, for example, would rank their tests among recent naturally occurring earthquakes, while others would take a ceremonial visit to the crater produced by the exploding bomb to gain an appreciation of its scale (see Figure 2.11; Bailey 1995: 76; Gusterson 1996a: 138). After 1963, weapons scientists would not know the yield of the explosion until days later, after radiochemical analysis of soil samples revealed the power of the event. This yield calculation was highly fetishized within the nuclear program, as the final number was important to military planners who might someday use the device. However, what could be appreciated with a glance in the above-ground test regime (the scale of destruction) was in the underground regime a subject of retrospective analysis and reconstruction. The yield calculation might be able to produce an experience of the mathematical sublime for weapons scientists focused on the complexity of the explosion, but the answer it

2.11. Nuclear weapon craters in Yucca Flats, Nevada Test Site. (U.S. Department of Energy photograph)

produced was simply a number, not a visceral understanding of the destructive power of the bomb in relation to the human body.

Consequently, while an above-ground explosion was always an exciting spectacle and marked event for weapons scientists, an underground detonation could be boring.[23] A number of scientists told me that the excitement from their point of view was in the buildup to the experiment—the deadline-driven effort to drill the hole, build the test rack, and array it with custom-built detector equipment and coordinate the efforts of physicists, chemists, engineers, and construction workers (Wolff 1984; LANL 1988). The intellectual excitement was also in the period after the test, when the data was in hand (sometimes days later). The sensory experience of an underground detonation (a monthly occurrence from 1963 to 1992) was the most predictable and normalized aspect of the experience. Thus, the underground test regime not only contained the radioactive effects of the bomb to the Nevada Test Site while shielding U.S. nuclear science from Soviet eyes, it also worked over time to make nuclear explosions routine.[24]

For Los Alamos weapons scientists, the technoaesthetic reinvention of the bomb during the underground test regime was enhanced by two factors: new arms control treaties and the commitment to designing an increasingly "safe" nuclear arsenal. In 1970, the United States signed on the Nuclear Nonproliferation Treaty, pledging to eliminate its nuclear arsenal at the earliest opportunity (formally making nuclear weapons as only a temporary solution to the global crisis). Then in 1974, the Threshold Test Ban Treaty prohibited all U.S. and Soviet nuclear tests over 150 kilotons. Neither treaty in practice prevented the United States from continuing to design and deploy weapons, even those with a destructive force greater than 150 kilotons. After 1974, weapons scientists simply did not detonate any nuclear devices above that range. Instead, they devised a multiple yield capability for nuclear weapons that could be determined prior to detonation, allowing testing at lower yields (see Garwin and Charpak 2001: 65). Thus, by the mid-1970s weapons scientists were "perfecting" military technologies that were never experimentally tested in the ways they would actually be used during a nuclear conflict. The last addition Los Alamos scientists made to the U.S. nuclear arsenal, for example, was the W-88 warhead. As many as twelve of these warheads can sit atop a Trident II missile, each possessing a yield of 475 kilotons (or over thirty times the size of the Hiroshima bomb; see Hansen 1988: 206).[25] As the state-of-the-art Los Alamos warhead, the W-88 is currently deployed on Trident submarines, the first leg of America's always on-alert nuclear triad. Yet, the W-88 has never been tested at its full explosive power, and the United States has conducted only one full-sequence launch and detonation of a missile and nuclear warhead combination.[26] I do not mean to suggest that the W-88 is not a viable weapon, or that a single Trident submarine (in 2001, carrying twenty-four missiles, each armed with eight warheads, capable of simultaneously destroying 196 targets/cities) is not the most destructive military machine ever devised. What I am suggesting is that the technoscientific production of "certainty" that had characterized the goal of Los Alamos weapons science since the Trinity test has, over time, developed an increasingly virtual dimension: first, because nuclear devices could not be tested in the way they would actually be used after 1963, which meant that military planners had to trust the expertise of Los Alamos scientists about how a Los Alamos–designed bomb would perform in a war; second, as Galison (1996) has shown, the increasing sophistication of computer simulation techniques encouraged theorists within the weapons program to confuse how their mathematical model of the bomb performed with the actual machine. In other words, the experimental proof of nuclear testing—the detonation that registered for a global audience the power of American nuclear technology—became only a partial demonstration of that power after the mid-1970s. The shifting experimental form of Los Alamos weapons science increasingly separated scientists from a full sensory or cognitive experience of the explosive power of the bombs they designed and maintained.

The underground test regime was also devoted to making the bomb, in the language of the nuclear complex, "safe, secure, and reliable"; that is, making deployed nuclear weapons safe from accident and theft, as well as perfectly able to deliver a specified amount of destructive force if used in combat. Inventing a "safe and secure" nuclear weapon during the Cold War involved adding Permissive Action Links (which prevent unauthorized use) and Enhanced Electrical Detonation Safety Systems (which prevent a lightning strike from accidentally detonating a nuclear weapon), using Insensitive High Explosives (which are much less likely to explode in an accident), and performing "one-point" tests (which ensure that a nuclear device will not produce a nuclear yield if just one of its explosive charges ignites; see Garwin and Charpak 2001: 77). As one senior Los Alamos weapons scientist told me, this Cold War pursuit of safety now presents serious technical challenges, as the complexity of the nuclear devices could make them temperamental over time, ultimately allowing "safety" to undermine "reliability":

> The problem is we've over-designed our weapons for safety reasons. It's part of the craziness surrounding nuclear weapons and there is a lot of that. For example, we were ordered to take beryllium out of nuclear weapons because it's a poison. Now think about it, you're worried about the health effects of a bomb that is in the megaton range! Today you could shoot a bullet through a weapon, light it on fire, drop it out of a plane, and it still won't go off or release its nuclear components. We developed a form of high explosive that will just barely go off as well. We also worried about how to prevent a weapon falling into the wrong hands—so we designed elaborate security systems and codes on each device that prevent that. Today these weapons will just barely detonate they're so complicated.

These weapons will just barely detonate they're so complicated. The problem is now not the exploding bomb that threatens the human body, but rather the dud—the bomb that is too "overdesigned" to explode. Thus, while expanding the destructive power of the bomb, and miniaturizing its form factor for missile delivery to any part of the planet in under thirty minutes, many Los Alamos scientists during the last decades of the Cold War were more self-consciously producing "safety" than unprecedented destructive power: safety in the form of a nuclear deterrent produced by nuclear devices that were highly optimized against accidental detonation and for military command and control. Each underground nuclear test was, thus, a highly productive event: it produced a community of expertise, as Gusterson has argued (1996a, 1996b); it also created "confidence" in the viability of the U.S. arsenal, making each device a complex experimental area in which deterrence, safety, and the aesthetic beauty of a highly optimized design were realized in the same explosive act.

I have argued, here, that changes in the experimental regime of Cold War nuclear weapons science have produced profound changes in the epistemic culture of the laboratory, most readily visible in the technoaesthetics of weapons science. The achievement of above-ground testing was to invent the atom and hydrogen bombs, and weaponize their form; it was also to dramatize the destructive power of these technologies in a way that brought their military reality home to all viewers. The achievement of the underground test regime was then to eliminate systematically those disturbing aspects of the bomb—nuclear fallout, as well as blast and radiation effects—from public view, allowing the challenge of weapons science to be in perfecting the bomb as a complex technology. The underground regime contained the bomb both physically and cognitively, allowing the process of conducting weapons research to be increasingly abstracted from the military reality of the technology. The difference between testing the explosive power of the bomb on a model American community in the midst of a nuclear war fighting exercise in 1955, and engineering a "safe and reliable" nuclear device through underground testing in 1975, is conceptually important, and reveals a deep domestication of the technology by the end of the Cold War. This cognitive shift is not readily apparent in the discourse of nuclear policy, which has always positioned the bomb as a tool of international relations, but is immediately visible in the technoaesthetic evolution of weapons science. Experienced through prosthetic senses, the bomb produced by underground testing became a philosophical project increasingly linked not to mass destruction or war but to complexity, safety, and deterrence within the laboratory, allowing new generations of scientists increasingly to invest in nuclear weapons as a patriotic intellectual enterprise to produce machines that could only prevent conflict.

The Soviet nuclear threat provided a counter to this ideological construction of the bomb within the laboratory, threatening discourses of deterrence and pure science with the possibility of a real war. The post–Cold War period is consequently the only time in which Los Alamos weapons science has not been justified in relation to an arms race. As we shall see, the post–Cold War experimental regime extends the aesthetic project of nuclear weapons science in new ways, eliminating not only the human body but also the nuclear explosion from the space of the experiment. In post–Cold War Los Alamos, each nuclear device has been purified of its destructive potential, allowing weapons scientists to approach the bomb as a complex universe of material science and virtual representations that offer potentially endless technoscientific pleasure. In other words, the bomb has been reinvented in Los Alamos in ways that free its aesthetic possibility from its destructive potential, finally allowing the bomb to cease being a bomb at all.

SCIENCE-BASED STOCKPILE STEWARDSHIP (1995–2010): VIRTUAL BOMBS AND PROSTHETIC SENSES

In Los Alamos, the post–Cold War period began not with the end of the Soviet Union but with the cessation of underground nuclear testing and nuclear weapons design work in 1992—an experimental regime and conceptual project that had defined generations of weapons scientists.[27] The Clinton administration's subsequent support for a Comprehensive Test Ban Treaty (signed in 1996, but voted down by the Senate in 1999) committed the weapons laboratories to maintaining the existing U.S. nuclear arsenal, as well as their nuclear weapons expertise, without conducting nuclear detonations.[28] The new experimental regime devoted to this task in Los Alamos was dubbed "Science-Based Stockpile Stewardship" (SBSS), an effort to maintain the Cold War U.S. nuclear arsenal through a combination of subcritical and non-nuclear explosive testing, a fleet of new experimental facilities, archiving Cold War experimental data, and modeling the combined insights on state-of-the-art computer simulations.[29] SBSS was conceived in 1995 as a fifteen-year project with a projected cost of $4.5 billion a year—making it significantly more expensive than the Cold War project of nuclear weapons design and testing it replaced.[30] As an experimental regime, SBSS is not only an effort to maintain U.S. nuclear weapons under a test ban, but also a programmatic effort to reconstitute the pleasures of conducting weapons science for nuclear experts confronting a radically changed mission. As we shall see, SBSS fundamentally alters the material form of Los Alamos weapons science, promoting a different concept of the bomb while reconfiguring sensory access to its destructive potential.

A deputy director of nuclear weapons technologies at Los Alamos offered this concise explanation of the consequences of the shift from underground nuclear testing to the "science-based" model for maintaining the U.S. nuclear arsenal:

For 50 years the Nuclear Weapons Program relied on nuclear testing, complemented by large-scale production, to guarantee a safe and reliable stockpile. New weapons were designed, tested, and manufactured on a regular basis. If the surveillance program discovered a defect, its significance could be established by nuclear testing. If the defect was serious, it could be repaired by the production complex. Even if the defect was not significant, the weapon was likely to be replaced by a more modern system in only a few years. As the stockpile ages far beyond its anticipated life, we can expect a variety of defects which will break the symmetries which were used in the design process. This means that weapons gerontology is far more challenging than designing new weapons. We are sometimes accused by anti-nuclear activists of wanting [new] facilities . . . in order to design new weapons. My answer is

Ave. Age (yrs.)

2.12. Aging chart of the U.S. nuclear arsenal. (*Source: 1998 U.S. Stockpile Stewardship Plan*)

that we know how to design new weapons. But we do not know how to certify the safety, reliability and performance of weapons as they age. Thus the SBSS challenge can be stated quite simply: "since we can't test them, we will have to understand them at a fundamental level." (Smith 1995: 1)

Weapons gerontology is far more challenging than designing new weapons. Instead of continuing the evolution of the bomb through new warhead designs, weapons scientists have become gerontologists, involved in studying how nuclear weapons age. While the Cold War experimental regime was based on the planned obsolescence of each weapon type (and an accelerated timetable of development), the SBSS program is designed to keep the current U.S. nuclear arsenal viable indefinitely. If the Cold War program speeded up time through constant production, as scientists rushed from one test to the next, the immediate post–Cold War project became to slow down time, to prevent nothing less than aging itself. The first articulations of the SBSS program seemed to hope for a kind of technological cryogenics where both bombs and the knowledge of bomb makers could be put into a deep freeze at 1992 levels, to be thawed in case of future nuclear emergency. However, the inability to stop time completely in Los Alamos—to keep bodies and machines safely on ice—promoted "aging" as the major threat to U.S. national security after the Cold War (see Figure 2.12). The arms race may be on hold in post–Cold War Los Alamos, but a new race against time is at the center of the laboratory's nuclear mission, a programmatic effort to defer endlessly a future of aged, and perhaps derelict, U.S. nuclear machines.

The vulnerable body, carefully scripted out of the Cold War experimental regime of underground testing, has also returned to the discourse of Los Alamos scientists. But the body in question is not the human body threatened by the exploding bomb; it is the bomb itself as fragile body, exposed to the elements, aging, and increasingly infirm. Within this post–Cold War program of weapons gerontology, nuclear weapons have "birth defects," require "care and feeding," "get sick" and "go to the hospital," get regular "checkups," "retire," and have "autopsies." Individual weapons systems are now undergoing formal "life extension" projects, new regimens of surveillance and component replacement to extend the viability of the oldest weapons in the U.S. nuclear arsenal past their planned deployment (see Figure 2.13). This use of productive bodily metaphors for supremely destructive technologies, which runs throughout the U.S. nuclear project, has always been part of the larger cognitive process of domesticating nuclear technology and giving machines a "life course"—literally translating nuclear weapon time into human time.

A strategic confusion of bodies and machines is a common technoaesthetic technique for internally controlling the meaning of laboratory work (see Knorr-Centina 1999; Traweek 1988). Within the nuclear complex, however, there is an added political consequence from confusing the animate and the inanimate, and deploying highly gendered categories for massively destructive technologies.[31] Cohn (1987) has demonstrated that the expert discourse of defense intellectuals grants military machines and not people agency, making it linguistically impossible to represent the victims of military technology. Gusterson has shown, in his study of Lawrence Livermore National Laboratory (LLNL), that when weapons scientists use birth metaphors to describe the bomb they are deploying "the connotative power of words to produce—and be produced by—a cosmological world where nuclear weapons tests symbolize not despair, destruction, and death but hope, renewal, and life" (1996b: 145). But while a combination of technoaesthetic discourse and successful experiments is the key to producing a community of experts, it is also important to underscore what is evacuated from the project of nuclear weapons science by these techniques, and to recognize its historical transformation in the post–Cold War period.

When Edward Teller announced the first successful detonation of a thermonuclear device in 1952 by cabling his Los Alamos colleagues the

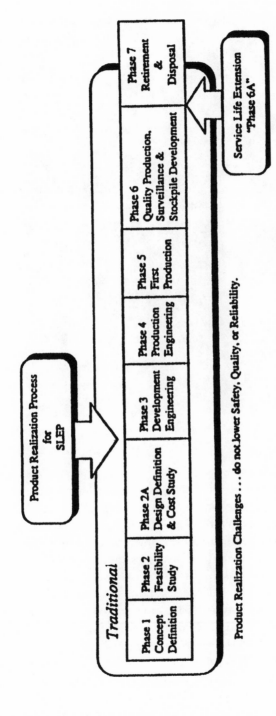

Traditional

| Phase 1 Concept Definition | Phase 2 Feasibility Study | Phase 2A Design Definition & Cost Study | Phase 3 Development Engineering | Phase 4 Production Engineering | Phase 5 First Production | Phase 6 Quality Production, Surveillance & Stockpile Development | Phase 7 Retirement & Disposal |

Product Realization Process for SLEP

Service Life Extension "Phase 6A"

Product Realization Challenges . . . do not lower Safety, Quality, or Reliability.

2.13. Stockpile Life Extension Program chart. (*Source:* 1998 *U.S. Stockpile Stewardship Plan*)

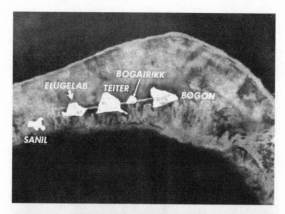

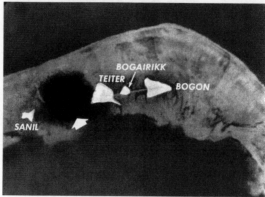

2.14. Portrait of Elugelab Island before and after the Mike Shot. (U.S. National Archives)

phrase "it's a boy" (see Ott 1999), he was not only linguistically transforming the most devastating force yet achieved into a purely productive event, he was deploying an image of the human body to enable the complete evacuation of people and the environment from the space of the experiment. At a yield of 10.4 megatons (five hundred times the bomb that destroyed Nagasaki), the Mike device vaporized the island of Elugelab, creating a fireball three and a half miles wide and sending a radioactive cloud twenty miles into the sky, contaminating a hundred-square-mile area around the Marshall Islands (see Hansen 1988: 58–61; Rhodes 1995; Ott 1999). Figure 2.14 presents an aerial view of that atoll before and after the Mike detonation, marking the crater. By describing a thermonuclear detonation through procreative and masculine metaphors (as presumably a "girl" would not explode), weapons scientists were not only positively valuing their achievement as a form of creation, but also working to contain linguistically the destructive reality of the event. The act of describing an exploding nuclear weapon as a biological being endows that machine and process at the level of discourse with sentient characteristics and empathic possibilities, allowing both a misrecognition of the relationship of the bomb to the human body and a powerful technoaesthetic identification with the technology. But if the Cold War discourse produced an image of the bomb as invulnerable body (the "boy" that can vaporize islands faster than a "shake of a lamb's tail"), the post–Cold War discourse has reversed the conceptual circuit of this logic, offering a image of the masculine bomb-body as senior citizen, so aged and weak as to be unable to perform. No longer the "baby boy," the bomb is now structurally positioned at the end of its life course, as the "old man," struggling against the progression of time and failing faculties. What is important for our purposes here is not the technical accuracy or political strategy of deploying this allegorical form to communicate the challenges of SBSS within the laboratory. Rather, by attending to the technoaesthetic production of the bomb we can see an important transformation in the everyday logics of laboratory life, as weapons scientists have become more directly concerned with protecting the vulnerable weapon of mass destruction from a catastrophic future than the human body.

Indeed, under SBSS, a sensory engagement with the bomb produces, not fear of the explosion, but rather an increasing concern about the viability of the machine as an embodied aesthetic form. The cornerstone of SBSS is a surveillance regime devoted to identifying how time and the elements are influencing each device in America's nuclear arsenal. Every year, eleven warheads from each of the eight deployed U.S. weapons systems are pulled from submarines, missile silos, bombers, and weapons storage and subjected to component-by-component inspection and testing (DOE 1998a, 1999e). Nuclear weapons have between six and seven thousand parts, and each part of each weapon under SBSS has a specific inspection program devoted to it (see Medalia 1998, 1994). Here, for example, is how one weapons scientist describes the post–Cold War project of "detonator surveillance":

> First we do a visual inspection to see how the detonators fared in the stockpile. Then we check the circuit resistance of each detonator cable assembly and compare that to the resistance measures when the detonator was first manufactured (yes, each one—and there are a lot of detonators). We x-ray all detonator cable assemblies in three views to check for voids, inclusions, cracks, or any other anomalies. We disassemble some of the detonators so we can visually inspect the subassemblies. We do chemical tests on the powders and perform scanning electron microscope and x-ray fluorescence spectroscopy inspections of the inner parts. Some of the detonators are recertified and sent to the Weapons Evaluation Test Laboratory at Sandia/Pantex. There

the detonators are test fired in conjunction with a real weapons fireset, simulating a full-up firing system test. The rest of the detonators are test fired here at our war reserve facility. We use a rotating mirror camera to record when the outbreak of light from each detonator occurs and compare that time to the start time of the firing pulse. This measurement, called transit time, must meet strict specifications. We also measure the simultaneity of the breakout of light from the detonators. The collected data are compiled and given to the design agency, which then compares the present condition and behavior of the detonators to those as-built and tracks any trends in the data (or changes due to aging). The design agency then issues a report that ultimately contributes to the weapons system certification. (LANL 2000: 4–5)

The production of scientific rigor here, in the recitation of inspection regimes, achieves fetishistic status, as scientists search for signs of aging in Cold War technology and wonder about how minute changes (cracks and abrasions) in individual components might affect the performance of each U.S. nuclear device during a war. While this inspection regime prioritizes surveillance, the problem of maintaining the U.S. arsenal has been reduced in some cases to the availability of specific components and materials. For example, after Dow Corning stopped making its "Silastic S-5370 RTV Foam" and its "281 Adhesive," weapons scientists devoted years to studying how a change in either the foam or adhesive used in a nuclear device might affect its performance (LANL 1996b: 2). Figure 2.15, from the *1998 Stockpile Stewardship Plan*, displays how this program of surveillance is designed to produce, out of the material analysis of component parts (depicted here as jigsaw puzzle pieces), an "integrated bomb"; however, the integrated bomb produced by SBSS is not one that explodes, it is one that can be identified as "safe and reliable." Thus, the Cold War world of weapons science, which was energized by regular nuclear detonations and the arms race, has been reduced for some weapons scientists to a long-term analysis of the compressibility of pieces of foam over time and an unending surveillance of aging machines. While this might seem a simple progression from the nuclear sublime to the nuclear banal, the logics behind the SBSS program are more complicated than they first appear.

If the Cold War project was simply to get new nuclear weapons to function as expected (i.e., explode on time and with the expected scale, and not explode at any other time), SBSS has promoted the question of aging in weapons as an opportunity for new kinds of basic scientific research. Rather than designing new nuclear devices to fit new military specifications as they did for nearly a half century, weapons scientists are now working to model all of the complex nanosecond processes that occur within a nuclear detonation. The formal goal of SBSS is to understand how aging effects on any single component might alter safety and

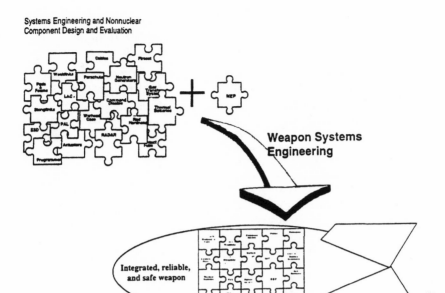

Systems Engineering and Nonnuclear
Component Design and Evaluation

Weapon Systems
Engineering

Integrated, reliable,
and safe weapon

2.15. Integrated bomb, SBSS. (*Source:* 1998 *U.S. Stockpile Stewardship Plan*)

performance over decades of storage.[32] But given the extreme pressures, velocities, and temperatures operating within a nuclear implosion/explosion, this effort to model the bomb also promises a new and more nuanced understanding of how a variety of materials behave in extreme conditions. The SBSS program promises weapons scientists the opportunity to replace nuclear production with what a former head of the Los Alamos weapons program has called the "holy grail of nuclear weapons theory" (Hopkins 2000); namely, a "first principles" understanding of nuclear processes. As an experimental regime, the intellectual appeal of SBSS is that weapons scientists can pursue the kinds of questions that would allow a totally scaleable understanding of what happens inside a thermonuclear blast, a generalized model applicable to all weapons systems. Since a first principles understanding of nuclear weapons is not necessary for producing a nuclear arsenal (as the Cold War arms race demonstrated), the decision to pursue the "equations of state" for U.S. nuclear weapons is an explicit effort to make nuclear weapons science compelling to scientists, to reenergize their nuclear imaginary in the absence of nuclear detonations and the arms race.

This focus on the component-by-component status of the U.S. nuclear arsenal has transformed the bomb from a device that explodes into one provoking a vast array of scientific questions about the behavior of plastics, metals, and nuclear materials over time. Uncertainty about the aging bomb-body has been mobilized, in other words, to turn each U.S. nuclear weapon into a potentially endless universe of basic questions about material science. I asked one weapons scientist if the known aging problems in the U.S. arsenal would simply reduce the yield or if they could actually stop a nuclear device from detonating:

> It is the latter case. Because of the specific details of how the weapon functions, and this energy amplification, this is not a gradual reduction in yield. If the primary doesn't achieve sufficient energy output, it will not light the secondary. So we're talking about cliffs here not gradual slopes. That's an important point—any further detail needs to get into weapons design and function [and is classified]. By the way, that's a terrible limitation to a discussion in an open society. I read things in the newspaper: The activists say, "We know everything we need to know about weapons"; I've seen members of the senate stand up and say, "We can just model it on the computer"—and I just want to tear my hair out. No! It's just factually wrong. We don't understand everything there is to know about basic properties. This is a good example: how does plutonium experience a known aging effect—that is, the growth of helium into the material from the radioactive decay—which could potentially change its property. Now what stockpile stewardship is having us do is take old plutonium and measure the compressibility, and then compare it with plutonium that is not aged. And then by knowing the physics, we put it in computer code (using the Accelerated Strategic Computing Initiative), and calculate just how old the plutonium can get before it unacceptably degrades the performance. So that, in a nutshell, is how stewardship works—but we had to invent the tools to measure all that compressibility. What I've just described to you explains why we are doing all these experiments in Nevada. You've heard of subcritical experiments at the UA1 facility? That's exactly what we are doing in Nevada—measuring the compressibility of plutonium.

We don't understand everything about basic properties. As I have argued, each new experimental regime in Los Alamos has produced not only new kinds of knowledge but also a new concept of the bomb. In this presentation the definition of an exploding bomb is one that reaches its assigned, militarily valued, yield. A device that only ignites its "primary"—the atomic bomb used to trigger a thermonuclear reaction, which might easily produce a yield similar to that of the Hiroshima bomb—is a total failure.[33] Moreover, a "first principles" understanding of nuclear technology produces, not a bomb that actually explodes, but rather a deep understanding of how plutonium behaves over time and under extreme conditions. There is no need to worry about the human body in this experimental regime, as there are only non-nuclear detonations occurring in Nevada, which are constituted as basic experiments in exotic material science. The nuclear weapon produced by SBSS is one that primarily exists in component parts, each framed by a discourse of uncertainty about aging, and the military value of each nuclear device is produced, not by an explosion, but through a high-tech inspection.

During the Cold War, Los Alamos scientists talked on occasion of designing what they called a "wooden bomb," a simplified and super-robust nuclear device that could be left on the shelf for a decades with no threat to its performance as a weapon (Hanson 1988). These experiments were consistently put off in favor of those exploring state-of-the-art concepts and exotic (and thus more volatile) materials, as Los Alamos scientists assumed that nuclear testing would not end. Weapons scientists were consequently caught off guard by the test moratorium of 1992, which left one Los Alamos test tower half completed in the Nevada desert. Weapons scientists also worked at such a pace during the Cold War that they did not always maintain detailed records about their experimental successes and failures in Nevada. As a result, one of the first SBSS projects was an effort simply to archive the knowledge that was produced by the Cold War nuclear complex, to record for posterity how to conduct underground nuclear detonations and build a highly optimized nuclear arsenal. By interviewing Cold War weapons scientists, and following the existing paper trail about U.S. nuclear weapons through office safes and file cabinets scattered throughout the laboratory, the Los Alamos Nuclear Weapons Archiving Project is the first effort to document formally the explicit as well as tacit knowledge about how to produce the bomb.[34] This historical assessment, as well as the new experimental knowledge produced by SBSS, will be consolidated in a new computer archive, which represents the first centralized database for the U.S. nuclear weapons program (see Stober 1999). The archiving project underscores that, from 1945 to 1992, confidence in the nuclear arsenal (for officials in Los Alamos, Washington, D.C., and internationally) was produced by the regular detonation of nuclear devices, not simply by the existence of nuclear experts. In the post–Cold War period, however, certainty comes not from an explosion but from a process of "certification"—a yearly report from the directors of the national laboratories stating that they see no reason why the U.S. nuclear arsenal would not function as planned during a nuclear war. While experimental "certainty" and "certification" may be different experimental and political concepts, we should remember that through the second half of the Cold War the United States was routinely deploying weapons that had not been tested in the ways in which they would actually be used in a nuclear war, and the nuclear device that destroyed the city of Hiroshima in 1945 was never tested prior to its military use. Thus, the current pursuit of a "first principles" understanding of nuclear weapons, while promising a host of new insights into how materials behave at extreme temperatures, pressures, and velocities, marks a significant change in the technoaesthetic construction of the bomb. Put simply, within the post–Cold War order the bomb is being evaluated not on its ability to be perfectly destructive but rather on the perfectibility of its form.

Nuclear weapons science has always been a compartmentalized experimental project in the United States, in which the rules of state secrecy as well as the division of expertise among theorists, physicists, chemists, and engineers has divided the bomb into a series of discrete experimental projects. The detonation of a nuclear device during the Cold War was thus a coordination of a vast array of scientific experiments distributed throughout the laboratory, which together constituted the technology as both a military machine and the material form of Mutual Assured Destruction (MAD). Under SBSS, the bomb is equally compartmentalized but there is no unifying moment in which the destructive power of the bomb is visible, in either an explosion or in after-effects, such as a desert valley pitted with test craters. In the absence of the arms race, as well as any material trace of the destructive power of the bomb, the SBSS focus on "first principles" fragments the bomb into a series of basic science questions that have no direct connection to the military reality of nuclear weapons. In post–Cold War Los Alamos, the bomb is consequently many things, but rarely a weapon of mass destruction. Consider, for example, how weapons scientists describe the Dual Axis Radiographic Hydrodynamic Test Facility (DARHT), a key tool in the SBSS regime for studying the effects of aging on the U.S. stockpile. When completed, DARHT will focus 40 billion watts of power in a 60 billionth-of-a-second (or 60-shake) burst to produce a three-dimensional X-ray image of a mock nuclear weapon primary during the implosion process (LANL 2001: 9). In the mid-1990s, project managers explained the need for DARHT through a variety of medical analogies, most prominently describing the explosives test facility as a "hospital for sick bombs." A former director of the Los Alamos nuclear weapons program suggested that the United States needed DARHT to allow "an assessment of the weapons we have before they get older—kind of like a CAT-scan baseline before someone develops heart disease—as [in the future] we might have to give these weapons a new heart." Mapping contemporary nuclear weapons science alongside modern heart transplant surgery, the bomb gains not only an organic form in this discourse but also an explicitly fragile (rather than a destructive) body. In post–Cold War Los Alamos, nuclear weapons are also frequently compared to a garaged automobile, often an ambulance that might not be able to start if one needed to race to the hospital in ten or twenty years. And as Jo Ann Shroyer learned from one weapons scientist (1998: 25), a nuclear weapon under stockpile stewardship is also like a fire extinguisher before an emergency:

> There's a fire and you have twenty fire extinguishers sitting there. You have a pretty good chance of finding one that works and you're going to put out the flames. But if you have only one fire extinguisher, you're going to want to test that thing, understand how it works, and make sure it's recharged.

This analogy, while focusing on the problem of knowing how and when a machine will work, also does the technoaesthetic work of transforming a nuclear weapon—whose central effect is the production of an explosion and massive fireball—into its opposite: a fire extinguisher.

An SBSS exhibit in the Bradbury Science Museum, which is the primary public space at Los Alamos National Laboratory, pushes this technoaesthetic project further, suggesting that a nuclear weapon is like a 911 emergency call (see Figure 2.16). The exhibit asks visitors to:

> pretend that this phone is going to be used by your local 911-emergency operator. Can you test it and verify that it will work whenever it is needed? There is one important rule. You are not allowed to make or receive a call to test it.

The exhibit then invites visitors to check the dial tone, to press the keys and listen to the key tones, as well as test the ringer. It then asks, "Are you confident that this phone will work if needed for an emergency?" and gives visitors a chance to vote on whether the phone could successfully complete a 911 call or not. To dramatize the technical problem of how to maintain nuclear weapons without actually detonating them, we see here an attempt to normalize the destructive power of the U.S. nuclear arsenal as, not the instrument that threatens the human body, but rather an institutional emergency response that attends to physical trauma—as ambulance, fire truck, or police action. Unlike in the 1950s experimental regime, in which the exploding bomb was tested on ambulances, fire trucks, police cars, and living beings to understand the physical effects of a nuclear attack, the bomb produced by SBSS can only be conceptualized as the institutional response to violence, not a means of enacting it. Weapons gerontology thus promotes an image of the aging bomb as body to mobilize a new kind of nuclear fear: fear not of the bomb that explodes but of the bomb that cannot.

This effort to underscore the fragility of nuclear weapons alongside the vast opportunities for basic research in the materials science through

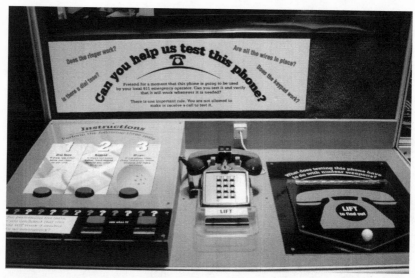

2.16. SBSS exhibit at the Bradbury Science Museum. (Photograph by Joseph Masco)

SBSS is, in part, tactical; for despite the rhetorical and technoscientific attention to aging weapons, the most profound question of aging at Los Alamos is among weapons scientists themselves. By the mid-1990s, the average age of Los Alamos weapon scientists in X Division, which is responsible for nuclear weapons design work, was over fifty years old.[35] Thus, just about the time when the last weapon in the current U.S. stockpile is going to exceed its planned design life in 2010, the last remaining weapons scientists with underground test experience are likely to be retiring. The SBSS program is consequently orchestrated around that 2010 date, when a whole generation of bombs and expert bodies is scheduled simultaneously to retire. As a result, the weapons laboratories have started a graduate program for new recruits who enter the weapons program knowing they are unlikely to ever conduct a nuclear detonation. A new academic program at Los Alamos—The Theoretical Institute for Thermonuclear and Nuclear Studies (or TITANS)—provides postdoctoral training in weapons physics for Los Alamos recruits who in previous experimental regimes would have undergone a multiyear apprenticeship with senior weapons scientists (LANL 1997a: 3; see Gusterson 1996a). However, the more immediate question is not how you train the bodies once you have them in the program, but how you get bodies into the program in the first place. After all, without an active nuclear weapons design project, it is difficult to sell a career in nuclear weapons physics/gerontology to new Ph.D.s, who are now more familiar with post–Cold War security scandals at Los Alamos (see chapter 6) than with the pleasures of conducting nuclear weapons science.

One of the immediate goals of the SBSS program is, therefore, to build a state-of-the-art infrastructure of experimental laboratories at Los Alamos and Lawrence Livermore National Laboratories that will be enticing to a new generation of scientists, and counter the banality of yearly surveillance reports with cutting-edge science. If the Cold War nuclear project was devoted to producing new generations of bombs, the post–Cold War project is to produce a new generation of nuclear weapons scientists capable of tending to those bombs. To this end, the Department of Energy (DOE) has committed to maintaining the fastest supercomputers in the world at the national laboratories through 2010.[36] The Accelerated Strategic Computing Initiative (ASCI) is intended to be not only a key tool for studying aging effects in nuclear weapons and pursuing a first principles understanding of nuclear processes, but also for recruiting scientists into the weapons programs.[37] In 1999, Los Alamos maintained a supercomputer running at one teraOPS (i.e., capable of running one trillion operations per second), a thirty-teraOPS system was under construction in 2001, and a one hundred-teraOPS computer was already on the drawing board. The goal of the ASCI program is to give weapons scientists over ten thousand times the computing power used to design the U.S. nuclear arsenal in the first place (GAO 1999a). Here, the Cold War commitment to speed of nuclear production has been transformed into a post–Cold War pursuit of computational speed, manifested in the ability to render three-dimensional simulations of nuclear explosions in ever-greater degrees of (temporal and spatial) resolution. The programmatic commitment to the ASCI program is not without controversy in Los Alamos; as one veteran of the underground test regime put it, the problem with simulation-based nuclear weapons research is:

> Truth. You can't test it. It might be highly precise but very inaccurate. Well, you can make a measurement very precise to four or five significant figures and because of something in your experiment it can be dead wrong. So your precision is very high, and your accuracy is very bad. So answers to questions are going to become more and more computational and hypothetical. Now there is nothing inherently wrong with that. We were getting more and more involved in simulating experiments before we would try them. The problem is that you lose sight of the fact that they are computational and not reality. So you start believing them. It becomes reality instead of being a virtual experiment.

It becomes reality instead of being a virtual experiment. The problem for post–Cold War weapons scientists is how to evaluate the meaning of the data produced by their various SBSS projects in relation to a military nuclear explosion. Without the "truth test" of the nuclear detonation to evaluate theoretical results, some senior Los Alamos scientists do not believe that future weapons scientists will have the right experimental expertise to evaluate U.S. nuclear weapons properly. Hardly a stable form, SBSS is simultaneously portrayed in Los Alamos as either a highly challenging means of perfecting nuclear technology or as simply an economy of appearances, a discrepancy that could be mobilized as a rationale for a return to U.S. underground nuclear testing in the near future.

It is important to recognize, however, that the theory, the instrumentation, and the experimental method of Los Alamos weapons science have changed in the post–Cold War era (see Galison 1997). SBSS assumes that one can test the components and processes in a nuclear weapon separately and assemble a picture of the military performance of the device from the collected data. The Cold War program was focused on the detonation of the actual weapons system, with success judged by how accurately weapons scientists were able to predict and reproduce the explosive yield. The instrumentation of nuclear weapons science is no longer a combination of the nuclear device, test sensors, and radiochemistry, but a series of discrete hydrodynamic test facilities, non-nuclear material science studies, and computer simulations. Finally, the experiment is no longer an earthshaking rumble in the Nevada desert registered on seismographs around the world, but is now a virtual nuclear explosion simulated on the world's fastest computers located in air-conditioned buildings at Los Alamos, Lawrence Livermore, and Sandia National Laboratories. Gusterson (2001) has argued that the knowledge produced by a more virtual weapons program is currently "hyperconstructible" because it remains an uncertain experiment, currently producing three competing scenarios about the future of the U.S. nuclear program: (1) that new design work will continue and be enhanced by a state-of-the-art nuclear complex, which would allow the United States to break the test ban treaty with maximal nuclear superiority at some date in the future; (2) that a new "virtual arms race" could take place in which nation-states stockpile advanced simulation facilities and new weapon designs, rather than actual bombs; or (3) that a "virtual disarmament" could inadvertently occur, as U.S. weapons scientists over decades lose key areas of "tacit" knowledge about how to build and maintain nuclear weapons. The range of possibilities here—from new forms of the arms race to the "uninvention" of nuclear weapons through atrophied expertise—is a register of the long-term uncertainty surrounding SBSS as an experimental enterprise, and underscores the profound nuclear policy implications of the program (see MacKenzie and Spinardi

1996). There is, however, a potentially more foundational structural effect of SBSS over time; namely, that the professionals most immediately responsible for the U.S. nuclear arsenal will embrace the aesthetic appeal of SBSS so completely as to lose cognitive access to the terror of the exploding bomb.

In Los Alamos, the pleasures of nuclear science have always been at odds with the destructive potential of the military machine, requiring a conceptual mediation of the project to transform a weapon of mass destruction into a purely productive scientific enterprise. The experimental trajectory of Cold War weapons science, as we have seen, diminished sensory access to the destructive power of the bomb with the move to underground testing, which encouraged a technoscientific focus on the internal characteristics of the explosion rather than its material effects. The post–Cold War regime of SBSS has taken this conceptual mediation of the enterprise one step further by eliminating nuclear detonations altogether while reinvesting in weapons science on a new scale. We can begin to assess the cognitive effects of this transformation in one of the major achievements of post–Cold War weapons science: the completion of the first three-dimensional computer simulation of a thermonuclear detonation in 2001. The simulation was jointly conducted on LLNL's 12.3-teraOPS ASCI White and on LANL's 3.1-teraOPS Blue Mountain supercomputers. Using a new secured network connecting the weapons laboratories, Los Alamos scientists engaged the Livermore system from their home laboratory in New Mexico. The simulation ran for 122.5 days and involved 35 times the total information in the Library of Congress. According to the Los Alamos press release, it would take a state-of-the-art home computer 750 years to complete the calculation (see NNSA 2002).

While the scale and sophistication of this simulation is a remarkable achievement in computer science, what is more important for our purposes is how weapons scientists tactilely experience the experimental results (see LLNL 2000). The three-dimensional simulation of the thermonuclear explosion (i.e., involving a coupled primary and secondary) is presented in the form of a movie, which is displayed in state-of-the-art "visualization centers" in Los Alamos. In these new SBSS facilities, scientists are positioned at the center of an "immersive theater," and oriented toward a Power Wall, the largest and most detailed projection screen on the planet. Standing in front of the sixteen by eight foot Power Wall, scientists are physically dwarfed by the microscopic processes that make up a simulated nuclear explosion, which are rendered in full color and projected on a massive scale (see Figure 2.17). Some interfaces allow scientists to manipulate the simulation through use of a virtual reality

2.17. Powerwall computer simulation of meteor hitting the earth, Los Alamos National Laboratory. (Courtesy of Los Alamos National Laboratory)

glove, and the national laboratories are all exploring ways of rendering nuclear simulations in ever-greater temporal and spatial detail, as well as with more interactive possibilities. The goal of this project in Los Alamos is to provide a "shake by shake" portrait of the densities, pressures, velocities, and turbulence that make up a nuclear implosion/explosion, and to be able to track all of these processes in three dimensions with perfect resolution. The first major achievement of the post–Cold War virtual laboratory is, thus, to have repositioned a nuclear explosion at the center of Los Alamos weapons science. However, this nuclear detonation is experienced not through vulnerable human senses that need to be protected from the blast, but rather through prosthetic devices that enable the body to interact with the simulated explosion within the safety of a secured room. The half century progression from protective goggles (necessary to prevent flashblindness during an above-ground event) to virtual reality gloves and goggles (needed to interact with the nuclear simulation) is the most significant evolution in the material form of Los Alamos weapons science, as this new experimental regime evacuates the destructive bomb entirely through a compelling new form of virtual embodiment.

SBSS ultimately promotes the possibility of a new kind of intimacy between scientists and the exploding bomb, allowing us to chart a logical conclusion to the multigenerational bomb-as-body concept in Los

Alamos. Looking past 2010, if the fifteen-year project of SBSS is successful, Los Alamos weapons scientists will be able to evaluate and account for the significant gerontological issues in the nuclear stockpile, as well as design new weapons in virtual reality with confidence that the systems would work if actually built and detonated. Thus, the last generation of Cold War weapons scientists will be retiring with most, if not all, the fundamental questions about nuclear weapons answered. The technical knowledge drawn from a half century of U.S. nuclear testing, as well as the advanced material science and computational achievements of SBSS, will be archived in permanent form—securing the technoscientific legacy of the Manhattan Project. Moreover, the next-generation supercomputers in combination with next-generation three-dimensional virtual reality technologies will complete the ongoing revolution in the body-bomb relationship for weapons scientists. Future weapons scientists will no longer interact with their experimental data via computer screens, which maintain a separation between the physical body of the scientist and the bomb as technoscientific project. Instead, the next generation visualization center will fulfill what is clearly the conceptual goal of the current system, which places scientists at the center of a highly sophisticated virtual space. In the near future, Los Alamos scientists will track specific particles, velocities, pressures, and flows through new, technologically mediated, but nonetheless felt senses, and they will do so not from office chairs and via computer screens, but from *inside* the nuclear explosion.

The weapons laboratory of the early twenty-first century will ultimately allow weapons scientists to walk inside a virtual hydrogen bomb, and experience the most extremely destructive force imaginable through physical senses that are not vaporized by the assault of the explosion but rather tuned to the aesthetic properties of the simulation. The promise of SBSS is, thus, not only to perfect and maintain indefinitely nuclear weapons technologies through non-nuclear testing, but also to resolve the multigenerational technoaesthetic confusion of bodies and machines in Los Alamos by creating a conceptual space in which weapons scientists and weapons of mass destruction can comfortably coexist—at the very moment of detonation. The bomb's new body is increasingly that of the weapons scientists themselves, as the intellectual pleasure of nuclear weapons science and a tactile sensory experience of the exploding bomb are being merged through a massively engineered technoaesthetic spectacle in virtual reality. The intimacy of this conceptual project—the desire to interact physically with a thermonuclear explosion in all its nanosecond and atomic detail—eliminates fear of the exploding bomb altogether in favor of a phantasmagoria. This flooding of the senses with virtual images of a detonating nuclear device reinvents the bomb as a purely creative project—more visible in its details, more compelling in its sensory form, and more attractive in its technoaesthetic performance than anything possible during the Cold War testing regimes. Purified of its military reality and its environmental effects in the virtual laboratory, the bomb that will ultimately be produced by SBSS is no longer geriatric or living on borrowed time: it will have an expanding future horizon, making weapons science no longer a temporary political solution to the global crisis but an aesthetic project capable of existing finally on its own terms. To this end, the bomb as aesthetic project is already a highly developed discourse in the laboratory; consider, for example, how two successful implosion studies were recently described in the laboratory's publication *Dateline: Los Alamos* (LANL 2001: 8):

> Two explosions rock two mesas at Los Alamos. Separated by a couple of chilly fall days and 10 miles, both experiments capture images of exploding objects very much like the primaries of nuclear weapons, absent the nuclear materials that produce criticality. Both are milestones in Los Alamos' efforts to focus the most sophisticated technology available onto its mission of maintaining the safety and reliability of an aging nuclear stockpile. And both experiments were looking for symmetry. Symmetry is beauty. Psychologists have found that the human eye judges a person attractive when it perceives symmetry in facial features. Los Alamos scientists and engineers also think symmetry is beautiful. Because without symmetry, nuclear weapons don't work.

Symmetry : implosion = beauty : human face. The pleasures of nuclear weapons science are being reinvented in post–Cold War Los Alamos through new experimental facilities that promise to free nuclear science from the politics of the bomb. However, this is a high-tech mystification, as the destructive reality of nuclear arsenals persists, despite, and in the future, because of this aestheticization of laboratory science.

OF BOMBS AND BODIES IN THE PLUTONIUM ECONOMY

The question SBSS ultimately poses, I would argue, is not how to maintain nuclear weapons as a technology—as machines—but how to maintain a conceptual understanding of what it means to detonate a nuclear device.[38] We have seen, through the shifting experimental regimes of Los Alamos weapons science, that even those most directly responsible for building the bomb have mediated their access to the reality of massively explosive technologies in profound ways, transforming weapons of mass destruction into purely productive forms. Each experimental regime from 1945 to 2001 has, in fact, produced a different articulation of the bomb, over time diminishing cognitive access to the destructive power of nuclear weapons in favor of an aesthetic-intellectual form. In another decade, when the bomb is closer to a perfected technoaesthetic form—lovingly rendered in virtual reality by scientists who are generations removed from those who last experienced the heat, shockwave, and atmospheric effects of a nuclear detonation—Los Alamos scientists will certainly know much more about how a thermonuclear device operates than they did during the 1950s era of nuclear testing in the Pacific. But who can argue that a computer simulation will offer the same level of conceptual understanding as did those above-ground detonations, where the destructive power of nuclear explosions was experienced not only as intellectually powerful but also as brutally, terrifyingly destructive? This slippage between the virtual and the real, which started with the first efforts to mathematically model nuclear explosions immediately after World War II in Los Alamos and continued through the Cold War testing regimes (Galison 1996), threatens now to become the ascendant aspect of weapons science in the twenty-first century and the ultimate institutional compensation for the terror of the nuclear sublime.

This is not to suggest that U.S. nuclear devices capable of exploding with massive destructive force will not be deployed around the globe or to argue for a return to underground nuclear testing; it is rather to point out that the expertise necessary to maintain those machines is in danger of being separated from an understanding of the consequences of using the technology. What, in other words, will make a nuclear device *the bomb*, if its primarily evaluative sphere is not informed by a need to protect the human body from the explosion, but rather by the aesthetic merits of a massively engineered three-dimensional simulation experienced from the comfort of a virtual space? An experience of the nuclear sublime provoked by an above-ground nuclear detonation involved a moment of terror that was ultimately resolved for scientists through an intellectual compensation, allowing the project of nuclear weapons science to continue. The need to manage terror at the center of the enterprise, however mediated, gave scientists momentary access to the possible real-world effects of their technoscientific work. SBSS, as an experimental regime, blocks access to any visceral understanding of the power of the U.S. nuclear arsenal, replacing it with sophisticated material science questions and a virtual spectacle, which together offer only complexity and aesthetic pleasure. Indeed, the nuclear weapon currently produced by the technoscientific and discursive practices of Los Alamos scientists is so compartmentalized and fetishized as a fragile form that it is increasingly difficult to identify *as a weapon*. The beauty of nuclear weapons science in Los Alamos has always been one of its most dangerous elements, allowing an aestheticization of scientific knowledge to circumvent the political import of engineering weapons of mass destruction. In his 1936 critique of the Italian Futurists' beautification of war and the machine body, Walter Benjamin argued that the movement revealed a "sense perception that has been changed by technology" and a European society on the eve of World War II whose "self-alienation has reached such a degree that it can experience its own destruction as an aesthetic pleasure of the first order" (1969b: 242). The bomb is America's response to forces unleashed at that historical moment, and the post–Cold War transformation of each U.S. nuclear device from a weapon of mass destruction into an opportunity for exotic material science and cutting-edge computer simulation advances the aestheticization of politics through a reconfigured sense perception to a new order for a new century. It is vital to recover the politics that SBSS works to erase, even as the future of the bomb in Los Alamos becomes no longer that of a bomb, but rather of America's technoaesthetic spectacle par excellence.

3 Econationalisms
First Nations in the Plutonium Economy

After the Second World War, Oppenheimer's slogan concerning Los
Alamos was "Let us give it back to the Indians." To his great credit Norris
Bradbury, as the first postwar director of Los Alamos, prevented that from
happening.
—Edward Teller, "The Laboratory of the Atomic Age"

The most important truth about Los Alamos National Laboratory is that it
has always been and still is a secret; a center whose work has always
been kept utterly shrouded from the view of the world; a place with no
public memory.
—Herman Agoyo (San Juan Pueblo), "Who Here Will Begin This Story?"

When the Manhattan Project arrived on the Pajarito Plateau in 1943 it
was to be a temporary U.S. intrusion into northern New Mexico, a necessary military undertaking that would disappear after the end of the
war. Few suspected at the time that the launch of the military atomic age,
and then the Cold War, would lead to a permanent technoscientific presence on the plateau, one that would make the plutonium economy a per-
petual feature of life along the northern Rio Grande. For those pursuing
military nuclear science, the future has always offered an unending possibility for self-reinvention, as each new technological advance participates in a modernist notion of progress that displaces the past in favor
of the future. Edward Teller offers us a perfect illustration of this logic—
and its hidden cost—in his contribution to an anniversary edition of *Los
Alamos Science* in 1993. Teller celebrates the fiftieth year of Los Alamos
by forecasting a bright post–Cold War future for the laboratory, involving "an open minded pursuit of the truly limitless possibilities presented
to inquiring minds by scientific and technological revolutions" (1993:
37). But in so doing, he also acknowledges a national-cultural rupture, a
spatial displacement enabling the U.S. progression into the nuclear age.
For Teller, the centrality of Los Alamos in the realm of military nuclear

science supplants all other claims to the Pajarito Plateau. He evokes an indigenous presence simply as counterexample, as a dramatic means of underscoring the ongoing achievement of the Manhattan Project, involving the transformation of a preindustrial space into a cutting-edge laboratory capable of unending technoscientific revolution. Teller's history of Los Alamos thus mirrors the history of the United States, as the logics of discovery—of both continents and isotopes—rely on simultaneous acts of colonialism, forgetting, and reinvention (cf. Carter 1988).

The doubled nature of this history is a visceral reality for those who have inhabited the northern Rio Grande valley "from time immemorial." For indigenous communities, the Manhattan Project is not usually located within a narrative of technoscientific progress or Cold War strategy or American military power, but in more exclusively local terms. The atomic bomb project figures as the source of important new jobs and cross-cultural contacts for Pueblo peoples, but also of profound rupture. Marking the fiftieth anniversary of the Manhattan Project from a different vantage point, Herman Agoyo (San Juan) engages these multiple registers of Pueblo experience, placing U.S. practices of secrecy and amnesia at the center of a process that has produced profound historical change along the northern Rio Grande.[1] In 1993, at the first public meeting between officials from Los Alamos National Laboratory (LANL) and the U.S. Department of Energy (DOE) and northern New Mexican community leaders, Agoyo takes advantage of the immediate post–Cold War moment to give voice to longstanding regional concerns. He begins his presentation by asking, "what should I tell my grandson" about Los Alamos? Agoyo's history of the Manhattan Project is, then, immediately grounded not in technoscientific achievement but in interpersonal relationships and generational reproduction. Acknowledging that when the Manhattan Project first arrived on the Pajarito Plateau many at the Pueblo thought it was going to be a "blessing," one that ensured jobs, education, and security, Agoyo concludes that Los Alamos's fifty-year legacy is one of "ashes":

> We have slowly realized that this work which started out to harness an unimaginable power has in fact harmed human beings and the planet beyond any calculation. It has harmed us all by the sickness, death, and destruction that has been the ultimate product of this work. It has harmed us by the nightmare fear instilled in the hearts and minds of all the world's peoples about nuclear war and radiation "accidents." It has violated and harmed us by the awful problems of pollution and defilement caused in handling and disposing of the radioactive materials dumped onto and into Mother Earth. (1995: 37)

It has violated and harmed us. Agoyo's initial description of Los Alamos as a "place with no public memory" shifts the terms of the Manhattan Project from a concern with military technoscience to local accountability, and from a global vision of American power to a regional assessment of the ecological and social impacts of that nuclear vision. What for Teller is a story of modernist progress, becomes for Agoyo an ongoing experience of radioactive colonization provoking a unique experience of the nuclear uncanny. Tribal rights, the politics of nuclear waste and war, as well as the possibility of extinction are linked processes in Agoyo's call to public memory, as the Manhattan Project is identified not as a source of global security, but rather of local defilement, pollution, and cultural disorientation.

If Teller ultimately argues that we forget the past to enable the future, Agoyo reminds us that the "past" is not so easily displaced, that LANL occupies a territorial space that remains vibrant within older, and substantially different, cosmological orders. This chapter explores northeastern Pueblo perspectives on the Manhattan Project, forwarding the realization that Los Alamos occupied a space richly animated within preexisting universes, intimate worlds now tied not only to modernist powers of self-reinvention but also energized by cyclic relations with nature. The U.S. nuclear project, from this perspective, is a new moment in the colonial history of the Southwest, as ecosystems, bodies, and cosmologies have been transformed by their biological, social, and spiritual engagement with the plutonium economy. For the Manhattan Project not only produced the bomb, it initiated an ongoing transformation of specific Pueblo universes. Agoyo's call to public memory thus engages not only the question of national sacrifice and citizenship, but also begins to chart a fundamentally different history of the nuclear age. From his perspective, the challenge of the nuclear age for indigenous communities involves balancing the local opportunities and hazards of U.S. military-industrial production, while maintaining the viability of political formations that predate the American, Mexican, and Spanish regimes. Put differently, the first international context the Manhattan Project engaged in 1943—but the very last to be recognized in 1993—involves the Pueblo communities that live at the foot of the Pajarito Plateau, who venerate the land now occupied by the laboratory as ancestral ground, and who are negotiating the biosocial effects of U.S. nuclear weapons science.

ECOLOGIES OF PLACE

The Pueblos all set careful limits to the boundaries of their world and order everything within it. These boundaries are not the same but, more important, the principles of setting boundaries are since all use phenomena in the four cardinal directions, either mountains or bodies of water, usually both to set them . . . All peoples try to bring their definitions of group space somehow into line with their cosmologies, but the Pueblos are unusually precise about it.

—Alfonso Ortiz (San Juan), "Ritual Drama and the Pueblo World View"

While Manhattan Project scientists began work in secret to produce security on a global scale in 1943, they unknowingly colonized a space that was already intricately involved in producing knowledge and security on uniquely local terms. U.S. military technoscience entered into a geographic space that was central to multiple Pueblo cultures, and that participated in a specific technology for producing security in everyday life. These indigenous technologies, as we shall see, were and are grounded in logics of ecological management and are protected by long-standing traditions of secrecy. Since 1943, dueling cultures of secrecy have worked on the Pajarito Plateau to mobilize nature for the benefits of their societies: as physicists worked to unlock the power of the atom in laboratories and test sites, Pueblo leaders sought to manage the ecological balance in their universe through the ritual maintenance of a complex system of shrines and sacred sites. The precision of nuclear weapons science collides here with the precision of Pueblo place making, which, as Alfonso Ortiz has argued, is a uniquely powerful aspect of northeastern Pueblo cosmology. The untold story of the Manhattan Project involves this collision between regimes of knowledge, concepts of nature, definitions of security, and secrecy societies on the Pajarito Plateau. In this section, I engage the basic structures of northeastern Pueblo cosmology to underscore the cultural and ecological effects of the arrival of the Manhattan Project in 1943. I forward the work of Pueblo intellectuals writing about their own traditions, noting that much of this knowledge remains protected within Pueblo societies. Indeed, as we shall see, for good reason it is often easier for an outsider to talk to a weapons scientist about the bomb at Los Alamos than to Pueblo leaders about their specific cultural investments in the land now occupied by LANL.

For the northeastern Pueblo nations, mythohistory begins with an emergence from inside the earth, a moment when—not unlike a plant seedling—each of the tribes left a dark underworld, and with the help of supernatural and animal guides, pushed up toward the daylight to inhabit the surface of the earth.[2] Each of the northeastern Pueblos has its own tale of emergence, which in general terms, relates how the tribe traveled on a difficult journey (for the Tewa, from underneath a lake; for the Keres, from a cave known as Shipapu), discovering witchcraft and death for the first time, but also the fertile river valley surrounded by the four sacred mountains where they now live. For the Tewa, the guardian spirits that accompanied the tribe from the underworld went directly to the four cardinal mountaintops to look after the people, and those that died on this first journey were buried near the Pueblo, returned to the earth where their spirits could be forever spoken to and taken care of (A. Ortiz 1969). The emergence stories tie the people in a unique manner to the earth, establishing their identity not simply within a specific geographical space, but also through maintaining an intimate, tactile engagement with a spiritually animated place. Some of the stories, for example, describe how the earth's surface was soft at the moment of emergence, leaving behind the footprints of the first people; marks that remain visible today in hardened rock and, through their continued visceral presence, provide a spatial mnemonic of that first journey. Similarly, the emergence stories describe how the people were directly involved in creating the divisions between summer and winter, male and female, as well as articulating the six cardinal directions and energizing specific relationships between all sentient beings, which include not only humans and supernatural spirits, but also animals, insects, rocks, plants and trees, rivers and springs, weather systems, and clouds. In this way, the emergence tales define an ecological universe and make the tribe intimately responsible for encouraging life and harmony between all the beings that populate the three levels of existence that make up that universe—the underworld, the surface of the earth, and the sky.

As a complicated philosophical system that locates humans as merely one element in a broader ecology, Pueblo cosmologies argue that the people are inseparable from the specific geographical space in which they now live, a place where their ancestors are buried and where the channels of power connecting the different levels of existence line up to focus life energy on their communities (A. Ortiz 1969: 141). The northern Rio Grande valley, thus, offers up sensual traces of the initial moment of world making through specific landmarks that remain part of everyday life and that, through mythohistory, emphasize the essential consanguinity of all aspects of nature. As Rina Swentzell (Santa Clara) describes it, for the Tewa:

> differences among the elements of the life force (or nature) are recognized and accepted, but essential characteristics are known to be the same. For instance, a lump of clay is recognized to be akin to the human holding it because the force which determines the essence of clay is identical to that which determines human beings. The Tewa word "nung" is translated to mean "us" or "clay" depending on the context. There is direct cross-communication possible between all elements of nature—human, plants, other animals, and even natural phenomena. (1982: 17; see also Naranjo 1992)

The essence of clay is identical to that which determines human beings. The intimacy of this universe is underscored by the emotional attributes given to all aspects of the natural world, which historically required people with the right heart to soothe powerful beings that can be lonely or vengeful as well as generous and caring (Parsons 1996: 198; also Laski 1958: 78).[3] A successful mediation of all these seen and unseen forces, enabled by the right mental attitude toward nature, produces a healthy ecospiritual system, which provides ample nourishment for all beings.[4]

Pueblo emergence stories articulate the fundamental coordinates of traditional Pueblo thought, defining specific cosmologies centered on maintaining intimate relations with all the beings that live within a fixed geographical space visibly bounded by the four cardinal mountains (see Hewett and Dutton 1945: 34–44). Alfonso Ortiz argues that the fundamental difference between Euro-American and Pueblo cosmologies is that Pueblo peoples emphasize an experience of space over time.[5] This is a profoundly different way of organizing both tactile experience and social history. Whereas a European metaphysics privileges a movement through linear time (in which each moment is unique and nonrepeatable), northeastern Pueblo cosmologies emphasize a spatiotemporal repetition based on a cyclical movement through a specific physical space (historically tied to the agricultural cycle). Within northeastern Pueblo cosmologies the past remains both fixed and animated within the landscape itself, allowing ongoing interactions with the first supernaturals as well as the entire ancestral lineage of the tribe and the ecosystem. Since the intent of this system is the stability of a specific moment of harmony in the system, radical historical change presents a special challenge to Pueblo thought. Ortiz has argued that northeastern Pueblo oral traditions endeavor to turn time into space by framing historical events in ways that reiterate the principles of the founding mythospatial charters.[6] He notes, for example, that ritual clowns burlesque and caricature those who have intruded on Pueblo life—Spanish explorers, missionaries, government agents, and anthropologists—and thereby incorporate these foreign elements into the ritual order, and through yearly repetition on the dance plaza, contain them within the Pueblo universe.[7] In a discussion of how Pueblo communities first negotiated requests that they perform their dances outside of the specific dance plaza where they are seasonally performed, Ortiz provides further insight into these spatiotemporal logics:

> Not only were their own traditional sacred dances rigidly locked into the seasonal cycle, but they could not be performed outside of a given sacred space within a Pueblo because it was believed that the dance would not only lose all its efficacy, but that it would have no meaning whatsoever outside of that sacred space. The reason they believed so is that a ceremonial

occasion is viewed metaphorically as being like a plant. When the date for the ceremony is set, it is believed that a crack appears in the earth where the seed of the dance has sprouted. The song-composing and practice sessions in preparation for the dance are viewed as being analogous to the states of growth of the plant. The day of the dance itself is considered the day when the plant bears fruit. Hence, through these powerful earth-bound metaphors the Pueblo peoples reinforced their sense of, and commitment to, the particular places they inhabit. They found it difficult to even think of these locale-centered ceremonies as having any meaning apart from the earth which gave them their being. (1977: 18)

Power, place, and identity are thus woven together in these traditions to promote a specific ecosocial order.

The overall effect of this philosophical system, in each of its manifestations along the Rio Grande, is to delineate clearly the borders of the Pueblo world and to focus Pueblo attention inward onto the village space. Historically, for example, the Tewa believed that the farther one traveled from the village center the more dangerous the world became, requiring ritual prohibitions on those that traveled into the mountains where the most powerful deities live (A. Ortiz 1969: 129; see also 1972: 157). Lakes, springs, and caves are sacred sites because they offer points of connection to the underworld; similarly, an elaborate system of shrines presents a symbolic means of channeling life energy or "healing" power onto the Pueblo (Naranjo and Swentzell 1989). At the top of the four cardinal mountains that orient northeastern Pueblo thought are sacred lakes where the supernaturals that led the tribe out of the underworld live, as well as *nan sipu*, or earth navels, where the ancestors live and watch over the Pueblo (A. Ortiz 1969: 19).[8] For the Tewa of San Juan, the hills between the sacred mountains and the village also have earth navels as well as caves or tunnels where specific supernatural beings live who visit the Pueblo during ceremonies in the form of masked dancers. At the very center of the village is the *sipapu*, the mythohistorical place of emergence, where all the directions come together (the cardinal points as well as the underworld and the sky). Energy flows out from the sipapu toward the mountain earth navels, which then return that energy toward the village, and in this constant flow of energy between sites, blessings are distributed over the entire Pueblo geospiritual system. The shrine system not only integrates Pueblo members into the local ecology, it is a technological means of producing security in their world.

Pueblo people know, then, exactly where the center of the universe is and work through yearly ritual cycles to channel the energy of that site for the benefit of the entire ecosystem. In the late winter, for example, the religious leaders at San Juan place seeds from all the village crops deep into the sipapu in the dead of night, and through this act, reach down into the underworld and wake up nature from its winter slumber, enabling Spring itself to begin (A. Ortiz 1969: 21, 114). The interconnectedness of this system makes life precarious, in that parts can influence the whole—that is, individual beings can affect the entire ecosystem (A. Ortiz 1972: 143). Northeastern Pueblo cosmologies ultimately rely on all sentient beings to participate productively in the flow of life, which requires that each being maintain a harmony of thought and action to produce a healthy ecology (Laski 1958). The philosophical beauty in these cosmologies is drawn from the way in which space, ecology, power, and action are consciously interconnected, placing humans within the center of an animate universe that requires the concerted action of all beings to continue life. Northeastern Pueblo cosmologies thus present a view of a rigorously ordered universe in which all beings have a specific role to play. Or, as Alfonso Ortiz once concluded, paraphrasing Albert Einstein, the physicist who helped launch the Manhattan Project, "the gods do not play dice with our universe" (1976: 38).

The seeming fragility of this cultural system is countered by the historical reality that northeastern Pueblo peoples have lived in the same territory, tended the same shrines, and successfully reproduced the natural order for over a millennium. With its fences and U.S. national security science, the Manhattan Project, however, introduced a rupture into this system, fundamentally altering how the shrine system could be engaged in everyday life. One Tewa resident of the valley described the technoscientific transformation of the Pajarito Plateau to me this way:

> The Forest Service had already taken all the land, so it made it easy for the government to transfer land from one organization to another. That's when the Pueblos lost a lot of their land. We lost an area that we used for ceremonial purposes. We've now got the right to go up there but we don't own it anymore. The mountain there was used for ceremonial purposes—for pilgrimages to shrines and other things. I remember my uncle going up to a site and crying because they had put in pipes that ruined the area. Once the buildings go in the religious character of the site is ruined. The MESON physics facility rests on a number of archaeological sites, as does Area G. They also do archaeological excavations up there. All of these are acts of desecration and none of the laws work to protect our interests. It's always the anthropologists, archaeologists, and engineers that have the legal advantage.

Once the buildings go in the religious character of the site is ruined. As a counterhistory of the Manhattan Project, this narrative moves from territorial colonization to religious and environmental desecration to interpersonal loss. It marks a collision in ecological and national regimes, and describes a cultural space transformed by military nuclear science. Whereas Pueblo cosmology emphasizes human participation in a broader ecosystem and reciprocal relations with nature, modernist techno-science at LANL assumes a position outside of nature, allowing a careful observation and manipulation of the basic building blocks of the universe (in which humans are not directly implicated in a system of reciprocal obligation). The collision between modernist technoscience and Pueblo ecology on the plateau is now a multigenerational process. A Tewa spokesman described his feelings about LANL to me this way: "Things have gotten better since the fences came down in the '50s, but it's like we had a shot-gun marriage 52 years ago that has not yet been consummated. We've lived side by side for 52 years and are just now learning to say hello to one another. But that doesn't mean that everything is good, or that war is still not possible."

Because the U.S. atomic bomb project occupied the top of one of the most prominent mountain ranges in the northern Rio Grande valley, it necessarily affected all those communities for whom mountains are sources of power. Los Alamos, in fact, occupies a place of particular importance within northeastern Pueblo thought—at the foot of the Valles Caldera Volcano, one of the largest in the Jemez Mountain Range. Greg Cajete (Santa Clara), while serving on the Santa Clara Tribal Council, discussed the implications of locating the laboratory at the foot of the volcano in his comments to the LANL 2000 conference in 1993:

> The lab itself is located in what we consider one of the most sacred areas among the northern Pueblos, located in a place of fire, it is right at the foot of a volcano. There is always reflection on exactly why the lab is there, because we as Pueblo peoples believe that nothing happens by accident, that situations evolve because in many ways they were meant to. So here you have basically an entity dealing with the very deepest secrets of nature which is, in a sense, releasing the eternal fire, which is the energy that is such an essential part of the life of the cosmos itself, and it being surrounded by some very, very sacred sites.

Nothing happens by accident. Here, the location of the U.S. nuclear project takes on specific meaning within the Pueblo universe, raising questions about the implications of weapons science within a specific georeligious topography. The Pajarito Plateau is that section of the eastern slope of Jemez Mountain Range that is located in a thirty-mile stretch between Santa Clara Pueblo and Cochiti Pueblo; it is visible from most of the northern Pueblos. It is one of the oldest inhabited areas in the Southwest, with signs of human occupation going back nearly ten thousand years. Today, thousands of archaeological and religious sites on the plateau are manifestations of both the millennial human investments in the region and the ongoing traditional use by indigenous peoples throughout the Southwest. Indeed, the Jemez Mountains remain an important cultural site not only for the Rio Grande Pueblos—which recognize them as a fundamental aspect of their geospiritual order—but also for the Acoma, Zuni, Hopi, Navajo, Mescalaro Apache, and Jicarilla Apache nations. Indigenous communities throughout the Southwest collect spring water, medicinal plants, minerals, and clay on the Jemez Range, and identify the plateau as a spiritually important site. The Pajarito Plateau participates in a complex universe of symbolic sites, including ruins, shrines, powerful natural elements (springs, caves, and lakes), as well as sites of mythohistorical emergence.[9]

The Manhattan Project landed within this multiply invested geospiritual space in 1943, eventually occupying 43 square miles on the Pajarito Plateau with some 150 miles of roads, 1,000 buildings, 400 miles of waste pipes (including 8 miles of radioactive waste lines), 123 liquid effluent discharge points, and 94 air emission sources. To this one needs to add the physical impact of the Los Alamos town site which, like the laboratory, has long since given up claims on being merely a temporary presence on the plateau, now maintaining a population of over 17,000. Thus, while northeastern Pueblo nations have experienced a rapid change in their own political and religious orders in the past fifty years, the Pajarito Plateau has been remade by the Manhattan Project into a major industrial site, transforming one-quarter of the northeastern Pueblos' symbolic universe into an experimental nuclear laboratory. Indeed, a curious feature of Pueblo country is that, with the exception of the Hopi and Zuni nations, all sixteen eastern Pueblo territories are located within the immediate orbit of a U.S. nuclear facility (either LANL or Sandia, in Albuquerque; see Figure 3.1). The Manhattan Project thus unleashed a physical assault on Pueblo geospiritual orders, denying tribal members access to certain sites while destroying others. Moreover, the indigenous nations that live downwind and downstream from the laboratory must now assess the ecological and health impacts of the atomic bomb project on their communities. Having survived Spanish and Mexican territorial governments, U.S. colonization, and the Cold War, Pueblo leaders are now asking what happens when the Manhattan Project finally ends, when, in perhaps a far distant future, the laboratory finally closes down and the cumulative ecological and spiritual legacies of U.S. nuclear science return to a uniquely Pueblo provenance.

A profound cosmological divide separates northeastern Pueblo concepts of nature from the new residents on the plateau. Part of the sacredness of mountains, lakes, springs, and caves for Pueblo peoples is their very wildness, their undisturbed nature, which participates in and

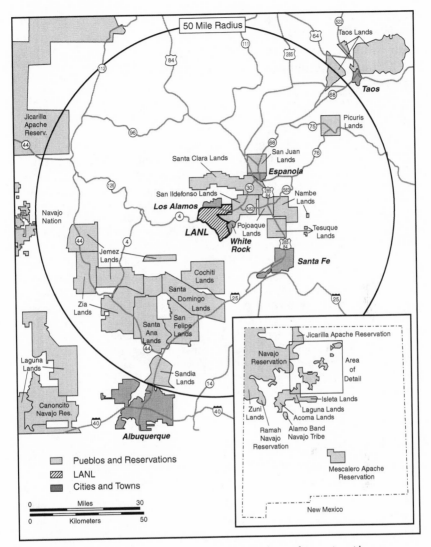

3.1. Indigenous nations in the vicinity of LANL. (Redrawn from a Los Alamos National Laboratory map)

enables a broader ecological reality. As Euro-American cultures emphasize the built over the natural, there is an enormous problem of translation for Pueblo communities who need to make the case that a specific area, devoid of any development or recreational use, is not merely of aesthetic value, but is profoundly powerful and necessary in a spiritual sense (see Naranjo and Swentzell 1989: 260–61). Pueblo officials often try to make this point by arguing that commercial development in some natural areas is the cultural equivalent of building a golf course, ski lodge, uranium mine, or nuclear weapons laboratory on top of Notre Dame Cathedral or Westminster Abby. Governor Walter Dasheno of Santa Clara Pueblo put it this way:

> The environment is an interaction of many forces, a unity of all things. There are the physical and there are the spiritual. And, I don't believe we can or should separate them. We have taken, as a major environmental theme, protection of our religious and cultural resources. We argue strenuously that equal consideration should be given to our religious concerns including practices that do not violate our sacred areas as a principle in environmental protection. This concept is difficult for governmental bureaucrats, business people and many other non-Indians to understand. We have suggested, however, that if a project were proposed underneath the National Cathedral or in Arlington National Cemetery, there would be a collective cry from all segments of our society. I submit that standards of respect and deference should be accorded the American Indian. When Los Alamos National Laboratories, for example, proposes to set off explosions on sacred ground, or to dump high level nuclear waste in sacred areas, the affront to our culture and religion is complete. We should not be required to specify in measurable terms why a sacred area is sacred. We should not have to fight for a law that segregates national protection of our religious beliefs from the same rights accorded other religious beliefs in America as outlined in our Constitution and Bill of Rights. We should not have to defend our cultural practices or sites in an environmental review process that is not required of any other American religion. (Quoted in South West Organizing Project 1993: 9)

We should not be required to specify in measurable terms why a sacred area is sacred. Governor Dasheno's statement underscores that Pueblo concepts of land and place inform uniquely Pueblo universes, and are largely irreconcilable with the Protestant notion of private property or the value of "improving" the land through commercial development or technoscience. Put somewhat differently, while Judeo-Christian traditions allow for an infinite production of sacred space through the consecration of built space, indigenous cosmologies ground the sacred within a natural ecology that is ultimately both fragile and irreproducible—once a lake, or spring, or shrine is destroyed it cannot be replaced. Thus, the arrival of the Manhattan Project on the Pajarito Plateau not only brought radically different concepts of nature, ecology, and power into collision, but also threatened (in just the act of building roads, facilities, and homes) indigenous connections to specific spiritually animated places.

Private property law (a radical change from previous regimes along the northern Rio Grande), as well as the enormous immigration into northern New Mexico after World War II, impacted water and land rights as well as access to religious sites throughout the northern Rio Grande valley. The Jemez nation, for example, has a shrine on the top of Redondo Peak, which is now in private ownership. Joe Sando (Jemez) reports that the Pueblo now "owns" a four feet by four feet section of the mountaintop where the shrine is located, but still must get permission to visit the site for ceremonial purposes (1982: 11). Similarly, Geronima Cruz Montoya (San Juan) has publicly commented on the difficulty San Juan religious leaders now have in completing their yearly pilgrimage to the top of Tsikumu P'in, a peak located just to the north of Los Alamos:

> Just recently—say in the last year or so—our people went on their annual pilgrimage and were shot at, so they really ran for cover in a hurry. Another time they asked ahead of time for clearance, so what did they find? White men waiting with cameras. Our people, of course, turned back disgustedly and disappointed and couldn't go to the top for their rituals. Now I understand, the shrine is full of beer cans and other trash. Desecration of such sacred places has inflicted deeper wounds on the Indian people than some of the worst political injustices. For the disappearance of such sanctuaries has left a vacuum which nothing the white man has to offer will fill. (Shutes and Mellick 1996: 142; see also Ford 1992)

The destruction or pollution of a shrine or natural resource (e.g., a lake, spring, or cave) is damaging to the entire system, as the power of these sites is drawn from the cumulative energy produced by generations of care given to those areas and the reciprocal relations with the supernatural entities and ancestors that inhabit them. Traditionally, the discovery of garbage within an earth navel was attributed to malevolent spirits or witchcraft, and was believed to influence directly the stability of the entire ecosystem (Curtis 1970: 12). Today, in addition to the problem of land ownership and the term of U.S. nuclear science, some New Age religious traditions have appropriated indigenous religious sites for their own use, leaving behind objects (candles, crystals, incense) that, for Pueblo peoples, pollute the shrine, and prevent it from being a conduit between entities and levels of existence. The conflict over who has the right to access and to use Pueblo religious sites is now a perennial problem in northern New Mexico, due to the expansion of mountaintop developments (for roads, ski areas, and homes, as well as projects of the national laboratory). Thus, in the nuclear age, it has become increasingly impossible for Pueblo nations to focus their energies inward (as they historically have done except in times of crisis), as relations with LANL have become an increasingly complex means of ensuring Pueblo cultural survival.

THE NEW WORLD: 1942/1992

In August 1993 at the first public meeting to discuss the historical impacts and future of LANL, local Pueblo and Nuevomexicano activists hung a huge banner behind the LANL 2000 conference stage that read:

"The Italian Navigator has landed in the New World."
"How did he find the natives?"
"Very friendly."—Manhattan Project, December 2, 1942: Dialogue between Enrico Fermi's laboratory in Chicago and Harvard University to announce the first self-sustaining fission chain reaction.

This quotation is from a coded exchange in the early days of the Manhattan Project between physicists Arthur Compton and James Conant, who immediately understood the achievement of nuclear fission in Chicago to be on par with Christopher Columbus's "discovery" of the New World in 1492. Here, indigenous activists capitalize on a remarkable scene in 1942, in which physicist Enrico Fermi is seen to be channeling the spirit of the "Italian Navigator" under Stag Field in Chicago as he enters the subatomic realm of neutrinos for the first time, an Edenic New World where the locals were, like Columbus's first contacts, always "friendly." The play of words involved in this wartime transmission of nuclear secrets between scientific elites illustrates in a remarkably concise gesture the convergence between the colonial imaginary of the western frontier and that which would come to inform the nuclear frontier. By forwarding the racial politics embedded within this founding moment of the Manhattan Project, indigenous activists in northern New Mexico sought quietly to derail the seamless authority of Los Alamos National Laboratory as a "U.S. national security" institution. Pueblo and Nuevomexicano representatives took advantage of the post–Cold War moment to shift the ideological terrain away from a Cold War logic prioritizing "national" security, in order to ask more fundamental questions about who is a citizen in the United States, and what kind of local sacrifices can be demanded of those living next to a nuclear weapons facility. In doing so, they also sought to put the laboratory on notice that the "natives" might not be "friendly" much longer.

Pueblo nations have always held a distinct place within U.S. law and history. As the oldest and most territorially rooted communities in the United States, they have maintained cultural integrity through three national regimes—the Spanish, Mexican, and American. But despite a millennium of residence along the northern Rio Grande River, Pueblo peoples have not always fallen into the category of the "Native American" within official U.S. discourse. Pueblo communities were incorporated into the

United States in 1848 with the conclusion of the war with Mexico. The Treaty of Guadalupe Hidalgo technically made all citizens of Mexico in the conquered territories into citizens of the United States. Pueblo peoples first entered the United States, then, not as indigenous communities but as Mexican citizens, and theoretically became full U.S. citizens at that moment. However, the legal status of Pueblo communities was debated from 1848 to 1913—a period in which they were neither U.S. citizens nor officially recognized as "Native American." In *United States v. Lucero* (1869), the first legal case to address the question of whether Pueblo peoples were "Indian" under U.S. law, the court concluded that their "Pueblo-ness" conflicted with their "Indian-ness":

> A law made for wild, wandering savages, to be extended over a people living for three centuries in fenced adobes and cultivating the soil for the maintenance of themselves and families and giving an example of virtue, honesty, and industry to their more civilized neighbors, in this enlightened age of progress and proper understanding of the civil rights of man, is considered by this court as wholly inapplicable to the pueblo Indians of New Mexico. (Quoted in F. Cohen 1986: 387)

Too "civilized" to be "Indians," while too "savage" to be truly "American," Pueblo communities exceeded the legal categories for identity in the nineteenth century, and were left in a state of legal limbo until 1913, when Pueblo nations were officially granted "Indian" status (cf. Pearce 1965). At that moment, they became "wards" of the federal government, gaining some legal protection and a limited recognition of their right to self-rule, but also giving up their claim to U.S. citizenship based on the terms of the Treaty of Guadalupe Hidalgo (see F. Cohen 1986: 385–88). During this period, Pueblo governments negotiated constant threats to their land base, and in the first decades of the twentieth century, direct legal attacks on Pueblo religion by those who considered Indian religious practices to be "anti-Christian" and "un-American" (Sando 1992: 90–96). The U.S. Congress granted full U.S. citizenship to all Native Americans in 1924. However, Pueblo communities in New Mexico were denied that most basic right of citizenship, the right to vote, until 1948, a full century after the Treaty of Guadalupe Hidalgo promised full citizenship, and five years after the start of the Manhattan Project in New Mexico.

Perhaps, then, it should not be so surprising to learn that the word that best characterizes the official relationship between LANL and adjacent Pueblo nations during the Cold War is *silence*. As the Soviet Union began to come apart, however, Pueblo leaders began to hear from Santa Fe–based activist groups of significant environmental problems at LANL, and began mobilizing for an accounting of the environmental and health impacts on their communities. San Ildefonso Pueblo, which shares a territorial boundary with the laboratory and claims the Pajarito Plateau as ancestral land, initiated conversations with LANL to address tribal concerns about radiological impacts on Pueblo lands. The resulting investigations of soil, water, air, specific ceremonial plants, and elk populations by LANL scientists concluded that there was "no health risk" to San Ildefonso residents posed by laboratory activities. These results, however, were almost immediately contested by studies conducted by the Eight Northern Pueblos Office of Environmental Protection, which showed "alarmingly high levels of radiation" on tribal lands. In October 1992, San Ildefonso challenged the veracity of LANL reports by cordoning off a section of its territory that borders the laboratory with a sign declaring: "Prolonged exposure to this area and gathering materials may be harmful to your health."[10] A few weeks later, a coalition of Pueblo, Nuevomexicano, and Anglo activists made a trip to Oakland, California, to confront the University of California board of regents, which has managed Los Alamos and Livermore National Laboratories since their inception. This New Mexican coalition pointed out that in the fifty-year history of Los Alamos, no UC representative had ever met with community groups in New Mexico to discuss laboratory issues. Herman Agoyo (San Juan) declared the people of the northern Rio Grande valley "the forgotten public"; Gilbert Sanchez, the lieutenant governor of San Ildefonso, stated that "local people have not been told what is going on" at Los Alamos; while Governor Walter Dasheno of Santa Clara wrote to the UC regents, declaring that "New Mexico is not a scientific colony to the State of California."[11]

As the Cold War came to a close, a host of new federal legislation also came into being, which provided Pueblo governments with new legal tools for engaging the nuclear complex. The Native American Graves and Repatriation Act (1990), Executive Order 13007 on Indian Sacred Sites (1996), and the Native American Religious Freedom Act (1978, Amended 1996) provide formal means of addressing cultural issues on the Pajarito Plateau, as federal agencies were now mandated to discuss cultural impacts with tribal governments. New environmental laws also came into being that allow indigenous nations to set environmental standards for their lands—standards that neighboring communities are obliged to meet. Changes in the Clean Air and Clean Water Acts, as well as Executive Order 12898 on Environmental Justice, mandate a new reciprocity between neighboring communities over environmental impacts, including an awareness of the racial and cultural dimensions of federal projects. Thus, as the Soviet Union dissolved into a series of new nation-states, LANL's position in New Mexico also fundamentally changed, requiring new sensitivity to the nations within: put simply, after a half century of federal silence, neighboring Pueblo nations were suddenly in a position not only to set environmental standards for their territories, but to affect the upwind, uphill activities of the laboratory—allowing those without a Cold War voice to impact the post–Cold War mission of the premier nuclear weapons facility in the United States.[12]

As a result of this new legal context, and rising regional concern about Cold War environmental effects, the legal position of Pueblo nations changed significantly in the post–Cold War period. In 1992, the DOE signed accords with the four Pueblos that immediately neighbor LANL— Santa Clara, San Ildefonso, Cochiti, and Jemez Pueblos—committing to a "government-to-government" relationship over laboratory impacts. In 1993, the University of California sent its first delegation to New Mexico to listen to community concerns about the laboratory. On November 12, 1994, LANL signed "government-to-government" cooperative agree- ments with Santa Clara, San Ildefonso, Cochiti, and Jemez Pueblos. In 1996, the State of New Mexico moved to resolve an eighty-four-year-old conceptual and legal ambiguity over the status of Indian tribes. Meeting at the State Capitol, the twenty governors and three presidents repre- senting territories within the State of New Mexico met for the first time to recognize each other's right to exist (see Figure 3.2). At this important post–Cold War moment, Pueblo governments were, thus, for the first time in American history, formally recognized by all the legal entities that directly impact their communities: the State of New Mexico, the Univer- sity of California, the DOE, and LANL.[13]

Collectively, these accords set up new lines of dialogue between four Pueblo governments and LANL, including plans for extensive environmen- tal monitoring of Accord Pueblo lands, a process of consultation over Pueblo cultural interests within LANL boundaries, emergency response training at the Accord Pueblos, environmental science training for Pueblo members, and ongoing discussion about new contracts and employment for Pueblo citizens (LANL 1995a; Shaner and Naranjo 1995). Thus, as neighboring Pueblo governments considered the types of environmental standards they wanted for tribal lands, they were also briefed for the first time about the environmental effects of fifty years of nuclear science on the plateau. Concurrently, laboratory officials learned about what it was like to live next to a nuclear facility and wonder about the physical and cultural impacts of nuclear science on a region of special importance to Pueblo peo- ples. These agreements represent a fundamental evolution in the history of LANL-Pueblo relations, which started in 1943 based on a "government-to- ward" relationship, were then remade over the course of the Cold War into a "government-to-citizen" dynamic (as Pueblo peoples became recognized

3.2. 1996 Mutual Recognition Meeting of the twenty governors and three presidents of territories in New Mexico. (Photograph by Joseph Masco)

U.S. citizens), and in the post–Cold War period, became centered around a new "government-to-government" relationship.

The trajectory of LANL-Pueblo relations was raised at the second executive meeting between the governments of Santa Clara, San Ildefonso, Cochiti, and Jemez Pueblos and LANL, a gathering that I attended at Cochiti Pueblo in 1995. Cochiti government officials began the session by discussing how for fifty years the people of Cochiti heard explosions and watched clouds of smoke drift over their land from Los Alamos, and wondered about the health effects of those clouds and their impacts on the people, water, crops, and land. Declaring that for over fifty years Los Alamos had been a "mystery" to the people of Cochiti, Governor Isaac Herrera underscored the need for government-to-government dialogue with the laboratory. The setting for this summit was particularly powerful, as the Pueblo de Cochiti Recreational Center provides a breathtaking view of the Pajarito Plateau, which rises immediately to the northwest. Pointing through an enormous glass window that directly frames the mountain, Governor Herrera visually demonstrated the proximity of the laboratory to the Pueblo, and emphasized that Cochiti religious leaders continue to traverse the Jemez Range for ceremonial purposes. His presentation underscored the cultural intimacy his people maintain with the

Pajarito Plateau, and simultaneously, the continuing "foreignness" of Los Alamos. This is important because the evidence of Cochiti Pueblo's participation in the nuclear age is not only social or spiritual, but also environmental, as traces of plutonium from military science at Los Alamos National Laboratory can now be found in the sediment of Cochiti Reservoir, located just above the Pueblo. The plutonium derives from the first decades of the Manhattan Project, when untreated radioactive effluent was discharged from laboratory facilities into canyons that ultimately flow into the Rio Grande River.[14]

In order to understand the combination of reticence and passion with which Pueblo leaders engaged LANL at the meeting, it is important to recognize the historical context of Cochiti-U.S. relations. Cochiti Reservoir was created by an act of Congress in the 1960s to relieve flooding downriver in Albuquerque. Built against the wishes of Cochiti Pueblo, the lake destroyed 50 percent of the tribe's farming land. Two years after the completion of the dam in the early 1970s, water began to seep through the retaining walls onto the remaining 50 percent of Cochiti farmland, eventually submerging it under a foot of standing water (see Sando 1998: 296–98). The plutonium from laboratory operations in Cochiti Lake, therefore, not only reveals a specific dimension of the plutonium economy—the remarkable mobility of radionuclides in the ecosystem—but also demonstrates the need to place the social and environmental effects of the laboratory in the broader historical contexts of both northeastern Pueblo cosmologies and U.S.-Pueblo relations. It also demonstrates why northeastern Pueblo engagements with Los Alamos are often interpreted as an index of U.S.-Pueblo relations more generally, standing not as an isolated relationship between a specific Pueblo and a specific laboratory project, but as a manifestation of a broader federal respect for Pueblo peoples.

Federal management of Pueblo lands produced fundamental changes in Pueblo societies during the twentieth century. In the decades preceding the launch of the Manhattan Project, the eight northern Pueblos, for example, lost title to over 18,000 acres of farmland in U.S. courts, just as their populations began to grow significantly. Unable to live off traditional farming practices for the first time, most of the eastern Pueblos turned to the cash economy for their livelihoods.[15] As Richard Clemmer (1984) has argued, the loss of the subsistence economy encouraged a number of Pueblos to lease their lands for coal and uranium mining, both tying their economic future to the world energy economy and placing their lands (and often bodies) in the hands of corporate mining interests.[16] For the northern Pueblos, the economic crisis led many to search out work at the area's largest employer, what was to become Los Alamos

Scientific Laboratory. Thus, one structural effect of U.S. policies toward Pueblo territories in the decades preceding the Manhattan Project was to help foment an economic crisis that coincidentally not only opened up tribal land to uranium mining, but also produced workers for those mining operations and for the construction of Los Alamos. Ultimately, Cold War New Mexico would produce half of the U.S. supply of uranium, providing the raw material for the U.S. nuclear weapons that were being designed at Los Alamos.

During World War II, Pueblo communities predominantly believed Los Alamos to be a temporary intrusion, one providing timely, if short-term, jobs in the laboratory and in the domestic economy of the town (Hawley 1948: 32–33).[17] Jobs included not only construction and support positions within the laboratory, but also domestic help in Los Alamos homes. A bus service was established to bring male construction crews from neighboring Pueblos and Nuevomexicano villages to the laboratory, as well as women, predominantly from the neighboring Pueblos of San Ildefonso and Santa Clara, to Los Alamos to help with childcare and household chores (Brode 1960). As Los Alamos became a permanent institution, communities throughout northern New Mexico began to see the laboratory as a source of financial stability, creating a new commuter economy for communities traditionally focused inward, and eventually a multigenerational, cross-cultural investment in the laboratory. First-generation employees encouraged their children to get technical training, hoping they could break out of the support jobs at the laboratory and move up the institutional hierarchy. Governor Dasheno of Santa Clara Pueblo, for example, has argued that the economic impact of the laboratory is a fundamental part of the larger environmental concerns of the Pueblo:

> The flip side of the environmental concerns is the economy. The national laboratories are major players. Any change in the direction, reduction in budgets, new mission, are of vital concern to New Mexico and the Pueblos. Downsizing Los Alamos, for example, could have a devastating impact on our economy. This, too, is an environmental issue. There is no question in my mind that steps must be taken to correct the adverse environmental conditions, a legacy of activities at Los Alamos and Sandia over 50 years. But, we must also be perceptive of the economic changes that will occur and see a plan of mitigation that does not compromise our quality of life. (Quoted in SouthWest Organizing Project 1993: 9)

Thus, while the Manhattan Project provided financial relief for neighboring communities suddenly reliant on a cash economy in the 1940s, it has evolved into a complex source both for maintaining local Pueblo life and for cultural assimilation in northern New Mexico.[18]

MIRRORS AND APPROPRIATIONS: THE SECRET SOCIETIES
OF THE PAJARITO PLATEAU

While there were no formal dialogues between LANL and neighboring
Pueblo nations during the Cold War, communities on and around the
plateau were acutely aware of and interested in one another. These logics
were not only interpersonal but also structured by the prevailing logic in
American society concerning Native American peoples. John Borneman
(1995) has argued that Native Americans were positioned in the nineteenth century as both the "first Americans" and as the counterconcept
to the American, creating a fundamental ambivalence about the legal
standing of indigenous peoples. This simultaneous discourse of genealogical connection and radical othering informed a number of Cold War
laboratory projects. Weapons scientists, for example, explicitly referenced Pueblo religion in their experimental work on nuclear fission,
naming the laboratories where they conduct criticality research "kivas."
Early criticality experiments involved moving blocks of fissile material
close enough together to start a chain reaction and allow neutrino
counts, while separating them before an explosion took place. This was
done by hand and was called "tickling the dragon's tail" due to its risk
factor (Rhodes 1986: 611–12). After physicists Harry Daghlian and
Louis Slotin were killed tickling the dragon in 1945 and 1946, Los
Alamos scientists built a new laboratory in Pajarito Canyon, the Critical
Experiments Facility, where criticality measurements could be performed
remotely in self-styled, high-tech kivas (Hacker 1987: 72–73). The first
kiva was built in 1947, the second in 1953, and the third in 1960.
Between 1947 and 1983 over 15,000 criticality experiments were performed in these kivas, divided between nuclear weapons projects, the
Rover nuclear rocket program, and nuclear reactor research (Paxton
1981; Mortensem 1983). Thus, much of the experimental work on
nuclear fission at Los Alamos was conducted in spaces explicitly referencing Pueblo traditions. Indeed, practices of naming, here, provide evidence of a curious cross-cultural investment on the plateau. An article in
the internal laboratory *Newsbulletin* imagined these high-tech kivas, and
their multicultural context, this way:

> The Pajarito Plateau is dotted with ruins of ancient stone kivas. Hundreds
> of years ago those secret ceremonial chambers witnessed Tewa Indian
> priests performing mysterious religious rituals. Today in the Pajarito
> Canyon, three concrete and steel kivas stand not far from many of their
> namesakes. These kivas have witnessed what (to the unknowing) may seem
> to be even more mysterious rites, such as metallic hemispheres moving
> together and apart in the absence of humans. These "mysterious rites" are

the activities of laboratory scientists working with critical assemblies, a mass of fissile material sufficient to sustain a nuclear chain reaction. (Mortensem 1983)

Mirroring an imagined Tewa ritual, which is both "ancient" and "mysterious," the author presents nuclear science as a new mysticism on the plateau. A laboratory history of the Pajarito Test Site pushed the analogy further, including a photograph of the first LANL kiva taken from within a nearby Pueblo ruin—visually emphasizing both the metaphorical connection between structures and the implied sense of technological evolution on the plateau (see Figure 3.3; Paxton 1981).

However, while it was possible for some LANL employees to imagine nuclear scientists channeling the spirits of Pueblo religious leaders within their high-tech kivas (see Figure 3.4), this demonstrates no engagement with the local, and living, Pueblo cultures. For example, it is quite possible that the ruins in Pajarito Canyon, which provided the symbolic points of reference for LANL's high-tech kivas, were utilized for ceremonial

3.3. LANL kiva from Pueblo ruin. (Courtesy of Los Alamos National Laboratory)

3.4. Interior view of LANL kiva. (Courtesy of Los Alamos National Laboratory)

purposes by neighboring Pueblos up to 1943 and the arrival of security fences, and would be used again if access were possible. Pueblo peoples venerate ruins because they are material points of connection to their ancestors, and are often burial sites as well (making them dangerous sites to disturb or discuss). Thus, the landscape used for the new criticality tests was not filled with the traces of a past civilization, but was part of an ongoing Pueblo cultural engagement with the plateau. Moreover, these high-tech kivas in their initial formation were also devoted to creating a military weapon, while Pueblo kivas are social spheres used both to define the community and to participate in a cosmogonic order that deifies nature and emphasizes "seeking life" (Laski 1958).[19]

LANL's high-tech kivas are, however, only one area where the multicultural context surrounding Los Alamos has been officially referenced in the culture of the laboratory. Street names in the town of Los Alamos and meeting rooms in the laboratory's Oppenheimer Conference Center also appear to honor local Pueblo nations. Thus, in the town of Los Alamos there is a San Ildefonso Lane, and you could meet someone at the corner of Tewa and Santa Clara Place or of Navajo and San Juan.

These asphalt streets cover areas of the plateau once embedded within indigenous practices, making their names a curious statement on the physical colonization of the Jemez range by the Manhattan Project. It is also, however, quite possible that these street names do not reference people at all, but rather nuclear explosions from the South Pacific above-ground testing regime, which provide names for several Los Alamos streets.

Operation Redwing was a test series conducted at the Bikini and Enewetok atolls in the South Pacific by Los Alamos Scientific Laboratory in 1956 (Hanson 1988: 69–75). Seventeen nuclear and thermonuclear explosions were performed between May 4 and July 17, each code-named after a Native American people. Operation Redwing was devoted to testing new weapons designs, and in doing so, unleashed over twenty megatons of power on the homelands of Pacific islanders (DOE 2000a). The initial test, Cherokee, was the first detonation of a B-52 dropped thermonuclear device, a 3.75-megaton reply to the Soviets' first test of a similar device five months earlier. The press (which had been banned from nuclear testing for several years) was invited to witness the explosion to make sure the message was delivered. Thus, the logics of U.S. national security produced a moment of explicit convergence: in order to send a message to the Soviet Union (the structural descendent of the "Indian" in the American oppositional imaginary) the genocidal potential of thermonuclear military technology was displayed on indigenous territories in the Pacific with devices evoking a claim on "Indian-ness" through the politics of naming. Even as North American indigenous nations—Lacrosse, Cherokee, Zuni, Yuma, Erie, Seminole, Flathead, Blackfoot, Kickapoo, Osage, Inca, Dakota, Mohawk, Apache, Navajo, Tewa, Huron—were appropriated for use as semiotic markers for the American bomb, the U.S. military personnel responsible for their use during war could imagine the nuclear battlefield itself as a kind of hostile "Indian country." At this moment in the nuclear age, indigenous communities provided both the explicit conceptual charter and absolute oppositional reference for the U.S. national security imaginary. The five-megaton shot on July 20, code-named Tewa, for example, evoked the "Tewa-speaking" Pueblo nations in New Mexico that then Los Alamos Scientific Laboratory bordered in northern New Mexico. Thus, just as the Tewa in New Mexico were dealing with the environmental and social effects of nuclear science at the laboratory, weapons scientists were evoking their name half a world away in an act of nuclear violence. The Tewa device (Figure 3.5) was detonated on a barge, creating a 129-foot-deep, 4,000-foot-diameter crater in the reef below and producing radioactive fallout that contaminated Bikini, Enewetok, and over two thousand

3.5. The five-megaton Tewa thermonuclear device, Bikini Island. (Courtesy of U.S. National Archives)

square miles of ocean—making it one of the most dangerous explosions in Operation Redwing (Hansen 1988: 74). Thus, from bombs to street names a misrecognition of Pueblo traditions prefigures its mirror-imaging in laboratory culture.

This symbolic evocation of Pueblo culture in Los Alamos, however, is echoed by moments of mirror-imaging from neighboring Pueblos. The forty-three square miles of LANL territory is extremely well marked by fences and warning signs, signs that alert visitors to the fact that they are

3.6. U.S. DOE No Trespassing Sign, Los Alamos County. (Photograph by Joseph Masco)

under new kinds of jurisdiction on LANL grounds, perhaps subject to search and seizure, and in some places, armed response (see Figure 3.6). Compare Figures 3.7 and 3.8. The first is a LANL road sign declaring "the roadway and surrounding lands are U.S. government property" and informing drivers to obey all federal, state, and laboratory rules. The second is a sign from Santa Clara Pueblo, alerting visitors to the fact that they are entering reservation lands, and are "subject to obey all Tribal and Federal laws within our boundaries." This type of sign (also marking San Ildefonso territories) is distinct in language and tone from the entrance signs at other Pueblos. Given that both Santa Clara and San Ildefonso identify the Jemez range as their homelands, and San Ildefonso claims the territory now occupied by LANL as ancestral lands, these signs of possession and jurisdiction take on a different political meaning, suggesting a colonial critique. Prohibitions on photography on Pueblo and LANL grounds also illustrate the mirrored levels of governmental power, as do the frequent road blocks along the Jemez: LANL shuts down roads while transporting dangerous materials each month, while neighboring Pueblos shut off access to their lands during ceremonial events they wish to keep private. In the mid-1990s, Pueblo governments established official Environmental Departments to engage the various environmental divisions at LANL, and the relationship between Los Alamos

3.7. Entering U.S. Territory Sign, Los Alamos County. (Photograph by Joseph Masco)

3.8. Entering Santa Clara Pueblo Territory Road Sign. (Photograph by Joseph Masco)

and the Accord Pueblos evolved from the previous period of silence, symbolic appropriation, and covert referencing, to one centered on official government-to-government process.

In the post–Cold War era, two potent sites of national cultural mirror-imaging have emerged on the plateau, concerning the politics of archival knowledge and secrecy. Nuclear weapons science and Pueblo religion are rooted in the same physical space in northern New Mexico, bringing these radically different means of achieving safety and security into direct engagement. Both cultures rely on secrecy, a compartmentalization of knowledge, and a social hierarchy of who knows what and why, to control access to social and material power. Similarly, both systems of knowledge make claims on controlling the essential powers of the universe: for scientists in the form of the atom, for eastern Pueblo religious leaders via intimate understanding of the reciprocal social bonds structuring nature. Technoscientific knowledge about the bomb may seem to be the most religiously protected secret in the world, but consider that almost every study of eastern Pueblo religion by a non-Pueblo author begins by acknowledging a profound cross-cultural rejection of that enterprise. Take, for example, William Douglass's 1915 essay on Tewa shrines, which begins: "The Pueblo Indians guard with great tenacity the secrets of their shrines. Even when the locations have been found, they will deny their existence, plead ignorance of their meaning, or refuse to discuss the subject in any form" (1915: 344). Secrecy is therefore a long-standing, and now cross-cultural, tradition on the Pajarito Plateau—a national-cultural practice that has often prevented LANL and neighboring Pueblo nations from talking to one another about their mutual investments in the same geographic space. Until 1957, Los Alamos was a gated community, completely cut off from neighboring communities except for those who worked in Los Alamos, and since 1957 the forty-three square miles of laboratory territory have been patrolled by armed guards and protected by electronic security systems. While fences have defended nuclear science from outside intervention, they have also enclosed a rival technology, an older system for maintaining balance in the world and creating security for the indigenous peoples of the northern Rio Grande.

Consider Figure 3.9, which is a laboratory illustration of the Pueblo cultural sites—ancestral ruins, petroglyphs, and shrines—located just within the fenced boundaries of what is now LANL property (Steen 1977). Numbering in the several thousand, these material traces of Pueblo culture document not only ancestral ties to the plateau but also participate in a geospiritual system for influencing nature and creating a harmonious ecosystem. For at the very least, the Pueblo shrine system is

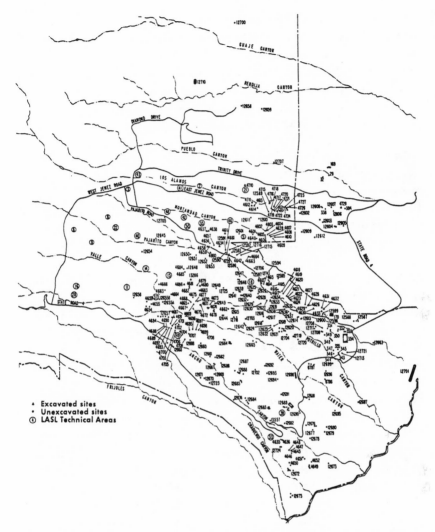

3.9. Archaeological site map of LANL territory. (*Source*: Charlie Steen, *Pajarito Plateau Archaeological Survey and Excavations*, Los Alamos Scientific Laboratory, 1977)

a technology that historically has been used by Pueblo religious leaders to engage nature, influence flows of energy in the northern Rio Grande valley, and thereby create security for their people. Paradoxically, those sites that have not been destroyed outright by laboratory activities have been uniquely protected, hidden from the destructive onslaught of pot hunters by U.S. national security systems. Thus, LANL has unintentionally preserved some Pueblo cultural sites, leaving them largely untouched since 1943, while bulldozing and polluting others. The forty-three square miles of LANL territory, therefore, gives staff archaeologists a unique archive of the past while offering Pueblo peoples on the opposite side of the fence the possibility of a renewed connection to those, now fenced but surviving, sites in the future. Ultimately, this means that the same territorial area responsible for inventing U.S. nuclear weapons remains active in an older system of cultural knowledge, setting the stage for a powerful post–Cold War negotiation over place, power, and secrecy on the plateau.

For weapons scientists, the end of the Cold War created a crisis of knowledge, as the moratorium on underground nuclear testing in 1992 caught scientists by surprise, changing the ground rules for conducting weapons science. During the Cold War, nuclear weapons science was based on speed of production, planned obsolescence, and the assumption that the pursuit of new nuclear weapons (and thus, the ability to conduct underground testing) was an unending project. Consequently, weapons scientists did not collectively archive all details of their work. Instead, information was scattered in various laboratory sites on the plateau, in notes stored in individual office safes and in the heads of several generations of weapons scientists. Realizing that in a few decades, those charged with maintaining the nuclear arsenal will have no direct experience with real (as opposed to virtual) nuclear detonations, LANL began the Nuclear Weapons Archiving Project in 1993, an attempt to archive all the data gleaned from a half century of nuclear testing. The project not only is gathering together papers and computer models stored at various laboratories, offices, and test sites on the plateau (and at Livermore and Sandia), but also seeking to record the technical and intuitive details generations of weapons scientists have relied on to design, test, and certify U.S. nuclear weapons. Weapons science has consequently been revealed to be a kind of folk art, grounded, at least in part, in long-term apprenticeships and oral culture, and located in multiple centers on the plateau. Once completed, the archived data will be accessible to weapons scientists via a secured Internet on a "need to know basis"; that is, only those maintaining the highest security clearances in the nuclear complex will be able to access the entire computer archive, which will stand as a unique record of one regime's activities on the plateau.

Concurrently, neighboring Pueblo nations began archiving their own cultural knowledge of the plateau in the 1990s, as part of an Environmental Impact Study (EIS) of LANL operations. The Accord Pueblos argued in 1994 for the inclusion of a "cultural impacts" report that would depict the unique consequences for Pueblo peoples of past and future laboratory activities. Pueblo officials began collecting tribal oral history of the plateau, documenting cultural uses of plants and animals while consulting religious leaders about the location and use of cultural sites. Given that the mountains are, at least within traditional Tewa culture, the spiritual responsibility of a specific class of religious leaders (see A. Ortiz 1969, 1972), this process mirrors the nuclear archive, in that, for those communities, a small group of people is responsible for maintaining the cumulative cultural knowledge produced on the plateau.[20] Moreover, given that in addition to the Tewa-speaking nations of Santa Clara and San Ildefonso, the Cochiti and Jemez nations are also involved in this archiving project, there are (like the nuclear project) multiple centers of information being explored, multiple communities being consulted about their investments in the plateau. Thus, for all regimes (U.S. technoscientific and Pueblo national) the question is now one of memory, of remembering the cultural import of sites that have been inaccessible to diverse Pueblo communities since 1943 and making sure that future generations understand cultural connections to those sites and that place now occupied by the laboratory.

The question of access to the cultural impact report also mirrors back to the nuclear complex the politics of secrecy informing U.S. weapons science. For despite the Accord Pueblos' interest in producing a cultural impacts document, Accord Pueblo cultural matters, especially those directly related to spiritual engagements with special places, are quite simply, top secret. Non-Pueblo recognition of cultural sites—and particularly the existence of detailed site maps—remains controversial and a subject of intense negotiation between LANL and neighboring Pueblo governments in the post–Cold War world. Under the Spanish colonial regime the Pueblos defended their religious system—first by military uprising in 1680 (that forced Spanish settlers out of New Mexico for twelve years), and then by closing their religious world off from public view, a tactic that endures. By preventing outsiders from viewing certain religious practices, Pueblo leaders sought to compartmentalize engagements with non-Pueblo ideas, shielding them from missionaries and from cultural diffusion. Many Pueblo scholars attribute the longevity and vitality of eastern Pueblo cultures to this system of compartmentalizing, and to the fact that Pueblo nations (unlike many other indigenous communities in the United States) were never forced from their ancestral lands (A. Ortiz 1994; Sando 1992; Dozier 1961). Former governor of Cochiti Pueblo Joseph Suina, speaking in the midst of spy allegations at LANL in 1999, offered this explanation of Pueblo secrecy:

There is still another reason why Pueblo peoples keep secret certain things. And that's because knowledge is used differently in the Pueblo world. In this world [the laboratory], anybody can know anything if they so desire. I was going to say, except for Top Secret things. But [it seems] anybody can know anything if you have the money and the desire and the connections. Sorry LANL, but I'm here to teach you a thing or two about secrets. Knowledge in the dominant world is of that nature—if somebody so desires to know about medicine, or about law, or about social work, it is a matter of taking time to study on your own, or with somebody, or in a course. But in the pueblo world, knowledge is not used that fluidly, that open. Knowledge is used in terms of funds of knowledge, if you can call it that. Sometimes knowledge is restricted because of gender. There are things that males know that females are not supposed to know. And there are things that women know, especially if you are a member of a religious society, that males are not supposed to know . . . My mother died many years ago, but she was a member of women's society. And my father, and we as children, had no right to know her business. So sometimes knowledge is withheld and then given. Knowledge is made accessible based on gender. Other times it is given when people mature, it is based on maturity. And still other times, it is based on commitment. Once a person made a commitment to serve in some capacity for the rest of their lives for the people, then they can have access to the knowledge. For anyone to tamper with knowledge, or to pry into, is courting serious, serious trouble.

Knowledge is not used that fluidly. The arrival of the Manhattan Project on the Pajarito Plateau thus not only brought together multiple secret societies—those supporting U.S. military nuclear science and Pueblo theocracies—but also rival systems of knowledge and knowing. Consequently, silence on a given topic can mean many things within Pueblo societies, and cannot be dismissed as either implicit support or a lack of interest, as secrecy is a longstanding strategy of cultural survival and internal social regulation.

Pueblo practices of secrecy are not only a means of negotiating a colonial experience, but are connected to Pueblo notions of power, which are connected to a unique combination of place and emotional clarity (see Pandey 1977).[21] Pilgrimages, for example, historically could not take place unless participants had a positive and undivided psychological investment in the purity of the process (e.g., Curtis 1970: 9). As Parsons noted in 1939, for the Pueblos, "secretiveness is founded on the concept or feeling that power communicated is power lost" (1996: 434). Thus, one of the central attributes of northeastern Pueblo secrecy is an emphasis on maintaining the quality of their engagement with specific places and ritual practices, which require that knowledge remains located within the ritual hierarchies of the tribe. In this sense, the national security culture of Los Alamos mirrors back to the Accord Pueblo nations their longstanding concerns about secrecy and power, as Parsons's quote could equally well be applied to how nuclear weapons data is treated in the United States: for in the world of military nuclear science "power communicated" is also experienced as power lost.[22] Accord Pueblo leaders have, therefore, made clear that the cultural impact report will only be pursued if it is kept secret, if they control who has access to the information and under what terms. Thus, in effect, they are mirroring what is done in the realm of U.S. military science, where information classified by the United States is written up in a separate document only accessible to those with the proper security clearances and on a "need to know" basis. The difference here is that four sovereign Pueblo governments will be in control of their own knowledge base, allowing future Pueblo leaders to evaluate laboratory activities, making the report a strategic—and highly classified—tool for the Accord Pueblos to use in their engagements with Los Alamos and DOE officials, who may or may not ever have access to the report.

Thus, in the immediate post–Cold War period, the national cultures on and around the Pajarito Plateau are archiving knowledge produced in their historic and everyday engagements with that shared space. While each of these national entities practice a compartmentalizing of knowledge as well as a ritual hierarchy limiting access to information, they are now directly concerned with generational reproduction—with maintaining cultural investments in specific sites and specific activities on the plateau. Pursuing their national security, then, from very different perspectives, all parties are now concerned about the long-term environmental and political viability of their engagement with that shared space. For mediating both of these archiving projects is, of course, a third: one involving the environmental impacts of Cold War nuclear science, which in the early 1990s was expected to be a $2 billion cleanup involving 2,100 sites on the plateau (DOE 1995a). From a cultural perspective, then, the ownership of the plateau remains in question, as two rival systems for achieving security require access to the same space. Some Pueblo nations are now reflecting back to Los Alamos the experience of being shut out of a national security culture, using religious secrecy to protect their investments in the plateau and take advantage of laboratory resources—gaining computers, environmental training, and cash in this post–Cold War cycle of exchange. Indeed, given that environmental and religious matters are so intertwined for Pueblo peoples, the key legal tools for Accord Pueblo engagements with LANL—environmental law and rights to religious freedom—force northeastern Pueblo governments to evoke secrecy rules in their political mobilizing. Thus, while Pueblo nations have used secrecy as a way of mediating a colonial experience since the seventeenth century, the top-secret projects of the twenty-first-century U.S. nuclear complex will be balanced by a rival system of national secrecy on the Pajarito Plateau capable of affecting laboratory operations. Thus, the future promises a more explicit mirror-imaging between neighboring regimes that are now engaged not only in "government-to-government" relationships but also in defining national security around centers of protected knowledge, knowledge produced on and embedded within the Pajarito Plateau.

EXPLOSIVE TESTING

The plutonium economy, however, has also created new millennial challenges for the Pueblo communities living adjacent to the Pajarito Plateau. For the Jemez range is now a sacred space invaded by the trace elements of military nuclear science—plutonium, strontium, cesium, tritium—a reality that not only threatens to disturb the relationship between humans, plants, animals, air, soil, and water by producing an increasingly toxic future, but also presents unknown spiritual consequences for Pueblo peoples. Gregory Cajete (Santa Clara) commented on the origins of Los Alamos at the LANL 2000 conference, noting not only the economic benefits of the laboratory and town site—a half century of employment for Santa Clara Pueblo—but also the environmental justice implications of locating a toxic military project on top of the northern Rio Grande valley:

Being from Santa Clara Pueblo, which is only about 19 miles away [from Los Alamos], I grew up very much within the context of the Los Alamos aura, so to speak. Very few people that I know in one way or another were not associated or were not in one way or another working for Los Alamos or working at Los Alamos. My mother, for instance, was a housekeeper for many, many years in Los Alamos and babysat and kept house for many of the scientists and technical people that were up there. I think my experience and my sense of Los Alamos has always been a very interesting one. We in the valley considered Los Alamos this very strange, almost like Mt. Olympus place. I remember that as I was growing up we used to talk and wonder about what was going on at Los Alamos. And also we would reflect on how different the people from Los Alamos were, not only in terms of students and people that were up there but also the kinds of things that were a part of that whole community, because largely Los Alamos kept to itself. It began primarily as a scientific city, a secret city. There are many stories as to why the lab was located at Los Alamos. One of them, of course, was because of its isolation, because of its ideal location [for military science]. But also I think because of the fact that it was being put in a place where if something did indeed go wrong it wouldn't affect too many people. And the people it would affect, in a sense, in that time and that place, were considered, I think, in some ways of thinking, almost expendable. I ultimately always reflected on that and thought about that orientation. If you're growing up in the valley you have a lot of relatives and people that work in Los Alamos but they always come back to the valley. Very, very few people from the valley moved up to Los Alamos and became a part of that community.[23]

There are many stories as to why the lab was located at Los Alamos. This articulation of local dependence and sacrifice simultaneously underscores the continuing "foreignness" of Los Alamos to many who live in the valley but also offers an evaluation of the meaning of U.S. citizenship for the northeastern Pueblos. Cajete suggests here that indigenous peoples were not officially part of the national order and therefore "expendable," making the long-term effects of LANL activities on the plateau also an index of the meaning of U.S. citizenship for Pueblo peoples, who are now intimately tied (by virtue of labor and place) to the production of U.S. national security. The plutonium economy therefore engages multiple registers of northeastern Pueblo experience, evoking a complex negotiation of economic advancement and colonialism, U.S. citizenship, and religious desecration—all of which problematize the future for communities who are uniquely invested in a specific territorial space, living in the shadow of a nuclear facility. Remarkably, it was only after the end of the Cold War that the first official discussion of the environmental and sociocultural impacts of locating the laboratory on the Pajarito Plateau took place, as communities throughout the northern Rio Grande valley pondered the future of LANL while learning new details about its past. The end of the Cold War thus began the local process of replacing official silence with proliferating fields of risk, concerning the environmental, economic, and sociocultural impacts of the laboratory.

We can see the logistics of this shift in perception in one of the first public confrontations between LANL and neighboring Pueblo nations at the end of the Cold War. A proposal by LANL scientists in 1992 to test the geothermal makeup of the Jemez Mountain Range by detonating a string of underground explosions along the Rio Grande Rift was vehemently protested by officials from Cochiti and Santa Clara Pueblos on religious grounds. The experiment was designed to test for molten rock underneath the Valles Caldera by detonating at least six one-ton charges of TNT in 140-foot-deep shafts along a 110-mile stretch of the Jemez Mountain Range. The collective seismic information gathered from these blasts would enable a three-dimensional portrait of the geology of the Valles Caldera. As a nonmilitary, non-nuclear project designed to understand geothermal energy—a potential new energy source—the experiment would seem to be less controversial than many Cold War nuclear experiments conducted on the plateau, but the end of the Cold War marked a dramatic shift in community engagements with the laboratory. The first explosion was to be conducted underneath Cochiti Lake, followed by a chain of explosions running the length of the Jemez range. Government leaders from Cochiti and Santa Clara Pueblos learned about the proposed tests in newspaper reports, just as an environmental impact assessment of the proposed experiment was coming to a close. Arguing not only that tribal governments had not been informed about the experiment but also that the explosions constituted an act of religious desecration, Pueblo officials threatened legal action. Santa Clara Governor Walter Dasheno stated that the vibrations from the explosions would impact shrines and archaeological sites on the Jemez range and unequivocally declared that the violation of the earth in these areas was in and of itself culturally destructive. LANL and the U.S. Forest Service countered that none of the tests took place on tribal property and pointed out that in 1991 the Jemez range had experienced some 230 earthquakes of equivalent or lesser force, assuring that the planned detonations would produce no damage to archaeological ruins or religious sites.

LANL arguments about the frequency of earthquakes did not, however, recognize the distinction that would be drawn in Pueblo traditions between a natural seismic event and an artificially created one. Eastern Pueblo cultures recognize—and venerate—the evolution in natural forms over time through erosion and decay; the cumulative impact of explosives testing on the ecosystem threatened the purity of those processes, potentially unleashing dangerous spiritual forces and affecting the larger chain of reciprocal relations in nature. LANL officials ultimately moved to accommodate Cochiti and Santa Clara concerns by eliminating the first proposed test underneath Cochiti Lake, and then by replacing several explosives tests in the central Jemez range with passive, nonexplosive experiments. The experiment continued but in a significantly abridged form, alerting all governmental and technoscientific agencies that communities along the northern Rio Grande were no longer passive witnesses to laboratory technoscience (Baldridge et al. 1997). Indeed, this collision between communities evoking radically different concepts of space—involving land as private property, as technoscientific project, and as sacred space—energized a new relationship between LANL and neighboring Pueblo governments. It also confirmed for many living around Los Alamos that northern New Mexico remains an experimental test area, raising new kinds of fears about what the future entails and about what the Cold War plutonium economy leaves in its wake.

Protests over the proposed Valles Caldera experiments also engaged longer-term concerns by neighboring communities over LANL experimentation on the Pajarito Plateau, concerns that were silenced by the national security logics of the Cold War. For in the realm of quotidian experience, one of the most visceral engagements with the plutonium economy for those living immediately adjacent to the laboratory has been the sound of explosions echoing from canyon test sites. The unannounced concussions from LANL explosives testing have become over the past half century a common intrusion into everyday life for those living in the shadow of the Pajarito Plateau, a startling reminder of LANL's presence and ongoing commitment to military technologies. Many of these explosions have been, and are, devoted to perfecting the military science and technology of implosion.

Implosion is a means of creating a nuclear chain reaction by encasing a sphere of plutonium within a shell of high explosives and then detonating the explosives in such a way that a highly symmetrical and inward-moving shockwave is produced. This shockwave uniformly compresses the plutonium sphere in an instant, triggering a chain reaction that releases energy on an unprecedented scale. An elegant, and economical, if technologically challenging design, implosion remains one of Los Alamos's unique contributions to the world and perhaps the first major achievement of the Manhattan Project. The first implosion device was also the first atomic bomb, detonated at the Trinity site in New Mexico on July 16, 1945; the second was detonated three weeks later over Nagasaki. As one of the key technologies of the Cold War, implosion designs not only enabled a sphere of plutonium the size of a grapefruit to level a city, but also allowed, through a constant refinement in the engineering process, nuclear weapons to shrink from several-ton behemoths to small devices that could be mounted on the tip of an intercontinental missile. Consequently, implosion technologies remain at the center of U.S. nuclear weapons science and a subject of ongoing research at LANL. Indeed, Los Alamos remains perhaps the world leader in the science and application of conventional high explosives, maintaining extensive explosive test areas on the Pajarito Plateau where the intricacies of creating perfectly symmetrical, inward-directed explosive charges are now a multigenerational project.

During the first two decades of the Manhattan Project, weapons scientists worked on improving implosion designs for U.S. nuclear weapons through explosives testing at Bayo Canyon, which is located three miles east of the Los Alamos town site and which runs eastward down the plateau onto the lands of San Ildefonso Pueblo. From September 1944 through March 1962, scientists conducted 254 implosion experiments using high explosives around a core of lanthanium-140 (used as a surrogate for plutonium, which was both too expensive and too dangerous for these tests; see Figure 3.10). Lanthanium-140 is an intensely radioactive but short-lived isotope, with a half-life of just forty hours. Averaging about one test a month during the eighteen-year life of the program, the RaLa experiments released a total of 250,000 curies of radioactive lanthanium, plus traces of strontium-90, barium-140, and cesium-140, into the local environment in the form of radioactive fallout. Fallout was blown over the plateau, requiring the fire department on at least one occasion to wash down the highways leading into Los Alamos, and on several other occasions to erect roadblocks. During several tests, fallout also was documented over the northern Rio Grande valley. In 1950, for example, the U.S. Air Force tracked fallout clouds from the RaLa program as a means of preparing for full-scale nuclear tests at the Enewetok Atoll in the South Pacific. On March 24, 1950, the U.S. Air Force measured fallout over San Ildefonso, Santa Clara, and Española (Dummer et al. 1997: 9–10). Cumulative doses to those living in Los Alamos and adjacent Pueblos are estimated (by recent LANL dose reconstruction studies) to have been low but the politics of the RaLa program nevertheless reveal how indigenous communities figured within a Cold War mind-set at Los Alamos, and correspondingly

3.10. RaLa Device, Bayo Canyon. (Courtesy of Los Alamos National Laboratory)

frame contemporary attitudes toward the laboratory from those who live the valley.

Test protocols for the RaLa experiments required wind to be moving in a northeasterly direction prior to the test, which would take fallout away from the Los Alamos town site (the most immediate populated area) but direct it toward the Pueblo communities of San Ildefonso, Santa Clara, and Pojoaque, as well as the town of Española. Describing the region to the north and northeast as "unpopulated areas," the test protocols appear to have ignored the existence of neighboring communities. Moreover, while scientists monitored for fallout, they did not inform tribal, state, or city governments about the test program. Indeed, the first communication between LANL and neighboring Pueblo nations about the environmental effects of the RaLa experiments came in 1994, thirty years after their completion, as a result of the President's Advisory Commission on Human Radiation Experiments.[24] At a volatile meeting of the advisory committee in Santa Fe, George Voelz, a LANL physician who studies the long-term effects of plutonium on the human body, explained the regional logics behind the test protocols in this way:

My own personal opinion, having known some of the people, was that the laboratory management really felt they had a responsibility for protecting the people who were in the area, and that was part of the planning and part of the checking in terms of these radiation measurements and things that were done at the time these tests were being run, and they were interpreting whether they were creating a problem or not, and I think they accepted that as part of their responsibility. Now, what they didn't do is what you asked earlier. As far as I know, there was not much communication going on with the people in the area, and that, in retrospect, was a mistake. It's something that we learned subsequently, and we now have laws and regulations and environmental impact statements and all of the rest that have come on, partly to amend some of these procedures that we didn't do earlier. Part of the protection, of course, as these tests went on was that the quadrant that we just talked about, that the cloud would go toward unpopulated areas, and so there were Native Americans (sic). I think kind of the generic term that was used was Española, but there is Santa Clara, San Juan—San Juan from above, and San Ildefonso Pueblo to the east, and we likely tried to exclude (I say "we," the laboratory—I don't have much party to any of these decisions) to exclude those populated areas the best they could. So, I think they were trying to meet their responsibilities, but they weren't talking about it.[25]

Given, however, that there are no documents—or local memory—of explicit engagement between the laboratory and neighboring communities over matters of health, safety, or emergency planning until the waning days of the Cold War in the late 1980s, Pueblo officials must take an astonishing leap of faith to accept that regional safety was of foremost concern during these experiments. At best the laboratory's stance toward neighboring communities during the first decades of the Manhattan Project was paternalistic. However, such a position is complicated by the fact that Pueblo people were involved in the RaLa project—hired in 1963 to clean up the Bayo Canyon site at the conclusion of the test series. Provided with film badges (for radiation dose calculations), work gloves, and burlap bags, Pueblo firefighting teams for Zia and Jemez Pueblos spent several weeks picking up debris from eighteen years of explosive testing, physically removing ninety truckloads of refuse from the canyon floor (see Figure 3.11). The material removed from Bayo Canyon was taken to Area G, one of the laboratory's radioactive waste burial sites located three canyons to the southwest of the test site (Courtright 1963; Ferenbaugh et al. 1982).

Thus, the RaLa tests exist simultaneously in two opposed narrative registers. A U.S. national narrative forwards the technoscientific value of the tests in enabling the development and refinement of implosive plutonium weapons at a time of intense national need—a time when the experiments were believed to pose little risk to the public, but when the fate of the entire United States seemed to be at stake. A more local post–Cold War narrative, however, forwards the effects of the RaLa tests on the valley and focuses on the environmental justice questions they raise. The RaLa experiments energize an experience of the nuclear uncanny for many, as the health risks from exposure to fallout and radioactive debris, and the long-term effects of explosive testing and nuclear waste storage on the mountain raise fundamental questions about the safety of Pueblo lived spaces. The logics of national sacrifice are manifold in these experiments, not only in terms of testing protocols, cleanup, and waste storage, but also in the spectacle of air force exercises over northern New Mexico to track fallout. Each aspect of the RaLa program therefore raises basic questions about the position of northeastern Pueblo communities within the United States, and can only be read in the context of the larger history of U.S. military practices in the Southwest. We should remember that when the RaLa experiments began in 1943 Pueblo peoples had only the promise of U.S. citizenship—not gaining the right to vote until 1948—and it was only after the Cold War that the Accord Pueblos began to be informed officially about the scope of laboratory activities. As the Advisory Commission on Human Radiation Experiments concluded about the RaLa tests, U.S. government "credibility is the casualty of silence and secrecy" along the northern Rio Grande (1996: 333).

One area where a loss of credibility is of immediate import is in evaluating the long-term health risks to neighboring communities of LANL

3.11. Pueblo cleanup crews, Bayo Canyon. (Courtesy of Los Alamos National Laboratory)

activities. Although the laboratory maintains world-class expertise in nuclear sciences, the official silence of the Cold War has made it difficult for many in the valley to accept laboratory statements about past or present environmental risks, fueling experiences of the nuclear uncanny. As one Tewa spokesman put it:

> I don't trust the lab leadership to deal honestly with the Pueblos and protect their interests. For 50 years we heard nothing from them. It took groups like the Los Alamos Study Group and Concerned Citizens for Nuclear Safety to alert us to the environmental dangers in the late 1980s. Prior to that nobody thought about health issues related to Los Alamos. Today, we are not really concerned about the politics of the bomb, as decisions to fight wars are made so far away from us. But we are scared about the environmental effects. We want to know why we have so many cancers.

We want to know why we have so many cancers. When I asked him about his own experience with LANL, he told me about two relatives who had worked at the laboratory in the first decades of the Manhattan Project. Both had held support jobs, and had not only enjoyed their work, but had also felt that people in Los Alamos always "treated them right." However, both developed cancer, which they, and their family, now attribute to their work at the laboratory. One relative remembers being asked to clean something up one day at the laboratory, only to discover later that he should have been wearing protective gear, initiating lifelong concerns about radiation exposure. In the northern Rio Grande valley, there are many similar stories about Pueblo, Nuevomexicano, and Anglo workers who were ill-trained or poorly supervised in how to deal with nuclear materials, and who now have cancer, fueling a racial and class critique of Los Alamos as a colonial institution. Such stories also reveal experiences of the nuclear uncanny, promoting fears not only about environmental contamination and a world filled with invisible dangers, but also of loved ones sacrificed to cancer by U.S. governmental neglect or malfeasance. A lived-space and a politicosocial sphere are equally contaminated by fears of radiation from U.S. national activities, making it difficult for many Pueblo members to accept the technoscientific conclusions of LANL scientists about health and safety.

Native Americans in New Mexico experience significantly higher rates of cancer than other ethnic groups. This is a startling change from the first decades of this century, when cancer was such a rare occurrence among Native Americans that some specialists thought they were "immune" to the disease (Manhoney and Michalek 1998). Since the dawn of the nuclear age, however, cancer has become a leading cause of death among Native Americans throughout North America. In New Mexico, this same period witnessed important changes in the local environment and the diet of Pueblo peoples as well as severely limited access to health care in some rural areas. Nevertheless, the rapid increase in cancer rates nationwide remains a largely unexplained phenomenon (Manhoney and Michalek 1998). In the context of Cold War secrecy and raising cancer rates, LANL has become a primary suspect for communities dealing with devastating illness. San Ildefonso Pueblo announced in the early 1990s that they have documented increased rates of cancer going back to the founding of the Manhattan Project; they also publicly questioned the veracity of LANL's health studies. Indeed, at the end of the Cold War, the immediate problem was that the laboratory had lost credibility on health and safety issues, but Pueblo nations had limited financial resources and technical expertise with which to conduct their own studies. Moreover, health studies of cancer rely on statistical portraits that are often irreconcilable with the small-scale communities of northern New Mexico. At one public hearing to discuss environmental LANL environmental impacts, a San Ildefonso official replied to a statistical portrait of health in the area by stating: "I don't agree with what you've said here tonight. For you one cancer out of 100,000 is justifiable, for me one cancer out of 700 (tribal members) is not acceptable. Your statistics do not take into account the proximity of the Pueblos to the land—we are the most impacted." At a similar hearing to discuss the statistically documented fourfold excess of thyroid cancer witnessed in Los Alamos, a Tewa resident of the valley sat quietly through a series of presentations largely attributing the cancer rates to aggressive screening for cancer at Los Alamos hospitals. In response, he said that many Pueblo do not trust the Indian Health Service to record accurately causes of death, claiming that some people who have died of cancer have had other causes of death listed on their death certificates, which has skewed the official cancer rates for those living in the shadow of Los Alamos. Storming out of the meeting in anger, he shouted, "We're sick, we know we're sick, and you hide behind these 'studies'!"

Thus, while the sound of explosives testing is the sign of technoscientific progress for those involved in military science, for neighboring communities, who are not often privy to the details of nuclear science at Los Alamos, these concussions figure on the periphery of daily life, as an unpredictable intrusion that startles, literally shaking one's home and raising a host of questions about environmental and religious desecration, U.S. governmental intent, and the possibility of life-changing illness. This auditory dimension of the plutonium economy, then, reiterates the foreignness of LANL to those living outside the national security fence, underscoring its power as a U.S. national space that, for many, is unknowable except in its after-effects, and thereby working to undermine how people experience their immediate tactile universe. For people who culturally identify with the land and live close to it—using adobe for their homes, making pots out of local clay for a living, using local plants for ceremonial purposes (for body paint, medicine, and religious practices) in addition to ranching, farming, and hunting—to raise fundamental questions about environmental safety is to challenge the viability of an entire way of life. In that light, consider the aftermath of an explosives test. Explosives testing disperses shrapnel and fallout over a wide area, producing elements that are subject to winds, water runoff, animal and plant consumption, and geological transport. Cleaning up test sites is an enormous technoscientific undertaking, an enterprise that is much more difficult than producing the explosion itself.

Consider Bayo Canyon, which has not served as a LANL test area since John F. Kennedy was president. It was first declared "clean" in 1963, then again in 1966, 1967, 1971, 1973, 1975, and 1976 after remediation efforts in each of those years (Ferenbaugh et al. 1982). New effects from those eighteen years of RaLa experiments in the canyon have continued to surface, requiring renewed action and regular monitoring throughout the 1980s and 1990s. Elk (a traditional food for the northeastern Pueblos) living on LANL property have been found to have higher levels of strontium-90 in their bones than elk living off-site. Noting that LANL security fences throughout the plateau have impacted the migratory patterns of animals, Pueblo representatives have voiced concerns about a declining elk population on the plateau over the past fifty years and also about the health risk to humans who eat elk wintering on laboratory land. Risks to game animals are not only from grazing on contaminated plants, but also from drinking liquid waste discharges from laboratory facilities (of which there are 123 on LANL property, some fenced, some not). Thus, even the first decades of implosive testing for U.S. nuclear weapons, taken in isolation from ongoing laboratory activities, have an enduring environmental and social legacy on the plateau (LANL 1995a; Shaner and Naranjo 1995; DOE 1998b).

Indeed, from this perspective, it is difficult to imagine what an end to the Manhattan Project would actually look like on the plateau, when exactly the trace elements of the first half century of the nuclear age will not be coursing through the Jemez Mountains' ecosystem. LANL has undertaken not only environmental studies of soil, water, and air on the Pajarito Plateau but also of fish (salmon, trout, catfish, and carp) from neighboring lakes, animals (elk and small mammals), plants (chamisa shrubs and piñon trees), and vegetables (pinto beans, sweet corn, and zucchini squash). Samples are taken not only from the Accord Pueblos and regional sources throughout northern New Mexico, but also from laboratory land. All show the traces of atmospheric fallout from above-ground nuclear explosions—a significant percentage of which were LANL designs—marking their baseline participation in the global plutonium economy. Vegetables grown on laboratory land in Los Alamos Canyon, however, which runs the length of the Jemez to the east through six and a half miles of LANL property, to San Ildefonso land, and eventually to the Rio Grande, are more distinct creatures of the nuclear age (Fresquez et al. 1997). In response to requests from San Ildefonso Pueblo, LANL scientists in 1996 mapped the most contaminated area of Los Alamos Canyon (which has received fifty years of radioactive discharge from laboratory facilities) and planted crops. The staple crops of the northeastern Pueblos—pinto beans, sweet corn, and zucchini squash—all revealed significantly elevated rates of radionuclides; strontium-90, cesium-132, americium-241, and pluto-nium-238, -239, -240 were absorbed from the soil into the crops in levels dangerous to people.[26] These gardens document a fundamental change in ecocultural regimes in the past half century. Prior crops grown in the area were for human sustenance and, in the case of Pueblo peoples, were tied to a specific, religiously sanctioned ecology (see Ford 1992). Today, however, the staple crops of northeastern Pueblo peoples are grown in Los Alamos Canyon simply to track radioactive contamination, to measure the impact of U.S. nuclear science on the mountain ecosystem.

The cumulative effects of nuclear science at LANL have produced a new intimacy with nature on the plateau as environmental scientists now seek out a portrait of the health of the entire ecosystem. Unlike the cultural intimacy of Pueblo cultures with this ecosystem (which involved neither industrial effects nor the unpredictable effects of new elements like plutonium), environmental scientists are now involved primarily in tracking damage to the ecosystem. The increase in environmental monitoring after the Cold War illustrates, then, not only a new priority in laboratory engagements with the plateau but also the fundamental concern local communities have about the world they live in, fundamental concerns about the toxicity of their environment and the safety of their daily food and water. Indeed, environmental sampling has become a new cross-cultural project in the post–Cold War era, as LANL scientists, Pueblo representatives, as well as officials from the Bureau of Indian Affairs are now conducting redundant tests of air, water, soil, plants, and animals as a way not only of defining the level of risk to Pueblo citizens, but also of documenting the veracity of LANL science for Accord Pueblo leaders.

Because public statements about the cultural consequences of environmental contamination or the disruption of sacred sites are restricted by Pueblo practices of secrecy and cultural compartmentalization, it is important to underscore that the full import of the Manhattan Project for these diverse communities is unknown to outsiders and may remain so. As Rina Swentzell (Santa Clara) reminds us:

> Pueblo reality is very much in the observable, sensory world—even the spirits dwell in the nearby mountains, lakes and streams. Within this sensory world, the possibility of multiple levels of existence are recognized. These levels, however, are not abstracted and relegated to a place after death, but rather are physically connected to this world through mountains, tunnels, and lakes. The structuring of the ecological environment corresponds with the notion that supernatural forces share the same physical, temporal world as natural forces, thereby creating an overall environment sometimes full of unexplainable events. The world, then, contains mysteries that cannot always be explained by rational human powers. Spiritual forces are a recognized part of everyday life and human beings are part of a sanctified life. (1982: 12)

The world, then, contains mysteries. In an animated universe where supernatural as well as quantifiable physical forces are at work, adherence to U.S. governmental standards for radiation exposure may only be a first step in evaluating the ecological integrity of the plateau.[27] As one northeastern Pueblo official related to me: "People up on the hill think of us down here in the valley as uneducated and not able to understand what they're doing. They always analyze. To me a miracle is a miracle. I'm not going to analyze it. But to them everything gets taken apart."

Thus, while LANL environmental monitoring can identify specific pathways at specific sites throughout the Pajarito Plateau (allowing an understanding of, say, the amount of beryllium in soil at "X" site), Accord Pueblo officials have been equally concerned with understanding the cumulative effects of all LANL activities on the total ecosystem. This is a much more difficult assignment, and one that requires a great deal of trust between laboratory scientists and Pueblo officials. Thus, even if Pueblo governments and LANL scientists can agree on the quantifiable health risks to Pueblo communities from past and present LANL activities, this only engages the most immediate set of concerns for Pueblo leaders, namely, the physical health of their communities. For nations who ground their identity on an intimate connection to the earth, and utilize plant metaphors to describe their origin and engagement with the universe, the effects of the plutonium economy are not only quantifiable health risks, but also the unique cosmological repercussions of a material and symbolic colonization, of discovering a radioactive plant, a vanished shrine, a polluted spring, or a toxic honeybee on ancestral lands.

NUCLEAR NATIONS: THE SOVEREIGNTY OF NUCLEAR WASTE

What we are told as children is that people, when we walk on the land, leave their sweat and leave their breath wherever they go. So that wherever we walk, the place, that particular spot on the earth never forgets us. And when we go back to those [ancestral] places we know that the people who lived there are in some ways, still there, and we can actually partake of their breath and of their spirit. And that's another incredible source of power.

—Rina Swentzell (Santa Clara) from the film, *Surviving Columbus: The Story of the Pueblo People*

Plutonium is eroding and being transported through the system at a rate not likely to exhaust the total inventory (including the fallout on the landscape of the upper watershed) for more than 2,000 years. If the rates of erosion and transport in Los Alamos canyon observed over the past 40 years prevail, the canyon will contribute plutonium from Los Alamos for 100 to 600 years depending on the magnitude of the original inventory . . . For the next several hundred years, Cochiti Reservoir will continue to store sediments and plutonium in increasing amounts from upstream sources. The continued pollution, albeit by small amounts, is a historical inevitability.

—William Graf, *Plutonium in the Rio Grande*

The Cold War plutonium economy inaugurated a multimillennial process along the northern Rio Grande, a new cycle of environmental and social exchange where radioactive materials from the U.S. nuclear project, injected into the mountain ecosystem, are now mobile elements, pursuing an unpredictable course dictated by invisible processes and environmental flows. Slowly working their way through and off the mountain, some of these radionuclides are now both unstoppable and all but eternal, thereby articulating a new, postnuclear ecosystem in New Mexico. The Manhattan Project transformed northern New Mexico into an enormous biosocial experiment, one in which toxic agents, military technoscience, and the cultural logics informing lived, indigenous spaces now interact in perpetuity. As Figure 3.12 demonstrates, plutonium is now more than merely a spectral presence on the plateau and in the valley. For the Pueblo nations who have lived in the shadow of the Pajarito Plateau since time immemorial the future now involves new kinds of risk. Indeed, the relationship between plutonium and the plateau—a 240,000-year engagement now barely fifty years old—is perhaps only matched by northeastern Pueblo cultural commitments to the same space, a region where they believe they always have lived and always will live. Now landlocked by historic colonial processes and private property law, most Pueblo nations have little space in which to move physically, making the plutonium economy also a form of toxic colonialism. For these island nations are defenseless from past and future radiological impacts, as the invisible materials from past and future U.S. national security practices cross their territories, revealing themselves only in their effects. Indeed, because the social and environmental effects of the Cold War plutonium economy will radiate long into the future, it is important to consider the futures now being made along the northern Rio Grande, and particularly the social mutations that necessarily follow in their wake.

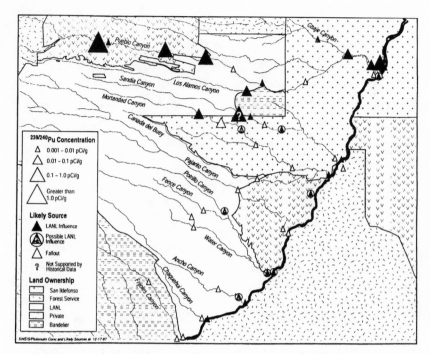

3.12. Plutonium concentration map of Los Alamos region. (Courtesy of Los Alamos National Laboratory)

The DOE has recently ruled that any permanent nuclear waste depository in the United States must have an operative plan that would make it safe for not a day less than ten thousand years. Such a plan is unprecedented in human history, though still accounting for only a fraction of the life span of the most dangerous nuclear materials, which will remain radioactive for hundreds of thousands of years. Nevertheless, consider the astonishing confidence the standard reveals, the certainty it registers about the future, and the eternal reliability of the American nation-state. Can we imagine a state that lasts one thousand years, let alone ten thousand? The closest we might come to such national cultural longevity in North America is the Pueblo nations of New Mexico, which have lived in their current areas at least since the twelfth century and inhabited the greater Southwest for perhaps seven thousand years. Thus, the communities now faced with the millennial threats of the nuclear complex are also the oldest communities in North America, peoples who maintain unique cultural commitments to living in the specific spaces they now occupy. It is necessary, then, to evaluate the regional effects of the Manhattan Project on a millennial time frame, not only because the nuclear materials will be circulating long into the future, but also because northeastern Pueblo nations remain committed to place on an equally millennial scale.

While stable at end of the twentieth century, the millennial future of these sites is subject to unpredictable natural processes making the safety of the plateau and larger ecosystem necessarily a matter of unending surveillance. In fact, the U.S. effort to contain the Soviet Union spatially and politically through nuclear weapons during the forty-plus years of the Cold War is now eclipsed by the millennial challenge of spatially containing the industrial effects of the U.S. nuclear arsenal at Los Alamos and other nuclear production sites. Off the Pajarito Plateau, the most immediate impacts of the plutonium economy fall on San Ildefonso Pueblo, which lies directly downwind and downstream from the laboratory. Officials at San Ildefonso self-identify as the only indigenous community in the United States sharing a territorial border with a DOE nuclear facility. Moreover, the Pajarito Plateau is San Ildefonso's ancestral homeland, a place tied to their emergence, populated with physical links to a unique geospiritual ecology. Pueblo officials have identified over 1,500 sites of cultural importance located within the current laboratory boundaries and have pursued an aboriginal land claim in U.S. courts since the mid-1960s for return of the plateau. The Pueblo is not only seeking legal recognition of its historic use of the plateau but also remuneration for a specific national exchange at the launch of the Manhattan Project. Oral history at San Ildefonso documents a gift of land in late 1942 from the Pueblo to the Manhattan Project to help in the war effort, land that Pueblo officials believed would be returned after the war, but which remains behind the U.S. national security fence to this day. San Ildefonso and Los Alamos are thus linked through their competing claims in the same physical space. Today, LANL occupies 27,832 acres of land, while San Ildefonso occupies some 28,136, but these boundaries are the result of a U.S. national process, not traditional use, making it difficult to identify realistically where Los Alamos ends and San Ildefonso begins. The environmental consequences of laboratory activities, therefore, engage a space that is multiply contested, making it uncertain whose national regime will ultimately bear the millennial costs of the U.S. plutonium economy.

Negotiating these multiple, and contradictory, claims on the plateau is a new, post–Cold War project, one requiring a delicate dance concerning cross-cultural issues of secrecy, respect, and national authority. At a meeting to discuss a transfer of land from the DOE to Los Alamos County, and potentially to San Ildefonso, a Pueblo representative engaged laboratory officials this way:

Even though that property sits now in the hands of the United States government . . . we would certainly like to have the opportunity to make sure they are protected to the best of our abilities, and to let the Department [of Energy] know that you have an enormous number of sites that have been identified through your professional services that are available, but there are still sites that we have not disclosed for reasons of our own secrecy and protection of those sites that we are not willing to disclose to anyone other than our own people. We need to have those things protected as best we can. It behooves me in the sense that we are looking at an area, and we are talking about 300 acres, and right within that 300 acres, I can say that there is something very significant that we have not told you about, and those areas adjacent as we see them. I think we need to make sure that we are protected. This great country of ours can go up there during the most recent war, the Gulf War, and tell its allies and its own soldiers not to destroy anything of religious significance in a time of war, but why can't we do it right in the back door where we are living in peace, and where we want to work together and do some of these things jointly? . . . When I go to the National Cemetery, I walk on the sidewalks or the paths that are there to go visit my uncles, or brother, or other relatives that are buried there. We just don't walk across those things. I think that is the dignity that we want to be at rest with, and that we want to share these situations with [you], to remind you. Remember in the back of your minds that, as you step on us, should you step on us, the only way down off that hill is through our lands. We have to work together and look at these things.[28]

The only way down off that hill is through our lands. The Pueblo representative concluded by stating that while occasionally there has been talk about blowing up the bridge that crosses San Ildefonso lands and allows commuter access to Los Alamos, tribal members are invested in building a healthy, respectful relationship with the laboratory and federal officials. Underscoring that the federal laws enabling and maintaining Los Alamos rarely recognize Pueblo claims, he evoked the sacrifices Pueblo members have made for the United States, not only in terms of land lost to Los Alamos but also in direct U.S. military service.[29] Asking for the same consideration given to U.S. enemies during wartime, he asks for the protection of sacred sites on indigenous territories colonized by a nuclear-powered regime. Defending the United States globally, while being threatened by the United States locally, are simultaneous realties for Pueblo communities living next to the laboratory, raising important issues about the meaning of U.S. citizenship and the future viability of the plateau and valley as lived spaces.

In this light, consider the reality of Area G, LANL's primary nuclear waste site: located on a thin mesa called the Mesita del Buey, Area G occupies a physical space that traverses the "official" border between LANL and San Ildefonso (see Figure 3.13).[30] Area G is a national

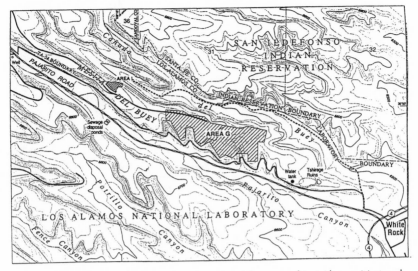

3.13. Area G nuclear waste site territory map. (Courtesy of Los Alamos National Laboratory)

sacrifice zone. The unresolved question is—for whose nation? A place that is now in the center of these rival claims on space, Area G opened in 1957 with the bulldozing of five Pueblo ruins. Each new burial pit has erased ruins and cultural sites that serve as points of reference for Pueblo peoples generally, and San Ildefonso in particular.[31] Area G grew throughout the Cold War to accommodate LANL's nuclear waste production, evolving from a five-acre site in 1957 to a thirty-seven-acre site in 1976 to a sixty-three-acre site in 1993, thereby offering a peculiar index of U.S. national investments in the plateau. The growth of Area G, however, comes at the expense of historical Pueblo investments in the plateau, which in 1957 included, by LANL measurements, sixty-nine archaeological sites. Area G became a highly politicized regional issue in the early 1990s, when antinuclear groups and Pueblo officials learned of plans to more than double the size of the nuclear waste site. The planned seventy-acre expansion would destroy more archaeological sites on the mesa and threaten a nearby spring, as well as make Area G the largest nuclear dump in New Mexico and perhaps the largest in the United States. In light of intense regional activism, the expansion has been put on hold until after an environmental impact study can be completed.[32]

What is difficult to communicate here is the startling beauty of the site. The mesa top provides breathtaking views of the valley and on the opposite side of the radiation warning fences are deep ravines filled with Ponderosa pine and piñon trees. Down below to the west is San Ildefonso land, an area used for ceremonial purposes, for hunting, and for the gathering of plants. If you visit Area G today you will pass by several Pueblo ruins (which are carefully flagged and fenced off) and see dozens of cement plugs sticking out of the ground, noting where shafts of tritium- and plutonium-contaminated waste were buried. Alongside the football field sized open pits, neatly packed with containers of radioactive contaminated waste, are fences posted with radioactive warning signs, and constant reminders to workers to promote safety, signs written in English and Spanish but not in Tewa or Keresan. Through these fences, the view of the plateau and the valley is fantastic. Ancient Pueblo peoples liked it too, taking advantage of an elevated site that was also one of the few naturally flat areas on the plateau for farming. Plants at Area G today, however, participate directly in the plutonium economy. The piñon trees that prior to the Manhattan Project fed Pueblo families now maintain plutonium in their circulatory system at a rate one hundred times greater than background levels, as do local grasses. Similarly, honeybees and honey collected from hives at Area G consistently record the highest levels of tritium contamination of any LANL site.[33]

The buried nuclear waste at Area G presents a multimillennial hazard. Indeed, the federal dream of a ten thousand-year safety net around these materials is already problematic. An underground plume of solvents and tritium from leaking canisters is making its way off the plateau, and there is evidence of tritium contamination in soils and runoff as well. Area G is of particular concern at San Ildefonso, not only because of the remaining cultural sites on and around the mesa, but also because traces of tritium have been found recently in water wells at San Ildefonso, suggesting that radioactive materials from LANL may be making their way through the mountain toward the deep aquifer.[34] The aquifer feeds the water system of the northern Rio Grande valley and is, from both a traditional Pueblo point of view and a technoscientific point of view, the source of life in the region. It is also ancient. Water in the main aquifer varies in age from one thousand years old under the western edge of the Pajarito Plateau to nearly thirty thousand years old underneath the valley (LANL 1995b: VII-31). It takes at least one thousand-years for surface water to work its way through the mountain to regenerate the deep aquifer, proving a new index of the possible effects of laboratory activities, which the DOE now acknowledges operate on a ten thousand-year time frame. Thus, from a northeastern Pueblo (indeed, a regional) perspective, Area G can appear as nothing less than a time bomb. LANL predicts, for example, that an earthquake capable of doing structural damage to all laboratory facilities will occur sometime during the next 2,300 to 14,000 years on the Pajarito Plateau (DOE 1998b: 5–84). While this offers a reasonable assurance of safety from a Euro-American, technoscientific focus on the present, Pueblo peoples can already claim a residence of nearly ten thousand years in the area, and proceed with the assumption that they will be living in the same spaces ten thousand years from now. The Accord Pueblos are now mobilizing to address the millennial threat by training a new generation of environmental scientists, whose job will largely be to monitor LANL's radioactive threats. Area G ensures that the past half century of social change caused by the Manhattan Project on the plateau is simply the first step in a millennial process in which local communities, and rooted Pueblo nations in particular, will be adapting to the new, postnuclear ecology of the northern Rio Grande valley.

If, for example, we follow the effects of the Cold War plutonium economy one community to the east in the northern Rio Grande valley, to Pojoaque Pueblo, which lies immediately adjacent to San Ildefonso and fifteen miles north of Santa Fe, we find a very different articulation of a plutonium-mediated national security. Pojoaque is a nation with a troubled history. It has, as Governor Jacob Viarrial says, "died twice" due to epidemics in the eighteenth and nineteenth centuries, and was only reconstituted in the 1930s, maintaining a population today of less than two hundred. A new, post–Cold War aspect of the plutonium economy was revealed at Pojoaque in the mid-1990s, with the announcement that the Pueblo planned to pursue storage of U.S. nuclear waste as a form of economic development. While shocking to many non-Pueblo residents of the valley, Pojoaque was merely responding to an invitation from the DOE, which in 1991 approached all Native American governments soliciting interest in nuclear waste storage projects on tribal lands. The DOE proposal was, and is, a response to the political gridlock surrounding the disposal of nuclear waste in the United States. It is also part of a larger post–Cold War process in which new recognition of the sovereignty of indigenous nations is quickly followed by invitations from federal bureaucracies and corporations for politically unpopular, environmentally dangerous projects.[35] In the Southwest, this trend promises to complete the nuclear life cycle in Indian country, performing the last step in a "cradle-to-grave" nuclear economy—from uranium mining to nuclear weapons design and testing to nuclear waste storage. The DOE plan promises financial independence for the small-scale communities of northern New Mexico. Indigenous nations interested merely in learning about "Monitored Retrievable Storage" (MRS) receive $100,000 up front from the DOE, and up to $3 million more—commitment-free—if willing to perform a formal site analysis. At least $10 million per year in profits can be expected from an MRS facility, whose lifetime is ultimately tied to the creation of a permanent U.S. nuclear waste site, which remains decades away (see Erickson et al. 1994: 78–82; Hanson 1998; Kuletz 1998). With potentially a quarter-billion dollars at stake over the next twenty-five years, it is not surprising, then, that when reporters asked Pojoaque Lieutenant Governor George Rivera why the Pueblo would even consider bringing nuclear materials onto tribal land, he simply replied, because "there's instant millions to be made."[36] Joe Sando (Jemez) has argued: "the most critical task facing the Pueblo Indians is the development of an economy capable of sustaining the people" (1992: 105). Lucrative nuclear projects have repeatedly presented themselves to indigenous communities in the wake of faltering or failed subsistence economies, offering immediate financial relief to those who are consistently among the poorest in the United States.[37] Indeed, as one northern Pueblo official confided to me in the mid-1990s, the primary grounds for publicly affirming Pueblo sovereignty in New Mexico are "nuclear waste and casino gaming."

This is important because Pojoaque's MRS announcement was, in large part, also a political tactic designed to underscore what was at stake for the Pueblo in debates over casino gaming. The government at Pojoaque Pueblo has been among the most vocal supporters of Indian gaming in New Mexico. Its "Cities of Gold" casino is among the most successful casinos in the state, playing off the ancient myth of the seven golden cities of Cibola that energized the Spanish conquest of the Southwest, and extracting money with almost surgical irony, from the mostly Spanish-speaking counties of northern New Mexico (see Figure 3.14). The legality of Pueblo gaming operations in U.S. courts, however, remained clouded throughout the 1990s, even though compacts had been signed by the governor of New Mexico and approved by the U.S. Secretary of the Interior and then renegotiated with the New Mexico state government. The ambiguity and indeterminacy of this political and legal process viscerally demonstrates how state and federal disagreements over the legal status of indigenous territories affect tribal efforts to pursue their own self-interest. Pojoaque Governor Viarrial vehemently protested state attacks on casino gambling in actions ranging from burning a ceremonial cane given to the Pueblo by then governor of New Mexico, Bruce King, to undertaking a hunger strike in 1994.[38] In 1996, when signed gaming compacts were once again thrown into legal doubt and tribal casinos were ordered by federal authorities to shut down, Governor Viarrial held political rallies in the state capital in Santa Fe. He also

3.14. Pojoaque Pueblo's "City of Gold" casino sign. (Photograph by Joseph Masco)

targeted the commuters to LANL, by threatening to post a toll on the main highway in northern New Mexico, which runs through Pojoaque land north and northwest to Los Alamos. On March 21, 1996, Pojoaque made good its threat, stopping the morning commute along highway 84/285, which runs from Santa Fe to Los Alamos, affecting about 40 percent of LANL's workforce. Tribal officials handed out leaflets (see Figure 3.15) to stalled motorists advocating the benefits of casino gaming for their community and promising toll roads as a replacement for confiscated slot machines.[39]

Nuclear waste storage projects remained a background threat throughout these negotiations. At a public hearing on the proposal, Governor Viarrial explained it this way:

> When we want to get something accomplished, we have plan A, and plan B. Long time ago we talked about the storage of nuclear waste. But we said let us try traditional economic development. So we opened up retail businesses. And like I said earlier they haven't always made a profit. They haven't given us enough money to send our kids to college, the things I mentioned earlier. And when the government decided about Indian Gaming, we said that's the way to go—let's do Indian Gaming. But we can't fight

PUBLIC NOTICE

INITIATION OF A TOLL ROAD ON THE PUEBLO OF POJOAQUE -- SUMMER 1996

Pojoaque Pueblo has faithfully followed the 1987 federal law regarding gaming. Federal law allows the State of New Mexico and the tribes to enter into gaming compacts. A compact was entered into by the State and the Pueblo in 1995. Based on the federally-approved compact, the Pueblo invested approximately $30 million in establishing gaming operations.

In a politically-motivated decision, the New Mexico Supreme Court ruled that the 1995 compact was illegal. The Court ruled that the New Mexico legislature must approve all compacts.

From 1987 to 1994, the New Mexico governors and the state legislators refused to act to resolve the gaming issue. This refusal forced the Pueblo to litigate the issue in state and federal court. Past and present gaming litigation has cost the Pueblo hundreds of thousands of dollars. Rather than pay these enormous amounts for lawyers and lobbyists, the Pueblos and other New Mexico tribes would rather see the money spent on all New Mexico citizens.

THE N.M. LEGISLATURE MUST TAKE IMMEDIATE ACTION ON GAMING!!!

The compacts provide much-needed money that goes directly to New Mexico state programs. Unfortunately, if the state legislature refuses to act, the Pueblo must seek innovative ways to repay its debts and create revenues to support its government.

THEREFORE, IF THE STATE LEGISLATURE REFUSES TO ACT, THE PUEBLO WILL BE FORCED TO COLLECT TOLLS AND PLACE AN UNWANTED BURDEN ON NEW MEXICO CITIZENS AND COMMUTERS!!!

IF YOU AGREE THAT TOLLS ARE AN UNNEEDED BURDEN, PLEASE CALL YOUR LEGISLATORS AND GOVERNOR OF NEW MEXICO AND DEMAND THEM TO DEAL WITH THE INDIAN GAMING ISSUE DURING THE SPECIAL SESSION!!!

Projected toll revenue will be used for:
$2 million to create jobs for Los Alamos Rifees and Northern NM residents
$1 million for the Pojoaque Valley School District
$1.5 million to Espanola and northern NM School Districts
$1 million to Espanola/Pojoaque Wastewater Project
$2 million to maintain highway 84/285
$6.5 million to retire debts incurred by the establishment of gaming operations

PLEASE WORK WITH US, WE DO NOT WISH TO INTERFERE WITH YOUR RIGHT TO TRAVEL AND WE APPRECIATE YOU TAKING THE TIME TO CONTACT YOUR LEGISLATORS. THANK YOU.

The Pueblo of Pojoaque Tribal Council and Employees

3.15. Pojoaque Pueblo leaflet of toll roads. (*Source*: Pojoaque Pueblo Government)

everybody . . . So that brings me to the issue of nuclear waste. We've looked at it in the past but just in passing, to get a feeling about what was out there in nuclear waste. But now that we are fighting this battle, and it appears that the legislators might take [gaming] away from us or dilute it, we are thinking about it again. And that's why I am asking you for your help in convincing the legislature to leave us alone, to let us try to accomplish what we need to accomplish through Indian Gaming in the way that Congress intended it to be done. We do have the legal authority to do it. We don't want nuclear waste more than anybody else, but we know it's very lucrative. And we are going to do a feasibility study. And if we are backed up into a corner, there is a good chance that within the next few months we will be deciding what kind of nuclear waste we are going to be putting in our lands. When we make that decision, the public is going to say "what can we do to change your minds?" I think by that time it will be too late; the time to help us make that decision is now. You need to help us change the attitude of the direction that the legislature is going now. Some people will call it blackmail, some people will say it's holding a hammer over somebody's head. Yes, it is. And it's survival.

We have the legal right to do it. In their public announcement, Pojoaque representatives specifically stated that they were interested in storing plutonium from dismantled U.S. nuclear weapons, precisely the weapons that were designed a few miles up the road at LANL. Pojoaque officials attempted to play off public fears of nuclear waste in nearby Santa Fe to press their claims about tribal gaming. At this raucous public hearing, residents of the valley were visibly upset and tried to talk Governor Viarrial out of the MRS plan. A six-year Anglo resident of the valley suggested that the tribe did not know what it was doing; stating that "the government promises you everything but twenty years down the line your children are being born without fingers," he argued that Pojoaque needed to be better capitalists, to "work harder than anybody else" and not take shortcuts to financial independence. A Nuevomexicana resident of the valley, on the other hand, argued against the MRS project by appealing to a shared citizenship and sense of neighborliness; she told Governor Viarrial, "There is such a thing as being a good American, and in being a true American, which I do believe you are."

What was implicit in this meeting was not only fear of nuclear material but also of Pojoaque's ability to handle it safely. Nobody commented on the fact that Los Alamos maintains large inventories of nuclear materials or has established at least eight nuclear waste sites less than twenty miles away on the Pajarito Plateau. Moreover, appeals to capitalism and American nationalism failed to recognize that these processes have explicitly worked against indigenous interests, creating the economic context that makes nuclear waste storage seem reasonable to some tribal authorities. Pojoaque Pueblo's tactical consideration of placing a nuclear waste site on tribal lands is both an example of the high-stakes international politics that have taken place around nuclear materials in New Mexico since 1943, and a new political strategy in which plutonium is one necessary tool of statecraft. Thus, as the national security of San Ildefonso is threatened by the environmental and social costs of the laboratory's nuclear waste sites, neighboring Pojoaque can forward nuclear waste storage as a means of achieving its own national security. For both Pueblos, their position is a direct consequence of the interior colonial dynamic between Native American nations and the United States: while no indigenous nation currently produces nuclear waste, all are potential candidates for the disposal of the nuclear materials produced by the U.S. nuclear complex.

While for the past five hundred years indigenous nations have been to one degree or another "risk societies," subject to colonization, dislocation, and legal disenfranchisement, the advent of the plutonium economy has brought new kinds of resources and risks, as the invisible toxins of the nuclear complex not only affect bodies and territories, but also national identities, experiences of citizenship, and systems of knowledge (see Beck 1992; Churchill 1997; Kuletz 1998; Petryna 2002). Some northeastern Pueblo communities are now remaking their nations to negotiate the effects of the nuclear age, producing among other things new constituencies of environmental scientists, and potentially, nuclear waste engineers. The millennial presence of nuclear materials in and along the northern Rio Grande will ensure that these social transformations are merely the first regional adaptation to a postnuclear ecology that is still in its infancy. Put differently, to understand the changing regimes on the plateau we might contemplate the future ruins that will populate that space. Joining Pueblo ancestral sites, which are part of an elaborate geospiritual order for controlling nature and endowing health on their communities, are now radioactive waste sites, housing in shafts, pits, trenches, and pads a legacy of U.S. national security that must now forever be contained. The distant future will still have to negotiate these sites, which will need to be tended, not as Pueblo sites have been tended in order to produce health, but rather to prevent illness and pollution. In this light, plutonium is revealed to transcend both time and space, becoming a material chronotope troubling Pueblo pasts, presents, and futures. For individual Pueblo nations, the consequences of this exchange will necessarily assume a millennial course, perhaps ensuring that plutonium, through an entirely subversive and dangerous course, proves a basic tenet of Pueblo cosmology: that part can indeed influence the whole.

ECONATIONALISMS IN THE PLUTONIUM ECONOMY

In the years to come, the invisibility of radiation in the northern Rio Grande valley will undoubtedly continue to make visible new forms of national consciousness among the northeastern Pueblos, as it already has in the post–Cold War period. This is not an unfamiliar phenomenon in the nuclear age. Jane Dawson (1996) has argued that a significant component in the dissolution of the Soviet Union was the econationalist sentiment engendered by the Chernobyl accident and the internal fear of similar nuclear disasters among member states. Tracing the development of antinuclear sentiment in several Soviet states during the perestroika period, Dawson documents how the unique psychosocial and ecological attributes of nuclear technologies can be turned on the national order that created them. Indeed, her reading of the tactical manipulation of nuclear fear in the states of the former Soviet Union, reveals that just as nuclear technologies are the basis for "super-power status," the constellation of issues nuclear technologies evoke—involving center/periphery politics, environmental justice, and everyday forms of (in)security—can also be mobilized by communities to attain new national standings. On these antinuclear econationalist movements, she writes (1996: 168–69):

> While Chernobyl and the threat of a nuclear disaster may have provided the initial impetus for mobilization, the movement eventually became a way in which participants came to understand their new identity in a rapidly changing world. As the old order was first challenged then rapidly discredited during the perestroika period and after, people were left disoriented. With their cognitive maps shattered, citizens of the former USSR were forced to take a new look at their world and reassess their own identity within it.

Dawson concludes that the econationalism engendered by nuclear politics in former Soviet states was ultimately based on a "superficial" investment in environmental politics, for after 1991, the newly independent states did not immediately eliminate their nuclear weapons or nuclear power plants, and energy-starved Ukraine even began discussing starting up the remaining nuclear reactors at the Chernobyl site (see also Petryna 2002). Thus, while demonstrating the power of nuclear politics in energizing national, econational, and counternational movements, the Soviet example nevertheless also illustrates how nuclear politics can serve also a merely tactical role in mobilizing public sentiment.

Northeastern Pueblo nations similarly awoke at the end of the Cold War in a very different world, one filled with the sudden revelations of past, present, and future threats from the U.S. nuclear complex. Unlike the tactical econationalist movements in the former Soviet Union, however, northeastern Pueblo nations maintain unique and long-term investments in the northern Rio Grande valley, which remains part of a geospiritual order founded in mythohistorical practice. Thus rather than mobilizing against the laboratory (which would threaten the largest employer in the region and leave behind the radioactive legacy of the Cold War), the Accord Pueblos used econationalist arguments to leverage a new political and legal standing in relation to LANL. The Cold War silence concerning LANL was transformed after 1992 into new federal, state, and laboratory recognitions of Pueblo sovereignty, creating new lines of dialogue as well as new exchanges of ideas, technology, jobs, and cash. The northeastern Pueblo communities who have lived with the local effects of nuclear science since the dawn of the atomic age now have every incentive to invest more thoroughly in LANL, looking to it for answers to a host of social, economic, and political problems while doing so in avowedly econationalist terms. For example, when I asked one Tewa spokesman if his government had ever considered succeeding from the United States, he replied: "we talk about it all of the time, but the question is—what will it get us, how would we be better off?" The new post–Cold War context around LANL now provides new means of articulating Pueblo nationalist sentiment, without giving up access to federal resources or embracing territorial isolation. In this sense, the new government-to-government relationships with the DOE and LANL are like a domestic Pueblo version of the 1991 Nunn-Lugar Amendment, which deployed Los Alamos expertise in the states of the former Soviet Union to secure nuclear materials after the Cold War. In both cases, the nuclear potential of another state is positioned as an immediate national security concern, requiring an explicit mobilization and engagement across international political lines.

New articulations of what might best be called eco-*ethno*-nationalism have allowed the Accord Pueblos to begin to chart a new future in regard to ongoing LANL activities as well as the environmental legacies of the Cold War. This new type of nationalist discourse (part ecological movement, part political strategy, and part cultural survival) is reinforced by the primary legal tools that Pueblo nations have for engaging the laboratory, which involve environmental standards and issues of religious freedom. These legal domains engage precisely the cultural logics of place that uniquely inform Pueblo investments in the mountains, rivers, plants, and animals of the northern Rio Grande valley. Thus, the experiences of life downwind and downstream from a major nuclear facility, in combination with the logics of federal Indian law, encourage new econationalist discourses in northern New Mexico. These new articulations of national belonging are not merely tactical attempts to mobilize regional sentiment but also strategic means of engaging the long-term effects of living within the plutonium economy. While LANL created the environmental risk in building the U.S. nuclear arsenal, it also maintains state-of-the-art expertise in environmental science and educational programs for Pueblo citizens. The post–Cold War period has revealed not only the multiple ecological, social, and political regimes on the Pajarito Plateau, but also the need for new cross-cultural exchanges. While negotiating the arrival of radioactive plants, animals, insects, and nuclear waste, Pueblo nations now have access to sites on the plateau that were fenced off for fifty-odd years, allowing indigenous communities to renew cultural connections to those ancestral places. Similarly, a new political and economic dynamic allows these same communities to pursue the technoscientific tools needed to monitor the physical health of their communities, their national territories, and their ancestral homelands. The nuclear materials buried on the plateau, however, remain in their infancy. Thus, while indigenous communities have entered an important new phase in the social life of plutonium along the northern Rio Grande, this post–Cold War moment remains a very early chapter in a multimillennial process, one promising many new biosocial orders yet to come.

4 Radioactive Nation-building in Northern New Mexico
A Nuclear Maquiladora?

I'll tell you what to write in your book—you write that the lab saved every-body in this valley! Without Los Alamos all these little Spanish villages wouldn't exist. Everybody tries to work at the laboratory because it is good steady work. Before the lab all the men in the valley had to go all over the country trying to find work—they would see their families only once or twice a year. With the lab we have good jobs that allow us to stay with our families. People from the valley built Los Alamos and there are always big construction projects there. Without the laboratory there is nothing, the village can't support us anymore.
—Hispano, from Rio Arriba County, who retired from a thirty five-year career as a construction foreman at LANL at the end of the Cold War

Los Alamos destroyed the diversity that existed in northern New Mexico, and in its place created an economy based on fantasy. Instead of preserv-ing the possibility of intimacy in land use, as dictated by the *Laws of the Indies*, Los Alamos created a consumer society interested in sterile or inconsequential intimacy. Lust for money supplanted intimacy with the land. Our economic system of *cambalache* [barter] was taken over by a money economy and greed . . . Although Los Alamos pays good wages, few locals can get past a certain wage level. What we have in the Rio Arriba Bioregion is a colonial economy and colonial economies place no value on caring for the land. They do not teach, encourage, reward nor protect. Now we have environmentalists who have no concept of our history and who want to teach how to care for the land.
—Juan Estevan Arellano, "La Querencia: La Raza Bioregionalism"

The epigraphs to this section reveal the complexity of contemporary Nuevomexicano investments in Los Alamos National Laboratory (LANL), an institution that exists simultaneously in local representations as a vital resource necessary for cultural survival and as a profoundly colonizing force in the northern Rio Grande valley. Referencing the high poverty rates in twentieth-century northern New Mexico, the first statement points to the material and imaginary effects of LANL on Nuevomexicano culture, an institution that not only has supported families economically in northern New Mexico for three generations but also has kept small-scale village life a viable enterprise since 1943. Offering a passionate pronouncement of investment and proprietary ownership in LANL, this Hispano resident of Rio Arriba County registers in no uncertain terms that LANL is too important to local communities to allow its misrepresentation; it affects too many people, defines too many local realities to allow an outsider to get it wrong, to misread or misrepresent its local value. Driving the point home by pounding an index finger onto my chest, his "I'll tell you what to write" is, then, also an index of the precarious place LANL occupies in post–Cold War New Mexico, for representations matter, revealing that a half century of LANL-Nuevomexicano engagements have produced a social sphere that is neither self-evident, nor transparent, nor secure.

For as the second epigraph testifies, LANL is not always understood to be a local institution in northern New Mexico, and can instead be experienced as an outside presence, one not attuned to local ecologies or cosmologies. As director of the Oñate Culture Center in Alcalde, New Mexico, Juan Estevan Arellano works to preserve and reinvigorate the unique cultural investments in the land that inform over four hundred years of Nuevomexicano life in the northern Rio Grande valley. Instead of forwarding the economic power of LANL—the region's largest employer—Arellano identifies the laboratory as a colonizing force, one that has erased a local diversity of everyday ecocultural practice in the act of creating U.S. national security. A culturally specific regional barter economy—which informed a unique pattern of land use and social organization—has, in his presentation, been usurped by the arrival of capitalism and a plutonium economy that maintains no particular investments in the land or people, homogenizing both as part of an American mainstream. Mourning a loss of cultural intimacy engendered by an economic dependence on U.S. nuclear science, Arellano points once again to how the bomb has created new social and material universes in northern New Mexico. By identifying LANL as a "colonial" institution he underscores that the Manhattan Project arrived in an area richly animated with distinct Nuevomexicano (and Pueblo) cultural investments in land, ecology, and everyday practice. Thus, the advent of the plutonium economy not only brought new jobs and cash, but also rival systems of knowledge and power, as well as new environmental pollutants into the northern Rio Grande valley.

What unites these two proclamations, however, is a feeling of unease about the present, a sense that something important is on the verge of being lost, of being controlled by outsiders (writers or nuclear scientists or environmentalists), or unwillingly forfeited after the Cold War. For while these statements approach LANL from radically different perspectives, both forward an implicit hope for a future of renewed Nuevomexicano power along the northern Rio Grande. The desire for class ascension meets here with the hope of regaining lost land, restoring traditions, and reembracing a community-centered lifestyle undermined by U.S. colonization in 1848. Both statements identify LANL as central to the problem of maintaining Nuevomexicano culture and village life, but for one this requires economic power in a capitalist system, while for the other it means restoring a uniquely Nuevomexicano lifestyle, one based on community land use and reinvigorated local political power rather than on nuclear science. Consequently, to talk about the post–Cold War future of LANL is also to talk about the viability of Nuevomexicano futures, to articulate a specific vision of power, place, and identity for those who claim a four-hundred-year presence along the northern Rio Grande. Indeed, LANL exists as a curious sign of the national for Nuevomexicano communities, evoking a complex constellation of issues involving colonization and class standing, as well as ecological and cultural integrity. But as we shall see, the unresolved question for many Nuevomexicano residents of the valley remains: Does LANL destroy the past by contaminating the future, or does it enable new kinds of futures by stabilizing the present?

RADIOACTIVE DEATH TRUCKS

If one were to look for the origin point of Nuevomexicano culture, one might choose July 10, 1598, the day that Don Juan de Oñate founded the first Spanish settlement at a site opposite San Juan Pueblo, just north of contemporary Española, at the foot of the Pajarito Plateau (see Figure 4.1; Agoyo and Brown 1987; Gutierrez 1991: 46–55). At that moment, Oñate not only fused Nuevomexicano and Pueblo experience, but also inaugurated a new system of land management and a new religious force along the northern Rio Grande. This new ecocultural regime was based on a system of land grants (which involved both large communal grazing lands and smaller individually controlled plots for farming), a new system of water management (known as the *acequia*, or ditch societies), and a sociopolitical sphere dominated by Catholic religious practices. This ecocultural regime, while responding to the political changes brought about

4.1. City of Española Welcome sign. (Photograph by Joseph Masco)

by three separate national regimes (Spanish, Mexican, and American), nevertheless evolved largely on local terms from the seventeenth to the twentieth centuries. Indeed, excluding the Pueblo Revolt of 1680–93 (which was an indigenous response to religious persecution and drought),[1] the most dramatic changes in the Nuevomexicano ecocultural regime after 1693 were probably initiated by the arrival of the railroad in 1870 and the Manhattan Project in 1943. Both of these events brought new technologies, people, and ideas into the northern Rio Grande valley, and with them, increasing pressures to transform local systems of knowledge and bring them into accord with U.S. law. Importantly, then, in 1943 the Manhattan Project engaged a cultural space that was already animated by the distinct ecocultural logics informing Nuevomexicano (as well as Pueblo) cosmologies. As we shall see, an ongoing project for the Nuevomexicanos of the northern Rio Grande valley is the problem of reconciling participation in the plutonium economy with a unique experience of place, of negotiating environmental and social change from within a lived space filled with social and cultural markers accrued from over four centuries of everyday practice.

Put somewhat differently, the arrival of the Manhattan Project grafted a technoscientific, U.S. national culture onto a predominantly land-based Nuevomexicano and Pueblo region (see Rothman 1992). In the post–Cold War period, about half of the economy of northern New Mexico was

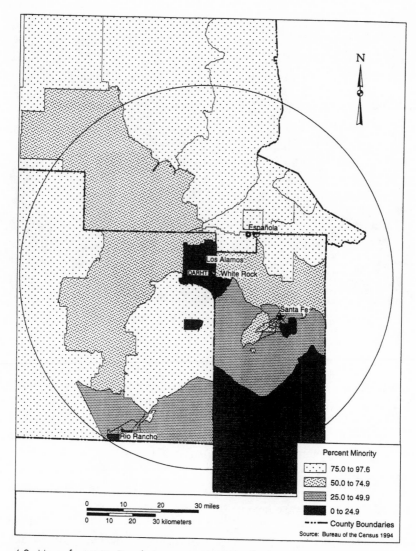

4.2. Map of minority Populations around DARHT facility. (*Source*: U.S. DOE, *DARHT Environmental Impact Study*)

directly tied to LANL, which remains the single largest employer in the region, while accounting for about 6 percent of the total New Mexican economy. Outside of Los Alamos County, Rio Arriba and Santa Fe counties provide the majority of the laboratory's workforce, creating profound geographical, racial, and economic differences between communities on "the hill" and those in "the valley."[2] Consider Figure 4.2, a map of the area immediately surrounding LANL. Part of a U.S. Department of Energy (DOE) environmental impact study of a post–Cold War nuclear weapons project at the laboratory known as DARHT (see chapter 5), this map charts the racial and ethnic diversity in a thirty-mile radius from the proposed nuclear weapons project. Showing the county boundaries of the state of New Mexico, but not the eight Pueblo nations overlapping the thirty-mile radius of the site, the map nonetheless documents a radical diversity: most of the region is marked as "50.0 to 74.9 percent minority," with Los Alamos bordered to the north and the south by areas that are designated as "75.0 to 97.6 percent minority." Thus, with the exception of Los Alamos County—which the U.S. Census identifies as 94 percent "white"—and the area immediately surrounding Santa Fe, the map argues that occupants of the northern Rio Grande valley are between 50 and 97.6 percent minority. But what does this mean to say that the people living in a region are potentially a 97.6 percent *minority*, or alternatively that 2.4 percent of the population represents a *majority*? As the advent of the plutonium economy brought new jobs, technologies, and people into the northern Rio Grande valley, it also engendered new class and racial divides in northern New Mexico. These divides are accentuated by the differences between rural and city populations as well as by the historical disfranchisement of Nuevomexicanos in the United States.

As LANL's billion-dollar-a-year budget has worked over three generations to facilitate the conversion of northern New Mexico from a predominately agricultural and barter economy to one largely reliant on cash, it has also made English the dominant language of the workplace. Thus, the broader effects of the plutonium economy are not only economic, political, and environmental but also profoundly cultural. As a consequence of increasing Nuevomexicano commitment to LANL during the Cold War, the post–Cold War uncertainty about the future of the laboratory necessarily raised important questions about cultural identity as well as economic security in the northern Rio Grande valley. For some in the valley, the psychological effect of the collision between land-based and technoscientific cultures assumes the shape of a kind of time travel or temporal rupture. Larry Torres, a prominent Taos educator, historian, and Penitente, put it this way:

> When you consider that the last Moorish stronghold at Granada fell in 1492, and that the Spanish start coming to conquer Mexico, and up the Rio Grande valley, they are coming straight out of the Middle Ages. They have not undergone the Renaissance, so that the people here are isolated for centuries. Our religion, our traditions, our customs, our way of looking at people are very medieval, still reflected in the language of today,

which is very archaic. Taos Spanish is three hundred years out of fashion, so that we have scholars from Spain, who come here to study the language of Cervantes here among us. What happens when you have a society that goes from this to that with no transition or stages? (Quoted in Rudnick 1996: 336)

What happens when you have a society that goes from this to that with no transition? Presenting the archaic form of Spanish still spoken by some in northern New Mexico as an index of temporal flux, Torres writes Taos culture out of the European Enlightenment, making contemporary Nuevomexicanos time travelers of a very particular sort. Other Nuevomexicano social commentators have echoed this sentiment, referencing not only a local sense of being on the periphery of world events but also the contemporary effects of Los Alamos on Nuevomexicano culture. A native of Española, for example, told me "prior to the laboratory, it was a pre-industrial existence here. We weren't part of the industrial age." Yet another Nuevomexicano, a resident of a tiny village in the northern Rio Grande valley, put this logic in more explicit terms:

Compare Los Alamos and the village of Truchas to see how much has changed [since 1943]. Both towns are at about the same elevation, and as the crow flies are right directly across from one another, but look at the differences, they are worlds apart. One is living in the 19th century, the other in the 22nd century. In Truchas, people are just trying to get by, making a living off the land. In Los Alamos, you have people who are thinking about space travel, which would be incomprehensible to the villagers in Truchas. They need to focus on putting food on the table.

Look at the differences, they are worlds apart. Comparing mountain villages (Los Alamos, west of the Rio Grande, Truchas to the east), this statement completes a regional portrait of northern New Mexico as a space of temporal/cultural collision. Disavowing Nuevomexicano participation in the Enlightenment, the industrial revolution, and, for some, the atomic and space ages as well, these self-representations reveal two things: first, a profound feeling of political and economic marginalization in northern New Mexico; and second, an intense personal commitment to local cultural history, as these statements also promote a distinct experience of place, one that makes Nuevomexicano culture absolutely unique and irreplaceable. In essence, these statements reveal a local belief that Nuevomexicano culture has evolved independently since 1598, on explicitly local terms, creating an entirely unique modernity that outsiders are not likely to understand or appreciate.

4.3. Descanso. (Photograph by Joseph Masco)

Signs of Nuevomexicano investments in place, however, are easy to find in the northern Rio Grande valley and constantly reiterate a religious topography. Driving to Los Alamos from Santa Fe, Española, or Taos, for example, one finds dozens of crosses lining the shoulders of roads and highways (see Figure 4.3). Placed at the site of traffic accidents, where someone died an unexpected and violent death, these roadside markers, known as *descansos*, or "resting-places," are part of a distinctly Nuevomexicano religious space. Descansos, importantly, address both the future and the past. As signs of danger, they warn future travelers to be careful. As signs of death, they also invite witnesses to say a prayer for those who may have died without the benefit of last rites. Moreover, the descansos are an ancient tradition, going back at least to the Spanish colonial period in northern New Mexico (Cordova 1994: 17–19); thus, they reveal a cultural continuity across generations even in the face of violent interpersonal loss. Descansos are not official state-ments, sponsored by neither the state nor the Catholic Church. Yet road-side property owners and highway construction crews do not disturb them. They mark a personal attachment, maintained over the seasons and years by the friends and family of the deceased as part of a larger cycle of commemoration. As shrines, descansos are indexes of cultural memory and are cross-culturally respected in northern New Mexico. As markers of loss, descansos add a powerful visual element to the New Mexican landscape, humanizing routes of everyday travel, and as such, acknowledging the visceral effects of social change. After the arrival of the Manhattan Project, northern New Mexico has become largely a com-muter economy, as workers travel daily from small villages to Los Alamos or other urban centers. As people have become increasingly dependent on cars, New Mexico has also gained the dubious distinction of maintaining one of the highest drunk driving rates in the United States, as well as being the state with the most highway fatalities. The descansos tradition, therefore, took on greater force in the latter half of the twentieth century, as thousands of daily commuters to Los Alamos passed by these after-images of violent loss. As such, descansos visually underscore the possibility of a sudden death in everyday life and partic-ipate in a broader Nuevomexicano cultural focus on the poetics of bod-ily sacrifice and death.[3]

In this light, consider the artwork of Nicholas Herrera, a Nuevomexi-cano from the village of El Rito who worked in construction at LANL for a number of years. His 1995 *Los Alamos Death Truck* (see Figure 4.4) addresses the regional fear of death on the highways by updating a tradi-tional Nuevomexicano folk image, often used in Penitente Holy Week pro-cessions, into the nuclear age. La Fraternidad Piadosa de Nuestro Padre Jesus Nasareno, also known as the Penitente brotherhoods, are a uniquely Nuevomexicano organization. These village-based, all-male religious organizations developed in the late eighteenth century, as a response to a dearth of official Catholic Church representation in northern New Mexico (see Steele and Rivera 1985). The Penitentes have been the subject of sen-sationalistic attention for their elaborate Easter activities, which include acts of self-mortification, cross bearing, and perhaps crucifixion (activities not unlike those still found among Catholic religious orders in Spain; see Weigle 1976); in response, they have hidden their religious practices since the late nineteenth century (adopting a familiar New Mexican strategy).[4] Identified by outsiders ever since as a "secret society," the Penitentes are a social organization culturally comparable with the other male-dominated "secret" societies in northern New Mexico, namely, the Pueblo religious societies and nuclear weapons scientists at LANL. Like those orders, the

4.4. Nicholas Herrera's *Los Alamos Death Truck*. (Photograph by Joseph Masco)

Penitentes are powerful cultural arbiters; they not only act as a kind of mutual aid society, they have been influential in land grant politics and maintain Nuevomexicano folk knowledge—from ceremonies to art forms to language to traditional land use. Participating in the religious topography of the descansos, Penitente rituals often focus on the vulnerability of the body and seek to prepare people for the inevitability of death. In some Good Friday processions, for example, Penitentes pull a cart with a carved image of a skeleton holding a bow and arrow. This so-called death cart is an image of the angel of death, known locally as Doña Sebastiana, whose arrow is drawn taut, poised to strike the unsuspecting down. Penitente scholars have argued that two visions of death are presented in this Easter ceremony: one involving the death and resurrection of Christ, which offers individuals the possibility of overcoming death and entering heaven through everyday Christian practice; the other, associated with the Doña Sebastiana figure, involves a sudden and unexpected death, in which a person's soul is unprepared and thus unable to enter heaven (Weigle 1976: 170). Herrera's *Los Alamos Death Truck* thus references the same kind of unpredictability of life that the Penitentes seek to confront and overcome through Christian practice and ritual preparation. His radioactive "death truck" is driven by a skeleton, and the arrow of death has been replaced by a devil that stands in the back threatening to throw nuclear waste barrels onto the road. Thus, Herrera evokes key Nuevomexicano cultural symbols to make the point that death roams the New Mexican roads in new forms in the post–Cold War period—specifically, in the form of radioactive waste trucks driving to and from Los Alamos.

If the descansos and death cart imagery are folk responses to a new, technologically mediated form of violence in the northern New Mexican landscape, both referencing a circulation of loss, other Nuevomexicano traditions offer a countermovement, a ritual circulation of bodies aimed at producing solace and a respite from suffering. Each year in the days leading up to Good Friday, the roads and highways are filled with tens of thousands of pilgrims walking to El Santuario de Chimayo, a shrine in the tiny village of Chimayo, widely known for its healing powers (see Figure 4.5). Pilgrims regularly walk the ninety miles from Albuquerque to Chimayo or the thirty miles from Santa Fe, traveling in small groups, usually with family members, often singing or praying together; some carry heavy crosses or images of saints; some walk barefoot. It is not uncommon to see the infirm, individuals on crutches or otherwise disabled, making the trek to Chimayo, enduring the physical pain of the journey as part of the larger ritual process. Dirt taken from within the Santuario is attributed with miraculous powers, and is rubbed on body parts or consumed with water in order to heal or ward off illness. Thus, many people on pilgrimage commit themselves to the journey in the name of family members who are suffering or in order to cure themselves of all manner of illness and loss. One room at the Santuario is filled with the devotional objects brought by pilgrims, creating an overpowering visual space filled with photographic images of loved ones needing miracles, religious statues, and prayers, as well as stacks of crutches, canes, braces, and eyeglasses from the cured. The Santuario has been an important aspect in Nuevomexicano culture since its founding in 1813, built on a site also recognized by the Tewa as sacred and valued for its healing powers.[5] Indeed, the hole from which dirt is taken at the Santuario is directly related to the Pueblo concept of the sipapu, a place of emergence from within the earth. Ramon Gutierrez has argued that the Santuario is an illustration of a more widespread effort by Spanish priests to "baptize" local traditions "by building a church over native religious sites, hoping thereby to fuse architectonically indigenous religious meanings and practices with those of the Christian faith" (1995: 74). The result of this fusion is a powerfully local symbol, one that plays an important role in a larger religious topography in northern New Mexico, and that has been increasingly linked (both symbolically and materially) to Los Alamos since 1943. Importantly, the Santuario is today both recognized by the Catholic Church but is also separate from it; it is made

4.5. Good Friday Pilgrimage to Chimayo. (Photographs by Joseph Masco)

powerful by individual acts of devotion rather than official sanction. As one Nuevomexicano pilgrim told me—"it's really of the people"—and thus, like the descansos, represents a colloquial, rather than official, investment in place.

Chimayo reveals Nuevomexicano investments in the northern Rio Grande valley in two ways: first, as a site of pilgrimage, it draws individuals from throughout northern New Mexico to one place, visually displaying on roadsides throughout the region each year a unique Nuevomexicano commitment to place; and second, the soil at the Santuario reveals northern New Mexico to be a place in which miracles can occur—where the earth itself is powerful. Listen to how this Nuevomexicano from Albuquerque described what it's like to participate in the Holy Week pilgrimage:

> Among the culture, it is something to be esteemed. One time we stopped and it was really very early in the morning, I'd say not even seven yet. There was a man outside and we asked "could we drink water from your hose" and he answered in Spanish and said: "No!" And we said "o.k." and started to leave. He then said: "No, I wouldn't think of it. You'll have to come inside." And then he offered us breakfast and everything and we were strangers. It was so nice. It was such a feeling of Hispanidad.

It was such a feeling of hispanidad.   The Santuario not only enables cultural belonging, it is also a place that people turn to in times of personal and regional crisis. Consider, for example, how this same Nuevomexicano family dealt with the traumatic impact of World War II:

> El Santuario de Chimayo was a local place where people could go to pray. People always have to ritualize big events because the need was so great. If a woman had a son or two sons in the war they made every effort to go, at a time when people didn't really travel. But at that time people were beginning to own cars, which made them more mobile. I have an aunt who married my uncle and a month later, of all places, he was sent to Pearl Harbor. He was there for one month and then it was bombed, and then a month after that, for the whole duration of the war, he was taken prisoner by the Japanese. So she didn't hear from him at all, and in fact, she had my oldest cousin, who never knew his father until he was almost five years old; he had never even seen him. One of the things that they did was that she had him hold a can after Mass, and tell people that the money they would give would be for his father. People knew the story, and they would throw in a dime or whatever. Well, she saved enough money to get on the bus to Santa Fe, and then somehow she got up to the Santuario, but she actually stayed in the homes of strangers. When she got there, there was nowhere to stay, but strangers put her up and fed her, and she went to pray for my uncle. The altars, she said, were plastered with pictures of service men. There were so many candles in there, she said you'd almost pass out from the heat.

What is revealed in this statement is not only a regional act of devotion, but also the intensity of World War II for Nuevomexicanos of the northern Rio Grande valley. For while wives and children prayed for the return of the vast number of men from the valley who participated in the war effort (of sixty thousand New Mexican recruits, 1,500 lost their lives in the war, many at Battaan and Corregidor; see Romero 1995), those who remained at home were recruited to work on the Manhattan Project at Los Alamos, to build in secret the physical infrastructure needed to produce the atomic bomb. As a result of this wartime service and sacrifice, many Nuevomexicanos of that generation take special pride in the achievements of the Manhattan Project, believing that it ended the war in Japan and saved local lives.

Perhaps it is not surprising, then, that Chimayo and Los Alamos became ceremonially linked during the Cold War. For in addition to the labor force circulating between Chimayo and Los Alamos, and their geographic locations on opposite sides of the Rio Grande valley, the symbolic centers of these communities—the Santuario and LANL—seem to engage in a kind of symbolic regional dialogue. In the Cold War context of Reagan-era militarism, an interfaith Pilgrimage for Peace was created in 1983 in which healing soil from the Santuario was taken in procession and ceremonially distributed in the center of Los Alamos at Ashley Pond—thus, "baptizing" Los Alamos on terms similar to those informing the founding of the Santuario (see R. Gutierrez 1995). At the time, LANL security officers conspicuously videotaped the procession from atop the Los Alamos city council building, marking it as a foreign intrusion. Now a yearly event, it has been officially sponsored by the Santa Fe Archdiocese since 1984, and attempts to serve as a vehicle for cross-cultural dialogue while confronting violence as a means of solving problems. The Pilgrimage for Peace begins with an early morning Mass at the Holy Family Church in Chimayo, followed by a two-mile processional to the Santuario de Chimayo, where dirt is collected and a torch lit from a Flame of Peace (which resides in the Santuario and is said to have "circled the globe" in 1986 as part of the First Earth Run, an aspect of the United Nation's International Year of Peace; cf. Kay 1987: 77–82). From the Santuario, twenty runners carry the soil and flame the twenty-eight miles to Los Alamos, where another procession ends at Ashley Pond with the distribution of the soil. In the year I attended, it concluded with Peter Garcia of San Juan Pueblo performing a blessing, distributing the soil from the Santuario, and a congregation forming a circle around Ashley Pond (see Figure 4.6). The Pilgrimage for Peace is not an explicitly antinuclear event, eschewing formal statements about nuclear weapons in favor of condemning acts of violence. For example, the archbishop of the Catholic Church began the pilgrimage with a discussion of violence in the former Yugoslavia and Somalia, the recent shooting of a policeman at Pojoaque Pueblo, and gang violence in Santa Fe. He merely identified Los Alamos as the "birthplace" of the atomic bomb, stating, "Los Alamos' was involved in some bad things. Less now, but I'm sure there are still things going on up there."[6]

4.6. Conclusion of Pilgrimage for Peace, Ashley Pond, Los Alamos. (Photograph by Joseph Masco)

The Pilgrimage for Peace can be read as an effort to locate Los Alamos within regional idioms of place and identity. The Mass and processional form, the sacred earth, the runners (a Pueblo tradition), the symbolic healing of Los Alamos through the Tewa blessing, and the distribution of the earth are all efforts to contain the foreignness of Los Alamos. The force of the pilgrimage argues that Los Alamos remains a problematic site within northern New Mexico, that the nuclear project is an external form that needs to be transformed through local ritual practice. The lack of any formal critique of the nuclear weapons mission of LANL within the event, however, also references the difficulty of publicly challenging the region's largest employer and most powerful institution, thus reiterating the subtle but ever-present power relations between the hill and villages in the valley.

Since 1943 Los Alamos and Chimayo have been intimately linked, dependent on each other for basic resources while remaining culturally in separate worlds. During the Cold War, LANL provided the major source of work for men and women not working in the traditional Chimayo industries of weaving and farming. Buses arrive daily to take workers from Chimayo and other villages to LANL, and now three generations of *Chimayosos* have worked at the laboratory. The economic stability of the Cold

War plutonium economy, and how it has enabled Nuevomexicano communities, is made more powerful in local imagination by the hard reality of life prior to Los Alamos. The Manhattan Project fundamentally changed the politics and economics of the valley. Between the arrival of the railroad in the 1870s and the Manhattan Project in 1943, it became difficult for many Nuevomexicanos to support their families through the land-based economy. Consequently, a majority of men from the villages of northern New Mexico were forced to ride the rails in search of jobs. The legal transition between Mexican and American regimes fundamentally affected the viability of the land-based communal social organizations of the northern Rio Grande valley, by divesting Nuevomexicanos of land and changing the resource base for the region. Overuse also reduced the productivity of lands, which were divided up within a growing Nuevomexicano population (see deBuys 1985). By 1930, of the 1,188 total population in Chimayo between 250 and 300 men left each year for seasonal labor in Colorado, Utah, and Wyoming (Weigle 1975: 88–92). By 1934, the Depression had destroyed the seasonal labor possibilities for Nuevomexicanos, leaving two-thirds of all Nuevomexicano families on some kind of federal relief (Weigle 1975: 360; see also Forrest 1989; Sanchez 1967).[7] Chimayo was one of the wealthier and more diversified village economies, and in the Depression years, locals relied on a barter economy with Española and Santa Fe stores (Usner 1995: 157; cf. Briggs 1988).

Thus, it was within this cultural, educational, economic crisis, that the technoscientific culture of Los Alamos took hold in 1943, creating an immediate social hierarchy in northern New Mexico but also providing the first real opportunity for Nuevomexicanos to enter and succeed in a local cash-based U.S. economy. The Manhattan Project provided a major new resource base for Nuevomexicano villages, quickly engendering a hybrid economy in which employment at the laboratory enabled new cash flows, while small-scale farming maintained individual ties to the land and traditional culture. For those within commuting distance of Los Alamos, the laboratory (and the domestic service economy) became a primary tool for maintaining the viability of village life, generating enough wealth to pay U.S. taxes on land, which had been falling out of Nuevomexicano ownership due to tax forfeiture since 1848 (see Forrest 1989), as well as creating a more diversified economic base. Over the next three generations, Nuevomexicano workers would become less satisfied simply with having stable jobs, and invest more thoroughly in the mission of the laboratory. Parents encouraged their children to get technical and scientific degrees, allowing access to better jobs at the laboratory, pursuing middle-class ascension through the plutonium economy. Consequently, LANL became tied to a broad set of Nuevomexicano cultural expectations and institutions during the Cold War, remaining the ultimate sign of the foreign (a place filled new people, ideas, and practices) but also the key to maintaining the local.

This collision between hypermodern technoscientific forms and Nuevomexicano investments that predate the United States creates a complicated notion of locality. In fact, a number of competing political and ecological regimes in northern New Mexico come into conflict at the foot of Los Alamos, at a placed called the Otowi Bridge. The Otowi Bridge crosses the Rio Grande near San Ildefonso Pueblo, on the main road up to Los Alamos. It was made famous for an English reading audience by Edith Warner, an Anglo writer who lived by the bridge during World War II and maintained strong ties both to San Ildefonso and to Los Alamos. She fed cakes to Robert Oppenhiemer, Niels Bohr, and Edward Teller during the Manhattan Project, wrote poetry about the bombing of Hiroshima, and became a romantic figure in the Anglo history of the Manhattan Project, after Peggy Pond Church's account of her life, *The House at Otowi Bridge* (1959). Today, the Otowi Bridge has been supplanted by a new highway to Los Alamos, and is important mostly as a jurisdictional cutoff, the point of separation between upriver and downriver politics along the Rio Grande. Specifically, the Otowi Bridge is a primary accounting point in the 1939 Rio Grande Compact— the agreement that divides surface water from the Rio Grande between Texas, Colorado, and New Mexico (DuMars et al. 1984: 83; Brown and Ingram 1987: 96). Consequently, it is also an important dividing line in the distribution of local water resources, most immediately between the predominantly Pueblo and Nuevomexicano agricultural interests north of Santa Fe, and the city of Albuquerque downriver.

Distribution of water is particularly complicated because water rights in northern New Mexico are recognized based on time of occupation, that is, on order of arrival into the northern Rio Grande valley. Thus, the Pueblos who claim a presence "from time immemorial" will usually have first water rights, followed by Spanish, Mexican, and American settlers in that order. Consequently, water rights in the north-central Rio Grande valley are among the most contested in the United States and involve legal claims dating back through Mexican and Spanish colonial regimes. In fact, the longest-running lawsuit in the United States involves water rights at the foot of the Pajarito Plateau in the Rio Grande valley, precisely the area that provides much of the labor force for LANL.[8] Water rights clearly reveal that the Spanish colonial system is still active in contemporary New Mexican politics, for disputes over water necessitate a determination of: first, how those rights were administered under Spanish and Mexican regimes; second, how the signing of the Treaty of

Guadalupe Hidalgo in 1848 influenced the transfer of title to those water rights; and only then a final determination of title under New Mexico territorial and state law. The administration of water rights in the north-central Rio Grande valley, especially for irrigation, is also complicated by the fact that local forms of water management are often founded in the face-to-face working of the acequia societies rather than on a well-documented bureaucracy.

The acequias define a predominantly Nuevomexicano ecocultural regime, and are important registers of local identity. As one Española city official told me: "The most valuable real estate in the world is the acequia-irrigated land of the northern Rio Grande valley." Acequias are both a technology for diverting water from rivers to farmland and the basis for a political organization in northern New Mexico. Rooted in medieval Spanish systems of water management, acequias are ditches that run throughout the farming country of the northern Rio Grande valley (see Simmons 1972). Each one is named and administered by an acequia society, made up of *parciantes* (irrigators) who elect a *comision* (of three parciantes) and a *mayordomo* each year (see Rivera 1998). Rights within and between acequias are determined by the age of the claim dating back to 1598.[9] In the mid-1990s, there were over one thousand acequias in New Mexico, which were recognized as subdivisions of the state of New Mexico in 1965, thus giving official sanction to the primary system of water management among farmers in northern New Mexico (Rivera 1998: 149). Acequia societies not only predate the United States as a political organization, but also remain the only nonstate or federal organizations in the United States that can levy taxes. Some ditches have been tended yearly since the Spanish returned to New Mexico in 1693 after the Pueblo revolt, and therefore represent a unique, Nuevomexicano ecocultural achievement in North America. Membership in the acequias also represents a very specific ecocultural claim on place in northern New Mexico, identifying members with a specific family lineage and, in terms of the age of the acequia, offering a precise register of regional identity. A Nuevomexicano involved in acequia politics in Española, describing a recent effort to determine the start date of an acequia just north of San Juan Pueblo, put it this way:

> The problem is that the documents that are available right now only go back to 1714 or so. But the people from that area go all the way back to Oñate, who first settled the area. It was Spanish people and Indian laborers that dug that ditch around 1600 for the first capital before Santa Fe. Now, an old Hispano was at the meeting and he refused to accept the 1717 date for the ditch, even though that was really old and not many claims were prior. When he was asked why he refused, he impressed the hell out of me. He said that

he couldn't accept that date because it would give Santa Fe an older claim, and that it would dishonor his ancestors to pretend that the first settlers of New Mexico were in Santa Fe and not near San Juan. He said that Santa Fe was water hungry and he would not disgrace his ancestors by accepting anything less than the truth: That the acequia had been maintained by Spanish and Indian laborers for over 400 years.

The documents only go back to 1714.   Acequia membership is one local mechanism for determining claims on place and structuring relations between communities. Similarly, care and maintenance of the acequias is recognized as one of the traditional mechanisms for bringing communities together. As such, the acequia societies represent a different concept of resource management, one not rooted in concepts of private property but grounded in a notion of the commons (see Rivera 1998; see also Rodriguez 1986: 14, and 1987).

The acequia societies, like the Pueblo shrine system, provide a local means of mediating ecological relations in the northern Rio Grande valley, one that exists alongside the technoscientific systems at LANL. As political bodies that mediate ecological impacts, the acequia societies maintain not only a cultural diversity but also a biodiversity, nourishing the broader ecosystem that surrounds the maze of ditches running through northern New Mexico (see Rivera 1998).[10] It is a system of ecological management that emphasizes interdependence, as those downstream are dependent on those upstream to ensure the system works properly, just as the entire acequia network relies on the right weather patterns to produce enough water for a season's crops. In a discussion about Nuevomexicano conceptions of the northern Rio Grande valley, one Nuevomexicano from Santa Fe put it this way:

Well, look at the ditch system: water is sacred, nobody messes with that. That is ancient Spanish law, ancient. I think even before the Romans, and each group that would come into Spain would bring a different set of laws but that was a constant—water use. I don't know if you've heard about last year there was a guy who bought property in Los Alamos County and in that area you have water rights according to the acreage that you have. And what he was going to do was just cut off the ditch system—which is unthinkable. Things like that have to be kept sacred because everyone's life will be affected; if one person gives up, we all go.

If one person gives up, we all go.   This narrative suggests that LANL, in taking over a major landmass in the midst of Pueblo and Nuevomexicano systems for ecological management, has had larger impacts than those usually attributed to the plutonium economy. As the most powerful institution in the region, LANL offers not only an alternative to a land-based livelihood, but also operates on a different concept of ecology and community. Each of these cultural transformations can affect the chain of relationships supporting local institutions like the acequias. Thus, just as LANL has pumped new cash into northern New Mexico, enabling many families to secure their hold on lands threatened by the transition to a cash-based economy, it also has brought a new population into the region, who may or may not be interested in maintaining ancient Nuevomexicano systems of water management. Los Alamos also directly affects water politics by drawing enough water to feed a 17,000-person town and a national laboratory out of the deep aquifer, and by distributing environmental contaminants from LANL into the local water system in the form of surface runoff.[11]

In other words, the acequias represent but one of several competing regional technological systems for promoting security that, like Pueblo ritual societies, rely on a communal intimacy with the specific ecology of the northern Rio Grande valley. Since 1943, the plutonium economy has not only brought needed economic resources into northern New Mexico, but also rival systems of knowledge, environmental pollutants, and people, all of which threaten the viability of traditional ecocultural systems. Within this context, the visibility of Nuevomexicano culture within a multicultural region has become more important, making descansos, pilgrimages, and folk traditions also highly politicized statements. Throughout the 1990s, Nuevomexicanos marked their awareness of the fragility of their culture by reasserting their claims on the northern Rio Grande valley in the face of accelerating social change.[12] Put differently, the end of the Cold War provoked anxiety in northern New Mexico about the stability of the future, and thus, also evoked what Marilyn Ivy (1995), in a radically different context, has called "discourses of the vanishing," a concern about cultural absence, the visibility of tradition, and the effects of social change. As we shall see, however, within the contested regional politics of northern New Mexico, the plutonium economy produces not simply nostalgia or a form of cultural mourning, but rather a renewed struggle to secure the northern Rio Grande valley on exclusively local terms.

ON INVASION AND ILLEGITIMACY

There are words hidden all over northern New Mexico, some on paper, some known only by heart. Even the tiniest adobe house in the smallest northern village is likely to have a stash of important words tucked into some hidey-hole, some safest place. There are four centuries of words in documents stuffed under mattresses, in deeds folded into drawers along

with land patents, titles, commissions from kings and queens. Some are documents from Spain and Mexico written in grand and formal language and spelled out in the graceful looping letters of other times and places; their dates are in the 1500s, 1600s, 1700s and early 1800s and they are the documents of presence, possession and entitlement, the Spanish words that link the people and the land. Then there is the Treaty of Guadalupe Hidalgo marking the end of the Mexican-American War in 1848, the document that claimed to turn these mountain Mexicans into New Mexicans. After that, the words are different, often in English, and tell a story of dispossession, loss, betrayal, disenfranchisement and separation. These words have been taken to heart.
—Walter Howerton Jr., "History's Ghosts"

This epigraph recognizes a certain national cultural uncertainty in northern New Mexico, a multiplicity of regimes that have not yet been consolidated or harmonized, preventing a purely American claim on the north-central Rio Grande valley from taking hold. In "History's Ghosts" Howerton implicitly recognizes that New Mexico has always been on the periphery of a larger national structure—Spanish, Mexican, or American—and that consequently the law has not always been attuned to the local, not always been able or willing to recognize Nuevomexicano claims on place. Maintaining documents of colonial orders now hundreds of years out of date, families in northern New Mexico can reach back through time and present clear title to lands now possessed by others, by the U.S. Forest Service, U.S. citizens, or even the U.S. national laboratory. Indeed, one attribute of the immediate post–Cold War period was a cross-cultural struggle over who rightfully owns the land occupied by LANL. This contest, over the legitimacy of U.S. national security claims on the local, was sparked by DOE efforts to make Los Alamos County a self-reliant entity for the first time in its history. Since 1945, the DOE has subsidized basic services in Los Alamos County, providing millions of dollars each year in support of school systems, basic utilities (water and power), as well as the airport and fire department. Richland, Washington, and Oak Ridge, Tennessee, received their last payments in 1969 and 1986, respectively, making Los Alamos the last of the Manhattan Project's "atomic cities" to be directly supported by the DOE. In 1996, the DOE offered a $22.6 million buyout to the county, as well as pursued plans to transfer title on some seven thousand possible acres on the Pajarito Plateau from the federal government to Los Alamos County. The cash and land transfers were intended to provide Los Alamos

County with a resource base large enough to support its growing population, to make it a permanent, self-supporting entity on the plateau. But instead, the end of DOE assistance payments reopened the question of ownership on the plateau, revealing a multiplicity of claims on the land occupied by LANL, claims that had been rendered mute during the nuclear standoff of the Cold War.

San Ildefonso Pueblo claimed first rights to any available land on the plateau, reiterating their 1967 aboriginal land claim for the entire area now occupied by LANL and the Los Alamos town site. In addition, Pueblo officials reminded all concerned that San Ildefonso had been waiting since 1943 for the return of specific tracts of land that had been loaned to the Manhattan Project with the understanding that they would be returned after the war. As officials for Los Alamos County, San Ildefonso Pueblo, and the DOE negotiated the terms of the land transfer in 1996, a rival territorial claim arose, made by a newly formed group, the Homestead Association of the Los Alamos Plateau. The Homestead Association is made up of descendents of the predominately Nuevomexicano ranchers that occupied parts of the plateau prior to the Manhattan Project. Like San Ildefonso, they claimed that the land transferred from their families to the Manhattan Project in 1942–43 had been accompanied by a U.S. promise that they would be able to return to their homesteads after the war was over.

Among these claimants were heirs to one of the three Spanish land grants that fall within what is now Los Alamos County.[13] In particular, the adjudication of lands within the Ramon Vigil Grant, which was founded in 1742 and is now largely incorporated within Los Alamos County, was called into question. This parcel of land was nearly as contested in the eighteenth century as it is today; Pedro Sanchez won the land grant in 1742 and immediately faced legal challenges over it from San Ildefonso Pueblo. He maintained title under Spanish law and his heirs eventually sold eight-elevenths of the grant to Ramon Vigil, who may or may not have forged key documents, but whose claim nevertheless was recognized by U.S. authorities in 1860. Vigil sold the land to Anglo land speculators from the East Coast in 1880, and it passed through several hands before coming into the possession of Ashley Pond, who created the Los Alamos Boys School, which eventually attracted the attention of Robert Oppenheimer as a possible site for the atomic bomb project.[14] Throughout this period, heirs to the three-eighth-share of the original Sanchez land grant both lived on the plateau and sought legal recognition of their claims. Some used U.S. homestead laws to reclaim part of the plateau in the American territorial period and were evicted in 1942, along with the Los Alamos Boys School by the Manhattan Project.

The Homestead Association presented several hundred individual claims on LANL property, including some from the heirs to the Ramon Vigil land grant. Evoking legal documents dating back to before the American War of Independence, the Homestead Association completed a kaleidoscopic moment in history, as Pueblo, Nuevomexicano, and Anglo-American territorial claims on the exact space now occupied by LANL came into simultaneous focus, with each community claiming a right of possession based on participation in a different legal regime—aboriginal, Spanish, Mexican, or American.[15]

If territorial politics around Los Alamos revealed a curious insufficiency in law and history, for Nuevomexicanos, this was only part of a larger discourse on illegitimacy and invasion in the northern Rio Grand valley. Negotiating post–Cold War downsizing at LANL, outsider gentrification of towns and villages, and ongoing struggles over the management of U.S. forest lands in northern New Mexico, the future viability of Nuevomexicano communities was challenged on multiple fronts at the end of the Cold War. For many in the valley, the proposed DOE land transfer to Los Alamos was particularly shocking, as land grant activists had been petitioning the U.S. government for decades, trying to recover land lost, stolen, or forfeited during the U.S. territorial period. Although the Treaty of Guadalupe Hidalgo promised that the property of former Mexican citizens would be maintained in the United States, only a fraction of Nuevomexicano land claims were upheld by the U.S. courts in the late nineteenth century and many were stolen outright by a corrupt legal system. Literally millions of acres changed hands, leaving almost every Nuevomexicano family in northern New Mexico with a story about how the U.S. government or someone manipulating the U.S. legal system took part of their land and impoverished their communities.[16] Poverty was an additional factor in the lost of land: Hal Rothman (1992: 179) reports that 80 percent of land owners in the north-central Rio Grande valley were delinquent in their taxes in the early 1930s, a fact that registers the intensity of the Depression years and the regional difficulty the land-based communities had in engaging a cash economy prior to Los Alamos. The resulting tax forfeiture to U.S. authorities was often done only on paper, meaning that many families only discovered they had lost title to their land decades later, when, for example, they were designated by the U.S. Forest Service as "squatters" on land their families had held for generations.

Thus, for land grant activists in the valley, the DOE proposal to give land back to Los Alamos County fulfilled a longstanding demand in the northern Rio Grande valley, a return to local ownership of federally held forest lands. But as one land grant activist put it to me, "the problem is that they're giving a land grant back to the wrong people." Thus, the newest community in the area, Los Alamos, was achieving one of the oldest regional desires, the recovery of lands from the federal government. With this example in mind, land grant activists began mobilizing with new intensity, knowing, for perhaps really the first time, that the U.S. government would transfer title to lands in northern New Mexico. As an explicitly U.S. national presence in northern New Mexico and the wealthiest community in the region, Los Alamos has always been a regional signifier in the land grant debate. At the height of the land grant struggle in the 1960s, for example, Reis Tijerina, head of the Alianza Federal de Mercedes, attempted with great fanfare to make a "citizen's arrest" on Norris Bradbury, director of Los Alamos Scientific Laboratory, for "trespassing" on the Ramon Vigil land grant and for creating "weapons of mass destruction."[17]

Informing a number of contemporary regional discourses about land and Los Alamos is a certain sense of invasion, concerning foreign people, ideas, and power structures. In this light, consider the import of Figure 4.7, an advertisement for a movie studio company located in Santa Fe. Declaring boldly in a full-page ad in the *Santa Fe New Mexican*, "not all foreign invasions are bad for the economy," Garson Studios plays off the theme of a television show—Earth 2—to make a point about local politics. Earth 2 is a science fiction series produced by Steven Spielberg, who maintains a house in Santa Fe. Shot entirely in New Mexico, Earth 2 imagines a future in which the earth is so polluted that humans abandon it, and follows the adventures of the first colonists of a planet, that may or may not be sentient. Referencing the Gaia hypothesis, while presenting an explicit allegorical reenactment of the European conquest of the New World, Earth 2 can itself be read as a remarkable allegory for local politics in New Mexico. At the time the ad appeared, Nuevomexicanos in Santa Fe were actively debating invasion, this time of wealthy foreigners. As Santa Fe became one of the favorite cities in the world for the wealthy elite—and a particular favorite of people in the film industry—a new cycle of gentrification threatened Nuevomexicano claims on the city.[18] In addition to Spielberg, for example, Ted Turner, founder of CNN, began buying property in New Mexico in the early 1990s. By 1996, Turner personally owned over one million acres, or 1,796 square miles of New Mexico—nearly 2 percent of the entire state.[19] Exponential growth in property values, and the resulting taxes, began forcing Nuevomexicanos from family homes and properties that predate the United States, fueling racial tensions throughout the region. In the summer of 1996, for example, a proposed national ad campaign by the Santa Fe tourist board forwarding the phrase "Mi casa es su casa" created a city furor and firings, as Nuevomexicanos in Santa Fe were literally witnessing

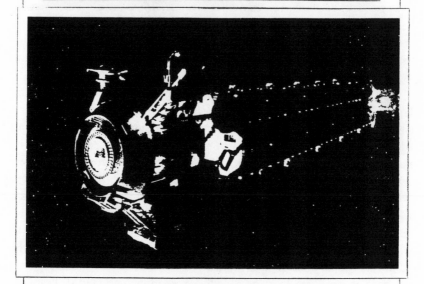

4.7. Garson Studios advertisement. (*Source: Santa Fe New Mexican*)

old neighborhoods changing hands. Thus, the "foreign invasion" referenced in the poster addresses not simply the theme of the show (the fictional colonization of a new planet), but also the broader effects of the production on New Mexico. Promising $25 million to the local economy, the poster offers an alternative narrative about invasion, arguing that it is "good" for the economy. When played against the history of local responses to U.S. colonization after 1848, and the specific debates over gentrification in Santa Fe occurring at the time, the poster also forwards the logic that money is everything, implicitly arguing that Nuevomexicanos should gladly accept an "invasion" in exchange for cash.

In the post–Cold War period, Nuevomexicano rhetorics of invasion and colonization were explicitly aimed at Anglo environmental and antinuclear groups, predominantly from Santa Fe, who were using the U.S. legal system to affect U.S. policy on forest service lands and at LANL. In the fall of 1995, as LANL faced its first round of post–Cold War layoffs, a coalition of southwestern environmental groups sued to enforce endangered species laws on national forest lands. One result was a ban on firewood gathering and logging in the Carson National Forest in northern New Mexico in order to protect the habit of the Mexican Spotted Owl, a rarely seen bird that activists acknowledged lives only in one corner of the national forest. Nuevomexicano loggers took this as a direct attack on their livelihood, as did residents of the thirty-eight villages dependent on the Carson National Forest for firewood. Heading into winter without enough firewood, residents of Truchas and other villages declared themselves to be the true environmentalists—having lived off the land for four hundred years—and declared that their cultural survival ought to be as important as that of the elusive Mexican Spotted Owl.[20] Longtime Nuevomexicano land grant activist Antonio "Ike" De Vargas formed a new group Herencia de Norteños Unidos to fight the new restriction, and in a commentary published in the *Santa Fe New Mexican* wrote:

The most irritating thing to me is the arrogance displayed by the enviro-maniacs in Santa Fe and their assertions that this land is their land. I think that is very important for these people to know and understand that many of our northern villages predated the U.S. Forest Service and the U.S. government and that any abuse of the land has been done by those two entities, not the people of these villages. It is extremely disturbing to me that these carpetbaggers from other states can come in and say that they are tired of the people living off the land . . . I think it is very important to note that the debate is not even about birds or other endangered species, the whole thing boils down to one simple equation: Who is to benefit from the management of the land? These people want to live in their cozy but closed and walled-in compounds so they do not come into contact with the poor and disenfranchised people who are native to the area. If they can keep the *norteños* ignorant and unemployed the inevitable result is the dislocation of the people from their villages and the eventual gentrification of all of Northern New Mexico.[21]

Fusing longstanding Nuevomexicano concerns about Anglo gentrification, legal disfranchisement, and ecological management (see Pulido 1996; deBuys 1985), DeVargas and Herencia de Norteños Unidos showed their rage. They staged a rally in Santa Fe in which members of the Santa Fe–based environmental groups pushing the legislation were hung in effigy (see Figure 4.8). At that event, members of Herencia de Norteños Unidos not only evoked their rights to the land under the Treaty of Guadalupe Hidalgo, but also argued that the new restrictions on forest use merely replicated the nineteenth-century land adjudication process, whereby Anglo outsiders used U.S. law to shut local communities out of the decision-making process about "their" lands.

This sense that outsiders were redefining the resource base of northern New Mexico involved not only forest lands but also LANL. New Santa Fe–based antinuclear groups—Concerned Citizens for Nuclear Safety (CCNS) and the Los Alamos Study Group (LASG)—were very effective in the post–Cold War period in using environmental protection laws to influence laboratory operations. With a membership consisting mostly of Anglo immigrants to the area, these groups pursued public information campaigns and lawsuits that identified LANL not as an economic resource but as a fundamental threat to the region. Several Nuevomexicano activists told me that while they appreciated the new information on LANL's environmental and health effects made available by antinuclear groups, they also saw them as a threat. As one put it:

> They don't represent us or our concerns. I like CCNS and LASG but shutting down the lab . . . that would be totally catastrophic for the valley. There would be no way we could recover. If the lab were to close down tomorrow, most of us would end up in some concrete jungle somewhere, or we would have to go to war here. Right now I would have to say that I think environmentalists and the government are the same—they're both the enemy. They don't represent our interests and are dangerous. Look at what Sam Hitt [of Forest Guardians] and his crowd did with the grazing, I mean everybody around here has some cattle that they graze on national forest grounds. It is our right by the Treaty of Guadalupe Hidalgo to make a living off that land. We're environmentalists, we have been for hundreds of years. Nobody around here wants to destroy the forest or the land—we live off it.

We would end up in a concrete jungle somewhere, or we would have to go to war here. In this statement, the plutonium and land-based economies are portrayed as equally threatened by Anglo outsiders, who claim an intimate concern for the land. Put differently, the new

4.8. Nuevomexicano logging activists hanging Santa Fe environmentalists in effigy. (Photograph by Joseph Masco)

environmental activism of the post–Cold War era has revealed the presence of rival ecocultural regimes in northern New Mexico, one fluent in U.S. law and empowered by it, one striving for legal recognition and protection from U.S. law.

In this light, Nuevomexicanos are caught in what John Bodine (1968) has called northern New Mexico's "tri-ethnic trap," a situation in which the legal and cultural position of Nuevomexicanos is doubly marginalized by white structures of power and by the cultural status of Native Americans as the "first Americans" (see also Rodriguez 1987). Thus, while the Pueblos as sovereign governments gained a new post–Cold War legal discourse with the laboratory—illustrated in the DOE/Tribal

Accords—equally affected Nuevomexicano communities gained no such legal voice. Similarly, they do not have a Nuevomexicano equivalent of the Bureau of Indian Affairs through which to engage the federal government. Likewise, while Anglo environmentalists can press for execution of endangered species laws on national forest lands, Nuevomexicanos who claim those lands as ancestral property have no legal recourse except to revisit the adjudication of the Treaty of Guadalupe Hidalgo and try to undo 150 years of U.S. law. While trying to mobilize unique cultural rights through legal structures that officially recognize all U.S. citizens as equal, Nuevomexicanos also have an ever-present example of what might have been in the form of Pueblo communities that maintain distinct territorial and legal structures. As one land grant activist told me: "The land grants are really sovereign. The people that live within the land grants should have sovereign rights, the same as the Pueblos. They were the same type of grants under the Spanish government." Thus, as Anglo groups pursued environmental laws on national forest land, and the Pueblos entered into formal negotiations with LANL over environmental and social impacts, Nuevomexicanos in the northern Rio Grande valley confronted a legal and political process that did not seem to recognize their unique cultural investments, allow their history, or care about their needs.

In part, this was also tied up in a complicated psychosocial dynamic by which Anglos shed responsibility for the American conquest of the Southwest by focusing on Spanish acts of imperialism.[22] This is evidenced by the lack of historical memory outside the Southwest about the Mexican-American war, and a common Anglo-American portrait of the territorial takeover of New Mexico as a "peaceful conquest," more a business transaction between neighboring states than an act of war. While disputing that image of the war, Nuevomexicanos nevertheless remember their own "peaceful" conquest of the northern Rio Grande valley.[23] Indeed, the central act of the Santa Fe Fiesta, which has been celebrated annually since 1712, is a reenactment of Don Diego De Vargas's reentry into Santa Fe after the Pueblo Revolt (see Grimes 1976). Vargas symbolically retakes Santa Fe each September, marching under the banner of La Conquistadora—Our Lady of the Conquest—a devotional statue of Mary believed to have protective powers (see Figure 4.9; also R. Gutierrez 1991: 143–46; Chavez 1975).[24] While these cross-cultural memories of conflict in 1693 and 1848 are often strategic, selectively informing particular visions of self and nation, Nuevomexicanos are caught once again in the tri-ethnic trap. The Santa Fe Fiesta—which in effect celebrates the establishment of Nuevomexicano culture in the region—has been criticized by Pueblo and Anglo residents of northern

4.9. La Conquistadora, Our Lady of the Conquest; Santa Fe Fiesta procession.
(Photograph by Joseph Masco)

New Mexico for glorifying an act of violence. In 1992, the year of the Columbus Quincentennary, Archbishop of Santa Fe Robert Sanchez attempted to address this controversy by bestowing a new name on La Conquistadora—calling her Nuestra Señora de la Paz, "Our Lady of Peace." While trying to shift cross-cultural understanding of that crucial moment in the history of the northern Rio Grande valley, perhaps it is not surprising that commissioners from Santa Fe and Rio Arriba Counties would soon also move to address the legacy of 1848. On October 26, 1995, in collaboration with La Herencia de Norteños Unidos and in the regional context of the first major layoff in LANL history, Rio Arriba County commissioners declared February 2, the anniversary of the signing of the Treaty of Guadalupe Hidalgo, a countywide holiday. Talking about it publicly as a "day of mourning," land grant activists and county officials sought to make the point that Nuevomexicanos maintain unique rights as citizens of the United States, as well as a unique claim on place in the northern Rio Grande valley, most clearly delineated in the land-based practices of the acequias and land grants (see Howerton 1996).

Concurrently, Nuevomexicanos from the valley began to talk openly about LANL as a part of this legacy of conquest, and began mobilizing to have an impact on the post–Cold War mission of the laboratory. In August 1995, Congressman Bill Richardson and Debbie Jaramillo, mayor of Santa Fe, co-sponsored an unprecedented public meeting to discuss the future of LANL. The hearing was called in response to a larger set of hearings (in Los Alamos and Albuquerque) sponsored by the DOE, as part of a Programmatic Environmental Impact Statement (PEIS) on Stockpile Steward-ship and Management, a study intended to provide a total portrait of the environmental effects of the post–Cold War U.S. nuclear complex. Since Santa Fe antinuclear groups had been instrumental in calling for the PEIS, the DOE's decision was interpreted as a sign that U.S. officials did not con-sider Santa Fe to be a community impacted by LANL activities. Mayor Jaramillo, whose family goes back to the early Spanish colonial period in New Mexico, and who was elected on an antigentrification ticket, responded by declaring Los Alamos a de facto suburb of Santa Fe. Describing the relationship between Los Alamos and Santa Fe as a "shot-gun marriage," she declared the two communities "permanently linked" and stated that Santa Fe is impacted "economically, environmentally and socially from everything that happens on the hill."

Identifying LANL as a threat as much as a resource for northern New Mexico, Jaramillo led the Santa Fe city council in passing a resolution criticizing LANL for its social and environmental effects on northern New Mexico, and demanding a voice in future policy studies concerning the laboratory. In her opening statement on August 5, 1995 (in the context of the fiftieth anniversary of the bombing of Hiroshima), she said:

> It appears, to some of us, that LANL is seeking a role as the central manu-facturing site for nuclear weapons components. If this happens this will continue to increase the environmental nightmare surrounding the lab. These include the possibility of radioactive waste landfills larger than WIPP and the transportation of nuclear and other hazardous waste products throughout our community. I ask you: Is this the kind of future we want for our beautiful and historical northern New Mexico? . . . But just as bad as the environmental threat is the cultural threat. If LANL is focused only on development and production of nuclear weapons, the lab will continue to be culturally and economically isolated from the rest of northern New Mexico. I don't want that. And I really don't think LANL wants that. I'd like to see more, not less, involvement of our citizens in the work of the national labo-ratory. I'd like to see Hispanics and people of color in management positions in numbers that reflect the make up of the surrounding region. And I'd like to see Los Alamos become not an island of paranoia and privilege but a place of hope and opportunity for the people of northern New Mexico, not only for northern New Mexico but also for our children and their children, and for the rest of the world. So let's make today a fresh honest start at working towards a good relationship. We must continue to turn away from the old assumptions of the Cold War. Let us turn away from the production of

nuclear weapons in the mountains above us. And let us, with this meeting, begin the process of integrating Los Alamos National Laboratory, with its fabulous technology and its gifted people, into a sustainable and diverse institution that will be truly an asset to the land and people of northern New Mexico.

I'd like to see Los Alamos become not an island of paranoia and privilege but a place of hope and opportunity. Breaking the codes of Cold War silence, Jaramillo was only one of several Nuevomexicano government officials to criticize LANL, giving voice to longstanding issues about class, culture, and regional security. Without the economic stability provided by the Cold War plutonium economy, residents of the valley began to discuss more openly the effects of having to speak English at the laboratory on Nuevomexicano culture, and to note publicly when LANL employees began pronouncing their Spanish surnames with an English accent. Jaramillo identifies LANL here as a cultural threat as well an economic resource and seeks to reverse the local cultural trajectory of the Cold War: that is, rather than locals assimilating to the imported culture of the laboratory, Jaramillo imagines a sustainable— non-nuclear—future, where LANL is integrated into northern New Mexico. Rather than presenting a new U.S. national security mission, Jaramillo stakes out a mission for LANL that is focused directly on local security—of jobs, cultures, and the environment.

This hearing, however, drew an audience composed almost entirely of Anglos, and the testimony, outside of Mayor Jaramillo's statement, rarely engaged Nuevomexicano experience. That is, until a former member of the Santa Fe City Council, who had discovered the hearing on television, rushed over to the city council chamber. Standing in front of the Santa Fe city seal (see Figure 4.10), which represents claims on three different national regimes (Spanish, Mexican, and American), he began his testimony by describing what it was like in Santa Fe during World War II, focusing on how, as a boy, he feared to come home from school each day because he did not want to hear that his father had been killed in the war. Expressing his family's profound relief at the conclusion of the war, he identified as a thirty-five-year employee of Los Alamos, and thereby implicitly praised LANL for stopping the war and saving his father. After asking that people remember those killed at Pearl Harbor as well as at Hiroshima and Nagasaki, he then addressed the composition of the audience directly:

Unlike 97% of you, I was born and raised in Santa Fe. Back in the 70s, I was on the city council; I used to sit right there. One thing I kind of feel sad about is people come up here and say "the city of Santa Fe's people"—this is what

4.10. Santa Fe City Seal, City Council Chambers. (Photograph by Joseph Masco)

we want and this is what we're telling the DOE. And yet when I look around, I don't know any of you. I've lived here for 62 years, except for the five years I spent in Boulder, Colorado getting educated and my service time, I've been here my whole life time. I don't know any of you. I've heard some of you say "Back in New York," or "I've been here three years." If I were the DOE honchos I wouldn't pay much attention to what is going on here today, because you are really not a cross-section of the city. You're a bunch of people who just moved in here, with your own little anti-nuclear agenda . . .

I don't know all the in and outs of everything that goes on at Los Alamos but after 35 years I kind of know my way around. I've seen [nuclear waste] up there in barrels in little old rusty, leaky shacks, sitting there with waste written on it. But you don't want WIPP [the Waste Isolation Pilot Plant]; you don't want it coming through here. So what is it you want? Do you want to leave it up there or take it away 200 miles down to WIPP or what? Because you can't have it both ways. If I were sitting up there listening to this I would say its more of the same old anti-squirrel, anti-mining, anti-nuclear, anti-everything, whatever comes down the pike—just against everything kind of folks is what we have in the room here.

I'm sure I agree with what you say about proliferation, but you've got to look at the other side of it. Los Alamos has provided an economic base. I know people that I went to school with that went into the Navy, got an education, came back and are making $50,000 a year, being technicians. I know a lot of them. Every morning I go to work I drive an old car and everybody passing me by is driving a real nice Mitsubishi or Lexus, or whatever. And it's a good place to work. The benefits are good. You downgrade Los Alamos because of its agenda, but Los Alamos has provided a terrific base for the people of northern New Mexico. Yes, we didn't go to Harvard and a lot of people didn't graduate high school, at Española High, but they make a heck of a good living at Los Alamos. They have beautiful homes in Chimayo, everywhere, built on what they made at Los Alamos. That's not to say there is not pollution, and that they don't need to tighten up what is going on up there but to condemn the whole thing . . . they need our support to clean it up and keep it clean.

I've been here my whole lifetime, but I don't know any of you. In this statement, Anglo gentrification in Santa Fe evolves into a threat not only to a local sense of community but also to the entire regional economy, from land-based practices to economic development to LANL. Identifying this vocal assembly of laboratory critics as illegitimate outsiders, this lifelong Santa Fe resident offers an alternative version of security—one based in the new cars and homes found the northern Rio Grande valley. But while fusing concerns about gentrification with restrictions on land-based practices and development, he also identifies LANL as a source of pollution, a place where the nuclear waste barrels are piling up. Anglo outsiders thus become linked to a chain of socioeconomic forces in the northern Rio Grande valley. Antinuclear activists do not protect the environment, in his presentation, but are instead a force keeping nuclear waste at LANL, preventing its evacuation to another part of the state, and thereby exacerbating the local risk. Job insecurity within the plutonium economy blurs with a broader regional and environmental insecurity in this narrative, marking the arrival of a complex new form of anxiety for Nuevomexicanos at the end of the Cold War.

Indeed, the end of the Cold War produced not only a regional uncertainty about the future of LANL, but also numerous revelations about its Cold War environmental impacts, for which Nuevomexicanos (workers and residents) were on the front lines. While many Nuevomexicanos from the valley have had longstanding health concerns about family members who worked at the laboratory, the early 1990s brought forth a series of revelations about the scale of environmental damage on the plateau—a projected $2 billion cleanup project—as well as discussion of atmospheric experiments conducted by LANL in the 1950s and 1960s that might have put northern New Mexico at risk (see Romero 1995). While assessing the cultural impacts of the first half century of the Manhattan Project, valley communities also worried that they may have been physically sacrificed to the Cold War national security project. As one Nuevomexicano, who does not work at LANL, described the post–Cold War reality of living underneath Los Alamos:

Now we wonder about the air we breathe, the water, the soil—we wonder what has happened to us. Today, every time a crop fails, every time a cow fails to give birth, or an animal's skin looks funny—we blame [he points up toward LANL]. When the lab came here, our people worked in the shit up there. We were the janitors, the plumbers, the laborers. But they made enough money to send their kids to school for an education, now we're doing better. But we don't know how much was done to us. The problem is that the health records aren't adequate to see what the effects were. So we have to say, "my parents, and me are screwed—we don't know what's happened to us" but we can get a baseline survey set up for our kids. So we need to do the medical survey now so that they have a baseline to work off of. I tell people that we don't even know what the lab has done yet—it could be worse in 50 years than it is now. Who knows what is working its way down that mountain, into our water supply, into our soil. There is no way of telling, so we had better prepare. We know that there was blue snow falling on Mora County. Now that's just one case, how many other [radioactive] releases happened when it wasn't snowing or raining— when you couldn't see it. We know that they released so many tons of iodine into the atmosphere as well. They did hundreds of tests that we know about. What else was going on up there that we don't know about? That's the question. In the early days they weren't too careful up there. Today, a lot of men from the valley work up in Los Alamos as plumbers and electricians, they're afraid of what they might dig into when they're working underneath people's houses, or what might be in the soil. We've always done the shit work up there and we don't know what the effects are.

We don't know how much was done to us—who knows what is working its way down that mountain? Here, Los Alamos appears primarily as a source of contamination, of invisible pollutants that are colonizing bodies in territories in the northern Rio Grande valley. Caught in an experience of the nuclear uncanny, the narrator fuses a concern about generational reproduction with the unknown effects of the laboratory, imagining invasive and radioactive elements to which his generation may already have been sacrificed. One long-term effect of living in the shadow of a major nuclear facility is revealed here in the form of a proliferating imaginary, one that is unable to contain the psychosocial, let alone environmental, effects of the plutonium economy.

In that light, let us consider the trajectory of another Nuevomexicano family that has been intimately involved in the plutonium economy right from the beginning of the nuclear age. As told in a special issue of *Los Alamos Science* devoted to exploring LANL's role in a series of covert human plutonium experiments (widely publicized by the *Albuquerque Tribune* in 1993), this multigenerational story about plutonium also documents a change in ecocultural regimes on the Pajarito Plateau (Inkret and Miller 1995: 125–54). Jose Gonzales's family homesteaded on the Pajarito Plateau before World War II, on Barranca Mesa to be precise, now one of the principal residential neighborhoods of Los Alamos. The

Gonzales family was evicted from the plateau by the Manhattan Project in 1943, and moved off the hill to El Rancho, which is the closest Nuevomexicano village to Los Alamos. Intimately involved in the founding act of the Manhattan Project in New Mexico, as a child, Jose Gonzales also remembers "the laboratory people would transport plutonium in convoys only fifteen feet from my kitchen door down the hill in El Rancho. I remember hearing those convoys passing our house at 1:00 A.M. in the morning" (135). Having lost his land-based livelihood, his father immediately took up work at the laboratory, participating in the early plutonium work on the first atomic bomb. In 1958, after a business failed in Pojoaque, Jose Gonzales also began work at the laboratory, taking a job in radiation monitoring; he described his first days on the job this way:

> I felt comfortable from the start even though I didn't know exactly what was going on in the experiments. I guess what made me feel good was that I had the equipment to protect myself and to protect those people that were out there. A lot of elderly people of Spanish descent were working there as laborers, electricians, craftsmen, and so on, and I was able to communicate with them in Spanish. (135)

However, this feeling of security was shattered at the end of his first month on the job as a weapons scientist was killed during a criticality experiment; Gonzales remarked that the death "shook me up" and he "learned from the experience that people can die from radiation—you can plan for a job for three weeks and it only takes one second to mess it up." Over the course of his thirty-three years at the lab he moved from radiation monitoring (helping people into and out of protective clothing and gauging laboratory work) to jobs in plutonium processing, and for a time, work on the Rover nuclear rocket program, a project designed to take people to Mars.

Though learning about radiation dangers on the job (in the context of a fatal injury), Gonzales underscores the sense of community he felt, not only because he could speak Spanish with many of the workers but also because in the 1950s everybody worked together at the plutonium facility, calling each by their first names—"none of this mister stuff," he remarks, thereby acknowledging a change in laboratory culture since the 1950s (136). Pursuing a successful and personally satisfying career at LANL, Gonzales was nevertheless asked to participate in this special issue of Los Alamos Science because he had been repeatedly contaminated with plutonium and other nuclear agents on the job. Thus, his presence in the major journal of the laboratory was also a document of his personal sacrifice to its mission. After describing numerous accidents, where containment vessels leaked or transport systems failed, dosing him with radioactive contaminants, he concludes:

> All the incidents happened, and still, I didn't want to quit my job. I have pride in my work. When I felt kind of bad, I talked to my family. I have two healthy children and two grandchildren and they understand. There were a few times when I had to leave my underwear at work, and my son would say, "Mom, daddy's hot again!" I'm so grateful that I can joke about those things today. At the time it happened, it was something serious. Today, I feel better physically, mentally, and spiritually than I ever have in my life. I'm still working at the Lab, helping to write a Lab report on the decommissioning of the metal prep line. I'm really proud to be doing that. (144)

"Mom, Daddy's hot again!" A lifetime of job security is balanced here by the reality of physical contamination and the unpredictable, long-term effects of radioactive toxins on the human body. For workers throughout the nuclear complex, the pleasures of job security are similarly measures against a lifetime negotiation of the nuclear uncanny.

I began this section with a discussion of the multiplicity of claims on the territorial space occupied by LANL and have argued that the incompatibility of these rival systems of legitimacy has produced explicit discourses about invasion and illegitimacy. The Gonzales family history brings these issues full circle, and returns us to the question of who defines cultural rights on the plateau and the regional effects of LANL. Specifically, one of the sites in which Jose Gonzales, and probably his father, worked is TA-21, a plutonium-processing facility and nuclear waste site. It was decommissioned in the early 1990s, and at that point became part of the DOE land tracts that were potential gifts to Los Alamos County. However, this area is one of the more contaminated sites at Los Alamos, requiring a multimillion-dollar cleanup operation before it is safe. Thus, Jose Gonzales has witnessed in the course of his lifetime a fundamental transfer of regimes on the Pajarito Plateau, from the land-based economy his father participated in, to the plutonium economy, and potentially back to the descendents of those who have claims on the plateau preceding the Manhattan Project—making his family intimately involved in this transfer of ecocultural regimes. Working for decades at a site a few miles from where his father homesteaded, Gonzales must now negotiate the physical after-effects of nuclear science, as does the plateau itself. Thus, the four-hundred-year history of overlapping national-cultural regimes on the plateau is eclipsed by the presence of a new invisible element, which marks both land and bodies on a permanent basis. For it is important to underscore that while territorial borders can be redrawn, and lifestyles and ownership can be renegotiated, the effects of plutonium are on a multimillennial trajectory. Thus, the plutonium economy is revealed in these workers' lives as a uniquely colonizing force, one that has complexly affected life in the northern Rio Grande valley, infiltrating a lived space with all its environmental, economic, and psychosocial effects.

LANL: A NUCLEAR MAQUILADORA?

The year is 2583. The past century has been one of political upheaval in what used to be known as the American Southwest. After centuries of wrangling about diverse interests, economic inequalities and political representation, the United States has fragmented into a cluster of smaller nation states. During this time period similar processes have affected the stability of Mexico, traditionally plagued by tensions between the relatively affluent North and centralized political control based in the South. Its northern Provinces have formed the Free State of Chihuahua with its capital in Chihuahua City, "the jewel of the north" . . . The maquiladora plants now lay idle, their semiskilled labor force unable to produce anything without a supply of prefabricated parts . . . Much of the Free State's intellectual resources are devoted to the location and recovery of usable articles, especially in the former U.S. territories, which had been inhabited by more highly developed technological societies and which are now constantly under the threat of invasion by the North American nation states . . . While making excavations at the site of the former Sandia National Laboratories, Free State resource archaeologists discover references to the WIPP site which include photographs of waste barrels filled with abandoned tools, cables, and clothing. Fragmentary maps are also found, which allow the location of the site to be established . . . To make a long story short, the WIPP site is intentionally mined by people unaware of the potential hazard, and all usable waste is exploited. During the mining operation, vessels containing transuranics are breached and contamination results.
—Harry Otway, "Altered Political Control: The Free State of Chihuahua"

This narrative is from a Sandia National Laboratory study entitled *Expert Judgment on Inadvertent Human Intrusion into the Waste Isolation Pilot Plant*, a serious exercise in government-sponsored science fiction, in which teams of scientists were challenged to imagine just what might evolve over the next ten thousand years that could lead to releases of the radioactive materials to be buried at the Waste Isolation Pilot Plant (WIPP) in southern New Mexico. This regulatory fiction is now mandated by the DOE, which requires a ten thousand-year safety plan to be established prior to the opening of any permanent U.S. repository for nuclear waste.[25] Recognizing the danger of nuclear materials that are radioactive for hundreds, and thousands, of years, the DOE has bureaucratically mobilized to address community fears by ordering safety precautions on an unprecedented scale. To put this requirement in some historical perspective, important human achievements in the past ten thousand years include not only the splitting of the atom but also the advent of writing and agriculture. Thus, the problem of what to do with the Cold War-era military and civilian nuclear waste in the United States poses an unparalleled material and conceptual problem, requiring policy makers to expand their concepts of time and risk exponentially, and imagine the social and environmental impacts of nuclear technologies far into a distant future—in this case, for the next *four hundred generations* of those living in what is now New Mexico. What is unique about this report is that it is perhaps the only genre of DOE policy documentation that contemplates a less than eternal American nation-state. Indeed, acknowledging that "no nation in recent memory has survived for more than a few centuries," Otway and his team conclude that the United States is unlikely to maintain control of the WIPP site, as the political and territorial borders in the region will eventually change, perhaps radically, leaving the radioactive legacies of the Cold War U.S. nuclear project under someone else's control (1991: D-34). Thus, the report strives to determine systems of warning (monuments, texts, symbolic markings) that will alert future generations, who are likely to be neither American nor English-speaking, of the dangers buried at the site. While this is a fascinating cultural enterprise in and of itself—imagining how to communicate to people in the year AD 12,000 that the carefully buried articles at the WIPP site are deadly refuse and not, say, like the currently prized relics buried within Egyptian pyramids—in the cultural context of the U.S. Southwest, this report takes on a different, and more temporally immediate, political light.

The "Free State of Chihuahua" scenario, in fact, can be read as a return of the repressed, an official science fiction that projects into the distant future the contemporary political tensions surrounding the U.S. nuclear complex in New Mexico. LANL is an implicit referent in this narrative, not only because Otway is a prominent Los Alamos scientist, and much of the waste (contaminated tools, clothing, and material) destined for WIPP is produced at LANL, but also because, as we've seen already, LANL is a potent symbol of national belonging in a region filled with competing national statuses. This science fiction is also one of the few moments in the official U.S. nuclear policy that recognizes the possibility of other national claims on the territory of New Mexico, that suggests the United States might be a temporary national-cultural formation, and that imagines a southern, rather than an eastern orbit of power. Presenting a future North America tragically transformed, not by nuclear war, but by internal economic and cultural fragmentation, Otway's narrative overturns the narrative assumptions of Cold War nuclear polity (about the eternal nature of America and the supreme power of its military complex) in order to deal with the radioactive legacies of the twentieth century. The scenario also demonstrates that while the Cold War rendered the national-cultural diversity of the northern Rio Grande valley invisible to U.S. policy makers, the multicultural, multinational context of life around LANL was nevertheless tacitly recognized by some at the laboratory, allowing its projection hundreds of years into the future in this report.

As a speculative planning document, set in a hypothetical distant future, the "Free State of Chihuahua" narrative would seem to be a peripheral statement on New Mexican politics; however, as I have noted, rather than presenting a future history, it can be read as an allegory for the first half century of the nuclear age. The Free State scenario posits a future where the United States collapses under the weight of internal division and economic crisis, fragmenting into a number of new nation-states. The twenty-two indigenous nations within New Mexico make the political fragmentation around the U.S. nuclear complex already a formal reality, but the land grant politics of northern New Mexico provide the more precise referent for the Free State allegory. Consider Figure 4.11, which is a hand-drawn map circulated in the late 1960s by the Alianza movement, declaring Santa Fe as the capital of Aztlan, the Chicano nation.[26] Indeed, there are striking historical parallels to this science fiction, for in 1967 the Alianza land grant movement declared six hundred thousand acres of Rio Arriba County the "Free City State of San Joaquin del Rio de Chama." Political leaders were elected, and efforts were made to take lumber from the former San Joaquin land grant, now "free city state," which was recognized by the U.S. government only as U.S. forestland. The resulting conflict had San Joaquin officials arresting U.S. Forest Service rangers for trespassing, and ultimately had the U.S. National Guard and U.S. tanks rolling through Rio Arriba County, pushing the poverty and political status of Nuevomexicanos onto an international stage for a brief moment.[27] Out of this period of activism also came the national-cultural formation known as Aztlan, a Chicano/a

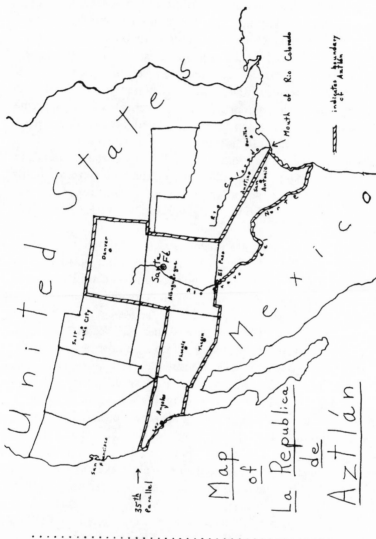

4.11. Map of La Republica de Aztlan; produced by the Alianza land grant movement circa 1968. (Courtesy of the Center for Southwest Research, University of New Mexico)

designation that remaps the territories currently occupied by the nuclear complex in the U.S. Southwest as part of a much older identification, one including the current Mexican State of Chihuahua (see Anaya and Lomeli 1989). Thus, the new national order projected into a distant future in the "Free State" scenario can be read as only a legitimization of the local processes already established in northern New Mexico. Nuevomexicano efforts to recover lost land and establish new kinds of political organizations remain vibrant after the Cold War, as evidenced by a new wave of political activism concerning the adjudication of land grants. In fact, New Mexico's congressional delegation began work in the late 1990s to reexamine the historical application of the Treaty of Guadalupe Hidalgo in northern New Mexico.[28]

The "Free State of Chihuahua" scenario also reveals an important aspect of the plutonium economy, one that is often hidden by the press of everyday deliberations about the U.S. nuclear complex, namely, the longevity of some nuclear materials and the multiple social formations that, over time, will necessarily be forced to deal with them. For while the Cold War nuclear complex was oriented toward protecting the United States in sequential units of fifteen to twenty minutes—the period of warning prior to an incoming nuclear strike—the "Free State" narrative transforms the scale of reference for dealing with the material legacies of the Cold War nuclear complex from minutes to centuries to millennia. In other words, the threat of a military nuclear strike is overcome in this official narrative by the day-to-day, century-to-century, millennium-to-millennium threat posed by the radioactive residues of the Cold War plutonium economy.

In this future history, the new state of Chihuahua is economically devastated, primarily because the maquiladora industry has collapsed, leaving locals with factories but no raw materials to process within them. The result, in this science fiction, is a region of scavengers, picking through the debris of a more technologically advanced, former United States for usable items and technology. Noting that Sandia National Laboratory is now a ruin, the Free State scenario offers no opinion about LANL, which is presumably in a similarly abandoned state in the year 2583. Scavenging through the wreckage of these former U.S. national laboratories, Free State archaeologists discover the location of the WIPP site, pictures of the clothing, tools, and machines buried there, leading to an excavation of the site and their own eventual contamination. The implied image is of Free State citizens walking home with radioactive tools, perhaps wearing the contaminated laboratory jackets and gloves of twentieth-century nuclear workers at Los Alamos, Sandia, and elsewhere. In this official fiction, the U.S. nuclear project has failed, leading not only to the collapse of the United States and the abandonment of the national laboratories, but also to the contamination of people. This scenario brings up a number of important issues in regard to contemporary New Mexico, not the least of which concerns the economic base of the region outside of the nuclear complex, and the more pointed question: Is LANL in its present or near future incarnation a de facto nuclear maquiladora?

For as scientists imagine a distant future in which the descendents of contemporary Nuevomexicanos scavenge through the debris of the twentieth-century nuclear complex (in a region destabilized by the disintegration of the United States, the loss of the national laboratories, and the collapse of the maquiladora system) they implicitly comment on their own value to social stability and project what the loss of the plutonium economy would mean for northern New Mexico. In that light, consider the comments of this Nuevomexicano (a longtime employee of LANL, who was born and raised in Santa Fe) about the material effects of participating in the Cold War plutonium economy:

Back in the early days [of Los Alamos], there was really no regulation, and I'm sure the lab was throwing a lot of stuff out in the public dump. They took no records, no need to keep records of anything. In fact, I shudder to think about what's over at Area G, which is their main disposal site. When I used to work in nuclear material safeguards, I went out there a couple of times. You read about people that used to see dead animals and see all sorts of unusual things being disposed of [at Area G]. I saw a brand new forklift. It must have been like a $200,000 forklift. I mean one of the big ones that had gotten contaminated. I don't know how it got contaminated but it was a brand new forklift that was just thrown in this open pit. In your mind you think to yourself: boy, this stuff must really be pretty difficult stuff to deal with if you are tossing out a brand new forklift. I saw that with my own two eyes.

My father, in order to make ends meet, was one of the first recyclers, except then we called it scavenging. Nowadays you have a lot of Mexican nationals going up to the dump. I used to do that as a kid, because that's how we used to make ends meet. We were pretty poor. People look at me now and thank goodness I don't have to do what my dad had to do to make ends meet. But I remember coming to Los Alamos as a kid because my dad worked in construction, but sometimes he worked, sometimes he didn't, and he had maybe a third grade education. So he used to do a lot of different things for the people up here. In our minds, the people of Los Alamos were rich. In fact, they were so rich they did things that we never even thought about doing in our own lives. They used to buy fertilizer. You know—they used to buy manure! We used to say: "why would anybody buy manure?" This was when I was a kid. So I used to go door to door. We used to go up to Taos and fill up a truckload of manure and then we would put the manure in 100-pound sacks, potato sacks. And I used to go door to door selling manure . . . When we used to come up here we used to go to the city dump up here to look for metals. And we used to find a lot. Los Alamos used to throw away a lot of good stuff—aluminum, stuff that they were fabricating, you know, really heavy aluminum, copper, and all this stuff. Back in those days nobody was into recycling, so we used to come to the dump. And I can just imagine what I got exposed to when I was out there at the dump—I played out in it. I think it will come back to haunt me as I get older.

I think it will come back to haunt me as I get older. Caught in the grip of the nuclear uncanny, this LANL employee reveals one of the most powerful and elusive costs of radioactive nation-building. Stories about locals unknowingly contaminated by materials found in Los Alamos dump sites (either at the laboratory or town site) are common in the northern Rio Grande valley, marking simultaneously the dangerous new material content of the nuclear age, involving invisible, polluting forces, as well as the profound economic disparities in northern New Mexico. In this narrative, the wealth of Los Alamos takes on nearly mythological proportions, in its official form allowing the discarding of $200,000 tools, and in its domestic form, with residents willing to buy manure for household gardens and lawns in a region largely devoted to ranching. Contrasting this island of affluence with local poverty—of cash, of knowledge, of security in everyday life—this Nuevomexicano portrays Los Alamos as a complicated dream space, one offering a new kind of lifestyle in northern New Mexico. Living off the refuse of the laboratory, the discriminatory income of the town, and ultimately creating a career at LANL itself, two generations of this Santa Fe family have been intimately involved in the Cold War plutonium economy. Mirroring the "Free State" scenario, however, scavenging in the nuclear complex produces radioactive exposure, as found objects become dangerous forces in everyday life, polluting and contaminating the future.

For both this LANL employee and the authors of the "Free State" narrative the question of how to evaluate a polluted future, of how to assess an exposure to radiation received as a child, or a yet immeasurable contamination of land and bodies in a distant future, is of paramount importance. What connects these narratives is their negotiation of the material and psychosocial effects of the same industry, and in this case, perhaps the same institution. In this light, the complicated story of investment, desire, and injury told by one Nuevomexicano employee accounts for merely the first two generations of what is now recognized as a ten thousand-year or four hundred-generation-long process along the Rio Grande. The ultimate conclusion of *Expert Judgment on Inadvertent Human Intrusion into the Waste Isolation Pilot Plant* is that the nuclear complex now necessarily needs to be as long-lived as the longest-lived materials produced during the Cold War. In a variety of scenarios leading to environmental contamination at the WIPP site, authors underscore how a lack of expert knowledge of the site will lead to disaster. Thus, they implicitly recognize that, in terms of military nuclear waste, the Manhattan Project is now all but eternal. Consequently, DOE officials are slowly beginning to mobilize the institutional and intellectual resources to deal with post–Cold War legacies of the nuclear complex in all of their regional and millennial specificities. In this light, they are following up on Thomas Sebeok's (1984) proposal that an "atomic priesthood" be established, one whose job would simply be to maintain the knowledge of where and how nuclear materials are buried, communicating from generation to generation over at least ten thousand years, in whatever local languages come into being, the radiating dangers of the twentieth-century American Cold War.[29]

If the millennial problems of nuclear waste now offer nuclear and environmental scientists a strange new kind of job security, the question of how local communities in northern New Mexico will negotiate the regional impacts of the nuclear industry requires further examination, returning us to the question of the nuclear maquiladora. In his remarkable study of the maquiladora phenomenon on the U.S.-Mexican border, *The Terror of the Machine*, Devon Peña has shown how this highly mobile form of assembly-line factory has initiated environmental, social, and political change along the border, participating in a new global/local dynamic. Emphasizing the ecocultural effects of this new form of industry, he writes:

> Maquiladoras are postmodern factory systems. By this I mean that they are characterized by fragmented and partialized labor process, by multinational workforces, and by a pastiche-like organizational culture. In the contemporary context of labor-market structures under conditions of "flexible accumulation," maquilas are part of the international strategy adopted by capital to promote "outsourcing" of production from core to peripheral locations and social classes. (1997: 45–46)

While noting that there is no single maquila organization, he characterizes maquilas as factories dependent on a profound division between management and labor, which display a disregard for the local environment, and are particularly reliant on national borders, as multinational corporations move their production facilities to where cheap labor and loose environmental standards will increase company profits. Consequently, maquilas are largely unsustainable industries and thus subject local areas to boom and bust economic cycles and potentially dangerous workplaces, and often leave profound environmental damage in their wake. Peña states, for example, that the nearly two thousand maquilas along the U.S.-Mexican border have made the border, as a National Toxic Campaign report recently concluded, a "2,000 mile Love Canal" (quoted in Peña 1997: 279), and argues that a true assessment of the impact of maquiladoras must include the environmental damage done to watersheds, plant and animal species, and local habitats. As a land grant activist who has been involved in acequia politics in the northernmost part of the community-based irrigation system built by Spanish and later Mexican settlers along the northern Rio Grande (now southern Colorado), Peña is particularly concerned with developing sustainable industries that support rather than replace local knowledge, by which he means ethnoscientific practices and traditional social forms. Thus, his reading of the maquiladora phenomenon in the U.S.-Mexican borderlands provides an important context in which to discuss Nuevomexicano investments in LANL.

For certainly his definition of the maquila—involving a partialized labor process, a multinational workforce, and a pastiche-like organization culture—could equally well be applied to LANL. And as the past and future histories discussed in this chapter reveal, the U.S.-Mexican border is in the long run a mobile demarcation, placing LANL not only in a contemporary national-cultural borderlands, but perhaps in the near future, on an altogether different border. But while the maquila industries are devoted to the mass production of consumer commodities, LANL as a U.S. national laboratory is a much more complex and multifaceted institution, with projects ranging from basic science research in numerous domains to maintenance of the U.S. nuclear arsenal. In the post–Cold War period, LANL was "dedicated to developing world class science and technology and applying them to the nation's security and well-being. Consistent with the DOE's mission, our core mission is reducing the nuclear danger to ensure a more secure future" (LANL 1995c: 1). Over 70 percent of LANL's budget in the late 1990s was devoted to nuclear technologies, nuclear proliferation issues, or environmental cleanup. Thus, one might say that the core product officially produced at LANL through a variety of technologies, projects, and research is "security." And certainly, the wages and benefits paid by the University of California as manager of LANL are among the best in the country, cutting against the maquila comparison. Nonetheless, because the central concept of the maquila is that its products are meant for a global not a local market, it is important now to examine how concepts of "security" circulate in northern New Mexico in regard to LANL. For one of the immediate developments of the post–Cold War era was a proliferating sense of unease among Nuevomexicanos about the laboratory's future and their own role in it. Indeed, one of the implicit concerns in the Rio Grande valley after the Cold War was the local sustainability of the plutonium economy, whether LANL was committed to local, as well as national, forms of security, and whether Nuevomexicanos would be sacrificed in a post–Cold War nuclear order.

Specifically, the end of the Cold War brought to the surface long-standing concerns in the northern Rio Grande valley about whether LANL is an exclusively U.S. national, or also a New Mexican, institution. Having physically built the laboratory with three generations of laborers, workers from the valley began to discuss openly longstanding environmental and economic justice concerns about LANL, pursuing discourses that were necessarily informed by the unresolved national-cultural status of northern New Mexico dating back to the Treaty of Guadalupe Hidalgo in 1848. The uncertain future of the laboratory after the demise of the Soviet Union mobilized Nuevomexicano employees to express their claims on LANL as a specifically New Mexican institution, just as a string of revelations about Cold War environmental damage raised regional concerns about laboratory safety. As laboratory management worked to define a post–Cold War mission for the laboratory, fifty years of regional silence was replaced by a vigorous debate about the economic sustainability, environmental impacts, and morality of weapons work at LANL. Within the laboratory, a Hispanic Roundtable took on the issue of a glass ceiling in promotions and began a public discussion of institutional bias against Nuevomexicanos. Nuevomexicano employees argued that LANL was profoundly divided between scientists and management who are largely from out of state, on the one hand, and the support staff, which is made up predominantly of locals, on the other. They pointed out that of the 2,760 LANL employees making over $60,000 a year, only 110 were Nuevomexicano, and attributed this disparity to a glass ceiling at the laboratory, and specifically to a LANL practice of hiring from outside the state rather than promoting from within.

Framing the debate as a "peasants revolt," the Hispanic Roundtable demanded access to management positions in equal proportions to the ethnic makeup of northern New Mexico. A member of the Roundtable put it to me this way:

> The laboratory is a victim of its own success, in terms of creating economic and intellectual freedom in northern New Mexico. We talked about how

the lab is an asset to northern New Mexico, such an asset that back in the early days you're not going to care much about rights or equity as long as you have a job and you can provide for your family. You now have a new generation that benefited from a lot of those jobs, and that economic development. You now have a second generation of northern New Mexicans, and now a third starting, that went out and got educated, and came back, and now their expectations are higher, higher than their parents', higher than my parents'. I think the concerns were always there, the concerns about the insensitivity to local cultures, the bias and lack of respect for the cultures of northern New Mexico. And the hurt and pain associated with that was always there. But my parents certainly would never have spoken up, they didn't have the education, they didn't have anything else to fall back on and they would have been eternally grateful for some kind of employment. And then there's my generation—we've put the lab on defense for the first time in 50 years. Again, they are a victim of their own success— they created me. They created economic opportunities in northern New Mexico. I was a product of that environment. They didn't keep me poor and dumb and ignorant and now I'm saying I want more. I expect to be treated like anybody else that is working up here. I'm tired of waiting. Have there been other uprisings by the "natives"? Yes, but never like today.

The laboratory is a victim of its own success. As a multigenerational process, Nuevomexicano commitment to LANL as an institution has only grown over time, as entire families have come to be employed at the laboratory or through its contractors. The debate over access to management status at the laboratory was thus also a debate over local control of the institution in the face of wide economic disparities in northern New Mexico. Indeed, as employees challenged the hiring and promotion practices inside the U.S. national laboratory, Nuevomexicano ranchers were also fighting the U.S. Forest Service and environmental groups over access to land in northern New Mexico. At stake was the basic viability of Nuevomexicano culture and economy, and U.S. recognition of it. As one Española official put it to me when I asked about the meaning of "national security" at LANL:

> You mean national *in*security. We're insecure because we don't know if the water is clean, or if the soil we work in has been contaminated, or the air we breathe. If the system was working, we would feel secure, but we don't. If the government or the environmentalists represented our interests, we would feel safe, but we don't. We're insecure. We don't know what's been done to us, or what's coming.

We don't know what's been done to us, or what's coming. This feeling that the national system—economic, political, legal—is not working for Nuevomexicanos in Española and greater Rio Arriba County reaches back to 1848, to the terms of New Mexico's incorporation into the United States, endowing contemporary politics with the weight of that history.

New Mexico remains the poorest state in America at the start of the twenty-first century, with 24 percent of its population living under the poverty level. In Rio Arriba County, one in three people live below the poverty line, making its citizens among the poorest of the poor in America. In contrast, Los Alamos is the wealthiest county in New Mexico, enjoying the highest median income of any county in the United States and a per capita income three times that of the valley.[30] These were some of the external social and economic forces informing the internal critique of the laboratory, where cultural, economic, and educational divisions have historically separated managers and scientists from technical workers and support staff.[31] Los Alamos County has the highest number of adults with at least a bachelor's degree in the United States (LANL 1994c: 63). By contrast, only 10 percent of the adult population in Rio Arriba County has a college degree of any kind (DOE 1998b, vol. 4: 165). Los Alamos schools, right from the beginning of the Manhattan Project, have been subsidized by the DOE, as a means of maintaining educational standards for the children of laboratory scientists. The Los Alamos schools, widely acknowledged as among the best in the country, have been a significant factor in recruiting scientists to the laboratory. In contrast, the valley school systems in Española and Pojoaque have struggled with a variety of long-term social issues and funding problems. People throughout the valley have tried to place their children in Los Alamos schools accordingly.[32] But in the mid-1990s, as the DOE discussed cutting off the $7-million-a-year subsidy to the Los Alamos school system after the Cold War, the issue took on another light, as LANL employees from the valley asked why their communities did not receive similar subsidies during the Cold War. Citing a chain of institutional forces that make Nuevomexicanos both dependent on LANL and trapped within the lower end of its hierarchy, community leaders argued that Nuevomexicanos have been essential to the success of the Manhattan Project since 1943 and deserved more. Thus, as LANL officials highlighted the education requirements necessary for conducting "world-class science" and subsequent access to the highest levels of the laboratory, Nuevomexicanos from the valley forwarded a more widespread, regional feeling of disfranchisement.

This regional debate exploded in the fall of 1995 as LANL undertook the first major layoffs in the history of the laboratory. Projecting falling budgets in a post–Cold War world, LANL management decided to change the ratio of scientists to staff at the laboratory in order to prioritize research dollars. In the context of Nuevomexicano concerns about race and hiring at the laboratory, however, the Workforce Productivity Initiative, and particularly its Reduction in Force (RIF), could not have been more poorly timed or poorly executed. Following the early retirement of 838 employees in 1994, the elimination of about 500 subcontractor positions, and the voluntary separation of 251 employees (enticed by cash and tuition benefits provided by the DOE) in the summer of 1995, 256 LANL employees were laid off. Of these, 164 worked in support positions, which meant that Nuevomexicanos felt the brunt of the downsizing. As the first significant layoffs in the history of the laboratory, and only the first in a projected post–Cold War cycle of restructuring, the RIF destabilized local expectations about the future. Indeed, it seemed to confirm the worst fears of those in the valley about LANL's ability to sustain their communities and revealed internal tensions about the influence LANL has had on Nuevomexicano culture. As one middle-aged Española resident (whose father worked in construction at the laboratory and encouraged him to get technical training to pursue a career at LANL, but who refused on ethnical grounds, because he did not want to work on weapons) commented:

> The last time I drove to Los Alamos was about quitting time. There was a line of cars coming off the hill from Los Alamos that was bumper to bumper all the way to down to Española. That's how many people work there. Everybody in the valley has gotten used to thinking that the lab is forever. We now have three generations of men who work at the lab. Men working alongside their fathers and grandfathers. Now with the lay-off it is like waking up with a bad hangover. The party is over. For those of us who don't work at Los Alamos it's hard to sympathize with all the complaining that's going on right now. I mean we lose our jobs and we don't get $20,000 in severance pay and a few months to look for a new job, we're just out on the street.

Everybody thinks the lab is forever. In all, nearly one thousand workers were off the laboratory payroll in 1995, demonstrating the first real instability in the plutonium economy, a growth industry since 1943, and giving the appearance that LANL was, if not a sinking ship, one that was no longer reliable. As the culmination of a fierce year of debate about race and hiring at the laboratory, some in the valley portrayed the RIF as nothing less than a "declaration of war" on northern New Mexico, and mobilized accordingly. In doing so, they implicitly refused to accept a future in which LANL performs locally as a de facto maquiladora. Former LANL employees banded together as Citizens for LANL Employee Rights

(CLER) and 102 of them sued, claiming that the layoffs were illegally executed and retaliatory, a purge of laboratory critics, older employees, and Nuevomexicanos.

In the post–Cold War period, Nuevomexicano activists pushed to address longstanding concerns about LANL along multiple fronts, emphasizing a need for regional control of the laboratory and for remedies to a perceived "second-class status" at the national laboratory. Nuevomexicano state legislators discussed taxing LANL and reworking school funding formulas to move, in effect, the DOE payments from Los Alamos schools to the valley. CLER took on the issue of laboratory management, appealing to the DOE in Washington directly. They also challenged the terms of the University of California management contract with LANL. Framed by recent California resolutions 187 and 209, which prevented illegal immigrants from receiving state services and which overturned affirmative action programs, activists argued that the current LANL contract made northern New Mexico a de facto "colony" of the University of California. As part of a larger campaign to "make LANL part of New Mexico," community activists argued in favor of local management of the laboratory, perhaps by the University of New Mexico, and demanded that the DOE put the LANL management contract out to an open bid. In an open letter to Secretary of Energy, Hazel O'Leary, in June 1996, CLER and nine other NGOs argued that:

> the 50-plus year practice of essentially automatically extending the LANL management contract to UC has perpetuated a status quo nurtured by a half a century of arrogance, secrecy, and privilege, a status quo represented by a corporate culture firmly rooted in denial. This lack of accountability has created an insensitive corporate culture that has virtually destroyed all trust between LANL and the leadership, people and communities of New Mexico, as well as with other stakeholders. It is a culture that can no longer be trusted to do the right thing, e.g. treat people fairly, pursue the "best science," respect the environment, and embrace meaningful contract reform.[33]

Meanwhile, LANL lawyers argued that in the present context, LANL could not get a "fair trial" in northern New Mexico and had the RIF trial moved south. CLER countered that "fairness" was indeed the issue, and pointed out that while the laboratory had unlimited tax dollars with which to fight the RIF lawsuit, many of those involved in the suit were unable to work and financially strapped. CLER representatives feared that LANL's billion-dollar-a-year budget and endless legal resources would prevent them from having their day in court, as financial limitations would force individuals out of the lawsuit. Thus, at this specific moment in the mid-1990s, LANL's legal engagement with Nuevomexicanos echoed the legal battles of the late nineteenth century in which Nuevomexicanos, unable to pay taxes or the legal fees necessary to secure title on land grants, lost their holdings to Anglo lawyers manipulating the U.S. legal system (see Ebright 1994).

While Nuevomexicanos challenged LANL in courts, events outside of New Mexico would fundamentally change the local context of the debates around LANL. The Clinton administration's commitment to a global Comprehensive Test Ban Treaty resulted in a new mission for the laboratory (SBSS) and a newfound financial security. For while underground nuclear testing was no longer possible, over the next decade the United States committed to spending over $70 billion in support of the SBSS program, thereby beginning work on a new nuclear complex for the twenty-first century. Thus, in contrast to immediate post–Cold War expectations of a major downsizing of the nuclear complex, by the late 1990s, the plutonium economy was once again a growth industry in New Mexico, promising larger budgets than at the height of the Cold War, at least until 2010. Local critics of the U.S. nuclear program portrayed the SBSS program as a "welfare" program for weapons scientists, who now have nothing left to do but watch nuclear weapons age (albeit through a new state-of-the-art nuclear complex). In doing so, critics of the SBSS program in New Mexico took issue with those in the laboratory that portrayed Nuevomexicano protests of the RIF as signs of a "welfare" state mentality in the valley. Each position has an element of truth, for life in northern New Mexico remains dependent on "foreign" capital, on money from Washington, D.C., or tourism. For those maintaining long-term cultural investments in the northern Rio Grande valley, or who have experienced national-cultural rupture and periodic invasion since 1848, the stark reality is that the economy of northern New Mexico is driven by outside funding, involving numerous forms of federal support, and thus is, in important ways, outside of local control. Without a federal commitment to military nuclear science or to fighting poverty, life in the northern Rio Grande valley for many would simply be unsustainable, a realization that energizes the vociferous regional debate about the future of LANL.

As the University of California renewed its first post–Cold War contract with the DOE for management of Los Alamos, Livermore, and Lawrence Berkeley National Laboratories in 1996, it made future contract renewals conditional on LANL addressing regional concerns in northern New Mexico about employment and environmental safety. The University of California established an office in Los Alamos, staking out its first permanent presence in New Mexico, and began to conduct community outreach efforts to engage local concerns. Similarly, LANL and the DOE set up offices in Taos, Española, and Santa Fe, making themselves available to local community interests and providing information about the environmental impacts of the laboratory. As part of this effort to integrate LANL into northern New Mexico, the University of California, LANL, and the DOE created the Los Alamos National Laboratory Foundation, a project to fund education and community groups in northern New Mexico. At the same time, the UC pushed to settle the ongoing RIF lawsuits. CLER eventually took its complaint about the RIF to the Department of Labor's Office of Federal Contract Compliance Programs, which in May 1998 ruled that LANL had not followed its own layoff criteria in the 1995 RIF, and had disproportionately laid off Hispanic employees. In settling the lawsuits, LANL agreed to pay nearly $3 million to the 102 employees involved in the suit and to rehire almost half of them.[34]

After more than fifty years of mutual investment, the debates between Nuevomexicanos and laboratory managers ultimately concerned whether LANL was exclusively a U.S. national, or also a New Mexican, institution. The terms of this debate were informed by historical engagements between Nuevomexicanos and the federal government, and implicitly interrogated whether the plutonium economy after the Cold War was to be based on a maquiladora kind of exploitation of local labor, or was to be a mutual project, one that addresses local concerns about economic and environmental justice. The RIF lawsuits, and the community activism they produced, demonstrated to all that Nuevomexicanos will now fight to maintain access to LANL and to have a role in shaping its post–Cold War future. Similarly, the scale of the plutonium economy was revealed to involve not just LANL and the residents of the Rio Grande valley, but also officials from the University of California and the DOE. Thus, much of the silence and insular character of LANL operations during the Cold War was broken, allowing a broader regional debate about the future of the laboratory and its local effects. As underscored by the "Free State of Chihuahua" narrative, the real challenge of the post–Cold War order in New Mexico is creating a plutonium economy that is as sustainable as the longest-lived radionuclides, ensuring that the tumultuous debates of the post–Cold War period are but the initial mobilizations of a multimillennial social process along the northern Rio Grande.

NUEVOMEXICANO FUTURES IN THE PLUTONIUM ECONOMY

An acquaintance at Los Alamos labs who engineers weapons black x'd a
mark where I live on his office map. Star-wars humor.
—Jimmy Santiago Baca, "Choices"

This passage from Albuquerque poet Jimmy Santiago Baca explores
the impact of the plutonium economy on Nuevomexicano experience,
marking the dual reality of new material possibilities (cultural, economic, technoscientific) since 1943 along the northern Rio Grande, but
also of new kinds of sacrifices. For the weapons scientist in this poem is
presented not as an Anglo outsider, an immigrant with no ties to the
land, but as a Nuevomexicano, one who works at Los Alamos, in part,
to maintain the financial viability of his ranch, exchanging "muddy
boots and patched jeans for a white intern's coat and black polished
shoes." Blurring the distinction between land-based and technoscientific
cultures, Baca asks what is now being given up in the negotiation of
modernity in northern New Mexico. His weapons scientist suggests later
in the poem that he would have lost his land without the money from a
Los Alamos job, and now he imagines buying more land and equipment.
But, for Baca, this is somehow not a story of advancement, but of loss,
of accepting a different way of being, one that Baca cannot share in.
Thus, the poem ultimately registers a loss of cultural cohesion, and articulates an illegitimacy, even as it acknowledges economic empowerment
and renewed commitment to the land. The X on the map, in the historical context of northern New Mexico, carries innumerable possible resonances—from military assault, to legal disfranchisement and loss of
land, to tourist gentrification and toxic contamination, to cultural assimilation—but in any case, it suggests the possibility of an absolute erasure,
of an external and unreachable force conspiring to control or eliminate
the local.

This is a particularly powerful, regionally inflected image of what I
have called radioactive nation-building. By this I mean the long-term
effects of participating in national-cultural logics that mobilize resources
in the name of security and community, but that do so in ways that are
unsustainable and that create both social and material toxicity. The
material, cultural, and psychological effects of the plutonium economy
on Nuevomexicano communities in northern New Mexico reveal the
complex ways in which plutonium has become a strange new signifier for
national standing in the early twenty-first century. Plutonium is now a

force that permeates cross-cultural relations along the northern Rio Grande, one that offers middle-class livelihoods, the possibility of taking back land and revitalizing Nuevomexicano culture through economic empowerment, or of losing it altogether through radioactive contamination, outsider gentrification, and cultural assimilation. While LANL has offered important economic opportunities for Nuevomexicanos since 1943, the end of the Cold War initiated a formal debate about the sustainability of the plutonium economy, and the long-term viability of Nuevomexicano culture within it. As such, Nuevomexicano engagements with LANL forward a new articulation of national security, defining it not simply as a question of how to protect the territorial borders of the state, but also as one of making a diverse citizenry feel politically, economically, culturally, and territorially secure within their nation.

5 Backtalking to the National Fetish
The Rise of Antinuclear Activism in Santa Fe

The most serious impediment to citizen participation has been secrecy. Although much technical data on nuclear weapons has been made public through the arms control process, there remains a dearth of information on the infrastructure, war plans, and the peacetime practices of the nuclear system. Officials have kept quiet for an obvious reason: It's going on in everyone's backyard. Secrecy obscures the link between a local inconvenience or eyesore and world events. It is the prime weapon in a calculated effort to discourage public inquiry.
—Willam Arkin and Richard Fieldhouse, *Nuclear Battlefields*

Assertive back talk turns a flat reading of signs into a performative space of claims and counterclaims, mutual misreadings, and momentary excesses that push things to the limit of the "ordinary" and draw attention to a space of unseen forces.
—Kathleen Stewart, *A Space on the Side of the Road*

Wearing matching blue windbreakers emblazoned with the icon of a Santa Fe–based antinuclear group, a seven-member "citizen verification team" arrived to conduct their first impromptu inspection of nuclear weapons programs at Los Alamos National Laboratory (LANL) (Figure 5.1) in March 1998. Modeled on the United Nations Special Commission (UNSCOM) investigators (then charged with monitoring Iraq's weapons of mass destruction programs), this self-authorized verification team identified the Plutonium Facility, the Chemistry and Metallurgy Research Building, and the Dual Axis Radiographic Hydrodynamic Test Facility as possible sites of U.S. nuclear proliferation, and demanded access to these buildings as well as to documents concerning the U.S. nuclear program. LANL officials refused each request from the citizen verification team, turning them away at the front gate of each facility, stating that it was against U.S. law for "uncleared" persons to be given access to classified

5.1. Citizen Verification Team at Los Alamos National Laboratory. (Photograph by Joseph Masco)

national security material.[1] The citizen inspection team hardly expected admittance. Rather, they sought to bring public attention to what they perceive to be dangerous contradictions in post–Cold War U.S. nuclear policy. Their actions were designed to underscore that U.S. national security is pursued in the name of citizens who have no access to its internal logics, costs, or future planning. They also sought to focus media attention on the fact that even as the United States threatens other nations with war and economic sanctions for pursuing weapons of mass destruction in the post–Cold War period, the United States remains not only committed to the bomb but also to modernizing the nuclear arsenal at LANL.

Linking the global and local through a performative nuclear critique, these activists place the bomb at the center of a world system based on secrecy, a military-industrial economy, and the threat of apocalyptic violence, rather than a democratic process. Organized by the Los Alamos Study Group (LASG), a Santa Fe-based NGO, the inspection team formally declared its purpose to be: "1) to educate the public about the United States' own weapons of mass destruction; 2) to call for international transparency regarding all programs which design, produce, or stockpile weapons of mass destruction; 3) to inspire a process of societal verification to bolster non-proliferation and disarmament efforts."[2] Thus, the activists not only argued that the world's state-of-the-art nuclear weapons program needs policing, they took their critique a step further. By blurring the distinction between Iraqi nuclear laboratories and LANL, activists mobilized to redeploy the concept of the "rogue or terrorist state," which has provided the primary public justification for maintaining the U.S. nuclear arsenal after the Cold War (Klare 1995). Indeed, by word and deed, these "UNSCOM-style" inspectors have identified the United States itself as a rogue nation, one that continues to threaten the world with weapons of mass destruction, even after signing nuclear nonproliferation agreements, a state that is modernizing its nuclear arsenal even while demanding the disarmament of other nations. LANL becomes, in this presentation, not a means of preserving global order (through deterrence and containment) but rather an instrument of nuclear proliferation, one continuing to fuel the arms race and increasing the risk of nuclear war.

This kind of theatrical backtalking to the nuclear complex is a post–Cold War phenomenon in northern New Mexico, marking a fundamental change in the regional politics surrounding LANL. Fusing environmental concerns with a moral critique of the bomb, Santa Fe NGOs mobilized in the 1990s to challenge the U.S. nuclear complex at every turn and articulate alternative notions of security. For unlike Nuevomexicano and Pueblo activists, who maintain complex investments in LANL requiring difficult (and at times impossible) acts of translation between communities, antinuclear NGOs in Santa Fe are more resolute in their condemnation of the laboratory. LANL is, for many Santa Fe–based antinuclear activists, a source of pollution: philosophically, as the origin point of the bomb; politically, as the center of the post–Cold War U.S. nuclear project; and literally, as the source of radioactive contamination. With full-time staffs and connections to a national network of antinuclear, peace, and environmental groups, Santa Fe NGOs have, in the post–Cold War period, provided the first consistent public oversight and critique of laboratory nuclear projects in New Mexico. Indeed, these NGOs mobilize to learn the language of the nuclear complex in order to provide a counterdiscourse, one grounded not in the logics of national security or technoscience but in radical democratic critique.

After a half century of classified nuclear weapons research in New Mexico, the first project for many activists at the end of the Cold War was simply to make the nuclear project visible, to reveal the size, scope, and legacies of the Cold War plutonium economy. Compare, for example, Figures 5.2 and 5.3. Figure 5.2 is a billboard located on the road from Santa Fe to Los Alamos promoting tourism in Los Alamos. Declaring "Explore Los Alamos: We've got Enchantment Down to a Science," the image plays off the official "land of enchantment" mythologizing of New Mexico, while

5.2. Los Alamos tourism billboard. (Photograph by Joseph Masco)

5.3. Los Alamos Study Group's "Welcome to New Mexico" billboard.
(Photograph by Joseph Masco)

portraying Los Alamos as a site of outdoor recreation and technoscience.
The billboard forwards an image of Los Alamos as a pristine natural space,
downplaying the presence of the nuclear weapons laboratory that has made
it world-famous. Figure 5.3, however, provides an activist counterdiscourse

to this kind of tourist promotion. Located on the main exit from the Albuquerque airport, the "Welcome to New Mexico" billboard thwarts the utopian image presented in the Los Alamos sign by declaring the state to be nothing less than the "America's Nuclear Weapons Colony."[3] The "Welcome to New Mexico" sign alerts visitors to a hidden radioactive presence in New Mexico, and is part of a larger activist campaign to mobilize New Mexico's tourist and commuter economies politically through nuclear critique. Another act of theatrical backtalking by the Los Alamos Study Group, the billboard campaign works to confront nuclear workers traveling between Los Alamos and Sandia National Laboratories, while also provoking tourists to look more closely at the romanticized New Mexican landscape. In doing so, it formally links the two largest sources of income in New Mexico—the bomb and tourism—fracturing a code of silence that has allowed the "land of enchantment" mythology to occlude nuclear weapons, waste, and militarism since 1943.

As a result of this kind of antinuclear activism, the Manhattan Project became more visible to communities across race and class lines in New Mexico after the Cold War, producing the first possibility of a regional critique of the U.S. nuclear project. However, while contributing to regional, national, and international debates about nuclear weapons, and articulating alternative definitions of security, Santa Fe NGOs also witnessed a resurgent nuclear mission in post–Cold War Los Alamos. Indeed, the post–Cold War period demonstrated that a smaller U.S. nuclear program nationally produced an expanded U.S. nuclear mission in New Mexico, as LANL became the consolidated center of the U.S. nuclear project. For New Mexican activists, the question that remains is whether or not the end of the Soviet Union can enable a real nuclear public sphere around LANL, a political space in which to engage the terms and local impacts of the U.S. nuclear project. For the paradox of antinuclear activism at the center of the nuclear complex has been that a successful mobilization at the national level produces an expanding local plutonium economy. The post–Cold War challenge for antinuclear NGOs has consequently been to pursue radical democratic action while negotiating diverse experiences of the nuclear uncanny in the face of an expanding U.S. nuclear mission at Los Alamos.

THE POST–COLD WAR MOMENT

As the birthplace of the atomic bomb, it is surprising that LANL did not provoke the kind of antinuclear activism evidenced at Lawrence Livermore National Laboratory (LLNL) or the Nevada Test Site during the

Cold War. Indeed, while these sites frequently evoked social protests involving thousands of people, and at times, nearly permanent activist encampments, LANL experienced only occasional signs of antinuclear organizing, usually around the anniversary of the bombing of Hiroshima, and even then, rarely exceeding two dozen people (see Rosenthal 1990: 117–22).[4] Although it is the center of the U.S. nuclear complex, New Mexico as a whole did not generate an internal antinuclear movement until the early 1980s, when the proposed construction of the Waste Isolation Pilot Plant (WIPP), a permanent nuclear waste facility, near Carlsbad promised to fill New Mexican roads with nuclear waste trucks, energizing the formation of several NGOs. At the same time, the Reagan-era arms race was provoking some of the largest social demonstrations ever seen either in the United States or in Europe: over 750,000 people marched against nuclear weapons in New York in June 1982, while millions participated in peace demonstrations in London, Rome, Madrid, and Amsterdam.[5] These social movements illustrate how profoundly American attitudes toward nuclear weapons as a whole have changed over the first half century of the nuclear age.

In 1954, half of all Americans believed that the development of the hydrogen bomb made World War less likely, and an equal number believed the United States could win a nuclear war.[6] By 1982, however, two-thirds of the American public felt that the atomic bomb was an "unfortunate" development, and 89 percent believed nuclear war to be fundamentally unwinnable, agreeing that a nuclear conflict with the Soviet Union would lead to the total destruction of both countries (Yankelovich, Kingston, and Garvey 1984). The most recent post–Cold War study of public attitudes toward nuclear weapons concludes that 77 percent of registered voters believe the world now would be safer without nuclear weapons, with two-thirds favoring a reduction or total elimination of the U.S. nuclear arsenal (Henry L. Stimson Center 1998).[7] Given this social trajectory, it is particularly striking, therefore, that for almost forty years weapons scientists in northern New Mexico worked in a largely uncritical social space. This reality both illustrates the economic power of the nuclear complex in northern New Mexico, and draws into sharper relief the proliferation of nuclear concerns witnessed in northern New Mexico at the end of the Cold War.

For by the mid-1990s, LANL weapons scientists could identify Santa Fe–based antinuclear NGOs to me as the single greatest threat to the implementation of LANL's post–Cold War nuclear mission. Within a few short years, in fact, antinuclear activists in northern New Mexico had mobilized from an occasional presence, easily ignored by the nuclear complex, into a significant regulatory voice in policy debates about the future mission of LANL. Clinton administration efforts to increase the declassification of Cold War materials as well as to assess the health and environmental costs of the Cold War nuclear project within the United States provided an entirely new political context for activism. The application of environmental protection laws to the nuclear complex after the Cold War required formal studies and public input on all new laboratory projects—opening up a new legal space for communities to engage LANL through a mandatory public hearing process. Indeed, the mid-1990s represent a rare moment in the nuclear age in which citizens representing a wide spectrum of interests were in direct conversation with policy makers over the environmental legacies and programmatic terms of the bomb. An eruption of post–Cold War discourse from local communities in New Mexico produced the first possibility of a nuclear public sphere around LANL, allowing activists to mobilize a diverse citizenry to take on the past and future terms of U.S. nuclear policy in the region. For northern New Mexicans, it was an unprecedented political moment, one that offered almost daily revelations about the effects of the plutonium economy on their lives, and that made the terms of the nuclear future an issue of profound cross-cultural negotiation and debate.

In part, this transformation in local attitudes participated in the broader shift in antinuclear activism in the late 1980s, from a primary concern with peace and disarmament issues to a larger engagement with the environmental and health effects of the nuclear complex. This shift in focus was a response both to the Chernobyl accident and to a series of revelations about serious environmental damage at several U.S. nuclear production sites. In 1988, Hanford, Rocky Flats, and the Fernald Feed Materials Production Center in Ohio were all shown to have unprecedented environmental contamination, resulting in lawsuits from impacted communities as well as the eventual reorientation of these Department of Energy (DOE) sites from nuclear production work to their own environmental cleanup. Across the United States, the scale of the plutonium economy was beginning to be revealed in its environmental impacts as the Cold War came to a close, replacing concerns of Soviet aggression in many U.S. communities with fear of the local health effects of the U.S. nuclear complex itself. Official estimates of the cost of cleaning up the Cold War nuclear complex ranged from $100 to $380 billion at the end of the Cold War, and the DOE was forced to admit that some sites were beyond environmental remediation given current technology, and were, thus, de facto national sacrifice zones.[8] Schwartz (1998: 355) has concluded that the total cost of dealing with the Cold War nuclear complex will be at least as great as the cost of building the Cold War arsenal itself, and given the multimillennial half-lives of some nuclear materials, presents a greater technoscientific challenge than designing the bomb.

In Santa Fe, fears about the environmental legacy of Cold War nuclear science at LANL fused with regional economic uncertainty about the future of LANL after the fall of the Soviet Union. In 1989, Concerned Citizens for Nuclear Safety (CCNS), which had been founded a decade earlier in response to the WIPP project, mobilized to stop a radioactive waste incinerator from starting operations at LANL. A year later, after the Berlin Wall came down, the LASG formed, also in Santa Fe, to foment a regional dialogue about nuclear disarmament and the conversion of LANL to a peacetime mission. These NGOs helped mobilize a regional coalition of thirty-two activist groups, not only to demand environmental analyses of LANL's Cold War legacies, but also to force the laboratory and DOE to justify new weapons projects, in terms of both their programmatic need and environmental safety. The All People's Coalition, for example, an Albuquerque-based group, produced a "tourist warning" map of New Mexico that declared it to be a "national nuclear sacrifice zone" (see Figure 5.4), illustrating not only the scale of the nuclear economy but also the statewide potential for political action. In aiming the map at tourists, activists sought to link formally the military and leisure economies in New Mexico in a new form of mutual critique. This kind of activism created a powerful new local dynamic, as the end of the Cold War coincided with the end of the design life of several LANL nuclear facilities. In the early 1990s, local communities were learning about the need for a projected $2 billion cleanup of the Pajarito Plateau at the same time laboratory officials began pursuing a new generation of nuclear facilities in a new political and regulatory environment and activists began mobilizing the first public critique of the laboratory.

The antinuclear critique gained new audiences in the fall of 1993 with the publication of Eileen Welsome's Pulitzer Prize–winning articles in the *Albuquerque Tribune*, detailing covert human plutonium experiments conducted on eighteen American citizens during the Cold War (see Welsome 1999). For the next several years, local papers in New Mexico ran almost daily stories on the effects of nuclear fallout, human experiments within the nuclear complex, and the environmental impacts of military nuclear science—revealing the cultural and material effects of a half century of government secrecy. The Welsome series also provoked a radical change in nuclear policy in Washington, D.C., where the first post–Cold War Secretary of Energy, Hazel O'Leary, committed to an unprecedented openness initiative at the DOE after reading about the human plutonium experiments. This involved a massive declassification project (using the

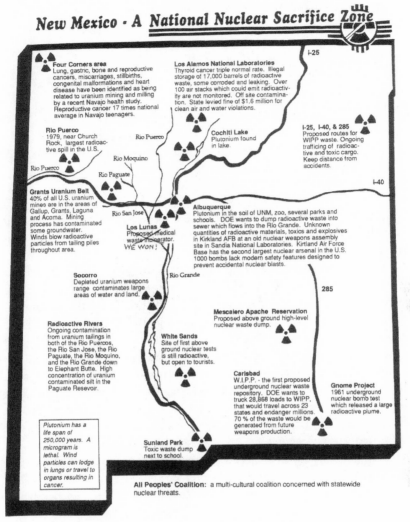

Four Corners area
Lung, gastric, bone and reproductive cancers, miscarriages, stillbirths, congenital malformations and heart disease have been identified as being related to uranium mining and milling by a recent Navajo health study. Reproductive cancer 17 times national average in Navajo teenagers.

Los Alamos National Laboratories
Thyroid cancer triple normal rate. Illegal storage of 17,000 barrels of radioactive waste, some corroded and leaking. Over 100 air stacks which could emit radioactivity are not monitored. Off site contamination. State levied fine of $1.6 million for clean air and water violations.

I-25

Rio Puerco
1979, near Church Rock, largest radioactive spill in the U.S.

Rio Puerco

Rio Puerco

Rio Moquino

Rio Paguate

Cochiti Lake
Plutonium found in lake.

I-25, I-40, & 285
Proposed routes for WIPP waste. Ongoing trafficking of radioactive and toxic cargo. Keep distance from accidents.

I-40

Grants Uranium Belt
40% of all U.S. uranium mines are in the areas of Gallup, Grants, Laguna and Acoma. Mining process has contaminated some groundwater. Winds blow radioactive particles from tailing piles throughout area.

Rio San Jose

Los Lunas
Proposed medical waste incinerator.
WE WON!

Albuquerque
Plutonium in the soil of UNM, zoo, several parks and schools. DOE wants to dump radioactive waste into sewer which flows into the Rio Grande. Unknown quantities of radioactive materials, toxics and explosives in Kirkland AFB at an old nuclear weapons assembly site in Sandia National Laboratories. Kirtland Air Force Base has the second largest nuclear arsenal in the U.S. 1000 bombs lack modern safety features designed to prevent accidental nuclear blasts.

Socorro
Depleted uranium weapons range contaminates large areas of water and land.

Rio Grande

285

Mescalero Apache Reservation
Proposed above ground high-level nuclear waste dump.

Radioactive Rivers
Ongoing contamination from uranium tailings in both of the Rio Puercos, the Rio San Jose, the Rio Paguate, the Rio Moquino, and the Rio Grande down to Elephant Butte. High concentration of uranium contaminated silt in the Paguate Resevoir.

White Sands
Site of first above ground nuclear tests is still radioactive, but open to tourists.

Carlsbad
W.I.P.P. - the first proposed underground nuclear waste repository. DOE wants to truck 28,868 loads to WIPP, that would travel across 23 states and endanger millions. 70 % of the waste would be generated from future weapons production.

Gnome Project
1961 underground nuclear bomb test which released a large radioactive plume.

Plutonium has a life span of 250,000 years. A microgram is lethal. Wind particles can lodge in lungs or travel to organs resulting in cancer.

Sunland Park
Toxic waste dump next to school.

All Peoples' Coalition: a multi-cultural coalition concerned with statewide nuclear threats.

5.4. "Tourist Warning" map. (Courtesy of All Peoples' Coalition)

World Wide Web), as well as a new emphasis on environmental review of DOE projects and greater engagement with local communities and antinuclear NGOs.[9]

Put simply, while LANL officials mobilized to define a new mission and build a post–Cold War nuclear complex, they were subjected to the first steady criticism and public review in the institution's history. Moreover, on environmental and health issues, the laboratory had simply lost credibility for many New Mexicans, becoming more associated with a half century of deception and public sacrifice than with a science-based form of national security. As one activist explained it:

> Los Alamos, and the nuclear weapons complex as a whole, has always privileged nuclear weapons research, design, and production way above safety and health concerns. I think there is a lack of political and cultural will to stringently meet environmental health and safety requirements. Without whistle blowers and citizen's suits, I don't think we would have progressed as far as we have today. Although, I would hasten to add, we still have a long, long way to go.

We have a long, long way to go. Or, as another Santa Fe activist concluded: "Hanford, Rocky Flats, the downwinders can all be laid at Los Alamos' doorstep. They were the technical oversight for the nuclear complex. People at Los Alamos knew what was going on and did nothing." As the intellectual center of the nuclear complex, all the deleterious effects of the national Cold War nuclear production are linked in these statements as a critique of LANL, making the pursuit of the bomb contingent on the sacrifice of communities and ecologies. Activists also present themselves here as the only oversight on a state nuclear project that uses secrecy and "national security" discourse to protect itself from basic forms of accountability. For antinuclear activists, an inherent problem in engaging the nuclear complex is its impenetrability, as classification and security measures are designed to prevent a public dialogue about the specific details of U.S. national security policy.

Consequently, opening up Los Alamos to dissenting viewpoints was part of a general activist project throughout the 1990s. CCNS was a principal organizer for a major 1993 conference entitled "LANL 2000: The Role of the Laboratory in the 21st Century," which included officials from LANL, the DOE, New Mexico's congressional delegation, Pueblo governments, Nuevomexicano representatives, and activist groups from throughout northern New Mexico. Taking place on the fiftieth anniversary of the start of the Manhattan Project, this was the first regional dialogue about the long-term effects, and future mission, of LANL. The LASG also sponsored panels in Los Alamos involving nationally recognized figures from the antinuclear and disarmament movements. In part, these efforts are a response to what Hugh Gusterson has called the "expert rationalism" informing military nuclear science (1996a: 204–5), an activist effort to rally outside experts (as well as local community leaders) to engage weapons scientists on their own terms. These strategies also reveal that for many Santa Fe activists the first achievement of the Manhattan Project was not the atomic bomb, but the institutionalization of a system of government secrecy, enabling a curtailing of democratic process when it comes to U.S. national security policy (see Adler 1994; Burr, Blanton, and Schwartz 1998). One activist described the importance of secrecy within the nuclear complex this way:

> Secrecy has multiple uses. It cordons off workers, keeps them under control, it keeps out the public, it creates a priesthood, it protects against inquiry, and can hide lousy work. Only those who are allowed into the system would actually know enough to actually criticize it, so the budget can't be attacked. The end result of all this is that secrecy is used to define the debate. We hear this all the time at the lab, about the "gulf of ignorance" that separates us from the scientists with the real knowledge. But everything to do with nuclear weapons is "born secret," meaning that it is classified without review, and the boundary between what is secret and what is not secret is also secret.

The boundary between what is secret and what is not secret is also secret. Thus, antinuclear activists feel that U.S. citizens are eliminated from the decision-making process because federal authorities can argue that by definition citizens never have the information necessary to make informed statements about U.S. national security policy. The bomb becomes, for these activists, the technoscientific evidence of a derailment in democratic process in the United States, making their work a means not only of dealing with nuclear fear but also of transforming society itself.

Santa Fe activists consequently engage the space of northern New Mexico with a very specific understanding of the linkages between local, national, and global processes. To challenge the terms of nuclear science at LANL is to open up a conceptual space for a new form of global security. Because of the classified nature of nuclear weapons work, NGOs are usually reacting to established policy, rather than shaping it. This means that there is a constant tension over where to address the nuclear complex: at LANL, where managers and weapons scientists work directly on the bomb; in Oakland, where the University of California executives who manage Los Alamos meet; in Washington, D.C., at the DOE, Department of Defense (DOD), and the White House; or internationally, at the United Nations and the World Court. In the 1990s, Santa Fe NGOs developed a multitiered approach to effecting change in the nuclear complex, relying on a combination of political mobilizing to affect key votes in Congress, negative publicity about LANL's environmental impacts in New Mexico, and lawsuits designed to force DOE and LANL officials to justify each new nuclear science project at LANL in terms of both national need and environmental safety. Thus, while uniformly acknowledging that nuclear weapons are abhorrent, antinuclear activists choose to learn the language of the nuclear complex in order to challenge its logics, and thus, paradoxically, choose to immerse themselves in the minute details of nuclear science, national security policy, and programmatic planning at LANL. This is a tedious pursuit, as activists patrol the field of public documentation looking for clues about U.S. nuclear policy, while deploying the Freedom of Information Act to force the declassification of policy documents.

Santa Fe NGOs also rely on national networks of peace and disarmament groups as sources of information and mobilization. In 1995, for example, activists in Santa Fe and Livermore discovered a document on a new DOE World Wide Web site that they interpreted as directly contradicting the current U.S. nuclear policy, which declared a moratorium on the production of new nuclear weapons. NGOs quickly mobilized this information into an international issue, entering into the global negotiation of a Comprehensive Test Ban Treaty. As one activist described this action:

> We downloaded this thing from the DOE website. And in this technical planning document they were describing future weapons projects, which made us angry because we had been told so many times, "oh no, we're not designing any new weapons." And now it is straightforwardly said that existing weapons will be replaced with updated weapons. But they're not going to be "new" weapons; they're just going to be "modifications." So after talking with another activist group, we e-mailed it to Greenpeace, who sent it to a long mail list around the world. And later we heard, that it had been the subject of a newspaper article in Bombay. We heard that people were waving this article in Washington at the Department of Energy telling them that their stockpile stewardship program was raising waves around the world. The DOE said the document was old, that it was up on the web site by mistake, and didn't really pertain to real things today. They said the document dates from 1993, but it had language in it that was not used in 1993. The language also closely paralleled language in the most recent congressional budget request, which was at that time a month or so old. So we had this battle about whether it was new or whether it was old. Eventually the DOE admitted they were wrong. The newspapers knew they weren't telling the truth. The DOE then shut down their web page for months to hunt through it for other incriminating documents. It was a big deal.

It was a big deal. What is remarkable in this narrative is the simple chain of events, as language within an obscure DOE planning document is mobilized into a global discussion of U.S. nuclear policy. It shows the political power of simply paying attention, of attending to the visible signs of the U.S. nuclear project, and of broadbanding the details to the world. Armed with this and other information about U.S. nuclear programs, India did, in fact, resist signing the Comprehensive Test Ban Treaty because they viewed it as a treaty that ensured the nuclear status quo, allowing nuclear powers to maintain their arsenals while denying non-nuclear powers the right to test their own.[10] In this case, Santa Fe activists mobilized locally to put international pressure on the U.S. nuclear complex. In the mid-1990s, Santa Fe NGOs continued this tactic by lobbying the World Court in The Hague to rule that a first-strike use of nuclear weapons is a violation of international law.[11] Activists reveal in each of these actions a basic distrust of U.S. officials when it comes to U.S. nuclear policy, noting a history of public deception and abuse of military power.

Santa Fe activists point out, for example, that the majority of weapons in the current U.S. nuclear stockpile were designed after the United States signed the Nuclear Non-Proliferation Treaty in 1970, in which the United States agreed to pursue nuclear disarmament at the earliest opportunity. Similarly, they critique the terms of post–Cold War arms reduction treaties as locking in place an excessive U.S. nuclear arsenal, making such agreements an act of preserving the nuclear status quo rather than reducing it. As one activist put it:

> If we should succeed in dismantling all the weapons that President Bush and President Yeltsin agreed to in the Start II Agreement—the most drastic reduction now envisioned—we will get down to a strategic arsenal of about 3,500 weapons and a number of other weapons on the side. If you add up the nuclear weapons of all the nuclear powers after the Start II reductions, you will find that even after 25 years of the nonproliferation treaty, we will have more nuclear weapons than we had when the treaty was signed . . . What can you do with those 3,500 weapons? Well, if you go through the explosive yield of those 3,500 weapons, you find that you can pretty much nuke every city in the world completely and simultaneously . . . Why would we ever need or want this many weapons?

The United States can nuke every city in the world. Like other residents of the northern Rio Grande valley who evoke international treaties (notably, the Treaty of Guadalupe Hidalgo) in their negotiations with federal authorities, members of Santa Fe–based, antinuclear NGOs want to hold the United States accountable to its agreements. However, antinuclear activists are a double-edged sword for many in northern New Mexico; they provide important environmental information, legal resources, and political mobilizations, but also threaten the stability of LANL and, thus, the regional economy. In part this regional tension is due to the fact that Santa Fe activists tend to advocate a global logic when it comes to nuclear weapons, replacing the nuanced claims on place that long-term New Mexican cultures maintain with a postnational vision of global security. Thus, while Santa Fe NGOs attempt to mobilize a multiracial, multi-interest coalition of activist groups in northern New Mexico, some Pueblo and Nuevomexicano residents see them as an unpredictable presence in their own right. For some, antinuclear NGOs mirror back the global-local logics of the nuclear complex but in inverted form, for rather than imagining nuclear weapons as a means of protecting the United States in a global order, they see the local work of Los Alamos weapons scientists as, perhaps, the greatest threat to global security. In both cases, the local can be overshadowed by the global, as specific cultural investments are bypassed in favor of a totalizing vision of (in)security.

THE PSYCHIC TOXICITY OF PLUTONIUM

While the end of the Cold War, and new public scrutiny of the U.S. nuclear complex as a whole, certainly informed the new antinuclear activism in Santa Fe, another important factor was the changing population of the city itself. Santa Fe County grew from 75, 000 in 1980 to over 120,000 by 1998. Much of this population growth was from Anglo immigration, responding to the city of Santa Fe's cultural cache, marking a profound shift in the cultural and racial makeup of the city. Thus, unlike Pueblo and Nuevomexicano activists, whose claim on the valley often predates the formation of the United States itself, many of the Anglo activists are the newest immigrants to the region. Only one Anglo activist I met, for example, could claim more than a third-generation family lineage in New Mexico. As many Anglo activists moved to Santa Fe to escape urban life, participating in a romantic vision of northern New Mexico (cf. Rudnick 1996), the proximity of a weapons laboratory and radioactive contamination in the northern Rio Grande valley registered as a profound psychic intrusion on an all but utopian space. Repeatedly, in my conversations with Santa Fe activists, the lights of Los Alamos, which are visible in the night sky from the city, were experienced as a daily provocation and source of distress. For one first-generation Santa Fe peace activist the central question became:

How are we going to put an end to this monstrous development of weapons? How are we going to put an end to an institution which so far has existed, as far as I can see, primarily as an institution developing means of threat, an institution which works to instill fear in people, an institution basically which has devoted itself for over fifty years now to violence? We're all very aware of the violence that we have around us. What is it like for young people to grow up in this city and to look out and see those lights every night and know what's going on up there, that [LANL] is an institution devoted to violence . . . that Los Alamos is a place of death?

What is it like for young people to see those lights every night? Here the nuclear uncanny is provoked by a light on the horizon, creating a sense that the world is dangerously out of balance. The unknown effects of military nuclear science are positioned here as a proliferating threat, linking nuclear war, radioactive contamination, and everyday violence within a corrupted regional space.

A core project for many activists is thus to register the psychosocial and cultural effects of the bomb on their lives, replacing a discourse of national security with a quotidian experience of nuclear terror. One laboratory critic, for example, declared herself to be the "potential mother of a mutant child." She narrated to DOE officials what it was like to be six months pregnant living beside a nuclear facility and worrying if her unborn fetus was mutating inside her. Imagining a future life caring for a deformed child, she decried the DOE for allowing "nuclear projects," "toxic dumps," and "bomb tests" to be performed in northern New Mexico, concluding that "maybe a country who planned to bomb and destroy whole countries deserves to bear monsters, a karma fitting to so monstrous a mentality. Maybe I deserve to have a mutant because once I was so casually uncaring about what these bombs were made for." As her womb is made foreign and dangerous to her, she is colonized by the psychosocial consequences of the nuclear security state. This activist articulates the proliferating anxiety felt by some in Santa Fe at the end of the Cold War, as news of environmental damage around the nuclear complex changed not only how they viewed Los Alamos but also their own lived spaces. The inability here to escape nuclear terror—in either the form of radioactive contamination or nuclear war—destabilizes a self that can no longer locate the boundaries between body and bomb. When pursued through a discourse of citizenship this process also illustrates one of the core effects of radioactive nation-building, a toxic public sphere where official statements are by definition suspect and discounted as conspiracy.

The question of veracity permeates activist engagements with federal nuclear discourse and the local statements of laboratory officials. In addition to official secrecy, the difficulty of translating technoscientific concepts into everyday discourse also fueled suspicions that the laboratory was more interested in managing public perception than dealing with community concerns. One former LANL employee, and longtime laboratory critic, explained the lack of Cold War critique to me as a combination of calculated public relations and the political effects of the nuclear economy. Noting that "doublespeak has always been important to the lab," he concluded that the economic impact of the laboratory had a silencing effect for decades in northern New Mexico because, as he put it, "around here, the lab is a taco stand—it brings in money to the community, that's all many people really care about." The issue of radioactive contamination, however, transformed these Cold War practices of silencing into a vociferous regional critique, mobilizing all communities to engage the laboratory through their own forms of insecurity. We can see here how easily the technological expertise of the laboratory is flipped into a moral critique of national security discourse, as the expert rationality of nuclear science is assumed to be able to account for all of its effects, making Los Alamos an institution that knowingly privileges production over environmental safety. Activists from all communities began to look at the Pajarito Plateau with new eyes after the Cold War, seeing not only technoscience and a billion-dollar-a-year boost to the economy but also the possibilities of regional contamination, increased cancer rates, and ecological mutation. As one activist put it:

> I think the lab has been able to coast along for 45 years without having any environmental accountability. They didn't even keep track of what was put at Area G until the late 50s. And until 1967 they had outfall pipes coming out of the canyon wall at Acid Canyon with untreated radioactive sewage. And I've seen these trees . . . go behind the Los Alamos Aquatic Center and you'll come to these two 45 or 50 year old Ponderosa Pines. And you know that the cross section of a Ponderosa is a circle—this is a star. The plates of the bark are at angles less than 90 degrees all the way around it. It is clearly a mutation. And there's just so much stuff like that—they don't even know what's there . . . But, of course, the real problem is that nobody really knows how to clean this stuff up. And the solutions that the Lab has come up with—accelerator transmutation of waste (which isn't even close to existing) relies on building reactors to generate the energy. It is a very sinister idea that they are promoting, and that a lot of New Age people in Santa Fe thought "this will be great." Very misleading—it's the dream of the alchemists. All they really know how to do is move nuclear waste around—nobody wants it.

A very sinister idea. Here, the recognition of deformed trees is mobilized into a broad-based political critique of laboratory discourse. Focusing on a widely publicized, but as yet technologically unfeasible, LANL proposal to develop a means of transforming nuclear waste into less volatile forms, the previous fifty years of environmental neglect is projected into an ongoing deception of the public. LANL public discourse is experienced here as a calculated deception that can only lead to increased nuclear projects, expanding the ecological risk and damage to northern New Mexico.

Santa Fe antinuclear NGOs have endeavored to channel this combination of anger and nuclear fear into political action at the regional level, mobilizing to enforce U.S. environmental laws on laboratory projects through a combination of publicity and lawsuits. For many of the Santa

Fe–based activists, the nuclear age can only be narrated via contamination, fear, and loss. Los Alamos becomes the literal and symbolic point of reference for addressing a lifetime of Cold War nuclear fear. As one activist described this:

> All my life, the two main things I've been concerned with have been nuclear weapons and social justice. I think we should stop all nuclear activities. There is something primordial and wrong about playing around with the stuff of the universe, the basic building blocks. That's part of the monster in Los Alamos. I always feel that there is a monster up there. My uncle used to graze his cattle up in the Valles Caldera, which is the largest caldera in the world. I always felt special up there, like I was back in the womb. It has a feeling of center place. I look at Los Alamos as a cancer eating away at that beauty. It's Sacred Ground. I think the land really belongs to San Ildefonso and should be returned to them.

There is a monster up there. The nuclear security state both colonizes and haunts the life histories of many activists. This is evidenced not only in the ability of many activists to narrate exactly where they were and what they were doing during the Cuban Missile Crisis or the Three Mile Island accident or Chernobyl, but also in more intimate social stories, in which they describe the trauma of watching friends or family members undertake careers within the nuclear complex. In these stories, the recruitment of friends or family into the nuclear complex is experienced as a personal loss, often first revealed in the form of a visit from FBI agents, conducting security checks on potential employees. Thus, representatives of the security state brought the news of a social rupture. As one activist described the experience of watching a close friend become a weapons scientist: "When the FBI came around to investigate my friend for his clearance, I felt that my world was collapsing. I felt a profound sense of betrayal." Thus, the Cold War nuclear state was experienced by these individuals not only as life-threatening (nuclear war) and polluting (nuclear contamination), but also as rupturing interpersonal relationships between friends and family. This dual sense of both global threat and the subversion of an intimate social sphere by the nuclear complex informs contemporary activism in Santa Fe. For some activists, this subversion of a local and intimate space is also revealed in continued fears of FBI intrusion into their lives, in the form of phone taps and surveillance, leading to an everyday life structure around a feeling of total surveillance.

For a number of Santa Fe activists the nuclear state is therefore a doubly invasive force, not only making war on the planet, but also seducing individuals into a banal acceptance of violence as the ultimate arbiter of social relations, corrupting science into military science, and mediating the minute-to-minute quality of everyday life. In this light, they experience the nuclear uncanny as a total gestalt, as nuclear fear comes to challenge their experience of social, material, and political spheres in the United States. As one Santa Fe activist described the psychic power of the bomb:

> Everybody who grew up through duck-and-cover drills, and saw how frightened the grownups were during the Cuban Missile Crisis, and how confused they were about the Vietnam War, somehow understood there was an enormous loss of faith, or of naiveté, in America. You couldn't be confident that the world would hold together long enough for you to grow up, to have a family and kids. I was one of those who found it uncertain about whether I would ever grow up or live out a normal life span. I remember one time during a lightning storm a lightning bolt hit near my house. I remember waking up to the explosion and thinking that it was a nuclear strike, thinking that the world was over. I also remember urging my parents to build a bomb shelter. First they told me it would be too expensive and then they told me it would be futile because we lived near a military base that was a first strike target.

I thought the world was over. As an adult, this activist transformed his sense of a futureless world into a direct confrontation with the bomb, declaring that "who we are is decided by our relationship to this militarism." Drawing on Catholic, Quaker, and Buddhist religious traditions, antinuclear activists in Santa Fe pursue a personal commitment quite literally to change the world, to channel nuclear fear and anger into a radical confrontation with the nuclear security state. Practicing a "think globally, act locally" campaign, founded in a personal rejection of violence in everyday life, Santa Fe activists challenge the moral legitimacy of the nation-state by articulating different concepts of security, democratic process, and technoscientific potential in everyday life.

In this regard, for Anglo Peace activists in Santa Fe, nuclear weapons are both the literal manifestation of a society in love with violence and the ultimate symbol of a corrupt democratic process. LANL exists within this worldview as a charged psychosocial signifier, representing the perversion of science to a destructive, rather than life-affirming, mission, becoming an institution that has consequences for every aspect of social life. Consequently, activists look for signs of another philosophical order both within themselves, in their own everyday practice, and in the international order of nation-states. One peace activist brought this sense of personal investigation home to me in a discussion of the genocidal aspects of the Cold War nuclear standoff, in which, seemingly off-topic, he began to talk about a recent experience he had in his garden. He had started a new garden at his home and had decided to grow squashes. Soon, however, he realized that insects were threatening his prized squashes. Not wanting to use pesticides, he slowly began to kill the squash bugs with his hands. Before long, he said he was seeing squash bugs everywhere—"even when I closed my eyes"—and he realized he wanted to annihilate them. He described this as an "extermination mode," which he was shocked to have discovered in himself. Finding this experience deeply disturbing, he discussed how seductive a genocidal mentality can be, and concluded that there was not much difference between his wish to kill all of the squash bugs in his garden, and General Curtis LeMay's (head of the Strategic Air Command) desire to eliminate the Soviet Union through preemptive nuclear strikes in the 1950s (see Rhodes 1996). He ended by saying, "I realized I was making war on the squash bugs, and in my own mind, I needed to find the king of the squash bugs and make a treaty. My decision was that I ultimately didn't need to participate in anything that evoked a genocidal impulse in me. I decided I didn't need the squash that much, and chose to let the bugs have them as a peace offering." What is important to underscore in this story is that world order is reduced to individual decisions, everyday actions that might have genocidal consequences and the decision to take personal responsibility for them. In this logic, the nation-state dissolves from a political entity with its own interests in a global sphere of completing nation-states, to a collection of individuals who have to evaluate each action in daily life based on its potential ecological, political, and moral consequences.

From this critical perspective, the post–Cold War opportunity for global nuclear disarmament becomes as much a referendum on the human species as on the willingness of nation-states to pursue other kinds of security. In that light, consider this activist's evaluation of international relations in the mid-1990s and its ecological orientation:

Nuclear weapons are like a self-destruction mechanism that reminds people that there is a price for failure, a price for failing to evolve the collective security and communication arrangements that would make nuclear weapons less necessary. I believe that there is a self-destruct mechanism inside most higher life forms. Catch an animal in a trap and it will have a heart attack and die before it dies of exposure or injury. If we fundamentally believe we are injuring the planet and we are doing something wrong, something that is ethically and spiritually wrong for another species, then we will consider ourselves unworthy of survival. On some deep level we will believe that there is nothing we can do to make it right, which will contribute to going down self-destructive paths with a vengeance, a "what the hell, it's happening anyhow, let's go for it, and enjoy the ride on our way out" kind of thinking. On the other hand, if people believe it is possible to be right in your heart about the way the human species is relating to the planet and the other species, then somehow we've got to find the evolutionary tools, the evolutionary steps. So I am now open-minded about how nuclear weapons might be part of that evolutionary step. I believe we are not going to have a world government but we are going to have to be completely multinational in specific areas. What we are seeing now is that the force of the non-weapons states was sufficient enough to get the nuclear weapons powers to agree to a Comprehensive Test Ban Treaty deadline—that's an evolutionary step. Nobody believed that was possible. So we are beginning to move, so grudgingly slowly, into a place where the collective agreements begin to mean something. And that's an evolutionary step that is more important than nuclear weapons by themselves.

That's an evolutionary step that is more important than nuclear weapons by themselves. This statement illustrates a desire to replace a vision of national security with a commitment to global security, and further, to adopt a "species" logic that is irreconcilable with national borders. For most Santa Fe activists, nuclear weapons are the ultimate representation of a chain of dangerous social processes, and thus, nuclear disarmament is similarly linked to a variety of environmental, social justice, and peace issues. As opposed to nuclear strategists who see weapons as specific tools of international relations, antinuclear activists see nuclear weapons as the most obvious sign of a society that has casually embraced a kind of death wish, at least since 1945. Confronting a $5.8 trillion national investment that is cloaked in secrecy, and articulated through a discourse of national security, as an individual citizen is, however, a daunting prospect.

Santa Fe antinuclear activists, consequently, often experience their work as a symbolic gesture of resistance, one that might result in greater public engagement with nuclear issues, but that might not fundamentally change U.S. nuclear policy. Several activists explained this stance to me by referring to an image from the Tiananmen Square uprising in China, when a student stood in front of a line of tanks and refused to move, temporarily stopping the convoy. Thus, an important aspect of the Santa Fe antinuclear movement is also to be visibly resistant, not just in public hearings and through lawsuits, but also by refusing nuclear weapons symbolically, as individuals standing against the nuclear state. Consider Figure 5.5, for example, a "die in" staged in the fall of 1995 on the Santa Fe plaza to protest the detonation of a French nuclear device in the South Pacific. During the last years of U.S. nuclear testing at the Nevada Test Site, Santa Fe activists "mourned" each underground test with similar performances, displaying the personal effects each test had on the group and theatrically making Santa Fe ground zero. Along similar lines, a Santa Fe activist began what she called her "Lone Ranger Project" in Los Alamos in 1995. To commemorate the fiftieth anniversary of Hiroshima and Nagasaki, each Friday she drove to Los Alamos and stood at a central intersection with a bright pink sign, asking "Why Do We Need

5.5. Antinuclear "Die in" on the Santa Fe Plaza. (Photograph by Joseph Masco)

Nuclear Weapons?"—a quotation she attributed to physicist Hans Bethe, who worked on the Manhattan Project but later advocated nuclear disarmament. Wearing a Lone Ranger style mask, she timed her action to coincide with the Friday afternoon commute. Standing alone or with another activist, she would wave back to critics and supporters from within the laboratory workforce. While laboratory workers undoubtedly understood the meaning of the sign as antinuclear critique—marking their feelings with signs of support, silence, as well as acts of profanity— the Lone Ranger mask was a personal effect. It suggested both that the nuclear complex needs patrolling and that she had crossed over into a new space, one in which she could not be herself. Though unlikely to change nuclear policy, the Lone Ranger action reveals that for some activists the everyday practice of resistance to nuclear logics is powerful in and of itself, part of a personal ecology as well as a political one.

While LANL managers, grounded in technoscience and expert knowledge, find it difficult to engage the often speculative criticisms of the Santa Fe antinuclear movement, for activists, secrecy and the inability to be heard are part of the same socially corrosive process, and they are often merged with fears about nuclear contamination. Indeed, secrecy and the invisibility of radiation become linked forces, which disturb how activists engage both their lived space and their government.

One Santa Fe activist explained the problematic nature of laboratory discourses this way:

> The lab seems so reasonable, and in a microcosm, usually is the more reasonable party when it comes to health and safety. But somehow macroscopically the citizens are more right, the hysterical people to which the lab always says "it's safe, it's safe, it's safe," are more right because the laboratory never wants to talk about the big picture. Well, the big picture is that we've created this toxic archipelago that will never be cleaned up. And that will cost this country an enormous fortune—cleaning it up is the largest civil engineering project in history, perhaps. This was all sustained by lies; it wasn't that people didn't know what they were doing. If you look at the record, they did know what they were doing, and they were lying in more cases than not.

It was all sustained by lies. Thus, current laboratory discourses about regional safety issues are destabilized by the psychosocial legacies of the Cold War nuclear complex. Government secrecy and the inability to maintain a dissenting public sphere within Los Alamos have come to invalidate scientific expertise in the eyes of some, fueling an experience of the nuclear uncanny. Explaining why some in Santa Fe cannot accept laboratory statements on regional safety at face value, this activist continues:

> When it comes to something like plutonium, well you know, the lab says "what is the inhaled dose that would have a certain probability of fatal cancers—at 27 micrograms or 81 micrograms." Well, these people don't want a single atom of plutonium in their lives. Even though we are bombarded by cosmic rays, and so forth, and we have plenty of plutonium in our bodies already (from atmospheric nuclear testing), which of course is a reason to be mad. The psychic toxicity of plutonium is very great. When people think about a plume from the incinerator or something like that it's connected with the atomic bombing of Hiroshima, which is seen both as an event in the past and a possible event in the future. They know the shape of that incinerator cloud, and they don't want anything to do with it. There is a sense that the enterprise that created this at its roots has a kind of mirror-like response to Nazi terrorism. They see something very unpleasant stepping out of the mirror. They don't want any part of this in their lives. They don't believe in the quantification that compares cancer risks from plutonium with dying from, say, radon in the generative life of one's own home; these deaths are not comparable. The quantification of them together is a kind of error. The DOE only allows health effects to be a legitimate discourse, so that's the way they have to talk. I think these people are sensitive instruments that are measuring something very important on the historical, psychic plane. They are calling attention to something that is happening in their lives; they have fear and they have grief and they have anger.

The psychic toxicity of plutonium is very great. Here, secrecy and the psychic effects of radiation combine to invalidate the technoscientific rationality of the laboratory. This process allows some citizens to experience the best efforts of laboratory scientists to document health risks in the valley as a kind of rupture and transgression in and of itself. The bomb here links past and future in a new kind of trauma, one that corrupts the possibility of an everyday life lived outside the plutonium economy. As we shall see, this post–Cold War recognition of the totalizing scope of the nuclear project produced new activist efforts to confront LANL in terms of both its historical contribution and its technoscientific form.

ANTI-ANTINUCLEAR ACTIVISTS

In 1989, after reading about a young girl who died from radiation effects after the Hiroshima bombing, a group of children from Arroy del Oso Elementary School in Albuquerque undertook to build a peace statue to be dedicated in Los Alamos on August 6, 1995, the fiftieth anniversary of the bombing of Hiroshima. By 1995, the Children's Peace Statue committee had gone global, attracting the participation of over 41,000 children worldwide and raising $20,000 in support of their project. In February 1995, the Los Alamos County Council held a meeting to discuss the peace statue, and in a tied vote, rejected it, denying the group land in Los Alamos. What was at stake in this negotiation was the identity of Los Alamos and its place within the peace movement. For many in Los Alamos, the city itself is a peace symbol, having participated, in their minds, in a national project that ended one World War and prevented another. Proponents of the Children's Peace Statue argued that it was simply a plea for peace, not an indictment of Los Alamos. They pointed out that the statue itself, a simple representation of the globe, had no writing on it addressing the Manhattan Project or Los Alamos, and thus simply represented a general wish for peace. At the Los Alamos County Council meeting, however, a majority of speakers viewed the statue as an attack on Los Alamos, emphasizing that the decision to dedicate the statue on August 6 was an implicit critique of the Manhattan Project. Additionally, Los Alamos critics of the project bristled at the thought of outsiders making so grand a statement in their community, and imagined the statue might become a center for peace demonstrations. One councilman argued: "the real backers of the project are the anti-nuke groups. I would tell children if they want to add to justice in the world they should not put their money into statues in Los Alamos but give their money to the poor. We need to recognize the role of defense in protecting America. People all over the world owe their existence to Los Alamos." A retired weapons scientist suggested that a statue celebrating LANL's achievements in arms control— a model of a defense monitoring satellite, for example—would be an appropriate commemoration. A Los Alamos high school student summed it up for many, however, when he declared: "I can't speak to the experience of World War II, but I can tell you what is going on today. The statue is an attempt by external forces to say that we should feel guilty for Hiroshima. If you want a peace statue I say look at the flag, or the models of Fat Man and Little Boy in the Bradbury Science Museum. This is an attempt by outsiders to invade our community." The Children's Peace Statue was ultimately installed at the Albuquerque Museum, and Los Alamos residents put up their own commemorative statement in the center of town later that year (see Figure 5.6), a rock with an embedded plaque thanking all the participants in the Manhattan Project for producing the weapons that ended World War II and that "deterred global conflict for the past fifty years."

This heated regional debate about how to commemorate the fiftieth anniversary of the bombing of Hiroshima and Nagasaki was influenced by two other controversies over history and display: the *Enola Gay* exhibit at the Smithsonian and Santa Fe activists' efforts to establish an "alternative display" at the Bradbury Science Museum in Los Alamos. The Air and Space Museum at the Smithsonian had planned to open a major exhibition exploring the decision to use the atomic bomb in Japan for the fiftieth anniversary of the war's end. The proposed exhibit addressed a number of controversies concerning the Hiroshima and Nagasaki bombings, including whether or not they were necessary to win the war, the casualty forecasts for an American invasion of Japan, the choice of those cities as targets, as well as the larger question of whether the dropping of the bomb was really the last event of World War II, or the first event of the Cold War.[12] The exhibition was designed by some of the leading historians of World War II, but was immediately met with resistance from veterans' groups. The battle over the exhibit came down to a struggle between archival sources mobilized by professional historians and the memories of soldiers who had experienced the trauma of World War. The battle over the exhibition eventually escalated to include members of Congress, the Air Force Association, and the American Legion, and it ended with the resignation of both the curator of the exhibit and the director of the Air and Space Museum. A much-reduced exhibit was opened in 1995, presenting a section of the *Enola Gay*, the plane that dropped the atomic bomb on Hiroshima, and videotaped statements from World War II veterans. As one of the most vociferous battles over public memory in recent history, the *Enola Gay* debate alerted communities throughout the United States that the fiftieth anniversary of the bombing of Hiroshima and Nagasaki was a particularly politicized event: veterans' groups decried a "revisionist" history that seemed to suggest that America was the aggressor in the war, while other parties viewed the *Enola*

THIS MONUMENT HONORS ALL
THOSE PEOPLE GATHERED
HERE AT LOS ALAMOS AND
DRAWN FROM ITS
NEIGHBORING COMMUNITIES
WHOSE WORK ON THE
MANHATTAN PROJECT
PRODUCED THE WEAPONS
THAT ENDED WORLD WAR II
AND WHO LATER HELPED
DEVELOP THE NUCLEAR
FORCES THAT DETERRED
GLOBAL CONFLICT FOR THE
PAST FIFTY YEARS.

DEDICATED BY
THE LOS ALAMOS EDUCATION GROUP
DECEMBER 7, 1995

5.6. Fiftieth Anniversary Monument to the Manhattan Project, Los Alamos. (Photograph by Joseph Masco)

Gay exhibit as a form of government censorship, demonstrating an unwillingness on the part of veterans and officials to look at the complexity of the historical event. At the Air and Space Museum the national fetish was ultimately protected by political interests who denied the possibility of interrogating the terms of World War, the meaning of the bomb, or the evolution of the nuclear security state. This confrontation in the nation's capital over the bomb also set the stage for a contest over public memory at the center of the nuclear complex.

The Bradbury Science Museum is the most public space at LANL, visited by about 120,000 people each year. It presents exhibits on the history of the Manhattan Project, current projects in non-nuclear sciences (on the human genome, lasers, and particle accelerators, for example) and in weapons science, presenting casings for Little Boy and Fat Man (the bombs dropped on Hiroshima and Nagasaki; see Figure 5.7), as well as displays on underground testing and basic weapons physics. It is a combination of history museum, science museum, visitors' center, and public relations wing for the laboratory. A post–Cold War plutonium exhibit, for example, discusses the long-term problem of dealing with nuclear waste and invites viewers to choose among three possible solutions, with the tabulated results forwarded to the DOE waste management departments to help in their decision-making process. The museum shows a film, *The Town That Never Was*, which focuses on the founding of Los Alamos and the rush to build the bomb, without mentioning Hiroshima or Nagasaki. The museum also conducts science demonstrations and tours for school groups. For most people who go to Los Alamos, it is the only laboratory site they will visit, and thus, it became an increasingly politicized space in the 1990s, following the rise of the Santa Fe–based NGOs.

Indeed, one of the first projects of the LASG in the early 1990s was to mobilize to gain space within the museum to offer an alternative display focusing on the human and environmental costs of nuclear weapons. LASG members argued that the museum presented a carefully sanitized view of the nuclear age, offering numerous photographs of above-ground nuclear detonations (the flash and mushroom cloud), for example, but none of the after-effects of the bomb at Hiroshima and Nagasaki. One LASG member told me that the alternative display idea was provoked by a brass plaque positioned near casings of the bombs dropped on Hiroshima and Nagasaki at the Bradbury Science Museum's first location, which declared "These bombs represent the highest achievement of the human intellect"—a statement that in their minds required a response.[13] Activist groups in California had demanded similar access to the museum at LLNL in the 1980s, and after a protracted court battle, had won rights to that museum's space. Using the Livermore

5.7. Casings of the first two atomic bombs, Fat Man and Little Boy; Bradbury Science Museum. (Photograph by Joseph Masco)

ruling as a legal precedent, the LASG argued that the museum was funded by taxpayer money and thus should be open to a diversity of public opinion about the value of the U.S. nuclear arsenal. The Bradbury Science Museum moved into a new location in 1993, becoming one of the most prominent buildings in Los Alamos. When its doors opened in April to begin the project of telling LANL's history from a post–Cold War perspective, the LASG owned an "alternative views" wall, on which they presented a nine-panel exhibit engaging the economic, environmental, and social legacies of the Manhattan Project. A comment book was placed in the exhibit encouraging viewers to respond to the display, and in August of each year (from 1992 to 1995) the LASG replaced its own exhibit with a display from the Hiroshima Peace Museum, which graphically relates the physical effects of the atomic bomb and radiation injury on the human body. The museum display was a major success in the eyes of the LASG because it gave visitors to Los Alamos a vision of an alternative history of the nuclear age, one not focused on technoscientific achievement but on damaged bodies and ecosystems. It was also a spectacular act of backtalking, one that gave antinuclear activists a small piece of landscape—a fifteen foot by eight foot wall to be precise—within Los Alamos on which to present their views.

For the managers of the Bradbury Science Museum, the alternative exhibit was an important display of openness within the laboratory after the Cold War, and a means of recognizing the mixed emotions that nuclear weapons provoke in visitors. The comment book, in fact, became a place where visitors, activists, military personnel, and Los Alamos residents conducted a fierce dialogue about the long-term meanings of the Manhattan Project, focusing on the implications of nationalist violence in Pearl Harbor, Hiroshima, Nanking, and Tokyo. In the context of the proposed Peace Monument and the *Enola Gay* controversy in Washington, however, the alternative space in the museum was destined to become a hugely contested site. In 1995, a group of LANL retirees and veterans demanded the right to present a counter-counterexhibition. Establishing themselves under the title Los Alamos Educator's Group (LAEG), the Los Alamos residents sought literally to educate Santa Fe activists about the horrors of World War II and the contribution of the Manhattan Project to world peace. They also criticized the Bradbury Science Museum for not dealing more directly with the reasons for using the bomb in 1945 in its exhibits, and for not celebrating Los Alamos's contribution to stopping one World War and preventing another. At a public conference on the issue in Los Alamos, one LAEG member criticized the museum for not depicting Japanese atrocities during World War II, Soviet aggression in Europe, or Soviet infiltration of peace groups in the United States, historical events that, she argued, justified the production of the U.S. nuclear arsenal. She concluded:

> It is as if the museum staff are afraid to be proud of war-time Los Alamos and its great and totally dangerous achievement. The bomb stopped the war with the Japanese. We must never forget that we did not start the war and we found no other way of stopping the war. And I hope no such situation ever exists again . . . This Laboratory and Livermore both have served the nation in War and in Peace. We should never be ashamed of our role in attaining peace and preserving it. One more thing: I have never ever, ever heard a nuclear scientist want to drop a bomb. My husband saw one out in the pacific, and he couldn't express how horrible it is. But we are stuck with knowledge. We have to learn how to deal with it better. And when we lie in our displays, when we do not tell the truth in our museums, we are doing no one a service.

Reacting to what they called "revisionist history," the veterans' group mobilized community support in Los Alamos for a new display, one focused on depicting Japanese atrocities during the war and the projected human cost of an American invasion of Japan. In establishing the "alternative" museum space, museum staff had never considered that a counter-counterexhibit would be proposed. They assumed that antinuclear voices would be the only force mobilizing for museum space, and agreed to allow the Santa Fe activists to determine the use of the space. Museum management was, thus, suddenly faced with rival constituencies—the laboratory and DOE, the Los Alamos community and LAEG, and the antinuclear community in Santa Fe—all deriving a different meaning from the Hiroshima and Nagasaki bombings, all demanding to see their point of view in the museum space (cf. Yoneyama 1999). The controversy gained additional heat when a letter to the veterans' group from former LANL director Harold Agnew (who took pictures of Hiroshima from within the *Enola Gay*, and ran the laboratory from 1970 to 1979) was sent to newspapers, in which he declared: "The only reason the laboratory was established was to help win the war as quickly as possible. We were successful in this endeavor and should be proud of the fact! If laboratory management and the museum manager don't understand this, they aren't fulfilling their responsibilities. We got rid of the Smithsonian curator over the Enola Gay fiasco. Hopefully, the Bradbury Science Museum staff will understand."[14] Pitting "pride" against historical documentation, the question of how to engage publicly the atomic bombings of Hiroshima and Nagasaki fifty years after the fact transformed the museum's alternative space into a potentially powerful arbiter of history.

In a Cold War-style confrontation over control of territory, namely, wall space, the LASG and the LAEG vied for control of the alternative museum exhibit space, each dancing around the issue of litigation. Santa Fe activists asked the museum to open up an equal amount of space for the veterans' group, arguing that they had fought and won rights to control the current exhibit space. Museum staff, however, feared an avalanche of competing, counter-counterexhibits if the alternative space was not clearly defined. The result was a split space, one depicting Japanese soldiers committing atrocities, the other depicting Japanese bodies charred by an atomic blast. The Santa Fe activists put a red screen over part of the Hiroshima Peace Museum exhibit asking "censored?" and depicting the controversy over the space. From their perspective losing half of their exhibit space to a pronuclear exhibit merely reinforced the message of the Bradbury Science Museum as a whole, violating the concept of the alternative space agreement. As a narrative space, the museum only got more complicated as an exhibit from the National Archives called "World War II: The World in Flames," which documented the historical progress of the war, was also installed. Thus, on the fiftieth anniversary of the Hiroshima and Nagasaki bombings, four rival exhibits were installed at the Bradbury Science Museum—the permanent museum exhibit on the Manhattan Project, the National Archives exhibit, the Santa Fe activist counterexhibit, and the Los Alamos activist counter-counterexhibit—each attributing a different emphasis to events in World War II, and thus, the meaning of the bomb.

For the Santa Fe activists, the core subject was the physical effects of the nuclear arsenal and the ongoing threat of nuclear war. For the veterans' group, the central issues were the morality of using the bomb in Japan and their own sacrifice at a time of World War. This contrast could also be seen in the two exhibits that occupied the alternative space after the fiftieth anniversary, the Santa Fe antinuclear group presenting a plea to "Never Again" witness the destruction of Hiroshima and Nagasaki, while the Los Alamos veterans' group declared that the "atom bomb saved civilian and military lives" (see Figures 5.8 and 5.9). In this discourse, counterdiscourse, give and take of pronuclear, antinuclear debate, the allocation of the Bradbury Science Museum's alternative space also became for many Santa Fe residents an issue of free speech rights and the willingness of LANL to engage in public debate about U.S. nuclear policy. Bradbury Science Museum staff eventually created a new policy in which alternative space exhibits would be rotated on a six-month cycle based on a lottery. This was intended as a means of handling multiple future requests for the space if they materialized, and was based on a laboratory legal judgment that LANL could not regulate the content of the exhibits for the alternative space. However, the LASG and the LAEG remained the only two claimants on the space, which meant that the alternative view space would be held for six months by a pronuclear organization. The LASG eventually boycotted the lottery, arguing that within the context of the Bradbury Science Museum, an alternative space must be devoted to antinuclear viewpoints to have any meaning. In winter of 1997, they removed their exhibit and the LAEG installed a new exhibit devoted to the benefits of nuclear energy. The LASG responded by initiating a leaflet campaign in front of the museum, which resulted in nine members of the group being arrested and charged with criminal trespassing for handing out the U.S. Bill of Rights.[15]

WHAT IS A "NEW" NUCLEAR WEAPON?

In September 1992, Los Alamos scientists conducted what proved to be the last U.S. underground nuclear test at the Nevada Test Site. The subsequent moratorium on underground nuclear testing, supported by both Bush and Clinton administrations, inaugurated a fundamental change in U.S. nuclear policy in the post–Cold War period. For weapons scientists, the loss of underground nuclear testing took away a primary laboratory, as underground testing was relied on both to test new designs and to confirm the performance of weapons in the existing nuclear stockpile. As the Clinton administration committed to a Comprehensive Test Ban

5.8. Los Alamos Study Group exhibit at the Bradbury Science Museum. (Photograph by Joseph Masco)

5.9. Los Alamos Educators Group exhibit at the Bradbury Science Museum.
(Photograph by Joseph Masco)

Treaty, the loss of underground testing signaled a major shift within the experimental conditions for U.S. nuclear science—moving from an empirical approach, grounded in the "truth test" of a nuclear detonation, to a "science-based" approach, largely dependent on computer modeling and simulated testing.[16] After 1992, the United States declared that it was no longer pursuing new weapons designs, and began a long-term project to dismantle parts of its nuclear stockpile. At the end of the Cold War, the United States maintained a nuclear arsenal of some twenty thousand weapons (made up of roughly twenty-five different weapons systems); by 1996, the U.S. arsenal had fallen to 12,000 weapons (consisting of eight weapons systems). Within this reconfigured weapons universe, LANL officials worked to articulate a new national mission for the laboratory, seeking public support for a new focus, perhaps on environmental and energy research, or technology transfers to private industry.

For Santa Fe activists this process represented both the best and the worst of possible worlds. The end to underground testing and a significant weapons dismantlement effort marked a promising shift in U.S. nuclear policy and the first real possibility for a full assessment of the Cold War nuclear project in the United States. In 1993, however, a classified LANL strategic plan was leaked to Santa Fe activists relating laboratory efforts to pursue a consolidation of U.S. nuclear projects at LANL. In 1994, LANL articulated its first post–Cold War mission as "reducing the global nuclear danger," an expansive project that refocused the laboratory on nuclear weapons, environmental cleanup of nuclear sites, and global nonproliferation efforts. By 1995, LANL was recognized as the indispensable institution within the nuclear complex, as the most diversified national laboratory, as well as the DOE institution capable of carrying out the greatest number of stockpile management projects. An independent review of the U.S. nuclear complex headed by Motorola chairman Robert Galvin, entitled *Alternative Futures for the Department of Energy National Laboratories*, formally recommended that Lawrence Livermore be phased out of nuclear weapons work altogether, and the remaining nuclear production work consolidated at LANL (Secretary of Energy Advisory Board 1995).[17] By the mid-1990s the consolidation of nuclear projects at LANL had already begun. Five of the eight nuclear weapons systems in the post–Cold War U.S. arsenal (the B-61, W-76, W-78, W-80, and W-88) are LANL designs.[18] Moreover, the laboratory began plans to start producing the plutonium "pits," which are the core components in nuclear weapons, for the first time in number since the late 1940s. This marked an important shift from an exclusive focus on research and design work in Los Alamos to the industrial production of nuclear weapons parts.[19] Other projects associated with non-nuclear weapons components also moved to LANL, while the nuclear weapons depot at Kirtland Air Force Base in Albuquerque took control of the single largest inventory of nuclear weapons in the United States. While LANL officials promised "cradle-to-grave" maintenance for the post–Cold War U.S. nuclear arsenal (thus, stabilizing its mission), activists saw the Cold War-era production complex with all its environmental wreckage being slowly relocated to New Mexico, albeit on a smaller scale.

Consequently, a coalition of over thirty NGOs and community groups from northern New Mexico petitioned both the University of California and the DOE to conduct an environmental impact study (EIS) of LANL activities. The application of the National Environmental Protection Act (NEPA) proved to be a fundamental tool for activists, allowing them to influence laboratory projects and schedules, as well as to articulate a rival definition of security, one based on protecting the environment rather than military force. The application of NEPA to the nuclear complex gained new prominence under Secretary of Energy James Watkins during the first Bush administration, as significant environmental damage revealed that U.S. nuclear sites had been exempted from environmental laws throughout the Cold War. External enforcement of NEPA, for Santa Fe activists, was also important because of evidence that laboratory personnel were not always committed to following the new environmental regulations. In 1990, David Nochumson, an environmental engineer at LANL, discovered the laboratory's air stacks were out of compliance with the Clean Air Act regulations. Rather than implementing his proposal to fix the problem, management harassed him on the job, eventually forcing him into another position. He sued, and after receiving whistleblower status from the DOE, was reinstated at the laboratory (1995b: 82).[20] CCNS immediately followed up on the radioactive air emission issue by getting the Environmental Protection Agency to audit LANL's radioactive emissions, and eventually by suing LANL for violations under the Clean Air Act. They won the suit and in an unprecedented settlement won DOE funds to set up an independent monitoring system of LANL's radioactive air emissions. By 1998, LANL was the first U.S. nuclear weapons facility in the country to have an independent system for monitoring air emissions, backed up with a promise from CCNS to sue for any discrepancies between activist and laboratory monitoring data. Newly empowered to sue the laboratory under NEPA, NGOs began a wide-ranging review of LANL's environmental effects in the 1990s, demanding everything from a full account of LANL impacts on the soil and ground water on the Pajarito Plateau, to an analysis of radiation in the Rio Grande River and possible damage to the regional aquifer. CCNS even led a campaign to shut down a "nuclear laundry" in Santa Fe, where LANL had sent its radioactive lab clothing to be washed for over thirty years.

This effort to bring environmental accountability to the nuclear complex produced a proliferation of public hearings in New Mexico— over eighty-five in 1995 alone dealing with LANL environmental impact studies. Thus, while activists had demanded greater information about LANL's environmental effects for years, by the mid-1990s the public hearing process under NEPA became a primary meeting ground for activists, scientists, and officials as well as an unexpected new burden. After fifty years of silence from the nuclear state, activists began saying that the laboratory was trying to "kill them" with public meetings. Many also began to wonder what was being accomplished by giving public testimony, asking whether it had any effect on laboratory policy at all. For LANL scientists many of the concerns, particularly of Santa Fe residents, about LANL's environmental impacts were overwrought and technically wrongheaded. Defenders of the laboratory frequently stated that the amount of radiation received from a particular project was the equivalent of taking a coast-to-coast airplane ride; some suggested that if Santa Fe residents were so concerned about radiation they should not have chosen to live in northern New Mexico at all, as the high elevation of the region increased exposure to natural radiation. But while LANL representatives tried to contextualize laboratory impacts by appealing to a notion of comparative risk, suggesting that residents could make decisions about radiation exposure, activists underscored their lack of choice in laboratory operations. This was exacerbated by the very language of the hearing process, which identified all interested parties as "stakeholders" and thereby seemed to suggest that a kind of rational choice, exchange logic informed people's engagement with the laboratory. For many Santa Fe activists, however, the laboratory remains simply a colonizing force, and each pico-curie of radiation released from LANL operations marks a new violation of the land and of their rights as citizens. The NEPA process was inherently valuable to them because it forced laboratory officials to look at environmental impacts before they proceeded with construction projects, and to create a formal record of that process. However, the ritualistic hearings—which once seemed to hold the promise of the first real dialogue with officials about the U.S. nuclear project in New Mexico— became instead, for many activists, a means simply of legitimizing state decisions at their time and expense. Rather than bringing a feeling of accountability to the nuclear complex, the hearing process ultimately had, for many activists, the opposite effect, confirming that decisions about health, safety, and nuclear policy were being made elsewhere without local input.

In the fall of 1994, Santa Fe NGOs injected themselves into the national policy debates over nuclear weapons by suing LANL and the DOE to stop construction of Dual Axis Radiographic Hydrodynamic Test Facility (DARHT). DARHT, which had already broken ground, was a new research facility designed to study plutonium pits, the primary mechanism within a nuclear weapon. The DARHT facility was originally conceptualized as a Cold War weapons design tool, but under the new test regime, was identified by the DOE as the central diagnostic technology for "maintaining the safety and reliability" of the U.S. nuclear stockpile. It was the first post–Cold War facility in the DOE's new Science Based Stockpile Stewardship (SBSS) program, a plan to maintain weapons technologies without underground testing. In an unprecedented action, Santa Fe NGOs secured a court injunction against DARHT, stopping construction until a full environmental analysis could be performed. It was a strategic intervention, as DARHT was linked up to a series of national policy decisions about the U.S. nuclear arsenal. Indeed, Hazel O'Leary, then Secretary of Energy, flew several Santa Fe activists to Washington to try to head off the suit. She agreed that an environmental impact study would be conducted not only of DARHT but also of the entire post–Cold War nuclear program, a longtime activist demand, but did not agree to stop construction on DARHT until these analyses were completed. As a result of the lawsuit, construction on the DARHT facility was delayed sixteen months and the relationship between activists and the laboratory was fundamentally changed. Antinuclear activists were no longer seen within the laboratory as simply misguided; they were dangerous, able to conduct negotiations directly with the Secretary of Energy over LANL projects, and to impact key LANL facilities. In a remarkable post–Cold War reversal, LANL employees began talking to me about being shut out of the U.S. national security debate. This resulted in the formation of another counteractivist group in Los Alamos—the Responsible Environmental Action League (REAL)—made up of past and present LANL employees, whose expressed purpose was to counter the testimony of Santa Fe NGOs in the public hearing process. Thus, the DARHT hearings presented a rather surreal scene, as activists with a pending lawsuit against DARHT interrogated LANL project managers, while laboratory personnel (including lawyers, weapons scientists, and DARHT scientists) presented testimony in favor of the project, speaking not as representatives of the laboratory, but rather as "citizens."

In the debate over DARHT that followed, a central issue was defining what constitutes a "new" nuclear bomb design, and in a broader sense, the purpose of the SBSS program under a Comprehensive Test Ban Treaty. For antinuclear activists, any new weapons capability represented a "new" design, and they interpreted DARHT as a weapons design facility, a means of creating new weapons by getting around the strict legal terms of the Nuclear Non-Proliferation Treaty and the Comprehensive Test Ban Treaty. Santa Fe activists had discovered U.S. plans to modify a nuclear weapon at LANL and Sandia National Laboratory in order to give it an "earth penetrating" capability (Mello 1997). The B61-11 earth penetrator was designed to destroy underground bunkers (like those used by Saddam Hussein during the first Persian Gulf War). For activists, the earth penetrator proved that the United States was interested in developing new weapons technologies, and the desire to have a bomb capable of destroying underground bunkers suggested that nuclear weapons remained full military tools, not just a nuclear deterrent force. Thus, the discovery of new, post–Cold war weapons programs seemed to confirm for activists that LANL was involved in increasing the global nuclear danger rather than reducing it. For weapons scientists, however, the earth penetrator was not a new weapon because its implosion system remained identical to that of an earlier model. They argued that a "new design" requires a new implosion mechanism (part of the seven formal steps—concept, feasibility, development engineering, production engineering, first production, quantity production, and retirement—in the production of a Cold War nuclear weapon). From this perspective, prototyping new weapons concepts or designing them in virtual reality would not be considered "new" production work, as these activities do not engage the full industrial cycle. Within this philosophical context, the regional debate over the purpose of DARHT focused on the technoscientific demands of maintaining "aging" weapons versus creating "new" ones.

At the DARHT hearings (see DOE 1995c), weapons scientists revealed that the intended design life of nuclear weapons in the post–Cold War stockpile was less than twenty-five years, and the average age of those weapons was twelve years. Thus, by 2010 the U.S. arsenal will have exceeded its projected design life. Weapons scientists argued that they needed DARHT and a number of other facilities to study how nuclear weapons age because the Cold War stockpile was going to outlive its design lifetime. They argued that aging studies had not been done on weapons during the Cold War because nuclear production was considered an unending process, with each new weapons design replacing an old one. An aging nuclear weapon was, then, inherently an unknown, and thus dangerous. DARHT could provide X-ray images of an implosion using a surrogate material for plutonium. The resulting computer data would then be compared to existing data about the weapon's implosion technology to look for signs of aging that might affect its military performance at a time of war. Searching for a variety of metaphors for DARHT—a tactic necessary for discussing classified nuclear weapons science, but also for controlling its political representation—LANL officials described DARHT as like an MRI, a CAT scan, as "a hospital for sick bombs," but then turned to a less anthropomorphized analogy. A LANL weapons scientist described the current problem this way:

> The problem that we face is that understanding the performance and safety of weapons as they age is actually a far harder task than designing brand new weapons. The reason for that is when you're designing new weapons, you can control things. When you are allowing weapons to age, you are no longer in control of the processes. Specifically, if you think of the problem that you might have with a new car, you can go turn the key on and expect that it will work. If you go out to my 25-year-old Ford and turn the key on, it may not. Without nuclear testing, we can't turn the key, so we're asked to rely on trying to understand how aging impacts the performance of these things. It's a very difficult task. Part of the process to understanding this will be to get basically zero time snapshots of what the weapons were supposed to look like, in order to understand how things will age.

We can't turn the key. For weapons scientists, the technoscientific problem of the post–Cold War era has thus become how to predict how small changes in the components of a bomb might function as the implosion takes place, when materials go into a plasma state and are subject to the most extreme temperatures and stresses. Here, the bomb as national fetish is revealed in the details of post–Cold War weapons science, as concerns about the minute changes in bomb parts over time are transformed into a $70 billion investment in nuclear infrastructure even as the United States pursues a Comprehensive Test Ban Treaty.

Critics of this SBSS program argue that the DOE has never documented aging effects so severe as to impair the detonation of a device, and they suggest easier solutions: disarmament, or a system to remanufacture weapon parts, machined to specifications learned during the forty-seven years of nuclear testing.[21] LANL weapons scientists argue, however, that the production complex for nuclear weapons is gone and there is no longer any way to maintain an exact match between Cold War-era bomb parts and today. In essence, they argue that bomb design is now less an industrial process than an art, and thus, expertise not technology is the key to maintaining the "safety and reliability" of the U.S. nuclear arsenal. For activists, it is precisely this "folk art" argument that is most suspect because it makes it impossible for anyone to validate laboratory statements about the arsenal. At the DARHT hearings, one activist, for example, spoke directly to the issue of "reliability":

> Reliability issues make people really nervous. But in fact, if you have a nuclear weapon that isn't reliable it means it doesn't explode, right, which for most people is considered safe. And since we are no longer in a nuclear war fighting situation where we want to launch thousands of weapons against an opponent to try to knock out his missile silos, and if we are only going to use nuclear weapons for deterrence, then in a situation where we really need to use nuclear weapons, if the first weapon didn't work, you could send a second one and it wouldn't make any difference in the outcome. So reliability is not what it sounds like. It's not that your car isn't going to start and you're going to be stuck in the middle of nowhere. The likelihood of a problem occurring in the stockpile where all the weapons go bad at once is extremely low.

So reliability is not what it sounds like. After redirecting the car analogy, the activist then exchanged the threat posed by aging weapons with one posed by weapons designers themselves:

> We have to consider the environmental impact of starting up another 20 years of the arms race without realizing it. That happened in the 1950s, when we developed hydrogen bombs. That happened in the 1960s when we designed multiple warheads. It happened when we went into Star Wars and antiballistic missiles. The likelihood of starting another arms race and having to go back into nuclear weapons production—which in this country is a $300 billion environmental impact for the cleanup of the last generation's nuclear weapons facilities—has to be considered.

The environmental impact of another arms race. Weapons scientists are identified here as the key to the arms race, dangerously authorized to pursue their technoscientific passions regardless of the global or local repercussions. In this light, antinuclear activists argue that Los Alamos weapons scientists push U.S. nuclear policy, rather than responding to it. They point to the lobbying by directors of the national laboratories against test ban treaties (Edward Teller in the 1960s and Harold Agnew in the 1970s), as well as Edward Teller's successful lobbying of the Reagan administration for the Strategic Defense Initiative (see DeWitt 1984; Broad 1992; Gusterson 1996a; FitzGerald 2000). Activists argue that because it is the director of each laboratory who certifies the military viability of the stockpile, it is simply a matter of self-interest for them to maintain anxiety and technoscientific questions about the status of the U.S. nuclear arsenal. Thus, Santa Fe NGOs interpreted the new SBSS facilities as part of a "deal" the DOE cut with weapons scientists to gain support for a Comprehensive Test Ban Treaty.[22] As one activist put it: "the AGEX [Above Ground Experiment] facilities, a suite of them of which DARHT is the flagship, followed by NIF [National Ignition Facility] and Atlas and Jupiter and so on, is a deal struck between the labs and Hazel O'Leary. Basically, the lab will give up their opposition to the comprehensive test ban in exchange for getting these new toys with which to design new weapons."

While the post–Cold War period began with talk of a new mission for the national laboratories (technology transfer, alternative energy, a "green" lab), by the mid-1990s the United States had recommitted to reinvigorating the nuclear complex at the national laboratories. The competitive relationship between LANL and Livermore during the Cold War, which left each laboratory vying for its designs to enter the stockpile, was transformed by 1996 into a "peer review" relationship, with each laboratory charged with watching over the other's stockpile maintenance. In support of this new arrangement, LANL and LLNL each received funding for new research facilities for the redundant study of weapons primaries and secondaries (in Los Alamos, DARHT and ATLAS; in Livermore, The Contained Firing Facility and the National Ignition Facility). Moreover, an Accelerated Strategic Computing Initiative (ASCI) was created to ensure that the national laboratories maintain the most powerful computers on the planet for at least the next decade.[23] Thus, the post–Cold War nuclear design complex remains not only intact but with significant technological upgrades. Los Alamos, Livermore, Sandia, and the Nevada Test Site all maintain a nuclear weapons focus, and have been charged by the White House to retain readiness to restart the nuclear test program. Since 1998, over 75 percent of LANL's total budget has been devoted to defense work, and the total laboratory budget has doubled.[24]

For antinuclear activists, the "deal" thus represents a significant expansion in the U.S. nuclear capability at exactly the moment the United States has agreed through international treaties to stop developing new nuclear technologies. In this light, activists marshaled evidence that there were no real aging problems in the U.S. nuclear stockpile, and challenged the need for new facilities like DARHT or the ASCI program.[25] They pointed out that the entire nuclear stockpile was designed on computers whose computation ability is easily replicated on store-bought machines today, and therefore wondered about the true intent of the new computer initiative. Arguing that the "computer is the ultimate bomb shelter," Santa Fe NGOs imagine a twenty-first-century U.S. nuclear complex in which new bomb designs are stockpiled in virtual reality, as nuclear devices were during the Cold War, awaiting the call to arms.[26] Thus, activists critique the proposition that SBSS is devoted to producing a "reliable and safe" U.S. nuclear arsenal, arguing instead that SBSS is a technoscientific way around the Nuclear Non-Proliferation Treaty and Comprehensive Test Ban Treaty, a means of covertly increasing U.S. nuclear capabilities. As one Santa Fe activist told me:

> Folks need to know that the three lab directors are required to "bless" the annual certification of nuclear weapons, stating the current weapons are "safe and reliable." This puts an awesome amount of power in their hands. And as we've already noted , these are directors from a culture that is inherently secretive and isolated. Who checks on them? Where is the accountability? The key word here is confidence. "Confidence" is a word of art rather than science; it is subjective. I think the "deal" consists of if you give the lab directors enough money they will be confident . . . "Reliability" is also a weaponeer's term of art. If a weapon goes off and it is more than 10% above or below its design yield, it is considered "unreliable." Well, I would contend that it would still be extremely reliable in killing thousands, if not millions, of people. Also take care with the idea of "safety." Nuclear weapons are safe: U.S. nuclear weapons are safe in the sense that they cannot be detonated without authorization. Specifically, they have Permissive Action Links that prohibit unauthorized detonations. You can shoot a bullet at them and it is not going to set them off. Lightning can hit them, and it is not going to set them off. They are not going to accidentally explode in a nuclear sense. You could have a plane crash, with an aviation fuel fire. The weapon could melt, and under the most extreme circumstance, yes, you could have severe radiological contamination. But will the weapon explode—ala Hiroshima and Nagasaki? No. Safety is not an issue. "Reliability" is a bit more of an issue. But if it is 10% over or under its design, it is still a weapon of mass destruction; it is still a credible deterrent. Which is supposedly the reason for the stockpile. The only reason you need a precision yield measurement and pin-point missile accuracy is for a first strike option—not a deterrent.

Weaponeer's terms of art that enable a nuclear first strike. Here, the language of the nuclear complex is deconstructed to reveal a larger program for U.S. nuclear hegemony. For activists, the move into virtual design work also leaves few exterior traces that could be monitored by external authorities, reducing the environmental impacts that NGOs have leveraged into a de facto oversight of the nuclear complex.

Thus, while weapons scientists experienced the new stockpile stewardship regime as a technoscientific challenge in which the key experimental tool—underground testing—was forbidden, eliminating certainty about nuclear performance in the process, antinuclear activists saw the weapons scientists using nuclear fear to scare federal authorities into a massive upgrade for the nuclear complex. At the DARHT hearings, for example, LANL weapons scientists accused activists of wanting the nuclear arsenal to become so unsafe and so unreliable that the U.S.

military would unilaterally disarm, having lost confidence in its nuclear stockpile. Activists countered that weapons scientists were really interested in slowly modifying the existing nuclear stockpile—adding new components and new military uses—so that in a few years laboratory directors could declare a lack of confidence in the U.S. nuclear stockpile (due to the unknown effect of cumulative upgrades), and force a return to underground nuclear testing. While each accused the other of a covert agenda, the DARHT lawsuit was settled in the DOE's favor in April 1996, after it filed a classified supplement to the environmental impact study. To mount an adequate rebuttal, NGOs asked for the right to present their own Q-cleared representative to review the classified supplement, but they were denied that option, allowing construction to resume on DARHT in April 1996. The DARHT lawsuit revealed both the new power of NGOs to impact nuclear projects at LANL and the limits on citizens' access to the nuclear complex, demonstrating that national security discourse and classification can always trump the public legal process.

The DARHT lawsuit articulated the post–Cold War power of both nuclear and antinuclear institutions in New Mexico. However, it was a highly mobile process. By the late 1990s, LANL officials were talking less about "reducing the global nuclear danger" than about "securing the global nuclear future," referencing a renewed confidence in the future of the laboratory and of nuclear sciences. Santa Fe activists, on the other hand, experienced the renewed U.S. commitment to nuclear weapons as a confirmation of their assumption about the lobbying power of the nuclear complex in Washington, and feared that the window for achieving a postnuclear concept of national security was closing with the U.S. commitment to a twenty-first-century nuclear program. Indeed, in October 1999, the Senate voted to reject the terms of the Comprehensive Test Ban Treaty, making it the first international arms control treaty in U.S. history to be signed by a president but rejected by Congress. The treaty remains in effect but is unratified, allowing the full spectrum of nuclear possibilities over the next decade, from a renewed U.S. commitment to disarmament to a return to full-scale nuclear weapons testing and production.

LOS ALAMOS: GROUND ZERO OF THE PEACE MOVEMENT

At the end of the Cold War, Santa Fe NGOs mobilized to change the nuclear mission of LANL by calling for a collective form of security, grounded not in the nation but in ecological sustainability and nonproliferation. A decade later, three of seven core U.S. nuclear production facilities were devoted to their own environmental cleanup, over eight thousand U.S. nuclear weapons had been dismantled, and the United States was seven years into a moratorium on underground nuclear testing. New Mexican activists had also significantly changed the political and environmental regulatory context in which LANL exists. However, these victories were balanced by the fact that budgets for nuclear weapons at LANL exceeded Cold War levels after 1995, and a new technoscientific infrastructure was coming on line to entice a new generation of weapons scientists into the U.S. nuclear complex. Rather than witnessing the end of the U.S. nuclear mission, activists instead watched its consolidation and technoscientific enhancement in New Mexico, as a new weapons complex using surrogate testing and virtual reality promised to be even more difficult for them to monitor. Over forty thousand barrels of nuclear waste from LANL activities were also marked for storage at the newly opened WIPP, meaning that more nuclear waste would soon be on the highways of New Mexico than ever before.[27] Thus, while the end of the Cold War seemingly held out the promise of moving beyond the nuclear arsenal as the basis for U.S. national security (at the regional, national, and international levels), the new stockpile stewardship program instead reenergized the national fetish—with a $70 billion investment in new technologies officially devoted to watching nuclear weapons age. As one Santa Fe activist told me as the decade came to a close: "I now think of Los Alamos as Dracula's Castle—as we proceed in progressive steps to eliminate nuclear weapons, it will be the very last to go." In response to this renewed commitment to the bomb, activists mobilized to make Los Alamos the central target of the nuclear disarmament and peace movement.

In 1998, the first New Mexican chapter of Peace Action formed, and immediately began organizing a national protest to take place in Los Alamos the following year. As an organization, Peace Action brings together two important historical strands of the antinuclear movement—SANE and FREEZE. The Committee for a SANE nuclear policy was founded in 1957 and led the campaign to stop above-ground testing on both moral and health grounds. By publicizing the effects of radioactive fallout on people and the environment, SANE mobilized a large coalition of citizens, NGOs, celebrities, and politicians to confront the Cold War nuclear arms race. This led to the Partial Test Ban Treaty in 1963, in which the United States and the Soviet Union agreed to cease detonating nuclear devices in the atmosphere, outer space, and underwater. The FREEZE movement began in 1981 in response to President Ronald Reagan's dramatic escalation in the Cold War arms race, growing into an international movement to stop the production of nuclear weapons and the Strategic Defense Initiative (FitzGerald 2000). Producing some of the

5.10. Peace Action march in Los Alamos. (Photograph by Joseph Masco)

largest peace demonstrations in U.S. history, the FREEZE campaign is credited with pushing Reagan and Gorbachev to the negotiating table in the 1980s, as well as changing public perceptions about the risks of nuclear war. SANE and FREEZE merged to become Peace Action in 1993, continuing to campaign for global nuclear disarmament and non-proliferation. Peace Action's arrival in New Mexico in 1998, thus, links the antinuclear campaigns of the 1950–80s with the post–Cold War movements in New Mexico, articulating a new national strategy for engagement with the bomb.

Coinciding with the anniversaries of the Hiroshima and Nagasaki bombings, Peace Action organized the largest protest in Los Alamos history in the summer of 1999 (cf. Guterson 1999b). Led by actor Martin Sheen (see Figure 5.10), the protest was unlike anything Los Alamos had seen in the six decades since the start of the Manhattan Project. The action involved more than four hundred people from across the United States as well as activists from half a dozen countries. As a new generation of weapons scientists was being trained behind closed doors at the new Theoretical Institute for Thermonuclear and Nuclear Studies (TITANS), two survivors of the Hiroshima bombing led a group of activists to the site where the first bombs had been assembled in Los Alamos to conduct a healing ceremony. The LASG's citizen inspection team gave a tour of

5.11. Peace activists confronting LANL employees, Peace Action march.
(Photograph by Joseph Masco)

laboratory facilities, pointing out sites of contamination and providing interviews about on-going weapons research projects. Eventually, hundreds of activists took over the center of Los Alamos and marched through town to the administration buildings. Once there, protesters were met by rows of Los Alamos police, who simply drew a line across the normally public parking lot and took into custody anyone who crossed it. While LANL employees watched from the top of the cafeteria, scores of protesters were handcuffed and detained for this act of civil disobedience (see Figure 5.11). Promising to return in future years with similar protests, the organizers of the event identified Los Alamos as the center of the nuclear complex and thus made it the focal point of their movement.

Thus, the programmatic effort by Santa Fe NGOs to articulate a rival definition of national security remains an ongoing project at the beginning of the twenty-first century. Despite more than a decade of post–Cold War backtalking to the nuclear complex, the categories of nuclear national security are now not just intact but are largely reinforced in the United States. From the theatrical efforts of UN-style citizen inspection teams and highway billboards to the detailed negotiation of nuclear bureaucracy and environmental standards, activists have sought to unsettle the normalizing effects of U.S. national security policy in northern

New Mexico after the Cold War. For Santa Fe NGOs, deterrence now addresses, not only foreign militaries, but also the U.S. nuclear complex itself, and the goal of building a twenty-first-century *anti*nuclear complex requires keeping the logics and practices of the U.S. nuclear program visible. The immediate project is to prevent LANL from returning to a normalized structure in everyday New Mexican life, as it was during the Cold War, and to maintain a critical public space in which to articulate alternative visions of security and risk, identity and nation. In this regard, the project of the twenty-first century for these groups is to create a peace complex on the scale of the Manhattan Project, making Los Alamos not only the birthplace of the bomb but also ground zero of the nonproliferation, peace, and environmental justice movements.

Part II
National Insecurities

II.1. Billboard by the Los Alamos Study Group, installed after the 2003 U.S. War With Iraq. (Photograph by Joseph Masco)

6 Lie Detectors

On Secrets and Hypersecurity in Los Alamos

The U.S. nuclear complex has always been haunted by the possibility of spies. At Los Alamos, some of these ghosts have names—Klaus Fuchs and Theodore Hall, for example—while others remain elusive, like the third Soviet agent long rumored to have worked at Los Alamos during the Manhattan Project.[1] With the end of the Cold War, however, espionage, like the U.S. nuclear arsenal itself, seemed to recede in the American imagination, psychically exiled as an increasingly quaint relic of a (nuclear) age assumed past. Hence the widespread shock and bewilderment in 1999, as accusations of atomic espionage arose from the center of a surprisingly vibrant U.S. nuclear complex in New Mexico. Even more sensational than the initial accusations in March 1999 that China had covertly attained design information about the most sophisticated nuclear warhead in the U.S. arsenal was the announcement a month later that a U.S. nuclear weapons scientist at Los Alamos National Laboratory (LANL) had illicitly downloaded to nonsecure computers almost the entire archive of nuclear weapons design codes developed during the Cold War era of nuclear testing. Of fourteen high-capacity computer tapes containing design codes for the U.S. nuclear arsenal, only seven could be accounted for, creating panic among officials about the missing tapes and their 806 megabytes of U.S. "nuclear secrets."

Suddenly the epicenter for nuclear fear at the national level, LANL became the focus of an intense post–Cold War public debate in 1999.[2] A presidential commission chaired by former Senator Warren Rudman concluded in June that LANL conducted "science at its best, security at its worst." The commission accused Los Alamos scientists of a profound, institutionalized arrogance concerning security and declared the U.S. Department of Energy (DOE) a "big, Byzantine, and bewildering bureaucracy," one that needed to be fundamentally reformed (PFIAB 1999: 8).[3]

By December, Wen Ho Lee, the chief suspect in the case, had become one of only a few people in U.S. history to be charged with gross negligence in handling classified information under the 1954 Atomic Energy Act. (The fifty-nine-count indictment, filed on December 19, 1999, promised a life sentence for Lee, if convicted; see *United States v. Wen Ho Lee* [79 F. Supp. 2d 1280 (D.N.M. 1999], *decided without published opinion*, 208 F.3d 228 [10th Cir. Feb. 29, 2000]). Testifying at Lee's indictment hearing, the director of the nuclear weapons programs at Los Alamos stated that the missing computer tapes could change "the global strategic balance," while the head of Sandia National Laboratory warned the judge that letting Wen Ho Lee out on bail was a "you bet your country decision" (from transcript of bail hearing, U.S. District Court for the District of New Mexico, December 27, 1999). Indeed, by the end of 1999, it seemed that all the repressed anxieties of a post–Cold War nuclear world order could be located in the mundane form of seven missing Los Alamos computer tapes and their digital arsenal of nuclear secrets.[4]

Over the course of the next nine months, however, the case against Lee began to unravel—fantastically—culminating on September 13, 2000, with an abrupt turnaround by federal prosecutors. After fighting bail for nine months (and after keeping Lee either in solitary confinement or shackled since his arrest), prosecutors accepted a plea agreement: Lee pleaded guilty to one of the original fifty-nine counts of mishandling classified information and was sentenced to time served (278 days). In the end, Wen Ho Lee—the man once portrayed by officials as the single greatest threat to U.S. national security in a half century—walked. Investigations into the case and how it was handled became the subject of congressional hearings, as well as of formal reviews at the FBI, the U.S. Justice Department, the DOE, and LANL. In the fall of 2000, Wen Ho Lee signed book and television movie deals to tell his story, while FBI agents entered a particular kind of purgatory: spending weeks methodically digging through the Los Alamos County landfill in hope of recovering the missing computer tapes (which Lee claims were thrown in the trash; see Pincus 2000).[5]

This chapter is less concerned with Lee's culpability than with interrogating what the institutional responses to the espionage allegations have revealed about America's nuclear project and the role of secrecy in enabling it. For while institutional responses to the Lee case played on the worst fears of the nuclear age—from atomic espionage to a new arms race to the possibility of nuclear war—they have also revealed important aspects of post–Cold War nuclear culture and policy in the United States and thus are well worth examining for their official, as well as more implicit, national cultural logics. Put another way, the search for the missing computer tapes at Los Alamos troubled a secret governmentality, revealing not only the terms of conducting U.S. nuclear science after the Cold War but also several different orders of nuclear secrets, secrets that have little to do with the production and maintenance of military machines.

Secrecy has always been a constitutive element in the U.S. nuclear complex. Indeed, with the invention of the atomic bomb in Los Alamos in 1945 came a powerful new kind of government secrecy and the very possibility of nuclear espionage.[6] During the Cold War, nuclear weapons took on the form of a national fetish in the United States, becoming simultaneously one of the largest and most dangerous industrial enterprises in U.S. history and a national project extravagantly protected from public discourse by official practices of secrecy. Nuclear weapons remain, therefore, ambiguous technosocial forms, simultaneously the material source of "national security"—the very arbiters of "superpower" status—and profoundly dangerous national products, which make claims on the life and death of citizens in a variety of ways. Secrecy has played a central role in mediating the national cultural contradictions embedded in the U.S. nuclear arsenal, a means of controlling the public discourse about radioactive nation-building. Consequently, it is primarily in moments of crisis that the nuclear complex becomes visible and its terms subject to analysis and renegotiation. The politics of keeping "nuclear secrets" and identifying "atomic spies" in Los Alamos, for example, have revealed the problematic identity politics operating within the U.S. nuclear complex at the end of the first nuclear century. Indeed, it is important now to recognize that the category known as "America's nuclear secrets" not only contains technoscientific information about how to build a nuclear weapon, but also addresses how race, citizenship, and security are defined at the very center of the U.S. nuclear complex.

WHAT IS A NUCLEAR SECRET?

The event that ultimately triggered the indictment of Wen Ho Lee in New Mexico for "gross negligence" in the handling of classified U.S. information actually took place seven years earlier at a place about as far away from Los Alamos as one can image, at Lop Nur, a nuclear test site in northwest China. There, on September 25, 1992, only a few days after Los Alamos scientists conducted what turned out to be the last U.S. underground nuclear test of the 1990s, China secretly exploded a nuclear device of its own. Both of these tests, however, were primarily secret to their own citizens, as seismic monitoring and satellite surveillance systems alerted governments around the world to both nuclear detonations.[7] Indeed, this was not a hugely significant event in the United States until a Chinese weapons scientist visiting LANL some months later happened to mention that the test had been exceptional: more precisely, it had involved a plutonium core that was not spherical but ovoid (a "watermelon not a grapefruit," as he put it), a major technological advance that suggested Chinese success in producing a miniaturized nuclear warhead (Broad 1999). In the world of nuclear policy, miniaturized warheads are important not only because insights into how to build them are among the most closely held nuclear secrets, but also because the possession of sophisticated nuclear technologies (like miniaturized warheads and intercontinental ballistic missiles) structures the power relations between nuclear states. Los Alamos weapons scientists began work on the first miniaturized nuclear warheads in the 1950s, part of a Cold War effort to increase exponentially the explosive power of nuclear weapons while simultaneously shrinking the weight and dimensions of nuclear warheads in order to place them on top of intercontinental ballistic missiles (Hansen 1988; MacKenzie 1990). By the mid-1960s, both Los Alamos and Livermore National Laboratories had succeeded in producing warheads that were thirty to fifty times as powerful as the bomb that destroyed the city of Hiroshima, yet so small that multiple warheads could be placed on a single missile, each capable of reaching a different target/city (Hansen 1988: 197–206).[8]

Since a miniaturized warhead has been part of the U.S., as well as Russian, nuclear arsenal for decades, China's 1992 test might seem a logical next step in the advancement of its own nuclear program, a basic technological milestone on the scientific path to nuclear superpower status.[9] But then the plot thickens. In 1995, a Chinese official handed over to a CIA operative in Taiwan a stack of Chinese state documents. Included in the "walk in" documents, as they are now known because they literally "walked in" the front door, was a manuscript describing the weapons that make up the U.S. nuclear arsenal. Most of the information was drawn from the "open" (i.e., unclassified) literature on U.S. nuclear weapons, with two key exceptions: one was the component layout of a miniaturized U.S. warhead, the other the measurements of a key weapons component within that system (Broad 1999). The documents immediately suggested to DOE counterintelligence officials that China had gained access to U.S. nuclear weapons schematics and specifically to the W-88 warhead designed at LANL. This conclusion launched the first nuclear espionage investigation of the post–Cold War period, which went public in the pages of the *New York Times* on March 6, 1999, with Los Alamos weapons scientist Wen Ho Lee, a naturalized Taiwanese-American, soon identified as the chief suspect in the case (see Risen and Gerth 1999).

It is important to underscore several elements in the development of this story. First, the United States was actively spying on Chinese weapons programs, monitoring their sites through satellite technology and inviting Chinese weapons scientists to Los Alamos just to chat. Second, Chinese officials went out of their way to make sure the United States understood the significance of their 1992 test. The CIA, in fact, now believes the "walk in" documents were offered by a Chinese triple agent—that is, the Chinese official was authorized by his government to give the documents covertly to the United States (Risen and Johnston 1999; Loeb and Pincus 1999). Third, the story was leaked to the *New York Times* by U.S. government officials. So what constitutes a nuclear secret if this kind of circulation is possible within and between rival nuclear states?

It turns out that almost everything to do with nuclear weapons in the United States has been historically constituted as a nuclear secret, making the category highly elastic and thus politically charged. Information relating to nuclear weapons in the United States is officially "born secret," meaning it is "restricted data" subject to automatic classification (DOE 1999a). This means that since 1943 a whole industrial infrastructure—a nearly $6 trillion national project and one of the largest industrial enterprises in U.S. history (Schwartz 1998)—has been shielded from public discourse. Consequently, nuclear secrecy evolved during the Cold War into an enormous state apparatus. By 1990, the DOE alone had hundreds of millions of pages of classified material to manage, in buildings scattered all over the country. These buildings were also filled with tens of thousands of workers, all of whom needed security clearances simply to be near the secrets (Burr, Blanton, and Schwartz 1998).[10] Nuclear secrecy, however, has protected not only information about how to build a nuclear bomb and deploy a nuclear arsenal but also information about the health and environmental effects of the nuclear complex itself and other matters that might generate lawsuits.[11] Indeed, at times, "national security" has meant protecting the U.S. nuclear complex from U.S. citizens, rather than from foreign adversaries. This dynamic is most clearly illustrated by a recent DOE disclosure that its agencies documented adverse health effects among nuclear workers at fourteen U.S. nuclear facilities dating back to the early 1960s (NEC 2000). This revelation contradicts the longstanding position within the U.S. nuclear complex that nuclear production had not affected workers' health.[12] Indeed, it now turns out that even as the DOE vigorously denied and legally challenged claims by workers who believed their cancers were job related, the department was collecting health data supporting those claims—data that immediately took the form of nuclear secrets, protected under national security protocols. Settlements over the next decade will be in the billions of dollars, involving workers and their families throughout the U.S. nuclear complex.[13]

Based on a compartmentalization of knowledge and a need-to-know logic of access, this system of secrecy was designed as a nationwide mechanism of social control, creating hierarchies within places like LANL that deal in classified material, while focusing workers' attention on the minute tasks at hand. For example, at LANL, while all nuclear workers need to have a "Q clearance" to move, as they say, "behind the fence," not all Q clearances provide the same levels of access to classified material. There are thirteen classificatory levels—or "Sigmas"—within the "Restricted Data" category and each Q-cleared weapons scientist is allowed access to information based on his or her Sigmas.[14] Thus, Sigma 1 has to do with nuclear weapons design information, but Sigma 5 has to do with numbers of weapons in the U.S. arsenal, and Sigma 10 has to do with chemistry and metallurgy of materials used in nuclear weapons (Burr, Blanton, and Schwartz 1998: 438–39). Thus, in conversation, U.S. weapons scientists must not only negotiate the need-to-know component of weapons work, but also make calculations about how information is divided under these security protocols (Gusterson 1996a: 79). In practice, this is a difficult cognitive process because nuclear weapons are integrated physical processes that do not always break down so easily along security lines.

Indeed, things are often classified in one context but not in another, which also makes the management of nuclear secrets a tricky business. For example, one weapons scientist explained to me how he breached security at Los Alamos simply by bringing a sack lunch into the plutonium facility. He left his lunch on his office desk and stepped out for a minute. He came back to find a commotion. A security officer informed him that the orange he left on his desk was, in fact, a classified object. He learned that any spherical object becomes a nuclear secret once it passes over the line demarcating the secure from the open areas of the laboratory, as it could be taken as a model for the plutonium pit that drives a nuclear weapon. The weapons scientist was told that in the future he could eat the fruit or store it inside his office safe with the rest of his classified documents, but if he left the orange out on his desk unsupervised it was a security infraction that could be referred to the FBI for investigation. Similarly, nuclear weapons information that is widely available to the public on the Internet becomes classified and is subject to all the security protocols and penalties for disclosure the moment it enters the weapons divisions at Los Alamos. This is the flip side of the "born secret" concept, that information can slip in and out of being a nuclear secret, depending on context and physical location.

But let us examine a more pertinent example in light of the espionage story: nuclear weapons computer codes. Computer codes were not only at the center of the allegations against Wen Ho Lee but also have become increasingly politicized technoscientific constructs within the U.S. nuclear complex. In the 1990s, they were identified as the "crown jewels" of U.S. national security in one official context and as profoundly "unreliable" technology in another.[15] At Los Alamos, physics information becomes automatically classified when it pertains to certain temperatures and energy regimes that are only possible in nuclear technologies. In a "security immersion" talk to laboratory personnel on April 21, 1999, Stephen Younger, the director of nuclear weapons programs at Los Alamos, described the complexity of a nuclear weapon this way: "While a nuclear weapon is operating, for the few nanoseconds it is really rolling, it is the brightest thing in the solar system, the hottest thing in the solar system. Some of them are the densest things in the solar system. So they achieve conditions that you just don't find in physics textbooks." The 1,030 nuclear tests that the United States conducted during the Cold War produced data about all these processes but did not produce what weapons scientists call a "first principle" understanding of nuclear explosions. This means that while the United States has been extremely successful in building highly sophisticated nuclear weapons, scientists cannot yet model with absolute precision all the physical processes that are important to achieving a nuclear explosion. Computer simulations have been used for decades to approximate the results achieved through nuclear tests at the Nevada Test Site, but have never produced perfectly reliable calculations. Indeed, weapons scientists will say privately that after each nuclear test they still had to "dial in" the results; that is, they had to manipulate the data in the computer simulation to match the experimental results.

What are now referred to as the *legacy codes* are the enormous computer programs (consisting of hundreds of thousands of lines of code) developed during the Cold War to simulate the extreme temperatures, pressures, and velocities that make up a nuclear explosion. Given the complexity of the physical processes involved in the milliseconds leading to a nuclear yield, the computer codes have long been recognized as temperamental approximations. Indeed, the punch line of a Cold War joke told among Los Alamos weapons scientists concluded that the fastest way to slow down the Russian nuclear program would be to send them a CRAY supercomputer to model their nuclear weapons on, as the amount of effort needed to create and then validate the computer codes would set the Russian nuclear program back years. Since Los Alamos weapons scientists no longer have the most direct experimental means of testing nuclear weapons or of improving the calibration of the legacy codes (i.e., detonating nuclear devices at the Nevada Test Site), one of the central post–Cold War weapons programs at Los Alamos is the new Accelerated Strategic Computing Initiative (ASCI). Under this program, the U.S. national laboratories maintain the fastest computers in the world and have new divisions devoted solely to interpreting the data produced by the weapons codes.[16] In the mid-1990s, weapons scientists lobbied for a long-term U.S. commitment to maintaining state-of-the-art computers at the national laboratories as well as for a fleet of new non-nuclear experimental facilities to replace underground testing. These efforts were successful (to the tune of well over $70 billion in new projects) largely because the legacy codes were convincingly portrayed as an insufficient means of evaluating and maintaining the U.S. nuclear arsenal on their own.[17] Thus, the legacy codes have served as political tools as well as technoscientific constructs and were deployed tactically throughout the 1990s as a means of shaping nuclear policy debates in Washington, D.C., after the Cold War.

In light of the espionage allegations, it is important to note that the technoscientific communities that wrote the legacy codes do not believe they are sufficient nuclear production tools on their own (May 1999: 13).[18] In our conversations, weapons scientists pointed out that the legacy codes rely on an interpretive framework that has evolved out of a half century of work at the U.S. national laboratories.[19] Consequently, weapons scientists were divided over how much the legacy codes would help a foreign weapons program. Weapons scientists tended to correlate the value of the legacy codes with the sophistication of that country's existing weapons program, suggesting that a successful effort to translate and interpret the codes would require advanced nuclear weapons knowledge. LANL weapons scientists agreed, however, that if U.S. computer codes were transferred to another country, that country would still need to conduct a range of physical tests—that is, a series of nuclear detonations—to achieve mechanically the technology modeled in the computer codes. Thus, it is unlikely that a country could produce a nuclear weapon derived from the legacy codes in perfect secrecy, given that the required nuclear tests would be world news. U.S. nuclear secrecy does not, then, in this case protect a set of specific industrial secrets, which if transferred to a foreign power could produce an overnight nuclear arsenal, but rather keeps foreign nuclear weapons programs from finding information that could, at best, speed up the developments of their own research programs by pointing them in the right technoscientific direction. In other words, it is quite possible for one nation to have another's nuclear secrets and not know what to do with them.

Concepts of security and practices of secrecy within the U.S. nuclear complex have consequently never been solely concerned with containing the spread of technoscientific data about nuclear devices. Indeed, the physical processes involved in producing a nuclear yield are not secrets in the traditional sense, as they are open to discovery by any party able

to conduct the appropriate scientific research. Nuclear secrecy has func-
tioned also as an internal mechanism of social definition and control
within the United States, becoming a national-cultural structure as well
as a means of protecting engineering data on how to build a nuclear
bomb. With this social context in mind, we can identify the first casualty
of the espionage allegations at Los Alamos: an openness initiative at the
DOE launched in 1994 as a direct response to revelations about covert
human plutonium experiments conducted during the Cold War on U.S.
citizens and to widespread concerns about environmental and worker
health effects from the nuclear complex (Welsome 1999). Between 1995
and 1998 over 600 million pages of documents dating from the first
twenty-five years of the nuclear age were declassified, part of a larger
effort to restore public trust in the DOE after the Cold War. But after the
espionage story broke in March 1999, all 600 million pages were quickly
reclassified and subjected to a second declassification process in the
search for errant nuclear secrets (see Aftergood 1999; Stober 1999).
Moreover, the DOE Office of Classification, which was famously
renamed the Office of Declassification by Secretary of Energy Hazel
O'Leary at the start of the openness initiative in 1994, was renamed once
again in 1999, this time as the Office of Nuclear and National Security
Information, a marker of the renewed importance of nuclear secrecy.
Finally, as a result of the espionage allegations, nuclear weapons programs were moved into their own "semiautonomous agency" within the
DOE. The new National Nuclear Security Agency is designed to build a
"higher fence" around the nuclear programs, to make the nuclear complex less visible, after nearly a decade of revelations about its Cold War
environmental, health, and security practices. Thus, one immediate consequence of the espionage allegations has been a programmatic effort to
rejuvenate the nuclear complex as a secret society, to redraw formally the
lines between public accountability and secret governmentality.

The recent national dialogue about "nuclear secrets" exemplifies what
Georg Simmel (1906: 465) wrote about secret societies almost a century
ago; namely, that people tend to commit the "logically fallacious, but
typical, error, that everything secret is something essential and significant."
Not all "nuclear secrets" involve usable technological information about
how to build a bomb. Indeed, nuclear secrecy can as easily conceal the
banal details of managing a large government bureaucracy, or more profound information regarding the health and environmental effects of
nuclear production on U.S. citizens. This new post–Cold War fixation on
security at precisely the moment when the United States by every measure
maintains the most powerful conventional and nuclear military presence on
the planet also demonstrates that secrecy is not merely a practical means of

containing military technology in a world of competing nation-states, but also a structural means of controlling the internal challenges and national cultural contradictions within the nuclear complex itself. Secrecy, however, is wildly productive: it creates not only hierarchies of power and repression but also unpredictable social effects, including new kinds of desire, fantasy, paranoia, and, above all, gossip.

ON RACIAL PROFILING

In his essay "Gossip and Scandal," Max Gluckman (1963: 309) argued that "the more highly organized the profession the more effective is the role of gossip" in defining a sense of membership and thus "a most important part of gaining membership in any group is to learn its scandals." The gossip among weapons scientists in Los Alamos in 1999 was, from this perspective, unsurprisingly unified. I could not find a single weapons scientist at Los Alamos who believed that espionage had actually taken place at the laboratory. Indeed, they countered that the information given to China about the W-88 warhead was not precise enough to have come from Los Alamos, and pointed to several hundred other possible sources for the information within the nuclear complex (see May 1999; Vrooman 1999). As one weapons scientist put it:

> If Wen Ho Lee had intended to divulge specific W-88 information, he certainly had access to stuff far more specific and far more useful. To put an analogy around it, what was told to the Chinese was "We can run a three-minute mile," but we didn't tell them how. You know, it's like "How do you run a three-minute mile? My God, what's your training regime, what's your diet? What are your running shoes?" That's the rough equivalent of what the Chinese learned, but we sure as heck didn't tell them how.

We didn't tell them how. In other words, because Los Alamos has designed the world's most sophisticated nuclear arsenal, the information leaked by a senior weapons scientist from such a facility would logically be not only perfectly accurate but also immediately helpful from a weapons design perspective.

Among weapons scientists, gossip focused on China and on Washington politics. Weapons scientists speculated that: (1) China leaked the documents to see if the information they had received about the W-88 was correct (an overreaction from the United States would demonstrate that it was correct); (2) China wanted to send a message to Taiwan about its nuclear capability and simply used the United States as a messenger; (3) China released this information to misdirect FBI attention to Los Alamos and thereby protect the real mole somewhere else in the nuclear complex; and (4) the entire affair was an elaborately staged ruse in which China predicted a powerfully xenophobic U.S. reaction. In this last scenario, the United States would respond to the nuclear scandal by expelling all foreign-born scientists now working within the nuclear complex and stop the technological brain drain of Chinese scientists to the United States. Thus, China would reclaim its own scientists and damage the U.S. national laboratories in a single brilliant stroke.

What is particularly remarkable about this last bit of gossip is that it exchanges one threat with another, replacing fears of nuclear espionage against the United States with fears of an attack on the laboratory's multinational workforce. U.S. national security at Los Alamos has always been produced by an international workforce. During the Manhattan Project, it was the European physicists—Enrico Fermi, Leo Szilard, Hans Bethe, Edward Teller, and others—who ultimately made the project a success. In the 1980s, both Los Alamos and Livermore National Laboratories had directors who were naturalized U.S. citizens. In the post–Cold War world, Los Alamos has come to rely even more heavily on foreign-born scientists to make up its workforce; today half of all Ph.D.s in engineering in the United States are foreign nationals (LANL Fellows 1999: 3).[20] As predicted, the nuclear espionage allegations did create an immediate backlash against foreign-born workers at the laboratory, with Asian and Asian American workers suffering an increasingly hostile work environment. By the end of 1999, the climate within the laboratory had become so bad that a number of prominent scientists left Los Alamos, while others, particularly in the nonclassified research areas, simply refused to recruit new scientists to the laboratory. This atmosphere of suspicion has profound implications for the future of the laboratory; for example, three of the top five recruits to the laboratory in 1999, all of whom were foreign nationals (from China, Russia, and India) refused offers, citing fears of a hostile racialized workplace as the reason (LANL Fellows 1999: 6). Indeed, laboratory gossip related stories of visas, postdoctoral positions, and offices being suddenly denied to foreign-born researchers; there were also fears that the new security badges, which encoded information about national origin, were being used to track electronically only certain scientists.

In the context of these fears, *racial profiling* became an explicit discourse within the laboratory and other U.S. nuclear facilities. In an appearance on the television program *60 Minutes* in August 1999, Wen Ho Lee claimed to be a victim of racial profiling, an accusation that was soon supported by the head of counterintelligence at LANL, who was one of the key figures in the DOE investigation of the "walk in" documents.[21] Lee was singled out in the investigation because he was a Taiwanese American who had made several trips to China in the late 1980s and because his wife, Sylvia Lee, also an Asian American laboratory employee with a Q clearance, had been an energetic host for Chinese officials visiting Los Alamos. Months after Lee's public indictment in the *New York Times*, however, and while he was under twenty-four-hour-a-day surveillance by the FBI, it was revealed that Lee had been given permission to go to meetings in China, and that several Anglo scientists had gone to similar meetings at the time and had not been subject to similar investigations. Moreover, Sylvia Lee was hosting the parties for Chinese visitors to Los Alamos at the behest of the FBI and was working as one of their agents, further troubling the investigation (Holscher 1999). Indeed, Wen Ho Lee also worked at times as a covert operative for the FBI. In a sting against a Chinese scientist working at Lawrence Livermore National Laboratory (LLNL) in the early 1980s, Lee wore a wire and pretended to be a Chinese agent seeking U.S. nuclear secrets. Thus, he performed—at the FBI's request—a role federal agents would later accuse him of playing in earnest: that of Chinese spy (Stober 2000; Holscher 1999). One of the central unresolved issues in Lee's case, therefore, is what kind of an agent he was and at what time—a double agent, a triple agent, a confusion of the two, or simply a fellow with profoundly bad judgment when it comes to managing U.S. computer codes. Lee has yet to explain fully why he moved the legacy codes from a secure to a nonsecure computer and to account adequately for the missing computer tapes containing the downloaded weapons codes. However, the investigation into his actions—his nuclear secrets—has revealed other nuclear secrets within the nuclear complex, secrets that compromise the legitimacy of the proceedings against him by virtue of their identity politics.

Lee consequently became a complex cultural icon after his arrest, simultaneously revealing a racial problem within the nuclear complex, the growing reliance of the national laboratories on foreign-born scientists, and the inherent dangers posed by scientists who understand nuclear weapons. Although he became the sole suspect in the investigation of the "walk in" documents in 1995, the FBI concluded four years later that Lee could not have transferred the W-88 information during the right window of time in the 1980s, and was also unable to show that Lee had transferred any classified information to a source outside the laboratory. Thus, even as the indictment process was warming up for Lee in 1999, the FBI was starting a brand-new investigation into the "walk in" documents.[22] The missing computer tapes remain, therefore, a separate matter from the espionage allegations that initiated the investigation into Wen Ho Lee in 1995. Determining Lee's civil rights also became part of a larger national debate about citizenship and race in the DOE, a conversation fueled by Lee's pretrial treatment.[23] During Lee's bail hearing, FBI agents argued against releasing him because, they said, any utterance by Lee in Chinese could be used as a signal to family or friends to deploy the missing computer tapes. Suggesting that a seemingly innocent phrase like "Uncle Wen says hello" could be a coded message, the FBI portrayed the entire Chinese language as a specially designed code for transferring U.S. nuclear secrets out of the country (a theory the FBI failed to apply equally to the English language). Lee was subsequently locked in solitary confinement awaiting his trial and allocated one hour a week with his family in the presence of an FBI agent during which the Lee family was restricted to speaking only English (see the transcript of bail hearing, U.S. District Court for the District of New Mexico, December 27, 1999).[24]

While the espionage allegations provoked newly racialized discourses within the nuclear complex nationally, they also revealed a deeper problem of race in Los Alamos. In July 1999, Secretary of Energy Bill Richardson traveled to Los Alamos to assure laboratory staff that they would not be singled out for investigation based on race or national affiliation. While categorically denying an official policy of racial profiling within the DOE, Richardson was confronted with not only foreign national workers' stories of harassment at the laboratory, but also more specifically New Mexican concerns. Members of neighboring Indian Pueblos discussed their longstanding issues with the laboratory over land rights, environmental effects, and hiring. Similarly, Nuevomexicano laboratory workers, who spent much of the 1990s fighting the laboratory over employment practices, reminded Richardson that major 1995 layoffs at the laboratory were overturned by the courts for disproportionately targeting "Hispanic" workers—demonstrating racial profiling of another kind in Los Alamos.

In the end, while trying to calm the fears of foreign national scientists at LANL, Secretary Richardson was confronted by the fact that the Manhattan Project has been a racialized project in New Mexico right from the very beginning. In addition to a longstanding aboriginal land claim by San Ildefonso Pueblo for return of the land now occupied by the laboratory, the descendents of Spanish and Mexican homesteaders on the Pajarito Plateau, evicted by the Manhattan Project in 1942, also mobilized in the 1990s to gain reparations for their loss. The homesteaders claimed that the U.S. government did not adequately compensate them for their lands in 1942 and then violated its agreement to return the Pajarito Plateau to homesteaders after the war was over. In the summer of

1999, the director of the Homesteaders Association, Joe Gutierrez (1999), asked concerned citizens to:

> reflect for a minute on the television [images from] three months ago, when we were seeing the images of the Kosovos leaving their native lands, at a moment's notice, or just overnight, with whatever they could carry, and at times, with perhaps nothing. That was pretty much the scene in November and December of 1942 when the homestead lands were taken here in northern New Mexico. Even though we were not under a foreign state or government, we were under siege by our own government. We now find that the establishment of the Manhattan Project was probably done under false pretenses. There was never a need for it. But the case I'm trying to make here is that there was loss of life in those days in 1942, when the homesteaders were run off at gunpoint from their lands.

We were under siege by our own government. In comparing the arrival of the Manhattan Project in northern New Mexico with ethnic cleansing campaigns in Kosovo, Gutierrez underscores the contested nature of the laboratory as a local cultural, national, and legal entity. To address racial tensions throughout the laboratory's multicultural, international workforce, Richardson commissioned a study on racial profiling within the DOE. The report concluded that Asian-Pacific Americans were experiencing a "hostile work environment" and a sudden "glass ceiling in promotions," and workers throughout the complex were experiencing an "atmosphere of distrust and suspicion" because of co-workers "questioning the loyalty and patriotism of some employees based on racial factors" (DOE 2000a). Acknowledging for the first time that racial profiling is a de facto reality within the nuclear complex, Richardson ordered a one-day stand-down of all DOE facilities to address the problem formally.[25]

What these events reveal is nothing less than the racialized context of the bomb itself. Because nuclear weapons are ultimately tools of "foreign relations"—that is, they are designed to threaten or kill foreign nationals—they have in their cultural makeup the fundamental question of the Other. This is a two-tiered logic, however, one involving not only other nation-states that are targeted with nuclear weapons, but also the industrial logistics of the nuclear complex itself, involving where nuclear facilities, tests, and waste are located in the United States and the specific communities they subject to risk. The environmental legacy of nuclear production from the Cold War is projected to be a half-trillion-dollar project over the next fifty years and presents a greater engineering challenge than the original Manhattan Project.[26] A recent DOE report, in fact, has revealed a once closely held U.S. nuclear secret; namely, that the cleanup of the Cold War nuclear complex is now a millennial project that ultimately relies on technologies that have yet to be invented. At 113 sites within the United States, the DOE is responsible for:

remediating 1.7 trillion gallons of contaminated ground water, an amount equal to approximately four times the daily U.S. water consumption; remediating 40 million cubic meters of contaminated soil and debris, enough to fill approximately 17 professional sports stadiums; safely storing and guarding more than 18 metric tons of weapons-usable plutonium, enough for thousands of nuclear weapons; managing over 2,000 tons of intensely radioactive spent nuclear fuel, some of which is corroding; storing, treating, and disposing of radioactive and hazardous waste, including over 160,000 cubic meters that are currently in storage and over 100 million gallons of liquid, high-level radioactive waste; deactivating and or decommissioning about 4,000 facilities that are no longer needed to support active DOE missions; implementing critical nuclear non-proliferation programs for accepting and safely managing spent nuclear fuel from foreign research reactors that contain weapons-usable highly enriched uranium; and providing long-term care and monitoring—or stewardship—for potentially hundreds of years at an estimated 109 sites following cleanup. (DOE 2000b: 1)

The DOE will provide long-term care and monitoring for hundreds of years. The internal cost of Cold War nuclear production thus presents an unprecedented kind of threat to U.S. national security.

The environmental legacy of the Cold War nuclear complex also disproportionately affects the poor and people of color, particularly in the West (see Churchill 1997; Kuletz 1998). New Mexico, for example, one of the poorest and most ethnically diverse states in the United States, has a cradle-to-grave nuclear economy—from uranium mining to nuclear weapons design and missile tests to nuclear waste storage—all within its borders. Thus, it is important to look at the nuclear complex as an arena in which the borders of the national community are defined in two ways: first, by explicit practices of nuclear targeting (i.e., who is threatened with nuclear weapons) and, second, by which communities are asked to bear the environmental and health costs of the nuclear complex itself—in other words, to risk their health for the "security" of the nation. This tension between national security and national sacrifice is what secrecy works to repress, forcing events—like an espionage scandal—that periodically open up the U.S. nuclear complex to scrutiny to evolve necessarily into much bigger debates about the terms of citizenship and the parameters of national identity supporting America's nuclear project. As a return of the repressed, however, this ambiguity between national security and national sacrifice is also immediately subject to new forms of regulation that once again attempt to resolve this contradiction through a national-cultural repression. This process is perfectly illustrated by the institutional response to the espionage allegations at Los Alamos in 1999.

HYPERSECURITY MEASURES

As the foreign national workers, primarily located in nonclassified research areas, negotiated the racialized context of work at Los Alamos in 1999, the core weapons scientist community also faced a newly politicized workplace. In a broad effort to control classified information, disk drives were pulled off computers, and a new rule was instituted requiring two people to be present whenever classified data was moved between machines. New DOE security regulations for weapons scientists were also announced, concerning everything from classification rules to computer use to travel, private conduct, and even sex. In an effort to define what kinds of personal interaction weapons scientists can have with members of other nations, the DOE issued a new rule entitled "Close and Continuing Contact with Foreign Nationals" (DOE 1999b). After defining a "close contact" with a foreign national as a relationship that involves "bonds of affection and/or personal obligation" or where employees share "private time" with a foreign national, the ruling then turns to "sexual or otherwise intimate relationships":

> Personnel do not have to report one-time sexual or otherwise intimate contact with a foreign national if (a) there will be no future contact with the foreign national, and (b) the foreign national does not seek classified or sensitive information, and (c) there is no indication that personnel are the target of actual or attempted exploitation. However, if it is likely that future social contact with the foreign national will occur—even if the future contact is expected to be in non-close (non-sexual) social settings—the relationship must be reported as a close and continuing contact. If personnel have sexual or otherwise intimate contact on more than one occasion with the same foreign national, regardless of circumstances of likelihood for follow-up contact, the relationship must be reported as a close and continuing contact, even if there is no expectation of future contact. Such contact must be reported regardless of whether the foreign national's full name and other biographic data are known or unknown.

If personnel have intimate contact on more than one occasion with the same foreign national. This policy declares that one-night sexual rendezvous between weapons scientists and foreign nationals are not a threat to U.S. national security but "close and continuing relationships" (i.e., two-night sexual meetings) are (Hoffman 1999a). It requires Q-cleared employees to report any repeated contacts, sexual in particular, that involve members on a list of twenty-five "sensitive country foreign nationals"—although the list itself remains classified. The "contact" rules stipulate what kinds of conversations and contacts are allowed, and what kinds require scientists to report immediately to their counterintelligence officer, or risk, as they now say, being "Wen Ho Lee-ed." These new regulations for weapons scientists supplement existing security protocols, including the standard FBI security review necessary to gain admission to the nuclear complex and the regular five-year follow-ups that investigate sexual and spousal relations, financial standing, drug and alcohol problems, and mental health. Within the nuclear complex, workers are expected to report on not only their own problems but also those of colleagues, neighbors, and family members.

These new regulations thus extend the expansive Cold War logics of security into a new realm of what we might call *hypersecurity*—an overdetermined effort to both mobilize and contain the nuclear referent through increasingly disciplinary structures of secrecy and threat. What the hypersecurity protocols reveal, however, is that the most portable nuclear secrets are not in documents but are locked up in the experience and knowledge of weapons scientists. So what happens when a nuclear weapons scientist is fired? Individuals are recruited into the weapons science community with an implicit promise of lifetime employment. In exchange, they relinquish their rights to publish in the open literature and agree to keep their entire work history classified.[27] Consequently, weapons scientists have been sheltered from the periodic layoffs at the national laboratories and have left the weapons programs primarily through retirement, through promotion, or by returning to basic scientific research at universities (which usually requires publishing in a second nonclassified research area while working as a weapons scientist). Wen Ho Lee is therefore not only one of the few citizens publicly tried for egregious mishandling of classified information under the 1954 Atomic Energy Act, he's one of the few senior U.S. nuclear weapons scientists who has been formally cast out of the program since Robert Oppenheimer in the mid-1950s.[28] Lee's work history is still classified and he may well be unemployable in the United States after the publicity of his trial. And of course, as the FBI so carefully noted, he speaks Chinese.

The nuclear fear generated by the Lee case manifested in official quarters as a need to further regulate weapons scientists, producing a major institutional change at the national laboratories in 1999: the introduction of lie detector tests. The proposed polygraphs met with immediate resistance from weapons scientists, provoking the first unionizing effort in Los Alamos history and contributing substantially to the overall climate of fear within the laboratory. While participation in the polygraph program was officially deemed "voluntary," Q-cleared employees were simultaneously informed that failure to take the test would result in a loss of access to classified material (DOE 1999c). In other words, individuals who did not submit to the tests would be effectively shut out of national security work. LANL scientists were concerned, however, not only about losing their jobs for not submitting to the tests, but also about the scientific validity of polygraph technology. They pointed out that Aldrich Ames, the convicted Soviet spy, passed four separate lie detector tests before he was arrested. As one young weapons scientist complained:

> The evidence indicates that polygraphs are ineffective and that polygraphs are unreliable. On a personal note, I also believe they are immoral. They take invasion of privacy to an entirely new level. It's one thing to look into my bank account, to search my briefcase, to scan my computer files, and to interview everybody I've known in the last ten years; but it's another thing to strap me up to a machine which claims to be able—and I'm quoting from the DOE's own briefing—to take a picture of my emotions. I love working at Los Alamos. I love the science, the community, the public schools, the mountains . . . But if I refuse to take a polygraph, if I refuse to be party to what I consider a grotesque invasion of privacy, then I may not be able to stay here. I may be forced to leave. (DOE 1999d: 96)

I may be forced to leave. Knowing that polygraph tests are not 100 percent accurate in determining truth from falsity and easily calculating the number of employees likely to be unfairly accused of hiding secrets, most Los Alamos scientists rejected polygraphs on the basis of their technological validity.[29] In doing so, however, they misrecognized one of the central ways in which lie detector tests are used and reiterated a basic contradiction within the logics of the nuclear complex itself.

Weapons scientists have assumed that polygraph technology is about detecting lies, making the central question the ability of the technology to perform that task. However, the CIA and FBI regularly use polygraphs not only as a measure of truth or falsity, but also as a tool of interrogation and intimidation (OTA 1983: 100). In fact, the polygraph was used this way in the Wen Ho Lee investigation. Lee passed his first lie detector test in December 1998, but in an interview with the FBI in March 1999 he was told that he failed.[30] He was then reminded of the fate of the executed atomic spies Julius and Ethel Rosenberg, and was told he had already lost his job and his retirement (see transcript of bail hearing, U.S. District Court for the District of New Mexico, December 27, 1999). To explain why he might have failed the polygraph (that he had, in fact, passed), Lee acknowledged that he had been contacted by Chinese officials interested in his Los Alamos work while on a trip to China in the late 1980s. Lee claims that he did not give the Chinese officials any information, but he also did not fully report this conversation to counterintelligence officers at the time. Lee was ultimately fired for this breach of the security regulations at LANL. (Lee's illegal file transfers were only discovered later and remain a separate matter from the investigation into the "walk in" documents.) The polygraph was clearly used in this case as an interrogation tool rather than a measure of truthfulness, a means of drawing out a confession rather than mechanically documenting the presence of untruths.

In a broader sense, the technoscientific politics of polygraph testing mirror those of the bomb itself. For just as polygraphs need not actually provide accurate data to evoke a confession—that is, to really detect lies with a spiking line on a piece of revolving graph paper—nuclear weapons need not actually be able to detonate to produce a nuclear deterrent. It is the *perception* that both technologies work that is the key to their success in achieving their stated social purposes: polygraphs in rooting out secrets, and nuclear weapons in deterring nuclear war. Both are also technologies that offer the illusion of a high-tech answer to the problem of the social but ultimately fall back on brute intimidation as the means to an end. But what social purpose do lie detector tests serve when aimed at the core culture of the weapons complex, the nuclear weapons scientists themselves?

Since the end of underground nuclear testing in 1992, weapons scientists have focused less on creating new technologies—new nuclear secrets—than on maintaining old ones. Quite literally the $70-plus billion in post–Cold War upgrades to the laboratories are designed to allow weapons scientists to watch nuclear weapons age, albeit through state-of-the-art technologies and the fastest computers in the world. Exploding nuclear weapons at the Nevada Test Site—detonations that demonstrated to the world the viability of the U.S. nuclear arsenal—have been replaced by a technoscientific concern with the effects of aging on plastic parts, electronic fuses, and nuclear components. During the Cold War, international confidence in U.S. nuclear weapons technologies was achieved through underground testing, which functioned as a kind of international political theater, in which each nuclear detonation communicated the capability of U.S. nuclear technology to a global audience.

But while the Cold War nuclear complex was energized by the constant production of new technologies, new nuclear secrets that signaled U.S. strength to a presumed insurgent Soviet Union, the post–Cold War order has had to search for an equivalent mechanism of threat for energizing the security logics that support the nuclear complex. In the 1990s, the national laboratories began replacing underground explosions with visits from foreign nuclear scientists as a mechanism for communicating the viability of U.S. nuclear technologies. However, what is missing from this equation is the international threat once provided by the Soviet Union, a perceived danger powerful enough to force conversations about nuclear fear to begin not in New Mexico where the nuclear waste is, for example, but to remain strictly outside U.S. borders. A combination of international threat and secrecy has always enabled this separation of spheres in the United States, where the accumulating sociocultural and environmental impacts of the nuclear complex here at home are not seen as connected to the potential danger posed by foreign nuclear arsenals located overseas.

The new polygraph program attempts, then, to reintroduce weapons scientists to a particular calculus of threat. Polygraphs accomplish this by underscoring that each nuclear scientist can, in the eyes of the complex itself, potentially change the "global strategic balance of power." By doing so, the new hypersecurity regulations argue that nuclear secrets are in fact still powerful and dangerous, allowing those on the inside of the complex to reclaim the right to determine access to this central U.S. national project. Hypersecurity measures not only make each weapons scientist more conscious of his or her importance to the national order, they also produce greater degrees of self-monitoring for those willing to submit to them, making the secret society all the more secret, homogeneous, and unified. Rather than simply watching weapons age, weapons scientists are being structurally reminded that they are responsible, in the language of the nuclear complex, for the "ultimate defense of the nation" and the safety of the "free world." The polygraph program attempts to accomplish this, however, by ratcheting up the level of risk in everyday life for weapons scientists—risk not only from foreign agents but also from the counterintelligence officers within the nuclear complex itself. Hypersecurity measures rely on structural intimidation to produce a productive paranoia, one requiring weapons scientists to imagine themselves as ever more at risk in everyday life, but also ever more powerful and important in their ability to influence global events.

At the height of the controversy over polygraph testing in Los Alamos in 1999, I (JM) had this exchange with a weapons scientist (WS):

WS: We've been trained a lot about security, and we get a lot of counterintelligence training. You know what's really depressing? Motivated spies will be able to get to you and open you up like [he snaps his fingers] like that and you won't even know it. If an intelligence service is so motivated they can infiltrate you, and they can get information out of you, and you won't even know it's happening.
JM: You mean like if you were traveling or kidnapped?
WS: No. Take this interview here. How do I know you're not working for a foreign intelligence service? You know this could be a very sophisticated way for a foreign intelligence service to come in and elicit information.
JM: Wouldn't they be less obvious in their approach? [In light of the espionage concerns I had arranged the interview through the laboratory's public relations office.]
WS: Maybe. But maybe if you are really good this is exactly how you would do it.

Maybe this is exactly how you would do it. On that note our conversation ended abruptly, as he became vulnerable to his own invented example, trapped by the possibility of an inadvertent confession—and the potential loss of nuclear secrets. Afraid that an inability to control his own speech might dangerously shift the global balance of power, this weapons scientist embodied the post–Cold War problem of how to deploy the perfect institutional response to a threat that is neither obvious nor specific but ever-present and potentially apocalyptic. In the context of hypersecurity measures, the test for weapons scientists becomes how to control oneself perfectly, to measure precisely risk in everyday-life interactions as well as internally, to find, in other words, a flawless technological and institutional mechanism for controlling psychosocial anxiety.

Thus, just as nuclear weapons have been repeatedly mobilized to deter social ambiguity on the world stage by increasing the technological ease/risk of nuclear war since 1945, so too are the new hypersecurity technologies intended to deter nuclear weapons scientists from stepping out of line by intensifying their experience of on-the-job risk. The new hypersecurity measures not only reinforce and reinvigorate the logics of nuclear secrecy at Los Alamos, however, they also effectively drive out those scientists unwilling to tolerate a hypersecure, racialized workplace.[31] Thus, hypersecurity measures reiterate the problem of the nuclear age itself, for just as the Cold War produced hundreds of contaminated sites—national sacrifice zones—within the United States in the pursuit of national security, so too do the hypersecurity measures further compromise the very scientific institutions they are intended to secure.

THE "NEW NORMAL"

> Secrecy sets barriers between men, but at the same time offers the seductive temptation to break through the barriers by gossip or confession. This temptation accompanies the psychical life of the secret like an overtone.
>
> —Georg Simmel, *On Secrecy and Secret Societies*

Simmel underscores the profound cultural work that goes into keeping secrets, for within secret societies there is always a corollary desire for revelation and exchange that must be constantly regulated for the organization to survive. I have examined some elements of this tension by showing how what may ultimately prove to have been an imagined loss of secrets at Los Alamos National Laboratory has nevertheless resulted in the entire U.S. nuclear complex reordering itself under hypersecurity measures. In Simmel's terms, I have argued that the particular "overtones" that resonate within the U.S. nuclear complex, and that constantly threaten to overturn its official secrecy, concern three linked areas: first, how secrecy performs as a general mode of social regulation within American society, not simply as a means of controlling technoscientific data about the bomb; second, the problematic foundations of race and citizenship within the nuclear complex; and third, how nuclear security relies on a misrecognition of technology's ability to perfectly control social relations and eliminate risk. The allegations of espionage at Los Alamos in 1999 put these repressed aspects of the nuclear complex on public display, briefly troubling a secret governmentality until unprecedented hypersecurity measures were mobilized to reestablish the nuclear complex as a secret society, one that controls not only how weapons scientists think and behave, but also how much of America's nuclear project remains accessible to a larger public sphere. In other words, the nuclear complex recapitulated its essential contradiction in 1999–2000: that official secrecy maintains the distinction between national security and national sacrifice. In striving to keep the internal (economic, environmental, and social) costs of the national security state invisible, state secrecy both produces and enforces an official fiction; namely, that the only legitimate forms of nuclear security and risk are located outside the territorial borders of the nation-state.

It is important, therefore, to recognize the social costs of legitimizing a new national discourse about the need to protect "America's secrets." The Wen Ho Lee affair was simply the first in a series of widely publicized U.S. "security scandals" in 1999–2000 involving a potential loss of classified information. Officials responded to these events by evoking "America's secrets" as a self-evident category, one needing no further explanation but that should be protected regardless of the cost to the nation. For example, in 2000, after John Deutch, former head of the Central Intelligence Agency, acknowledged that he had illegally stored classified information about CIA covert activities on his unsecured home computer, and after a State Department laptop computer containing "above top secret" information was lost, Secretary of State Madeleine K. Albright intoned: "This is inexcusable and intolerable. Such failures put our nation's secrets at risk."[32] That no one even bothered to question this open declaration from the State Department that the United States keeps "secrets" reveals perhaps the truest legacy of the Cold War—after all, the fact that states keep secrets is supposed to be a secret! But as America's first multigenerational, global conflict, the Cold War, with all its expansive new forms of secrecy, became nothing less than an organizing principle in American society. One cultural legacy of that nuclear standoff is that an "at war" mentality is now a basic feature of the U.S. national imaginary, one that is easily provoked, deployed, and acquiesced to.

One of the most remarkable aspects of the U.S. response to the September 11 attacks on New York and Washington, for example, was the speed with which America went to war. Before the attackers had been identified, and therefore before the nature of the conflict or victory could even be imagined, President George W. Bush committed the United States to an all-out struggle against "terror"—a vague if powerful concept, more a structure of feeling than a military foe. Bush's "war on terror" was inaugurated, then, not as a battle with a specific enemy or state (one definition of a war) but instead as a future-oriented governmental structure. Indeed, citizens were informed immediately by officials that this "new" war would be: (1) planetary in its scope (merely starting in Afghanistan), (2) expensive (requiring vast new military expenditures), and (3) potentially unending (at the very least, occupying the foreseeable future).[33] Speaking theatrically from various "undisclosed locations" in the fall of 2001, Vice President Dick Cheney named this dual reconfiguration of U.S. geopolitical policy and everyday American life as nothing less than "the new normal."[34] Thus, the necessary project of responding to the unprecedented attacks on two American cities was formally linked right from the start to a broader domestic project of normalization and regularization of a specific wartime economy; in other words, hypersecurity became an explicit national structure after September 11.

The "new normal" elevated many of the concerns of the hypersecurity state evidenced two years earlier in Los Alamos to the national level. Racial profiling took the form of a nationwide dragnet for Arab nationals between the ages of eighteen and thirty-five, resulting in over 1,200 men being "detained" in secret by the Justice Department without being charged. Similarly, secrecy became an overdetermined project of the post-9/11 American state. It began with an immediate effort to remove information from libraries and Web sites that might be useful to terrorists, but became a broader purge of government information from public access. In October, President Bush signed Executive Order 13233, which in effect seals presidential records (after the Reagan administration), and he proposed a new form of military tribunal for captured "terrorists" to ensure that trials could be conducted quickly, in secret, and rely on classified information.[35] Attorney General Ashcroft concurrently announced in a memorandum to all government agencies that the Justice Department would support official efforts to resist Freedom of Information Act requests from citizens and, in the form of the quickly passed Patriot Act, received expansive new powers for wiretapping and surveillance of U.S. residents.[36] In a congressional hearing on November 9, 2001, Ashcroft offered this perspective on critics of this expanded program of governmental security: "To those who scare peace-loving people with phantoms of lost liberty, my message is this: your tactics only aid terrorists."[37] After 9/11, secrecy was thus formally linked with silencing as a mode of controlling debate about not only the war effort but also America's presidential past and its militarized future.

Hypersecurity in perhaps its purest form, however, was evidenced by a series of terrorist "warnings" issued by the Justice Department and the newly formed Department of Homeland Security. These alerts were characterized by an absence of information about the source of the threat, the longevity of the risk, or the rationale for the warning. In essence, these state declarations of risk simply presented citizens with the category of "threat" itself (i.e., the official message was: something terrible might happen, somewhere, any second now); the alerts provided citizens with no conceptual tools for evaluating or accommodating this new danger. It was danger itself purified and amplified as national discourse. In March 2002, these terrorist warnings were institutionalized by the new director of homeland security, Tom Ridge, when he presented a color-coded ranking of the terrorist danger to citizens and state agencies, offering a hierarchy of risk in categories from red (severe risk), to orange (high risk), to yellow (elevated risk), to blue (significant risk), to green (general risk).[38] Thus, the terrorist danger of 9/11 is now officially codified as a permanent aspect of everyday life. Paired with President Bush's statement that nations are either "with" the United States, or "with the terrorists," this new domestic warning system elevates "terror" to the defining category of an American world system, structuring both international relations and everyday American life. Consequently, hypersecurity has become a dominant mode of governmentality after 9/11, a series of linked discourses and official practices that work through the mobilization of a named or unnamed, but always totalizing, threat.

Within this context, nuclear weapons, as the ultimate tools of threat, not surprisingly resurfaced as a central organizing principle in the U.S. war on terror. In his 2002 State of the Union address, President Bush formally linked terrorism with weapons of mass destruction, arguing that non-nuclear states that pursue nuclear weapons are a threat to civilization itself:

> States like these, and their terrorist allies, constitute an axis of evil, arming to threaten the peace of the world. By seeking weapons of mass destruction, these regimes pose a grave and growing danger. They could provide these arms to terrorists, giving them the means to match their hatred. They could attack our allies or attempt to blackmail the United States. In any of these cases, the price of indifference would be catastrophic. We will work closely with our coalition to deny terrorists and their state sponsors the materials, technology, and expertise to make and deliver weapons of mass destruction.

We will develop and deploy effective missile defenses to protect America and our allies from sudden attack. And all nations should know: America will do what is necessary to ensure our nation's security. We'll be deliberate, yet time is not on our side. I will not wait on events, while dangers gather. I will not stand by, as peril draws closer and closer. The United States of America will not permit the world's most dangerous regimes to threaten us with the world's most destructive weapons.[39]

While threatening preemptive strikes against regimes seeking weapons of mass destruction, and identifying Iran, Iraq, and North Korea by name as this new "axis of evil," Bush seemed also to be identifying nuclear weapons as tools of terror. However, the concurrent 2002 Nuclear Policy Review revealed that the administration was committed not to reducing but to expanding the use of the U.S. nuclear arsenal. In addition to taking all the steps necessary to go back into general nuclear weapons production, the Nuclear Policy Review identified the need for new generations of nuclear weapons (mini-nukes and earth penetrators) for potential use against the "axis of evil," argued for targeting nuclear weapons against non-nuclear states for the first time in U.S. history, and recommitted the United States to a national missile defense system.[40] This increasingly expansive vision of the nuclear state is revealed most directly by U.S. military budgets, which before 9/11 were roughly $330 billion a year, already higher than the military budgets of all of America's NATO allies, Russia, China, and the so-called rogue states *combined* (*Bulletin of the Atomic Scientists* 2001). After 9/11, the Bush administration asked for and received an immediate $48 billion increase, and projected annual increases leading to defense budgets of close to half a trillion dollars a year by 2007 (Dao 2002).

At the start of the twenty-first century, then, the United States exists in the contradictory position of waging a global campaign against "terror," focusing on states with nuclear ambitions, while simultaneously enhancing its own reliance on weapons of mass destruction. Rather than delegitimating nuclear weapons within the international order, the terrorist attacks of September 11 have been mobilized to reenergize the nuclear fetish at home and abroad. The "new normal," however, presents merely a purified version of the Cold War geostrategic program of global containment and technological control (but one not dependent on the future stability of any specific state). To this end, nuclear "terror" has been reconfigured as an infinitely expandable concept in the United States, one that links domestic and international politics, that ensures record defense budgets for years to come, and that ultimately empowers the hypersecurity state (through the linked deployment of secrecy and threat) to imagine, perhaps really for the first time in history, a truly unlimited field of planetary action. Thus, it is important to interrogate the national insecurity about LANL not only in terms of its formal features but also in terms of how a discourse of "insecurity" informs larger policy debates over how to define the current position the United States holds as the world's sole military "superpower." The strategic manipulation of real or imagined "threat" is enabled by a secret governmentality (as the details are always "top secret"), but that secret governmentality is also further legitimated by the constant evocation of new threats (such as missing computer codes, phantom "wmds," and the always "imminent" terrorist act). If this circuit continues, then how the nuclear weapons complex evolves in U.S. policy and practice, and how citizens are positioned in regard to U.S. national (in)security over the next few decades, is very likely to be nothing less than an ever more strictly policed, ever more powerfully protected, nuclear secret.

7 Mutant Ecologies
Radioactive Life in Post–Cold War New Mexico

After more than five decades focused on a specific kind of apocalypse in Los Alamos, the firestorms of spring 2000 could not have come from a more unexpected source. On May 4, the U.S. Forest Service lost control of an effort to reduce the risk of forest fire in Bandelier National Monument by burning underbrush. Over the next week, winds gusting to over sixty miles per hour turned the "controlled burn" into a raging firestorm, forcing the evacuation of Los Alamos County. In addition to displacing over 25,000 people, the fire forced Los Alamos National Laboratory (LANL) to close for the first time in its history, leaving scientists to worry about ongoing research projects, the security of their experimental data, as well as the safety of nuclear materials.[1] Meanwhile, thousands of residents of northern New Mexico fled the region, fearing the health effects of the smoke and ash. By the time the fire was contained some 48,000 acres had burned, making the Cerro Grande blaze the most damaging forest fire in New Mexican history. The town of Los Alamos was the hardest hit, with hundreds of homes reduced to smoldering ruins (see Figure 7.1). Almost a third of Los Alamos National Laboratory's 27,000 acres burned, causing over $300 million in damage and the loss of three dozen buildings (including several involved in assembling the original Trinity device). Significant areas of both Santa Clara Pueblo and San Ildefonso Pueblo were also scorched, damaging water supplies as well as sacred sites. Concerns about how the charred mountain landscape would handle the torrential summer rains kept residents in fear of flooding for months afterward, hampering rebuilding efforts and extending the scope of the tragedy.

A natural disaster of this magnitude is terrifying, and undeniably traumatic, for all involved. One of the most striking cultural aspects of the Cerro Grande fire, however, was how many New Mexicans experienced the blaze as nothing less than a nuclear apocalypse. During the midst of

7.1. Cerro Grande fire aftermath, Los Alamos. (Courtesy of Los Alamos National Laboratory)

the crisis, conversation among many New Mexicans focused on how the melted ash of burned Los Alamos homes was like the melted sand created by the first atomic bomb, which was detonated by Los Alamos scientists in the deserts of central New Mexico in July 1945. Similarly, some laboratory scientists took pains to calculate the heat of the Los Alamos firestorm so as to compare it to the firestorms created in Hiroshima and Nagasaki in August 1945. Hundreds of Santa Fe residents, fearful of "radioactive" smoke and ash from the fire, fled the area. When asked how people were coping with the disaster, one laboratory employee and Los Alamos resident put it succinctly: "All of us are thinking of Hiroshima. Now we know what that was like." But while four hundred Los Alamos families tragically lost their homes, and residents of northern New Mexico breathed smoke-filled air for weeks, and the regional environment was heavily damaged, miraculously no one was killed or suffered a serious physical injury during the fire. So what does it mean that residents immediately negotiated their charred mountain landscape by referring to themselves as "survivors" and evoking the atomic bombings of Hiroshima and Nagasaki (events in which some two hundred thousand people lost their lives) as a point of reference? What does it mean that ten years after the Cold War, and the most overt national fears of a nuclear apocalypse, so many New Mexicans came to inhabit a post-nuclear landscape in May 2000 and to understand a most terrible forest fire in decidedly nuclear terms?

In *After The End: Representations Of The Post-Apocalypse*, James Berger explores the linkage between concepts of "trauma" and "apocalypse" by analyzing how temporality and perception function in regard to painful experience. He argues that:

> trauma is the psychoanalytic form of apocalypse, its temporal inversion. Trauma produces symptoms in its wake, after the event, and we reconstruct trauma by interpreting its symptoms, reading back in time. Apocalypse, on the other hand, is preceded by signs and portents whose interpretation defines the event in the future. The apocalyptic sign is the mirror image of the traumatic symptom. In both cases, the event itself is so overwhelming as to be fundamentally unreadable: it can only be understood through the portents and symptoms that precede and follow it. (1999: 20–21)

Thus, like Elaine Scarry (1985), Berger argues that the experience of pain is unrepresentable in the moment of its occurrence; it is only through its displaced effects in time that suffering takes on its psychosocial shape, becoming imbued both with language and with psychodynamic processes. Community responses to the Cerro Grande fire revealed not only that New Mexicans can work together with strength and compassion during a time of crisis, but also that a nuclear subtext informs everyday life in northern New Mexico, linking trauma and apocalypse—past and future—in a specific constellation. I want to examine the terms of this nuclear subtext, arguing that the normalization of life within New Mexico's nuclear economy is neither complete nor free of nuclear fear. Indeed, reactions to the Cerro Grande fire gave expression to the traumatic residues of the Cold War nuclear project, while articulating broad-based ecological fears about the long-term nuclear effects of LANL.

The smoke from the Cerro Grande Fire, for example, was immediately mapped as dangerous in New Mexico not because of the usual health concerns about smoke inhalation, but because it was taken by many to be radioactive. The plumes of smoke created the effect, for many, of atmospheric fallout from a nuclear explosion, as the particulate matter

7.2. Smoke from Cerro Grande fire. (Courtesy of Los Alamos National Laboratory)

within the clouds from destroyed buildings and from radioactive ecologies within the laboratory generated regional concerns about radiation effects (see Figure 7.2). The billowing smoke, thus, not only drew visible attention to LANL as a threatened site, but also revealed a widespread regional concern about the ecological effects of a half century of nuclear research.[2] The fire demonstrated the willingness of many New Mexicans to experience any ecological event involving LANL through the lens of nuclear trauma.[3] And indeed, there were subtle nuclear logics informing the event: after President Clinton declared Los Alamos County a Federal Disaster Area, for example, residents of Los Alamos became dependent on the Federal Emergency Management Agency (FEMA), an organization formed for nuclear civil defense planning during the height of the Cold War. But to understand the nuclear fears evoked by the Cerro Grande fire, I suggest we must first understand the historical production of nuclear natures, and recognize the cultural processes that have evolved since 1945 to manage life within a radioactive biosphere. For reactions to the fire reveal not only a specific apocalyptic sensibility in northern

New Mexico, but also a structural change in how nature is now constituted and experienced. This effort to normalize nuclear nature has been a multigenerational process in New Mexico—one affecting concepts of social order, ecology, health, and security—producing in the aftermath of the fire multiple experiences of the nuclear uncanny.

In this chapter, I interrogate the production of nuclear natures in the New Mexico context, arguing that one of the most profound aspects of the Manhattan Project has been to put in motion changes in specific social and biological ecologies that are highly mutable. To understand these new formations, however, we need a political ecology that can forward multigenerational reproduction. I argue that a theory of mutation allows us to assess the quality of biosocial transformations over time—as alternatively injury, improvement, or noise. I begin by revisiting the 1950s debates about the global effects of the bomb, a moment when the discourse about mutation was both explicit and transformative in American culture. I then explore the politics of mutation first by examining the traumatic effects of blast and radiation on living beings produced during the Cold War U.S. nuclear testing program; then by interrogating how specific radioactive environments have been officially rescripted in the post–Cold War period as ecological "improvements"; and finally, by looking at how the idea of the "nuclear worker" now links humans and wildlife within a shared genetic experiment in northern New Mexico, one producing a highly ambiguous and charged social space. Assessing the scale of this biosocial process requires us to unpack contemporary assumptions about the bomb as a technology while interrogating the historical terms and parameters of the Cold War nuclear program as a global ecological experiment. For reactions to the Cerro Grande fire revealed not only widespread nuclear fear, but also repression about the historical production of nuclear nature. Thus, it is important now to ask: How have Americans come to understand their place within a radioactive environment since 1945? What does a shift in knowledge about nuclear nature tell us about the long-term transformations of both the nation-state and the state of nature in the nuclear age?

OF MEN AND ANTS

> It is a curious phenomenon of nature that only two species practice the
> art of war—men and ants.
> —Norman Cousins, *Modern Man is Obsolete* (1945)

A full-scale nuclear attack on the United States would devastate the natural environment on a scale unknown since early geological times, when, in response to natural catastrophes whose nature has not been determined, sudden mass extinctions of species and whole ecosystems occurred all over the earth ... It appears that at the outset the United States would be a republic of insects and grass.

—Jonathan Schell, *The Fate of the Earth* (1982)

In the classic Hollywood science fiction film, *Them!* (dir. Douglas, 1954), Los Alamos weapons science and Cold War logics of "containment" are turned quite sensationally on their heads. Rather than producing international security in the form of a military nuclear deterrent, the American nuclear complex is portrayed as the domestic source of proliferating radiation effects, creating an entirely new ecology of risk in the form of gigantic mutant carnivorous ants. These fantastic creatures are identified, in the film, as the products of the very first atomic explosion in central New Mexico on July 16, 1945. The Trinity test is portrayed, then, not as the first triumph of American big science, nor as the technoscientific means of ending World War II, nor as the military foundation of the world's first nuclear superpower. Rather, the first atomic explosion, in this science fiction, is the source of an inverted natural order, in which the smallest of creatures can become a totalizing threat, and where the security state must be deployed to protect citizens from the unintended consequences of Los Alamos science. *Them!* engaged a new kind of nuclear fear in 1954, one based not on the apocalypse of nuclear war but on the everyday transformation of self and nature through an irradiated landscape. Remembered today mostly for its McCarthy-era theatrics in which the giant ants play a thinly veiled allegory for the communist "menace," the film more subtly presents a devastating critique of U.S. nuclear policy at the very height of the Cold War: it argues that on July 16, 1945, Americans entered a postnuclear environment of their own invention. From this perspective, the nuclear apocalypse is not in the future—a thing to be endlessly deterred through nuclear weapons and international relations—it is already here, being played out in the unpredictable movement of radioactive materials moving through bodies and biosphere.

Them! arrived on American movie screens in June 1954, just three months after Los Alamos scientists conducted the largest thermonuclear explosion of the Cold War at Bikini Island in the Marshall Islands. Detonating with 2.5 times its expected force, the Bravo event produced a fifteen-megaton yield and vast atmospheric fallout (see Figure 7.3), as Chuck Hansen (1988: 65) describes it:

Within a second, a fireball nearly three miles in diameter was formed and a crater more than a mile wide and over 200 ft. deep was gouged from the

7.3. The fifteen-megaton Bravo thermonuclear event; Operation Castle, Bikini Atoll, 1954. (U.S. Department of Energy Photograph)

reef. The light from the fireball was visible for nearly a minute on Rongerik atoll 155 miles to the east, and was observed clearly by military personnel at Kwajalein Island over 250 miles southeast of Bikini . . . Within a minute, the fireball had risen to 47,000 ft. and the pulverized coral from the crater was pulled up into a cloud that was already more than seven miles across with a stem 2,000 ft. wide. In this same minute, the blast wave from the explosion moved outward from the burst point, stripping the nearby islands of vegetation and animals. Ten minutes after zero hour, the mushroom cloud was 70 miles across and rising swiftly, a minute later, windows in buildings at Rongerik atoll rattled as the blast wave hit.

Stripping the nearby islands of vegetation and animals. The Bravo test ultimately contaminated fifty thousand square miles of the Pacific with "serious to lethal levels of radioactivity" (Weisgall 1994: 305). Among the exposed were 223 indigenous residents of Rongerik, Rongelap, Ailinginae, and Utirik Atolls as well as the twenty-three-member crew of the Japanese fishing boat, *The Lucky Dragon*, which was over eighty miles from ground zero at the time of detonation. Thus, as American theatergoers flocked to *Them!* in the summer of 1954, making it one of the most successful films of the year, news reports were simultaneously following the progression of radiation sickness among the Marshall Islanders and *Lucky Dragon* crew—educating many Americans, for the first time, about the biological effects of radioactive fallout.[4] This graphic documentation of the ecological costs of nuclear testing, as brute reality as well as cinematic fantasy, worked to transform America's nuclear program for many individuals from an exclusively military project to a global environmental threat. After Bravo, the bomb was increasingly recognized to be both an explosive and, in the form of fallout, a chemical/biological weapon in the United States, challenging the nature of the "experiment" being conducted by Los Alamos weapon scientists. For if each U.S. nuclear detonation advanced the potential of the bomb as a military machine, each test also added to the global burden of radioactive elements in the biosphere, overturning the "national security" logics of the U.S. nuclear arsenal by introducing the possibility of cellular mutations in plants, animals, and people on a global scale.

As the first U.S. popular culture text to engage the bomb not as a military weapon but as an ecological threat, *Them!* is worth revisiting in post–Cold War America. The film is important not only because it reveals a moment when the U.S. nuclear arsenal was not yet a normalized (all but invisible) aspect of everyday life, but also because it is the *Ur*-text for an ongoing fascination with mutation in American popular culture, an important cultural legacy of the Manhattan Project.[5] Although it appears today as a form of atomic kitsch, the film (an academy award winner for its one special effect: the giant ants) is played straight, and remains a compelling textual effort to assess the "newness" of the atomic age. *Them!* begins, quite hauntingly, as a crime story. The police encounter a young girl, wandering the New Mexican desert alone in her bathrobe, too traumatized to speak (the image of a postnuclear survivor). Discovering a series of bizarre and violent murders in the area, including those of the girl's parents, the police struggle to make sense of crime-scene evidence (buildings destroyed from the inside out, recurring traces of sugar and formic acid, and an apparent lack of motive). The police soon call in the FBI, but these domestic agents of the security state are equally limited in their ability to assess the "crime," also unable to make the imaginative leap required to see mutant nature as the cause. Frustrated by a lack of fingerprints, for example, the police and FBI agents stare without recognition at a strange impression found in the earth. The plaster cast of the impression reveals the footprint of a giant ant, constituting a criminal signature literally too large for the police to comprehend. Nuclear nature simply baffles; as one policeman puts it, "Lots of evidence, loaded with clues, but nothing adds up." The problem here is that the crimes are "unnatural" by the standards of prenuclear

America, making the first problem of the nuclear age one of linking perception and imagination in a world operating by new horizons of possibility.

A father-daughter team of entomologists from the Department of Agriculture eventually identify the footprints, and lead the police back through the "crime scenes" looking for evidence of a natural order transformed. In the fallout zone from the 1945 Trinity test, an area untouched by people in nine years, they discover strange mound formations that signal the arrival of a new species and trigger the first confrontation with the giant ants. The film suggests that the nuclear transformation of everyday life can occur at any time, and anywhere, even in the silence of an eerie, and seemingly empty, desert. As the security/science operatives attempt to contain the ants (using chemical weapons and flamethrowers to destroy the nests), they discover that several queen ants are already airborne, flying away to establish new colonies. Evoking all the logics of the Cold War nuclear state in dealing with a radioactive threat—the need for complete secrecy to prevent panic in the citizenry, a total mobilization of the military, and an apocalyptic rhetoric of failure—the film systematically turns the logics of the nuclear state on its own unintended creations. Noting, for example, that it is the nature of ants (as with humans) to conduct aggressive military campaigns, the emissaries of the science/security state both demonize and admire the giant ants as "ruthless" and "efficient" killers, and conclude that if the giant ants are not stopped immediately, "mankind will be extinct within a year." The final third of the film then becomes an arms race of a different kind, as the military mobilization follows the giant ants from New Mexico to the storm drains underneath Los Angles, where the climactic battle takes place to prevent a next generation of mutant insects (introducing a new kind of nuclear proliferation).

Them! both deploys and ridicules the military logics of containment by asking: If the giant ants are a crime, then who is responsible? The film enacts a split vision, both demonizing the ants as an external other, while recognizing that they are a creation of the U.S. security state. Thus, the terrible joke embedded in the title of the film—*Them!*—which suggests that the agents of destruction are foreign-born rather than domestic, "theirs" rather than "ours." The film ultimately argues that the dispersal of nuclear materials in the environment (recognized as a global phenomenon by 1954) is the source of a new kind of nature, mutant, wild, and *un*containable by the state. As imagined here, the U.S. nuclear complex is responsible not only for new technologies of mass death but also of producing new kinds of mutant life, as species are reinvented at the genetic level. As nuclear allegory and ecological critique, *Them!* also implicitly argues that human beings are not only responsible for creating a mutant ecology via the bomb, they are also part of this ecology, producing a future that is as unpredictable at the level of genetic stability as it is at the level of international relations.

Them! is the cinematic instantiation of a larger cultural discourse in the United States about the bomb, in which nuclear critics have deployed insects as a means of engaging the philosophical status of the nuclear age. From Norman Cousins's 1945 essay "Modern Man is Obsolete," written days after the atomic bombings of Hiroshima and Nagasaki, to Jonathan Schell's 1982 portrayal of a postnuclear American republic of "insects and grass," insects have been used to articulate a "species" knowledge in relation to the nuclear. The "nature" of nature is interrogated in these discourses, as the power of atomic energy, the "purity" of ecosystems, and the adaptability of certain organisms to a radioactive environment are positioned against human "nature." Cousins's argument that only "men and ants" make war asks if it is a biological imperative to organize conflict in both species (as highly organized but ultimately mindless beings), while Schell argues that humans are too fragile a species to survive a nuclear war, and that the only victors would be the insects that could withstand and adapt to a radioactive environment. Both authors argue that the destructive power of the bomb demands social evolution, and deploy insects as a mirror to humanity. Edmund Russell has tracked this historical impulse to link people and insects in a remarkable analysis of chemical weapons and pest control in twentieth-century America. Tracking the technoscientific, organizational, and ideological tools used in military and public health campaigns against human and insect "enemies," he documents a structural interaction between species under the concept of "extermination," concluding that "war and control of nature coevolved: the control of nature expanded the scale of war, and war expanded the scale on which people controlled nature" (2001: 2). Technoscience militarizes nature in these discourses, enabling a dual deployment of social evolution and biological extinction as the focal points of a new kind of modernity. In other words, the atomic bomb produces not only new understandings of self, nature, and society but also (as *Them!* argues) initiates a profound mutation in each of these terms.

Consider, for example, the concept of "background radiation," which references the baseline level of radiation considered to be inherent in the environment by federal authorities. The background radiation figure is the amount of radiation the average American receives in a given year from all sources; it is also the standard with which U.S. industrial radiation exposure rates are measured. The current background radiation rate for U.S. citizens is 360 millirems per year. Of this, 300 millirems come from "naturally" occurring sources, such as cosmic rays, radon, radiation from the surface of the earth, and potassium-40 in our bodies. The remaining 60 millirems come from the cumulative atmospheric effects of industry—including nuclear medicine, nuclear power, and nuclear weapons testing (Wolfson 1991: 60–63). What now constitutes the "background" field for all studies of radiation effects is a mix of naturally occurring and industrial effects. More specifically, the trace elements of Los Alamos weapons science now saturate the biosphere, creating an atomic signature found in people, plants, animals, soils, and waterways. The Manhattan Project not only unlocked the power of the atom, creating new industries and military machines, it also inaugurated a subtle but total transformation of the biosphere. But if nature entered a new kind of nuclear regime in 1945, then how should we now assess that transformation? After all, the very idea of a background radiation standard is to establish a norm, a new definition of the "natural" in which the past effects of the nuclear complex are embedded as a fundamental aspect of the ecosystem. To appreciate the full scope of this nuclear revolution, we need to examine the effects of the bomb not only at the level of the nation-state but also at the level of the local ecosystem, the organism, and, ultimately, the cell.

The background radiation rate constitutes an average and thus does not apply to any specific individual.[6] The true evaluation of nuclear risk is tied to specific exposures rather than the background radiation count (which, although measurable, constitutes a negligible health risk). Makhijani and Schwartz, for example, identify seven classes of people negotiating health risks from U.S. nuclear production:

> (1) Workers in uranium mines and mills and in nuclear weapons design, production and testing facilities; (2) armed forces personnel who participated in atmospheric weapons testing; (3) people living near nuclear weapons sites; (4) human experiment subjects; (5) armed forces personnel and other workers who were exposed during the deployment, transportation and other handling and maintenance of weapons within the Department of Defense; (6) residents of Hiroshima and Nagasaki in August 1945; and (7) the world inhabitants for centuries to come. (1998: 396)

The enormous difference in the types and degrees of exposures among these populations demonstrates both the generality and the specificity of the nuclear age: exposures are simultaneously collective (involving everyone on the planet) and highly individualized (involving specific classes of people—soldiers, miners, nuclear workers). While we all have trace elements from the Cold War nuclear project in our bodies, no two exposure rates are identical, as geographical location, occupation, and nuclear events (whether from nuclear industry, atmospheric nuclear tests, or accidents such as

Chernobyl) combine with individual physiology and specific ecosystems to define actual rates and degrees of risk. Nevertheless, if we were able to track back in time and space, following the trajectory of the various chemicals and nuclear materials now in each of our bodies, one subset of these industrial signatures would lead back to Los Alamos and the Cold War national security project, offering a different vantage point from which to assess the nuclear age. From this perspective, America's nuclear project has witnessed the transformation of human "nature" at the level of both biology and culture, leading to the formation of new kinds of risk societies, unified not by national affiliation, but by exposure levels, health effects, and nuclear fear.[7]

These ever-present signatures of the nuclear security state constitute, for the vast majority of people, a theoretical rather than a known health risk. However, while studies of the survivors of Hiroshima, Nagasaki, the Marshall Islands, and Chernobyl, as well as of nuclear workers, have produced a detailed scientific understanding of the effects of high levels of radiation exposure, the effects of low-level radiation remain a subject of intense scientific debate.[8] It exists, as Adriana Petryna (2002) has put it, at the level of "partial knowledge," making the challenge of the nuclear age as much the regulation of uncertainty as the documentation of biological effects. This uncertainty is intensified by the specific attributes of radiation-induced illness, which includes a displacement in time (sometimes occurring decades after exposure) and a potential to be genetically transferred across generations. Recognizing the subtle but totalizing scope of the nuclear transformation of nature—the dispersion of plutonium, strontium, cesium, and other elements into the biosphere—challenges the traditional concept of a "nuclear test," which in Los Alamos has referred most prominently to the detonation of a nuclear device: For how does one define or limit the scope of the nuclear laboratory when its trace elements can be found literally everywhere on the planet? Thus, while Los Alamos scientists worked through the Cold War to perfect nuclear weapons as the core technology in a "closed world" system of military command, control, and surveillance (see Edwards 1996), their testing regime also transformed the biosphere itself, turning the earth into a vast laboratory of nuclear effects that maintain an unpredictable claim on a deep future.[9]

A concept of hybridity for scholars as diverse as Latour (1996), Haraway (1997), and Rabinow (1999) has been highly productive in revealing technoscientific objects to be complex fusions of nature and culture.[10] In thinking about radioactive natures, however, the concept of hybridity—with its focus on parental elements and temporal orientation toward the present—limits our ability to recognize multigenerational reproduction across technoscientific forms and effects. As Young (1995) reminds us, the original definition of the biological hybrid is tied to a concept of species. In sum, a species is that which can reproduce, while the hybrid is the infertile offspring of two different species or subspecies. Thus, the hybrid is in a strict sense a form of generational stasis, allowing one to separate analytically the distinct genetic lines that came together to create the infertile being. The world produced by the bomb, however, is structured by its totalizing scale (the entire planet) and by more localized, multigenerational effects that are highly changeable, rooted in any given moment as much in ambiguity or latency as in material fact. The 24,000-year half-life of plutonium, for example, presents a multimillennial colonization of the future, requiring a different temporal analytic for investigating radioactive ecologies.

To this end, I propose extending our theorization of the complexity of nature-culture forms via the concept of mutation. A mutation occurs when the ionization of an atom changes the genetic coding of a cell, producing a new reproductive outcome. As cells replicate over time, mutagenic effects can have three possible outcomes: (1) evolution, or an enhancing of the organism through a new adaptation to the environment; (2) injury, such as cancer or deformity; or (3) genetic noise, that is, changes that neither improve nor injure the organism but can still affect future generations. A concept of mutation implies, then, a complex coding of time (both past and future); it assumes change, but it does not from the outset judge either the temporal scale or the type of change that will take place. It also marks a transformation that is reproduced generationally, making the mutation a specific kind of break with the past that reinvents the future. Engaging the U.S. nuclear project through the lens of mutation, rather than hybridity, privileges not only the institutional and technoscientific networks needed to construct the bomb but also the long-term social and environmental effects of the production complex itself. The ecological effects of atmospheric nuclear testing, for example, may not be fully realized for decades, and an understanding of their cultural effects requires an investigation into the different conceptions of nature that inform local forms of knowledge. Post–Cold War studies at the Semipalatinsk nuclear test site in Russia, for example, have demonstrated elevated mutation rates in the children of populations exposed to fallout during the 1950s (see Dubrova et al.1996, 2002). Similarly, Petryna (2002) has shown how exposed populations near Chernobyl now pursue a "biological citizenship" in which everyday life is centered on the negotiation of risk, health care access, and the psychosocial effects of radiation-induced trauma (see also Lifton 1991). Nuclear science has transformed human culture at the cellular level in each of these cases, producing new kinds of ecologies, bodies, and social orders.

Thus, while the Cold War American nuclear project has not yet produced any giant ants, it has distributed new material and ideological elements into the biological bodies of citizens and the social body of the nation that continue to proliferate, promising unpredictable outcomes. As such, the Manhattan Project remains an unending experiment: nuclear war is still possible today, just as the biosphere and specific social orders continue to be transformed by the accumulating effects of (post)–Cold War military nuclear science. While each U.S. citizen negotiates the traces of Los Alamos science in their bodies and biosphere—making each of us real or potential mutants—the nuclear future remains highly mobile. Consequently, the remainder of this chapter investigates debates and practices involving new "species" logics in the nuclear age, examining how the pursuit of security through military technoscience has raised questions about the structural integrity of plants, animals, and people. As we shall see, the nuclear saturates both environments and social imaginations in New Mexico, revealing mutant ecologies subject to new possibilities. The ethnographic challenge, I suggest, is to realize a deep sense of this mutating future and assess how life is currently structured within specific locales.

NUCLEAR TEST SUBJECTS

Any person living in the contiguous United States since 1951 has been exposed to radioactive fallout, and all organs and tissues of the body have received some radiation exposure.

—Department of Health and Human Services, Centers for Disease Control and Prevention and the National Cancer Institute (2001)

Radiation can make cells lose their memory, and loss of memory seems to be one of the cultural effects of the bombs too, for Americans forgot that bomb after bomb was being exploded here.

—Rebecca Solnit, *Savage Dreams* (1994)

As a state project, the Cold War nuclear arsenal seems to have distributed risk to human populations on a species scale. As the Department of Health and Human Services (DHHS), the Centers for Disease Control and Prevention (CDC), and the National Cancer Institute (NCI) underscore in a 2001 joint report, all Americans maintain traces of U.S. nuclear testing in their bodies—"all organs and tissues" have been exposed. However, as Rebecca Solnit reminds us, this national exposure also became an exercise in national amnesia over the long course of the Cold War, as U.S. citizens seemed to forget or repress the implications of living within a national nuclear complex. Much of this can be traced to the cultural repercussions of the move to underground nuclear testing in 1963, which was both a public health initiative and a means of making nuclear testing more covert in a world of competing states. Without the visible effects of the mushroom cloud to remind citizens of the ongoing American nuclear project, the discourse of mutation became a generalized concern in American culture, rather than an explicit critique of the nuclear security state. The post–Cold War period, however, has witnessed a renewed awareness of the ecological effects of the nuclear complex as a result of new environmental laws, the declassification of information about Cold War nuclear projects, as well as the mounting human and environmental cost of nuclear production itself. The new visibility of America's Cold War nuclear project, however, does not take the shape of a mushroom cloud but is instead measured in terms of toxicity levels, cancer rates for certain populations, and the ecological challenges of Cold War nuclear production sites. The DHHS, CDC, and NCI report (2001: 6–7) concludes that above-ground nuclear testing in the continental United States (1951–63) produced 11,000 cancer deaths, and somewhere between 11,300 and 212,000 thyroid cancers among U.S. citizens (see Figure 7.4). As participants in this radioactive ecology, how should we—as citizens, residents, and biological beings—now evaluate the dialectics of survival and sacrifice that remains at the center of the nuclear state? And what has changed about this dialectic since the demise of the Soviet Union and the orchestration of a post–Cold War American nuclear complex?

Let us start with two specific illustrations of radioactive nature taken from opposite ends of the Cold War: the first involves a fish, the second, a bull—one an image of radioactive death, the other an image of radioactive life. In 1946, Operation Crossroads was designed to sink the remnants of the Japanese, German, and American navies and to display American nuclear power for a global audience (Figure 7.5). For scientists, it was also an opportunity to study the biological effects of America's fourth and fifth nuclear explosions (after Trinity, Hiroshima, and Nagasaki) on a wide variety of test animals as well as on the environment of the Marshall Islands. In his memoir of radiation science on Operation Crossroads (ominously titled *No Place to Hide*), David Bradley assesses the ecological effects of the bomb and offers a startling new register of the nuclear age—the "radio-autograph":

Radio-autographs are made by taking a small fish, slicing it longitudinally down the middle, drying it in a blast of warm air, and then placing the fish, cut side down, on a photographic plate. After a suitable time the radioactivity

Per capita thyroid doses resulting from
all exposure routes from all tests

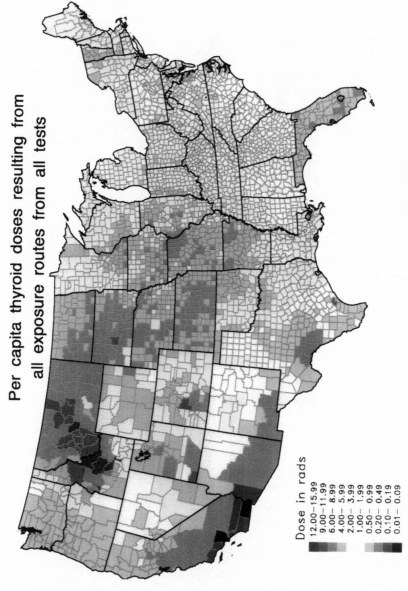

Dose in rads

12.00–15.99
9.00–11.99
6.00– 8.99
4.00– 5.99
2.00– 3.99
1.00– 1.99
0.50– 0.99
0.20– 0.49
0.10– 0.19
0.01– 0.09

7.4. National Cancer Institute map of iodine-131 contamination from above-ground U.S. nuclear testing (1945–63).
(Courtesy of the National Cancer Institute, 1997)

7.5. Shot Baker, Operation Crossroads, July 1946. (U.S. National Archives)

present in the tissues of the fish will have exposed the adjacent film, which, when developed, will then outline the fish in tones which are proportional to the radioactivity present . . . Almost all seagoing fish recently caught around the atoll of Bikini have been radioactive. Thus the disease is passed on from species to species like an epizootic. The only factors which tend to limit the disease, as distinguished from infectious diseases are the half-lives of the material involved, and the degree of dilution and dissemination of the fission products. (1948: 125–26)

Almost all seagoing fish have been radioactive. The radio-autograph constitutes a new sign of modernity, one made visible simply by placing the biological being on photographic film. The unnatural energy signature of the creature then produces its own negative image, drawn in the mirrored form of contaminated organs and orifices. Bradley approaches radiation exposure as a disease and is concerned with how it moves through the food chain; he sees no technological possibility of containing exposure rates other than the one intrinsically provided by the half-lives of the involved nuclear materials. While Bradley's radio-autographs document radiation exposure rates at a specific moment in time, they are also dialectically related to the future, as the Bikini Island ecosystem continues to negotiate the eight-day half-life of iodine-131, the 28.5-year half-life of strontium-90, and the 24,500-year half-life of plutonium. Radiation exposure is presented here as a form of incipient death, moving through the biosphere as contamination or infectious disease. The human populations affected by Operation Crossroads, including Marshall Islanders and U.S. military personnel, are still negotiating their entry into this radioactive ecology (Weisgall 1980, 1994). Concerned now with what their own radio-autographs might document, they constitute (along with the survivors of Hiroshima and Nagasaki and Manhattan Project personnel) the first distinct classes of a new global nuclear "risk society" (Beck 1992).

If the pre–Cold War radio-autographs of irradiated fish from Operation Crossroads offer us an image of a nuclear ecology of damaged organs, a corrupted food chain, and death, another image of radioactive nature in the post–Cold War period privileges survival. The Chernobyl site, which is, for many people, now the primary reference for radiation exposure, provides perhaps the clearest illustration of this new formation. After the meltdown and fire in one of the four nuclear reactors in 1986, a thirty-kilometer "zone of exclusion" was created around the Chernobyl facility, which was also encased in a concrete shell known as the "sarcophagus." By the late 1990s, 3.5 million Ukrainians had obtained legal recognition as "sufferers" of what the Soviet state had first referred to as a "controlled biomedical crisis" (Petryna 2002: 4–5). During the 1990s, a bull was found grazing in the contaminated grasses within the zone of exclusion. The apparent health of the animal became a source of commentary and pleasure for workers and neighboring communities who were dealing with the daily effects of radiation exposures and uncertainty in their lives. However, radioecologists named the bull Uran (after uranium), because of the amount of radionuclides in its system, and they began breeding the bull to study the genetic effects of radiation exposure.[11] Unlike the radioactive fish from Operation Crossroads, the cattle from the exclusion zone sired by Uran were immediately valued not as signs of damaged nature but as "survivals," illustrations of a natural adaptation to a radioactive environment.

To be sure, the four decades separating the Crossroads and Chernobyl events involve a complicated history of nuclear imagery, science, and Cold War public policy. Yet these cases are linked, as they demonstrate the progression of a new kind of "species" knowledge: if the Cold War logics of deterrence sought to preserve the stability of the present through nuclear weapons, the power of the radioactive, yet thriving, bull is that it is neither pure nor hybrid but alive and potentially mutant. Life within a radioactive zone changes the terms by which we can evaluate the nuclear revolution; it cannot be narrated within a discourse of purity—of either the nation-state or the state of nature. The question increasingly asked today concerns the quality of biosocial transformations set in motion by nuclear science. The nuclear age, from this perspective, still involves a dialectic of survival and sacrifice, but this process has expanded to include an ecological dynamic that is both external to, and preceding, the possibility of nuclear war. Recognizing radioactive natures redefines the question of nuclear security, linking the survival of the nuclear-powered state to the integrity of both social and cellular reproduction over time.

Los Alamos scientists recognized the biological effects of radiation from the start of the Manhattan Project, making Operation Crossroads an early step in an ongoing biological as well as military experiment. The goal of this research was not to stop the exposure rates, however, but to figure out how to mitigate the ecological effects of the bomb during an escalating Cold War arms race. In fact, there was no separation between the experiment and its real-world effects during the above-ground testing regime of 1945–63. Operation Plumbbob, a series of thirty nuclear detonations conducted at the Nevada Proving Grounds in 1957, for example, was designed to advance nuclear weapons science as well as study the effects of a nuclear explosion on a variety of military machines (planes, helicopters, blimps, and tanks), shelters (military bunkers, foxholes, and ammunition depots), and weapons (land mines and missile guidance systems). A significant part of the test series was also devoted to investigating the environmental and biological effects of nuclear radiation (U.S. Defense Nuclear Agency 1981a). The Department of Defense produced a thirty-one-minute film of the test series entitled *Operation Plumbbob: Military Effects Studies,* which was declassified in 1997. Under the subheading of "Biomedical Testing," the narrator states that a "major portion of the experiment was devoted to testing the effects of nuclear weapons on a large biological specimen: the pig."

Prior to Shot Wilson, 135 pigs were placed in individual aluminum containers and distributed in a large grid formation on the test site (see Figure 7.6).[12] The bomb exploded with a greater than expected force (10 kilotons), exposing the pigs to high levels of gamma radiation. Only 2 of the 135 pigs lived more than 30 days, making the experiment, by its own terms, a failure. Shot Priscilla, a Los Alamos project to study how to reduce atmospheric fallout, was also designed to study "radiation, thermal, and mechanical injury effects" on living beings (DOD 1957; see Figure 7.7). Seventy-eight pigs were shaved (to simulate human skin), painted with various materials or covered in fabric, placed in elevated boxes, and then exposed to the nuclear blast (see Figure 7.8). The pigs were used to research protective fabrics for military uniforms, as well as various flash-burn creams and different types of thermal shielding

7.6. Radiation tests on pigs in metal containers, Nevada Test Site. (Still from the DOD film, *Operation Plumbbob: Military Effects*)

7.7. Shot Priscilla, thirty-seven Kilotons; Nevada Test Site, June 1957. (U.S. Department of Energy Photograph)

7.8. Radiation and blast tests on pigs in boxes, Nevada Test Site. (Still from the DOD film, *Operation Plumbbob: Military Effects*)

(Defense Nuclear Agency 1981c: 52–53). Moreover, 710 pigs were distributed in open pens and in small open-faced boxes placed various distances behind sheets of glass. The experiment exposed one group of pigs to radiation effects, while creating shrapnel injuries in others, of the kind soldiers might experience in a nuclear strike. The irradiated and wounded pigs were then used to field-test surgical techniques. As with Shot Wilson, Shot Priscilla was a failure in the biomedical arena due to the nearly 100 percent fatality rate caused by "mechanical injury to the organism" and "massive radiation" exposure.

The DOD film presents a slow-motion image of the blast wave hitting a pen filled with the animals and then documents the efforts of scientists to collect the injured and dead bodies after the test. In describing the experiment, the DOD narration identifies the pig as "an instrument" for radiation research, and in one close-up, the film shows a chart outlining the body of a pig—used by radiation scientists to mark the injury and radiation effects on each of the animals. The rationality of this preprinted form (see Figure 7.9), which suggests an industrial logic of production and control, is at odds with the chaos documented in the postexplosion scenes of technicians in white anticontamination suits and ventilators trying to round up the visibly wounded and dying animals. The effects of the nuclear blast on the instrument-body of the pig is portrayed in the film

7.9. Chart of pig for radiation and blast studies, Nevada Test Site. (Still from the DOD film, *Operation Plumbbob: Military Effects*)

with the same efficiency as those demonstrated on various kinds of machinery. In Operation Plumbbob, the nuclear age involves not only military technoscience (the Los Alamos–designed nuclear device) and military capability (tanks and planes) but also the fragility of the biological being to blast, thermal, and radiation effects. Concluding that the nearly 100 percent death rate among the 845 pigs can also "be applied to man," the biomedical project of Operation Plumbbob seems successful only in constructing the traumatized organism as an institutional project—involving the deliberate application of the exploding bomb to a variety of living beings. Nuclear trauma is not to be avoided here—indeed, it is instrumentally and methodically pursued—in an effort to test the fragility of human and animal bodies to nuclear radiation and blast effects.

Each above-ground nuclear test was a biomedical experiment that explicitly sought to mitigate the effects of the bomb by methodically applying its force to plants, animals, and ultimately people. Pigs, dogs, sheep, cows, monkeys, and mice were used to test the effects of radiation on different species, utilizing skin, lungs, eyes, blood, and genetic material to explore how radiation exposure traumatizes a biological being in the millisecond of an atomic blast and over longer periods of time as the mutagenic effects of radiation exposure occur. The protected body of the Cold Warrior, increasingly rendered as cyborg in the cockpit of planes and other military machines, was thus prefigured by the vaporized, mutilated, and traumatized animal body. The instrumentalization of the pig in Operation Plumbbob is not only a marker of the enormous stakes of the Cold War nuclear arms race, but it is also an important illustration of a larger production and deployment of radioactive natures since 1945. In a variety of ways, soldiers and citizens were also part of this experimental regime, exponentially expanding the frame of the nuclear experiment from the confines of the Nevada Test Site to the global biosphere: as the DHHS, CDC, and NCI remind us, "all organs and tissues of the body have received some radiation exposure" (2001: 2).[13] If, however, the Cold War nuclear project began with a pursuit of the traumatized body, then what has happened to these nuclear natures in the subsequent decades? As we shall see, the radioactive body once studied for its injury is now celebrated as a Cold War survival and embedded within a new discourse of ecological purity.

THE WILDLIFE/SACRIFICE ZONE

At the end of the Cold War, the U.S. nuclear complex formally occupied a total continental landmass of over 3,300 square miles, involving thirteen major institutions and dozens of smaller production facilities and laboratories (O'Neill 1998: 35). These production sites were predominantly located in isolated, rural areas as a complex form of domestic development. Huge new industrial economies were created in Oak Ridge (Tennessee), Hanford (Washington), and Los Alamos (New Mexico) in 1943 and later in Aiken (South Carolina), Amarillo (Texas), Idaho Falls (Idaho), Rocky Flats (Colorado), and at what became the Nevada Test Site (see Hales 1997; O'Neill 1998). It was in these mostly rural, nonindustrial locations that nuclear materials were mass-produced, nuclear weapons were built and tested, and nuclear waste was stored, fusing local ecologies and local communities with the American nuclear project. The internal logics of nuclear development required deliberate acts of territorial devastation, producing an archipelago of contaminated sites stretching across the continental United States from South Carolina to Nevada, from Kentucky to Washington, and from Alaska to the Marshall Islands. This "geography of sacrifice," as Valerie Kuletz (1998) has called it, is currently estimated to entail a $216 to $400 billion environmental restoration project for those sites that can, in fact, be "remediated," and it is likely to cost more than the Cold War nuclear arsenal itself (see Schwartz 1998; DOE 1995a, 1995b). Nuclear security has required complex new forms of internal cannibalism, as both the biology of citizens and the territories of the state encounter an array of new nuclear signatures after 1943.

In the post–Cold War period, the U.S. nuclear complex has implicitly recognized these transformations through a new type of territorial reinscription. On October 30, 1999, for example, Secretary of Energy Bill Richardson announced the formation of a thousand-acre wildlife preserve within the forty-three-square-mile territory of LANL. The new White Rock Canyon Preserve was singled out by the U.S. Department of Energy (DOE) as a "unique ecosystem," one that is "home to bald eagles, peregrine falcons, southwestern flycatchers, 300 other species of mammals, birds, reptiles, and amphibians, as well as 900 species of plants" (DOE, LAAO 1999: 1). As Secretary Richardson explained:

> How fitting that we are here today at Los Alamos, the place that witnessed the dawn of the atomic age . . . In places of rare environmental resources, we have a special responsibility to the states and communities that have supported and hosted America's long effort to win the Cold War—and we owe it to future generations to protect these precious places so that they can enjoy nature's plenty just as we do. Los Alamos's White Rock Canyon is such a place, an able bearer of New Mexico's legacy of enchantment. After today, it will be more so as we celebrate the reunification of land and community.

We celebrate the reunification of land and community. The "wildlife preserve" as a concept forwards a claim on purity, marking specific ecologies worth preserving as precious resources in a "state of nature." What can such a claim mean, however, in the context of a U.S. nuclear site? Richardson's appeal to a "legacy of enchantment" as well as to the reunification of land and community in New Mexico comes after a decade of intense environmental politics concerning the Cold War legacies of nuclear weapons work at Los Alamos. The post–Cold War period began in New Mexico with the near simultaneous announcements of a moratorium on nuclear weapons tests and the designation of 2,200 contaminated sites within LANL, requiring an estimated cleanup of over $3.3 billion (DOE 1995a: xiv). While many New Mexicans discovered the scale of Cold War nuclear research at Los Alamos through its environmental costs, community groups throughout northern New Mexico began mobilizing for health studies as well as increased surveillance of water, soil, and air quality. The reunification of land and people proposed by the "wildlife preserve" recognizes the unique cultural investments of Pueblo and Nuevomexicano communities in the area now occupied by Los Alamos. However, the discourse of "preservation" enabling such recognition can only do so by ignoring the longstanding practices of environmental ruin, informing past and present research at the laboratory.

Rather than focusing on the radio-autographs of fish from Bikini Island or the instrumentalization of the pig in Nevada, the DOE now assumes responsibility for preserving the southwestern flycatcher and the peregrine falcon in northern New Mexico. In doing so, the DOE attempts to expand retroactively its Cold War mission from nuclear deterrence to environmental protection. This ideological project to link the "national security" offered by the atomic bomb during the Cold War to sustaining the biodiversity of U.S. territories, however, forwards a deep structural contradiction. The global effects of nuclear production have transformed the global environment, making the biosphere itself a postnuclear formation. Since the trace elements of atmospheric fallout are now ubiquitous in soils and waterways, flora and fauna, the "nature" of wildlife as a concept has changed in the nuclear age. If exposure is now a general condition—a question of degree rather than kind—then what does it mean to promote such images of survival in the midst of contamination?

This recuperation of "nature" within post–Cold War debates about the environmental and health dangers of nuclear production articulates a new form of state territoriality. In the continental United States alone, the DOE has recently transformed over 175,800 acres of land by legislative fiat from industrial nuclear sites to wildlife preserves. Carved out of the vast security buffer zones established around nuclear sites, most of these areas were fenced off in the middle of the twentieth century and isolated from human contact during the Cold War. Consequently, these sites were among the most heavily fortified wilderness areas in the world. By presenting these sites as untouched in over fifty years, the DOE seeks to redefine the value and object of that military fortification, replacing nuclear weapons systems with biodiversity as the security object of the nuclear state. This suturing together of wildlife preserve and national sacrifice zone has become an expansive post–Cold War project.

At the Savannah River Site, which produced plutonium and tritium for the U.S. nuclear arsenal, ten thousand acres (of the two hundred thousand-acre nuclear facility) became the Crackerneck Wildlife Management Area and Ecological Reserve in 1999 (DOE, SROO 1999). Celebrating some 650 species of aquatic life found on the site, the DOE presented a remarkable image of biodiversity to the public. DOE representatives failed to mention, however, that the unusually healthy alligators and rather large bass found at the Savannah River Site are also unusually radioactive (Associated Press 1999). Their bodies contain cesium-137, a byproduct of nuclear material production on the site, which is home to five nuclear reactors. The Savannah River Site now presents a uniquely modern contradiction: the site maintains a massive environmental problem in the form of thirty-four million gallons of high-level radioactive waste, a multimillennial challenge to the future, but it has been rescripted by the nuclear state as an ecological reserve preserved, as the DOE notes, for "future generations."

At the Idaho National Engineering and Environmental Laboratory (INEEL), 74,000 acres are now included in the Sagebrush Steppe Ecosystem Reserve. The DOE has devoted this preserve to the protection of some 4,000 species of plants and 270 species of animals—including the ferruginous hawk, the pygmy rabbit, and Townsend's big-eared bat (DOE, INEEL 1999). Inaugurating the reserve, Secretary Richardson remarked:

> The Department of Interior estimates that 98 percent of intact sagebrush steppe ecosystems have been destroyed or significantly altered since European settlement of this country. Because the INEEL has been a largely protected and secure facility for 50 years, it is still home to a large section of unimpacted sagebrush habitat. Our action today will help preserve for future generations one of the last vestiges of this important system. (1999: 1)

INEEL—a largely protected and secure facility. With fifty-two nuclear reactors, and eleven gigantic tanks filled with 580,000 gallons of high-level nuclear waste, INEEL is redefining the definition of "protected" and "secure"—as well as "impact" and "risk"—for distant future generations. Townsend's big-eared bat and the pygmy rabbit may have gained new state recognition via the reserve, but their new status is primarily a bureaucratic one that does not address the mobility of animals, ecosystems, and radionuclides between territories identified as wildlife reserves and nuclear production sites.

The hard insight informing these new wildlife preserves is that isolation from human traffic provides an enormous ecological benefit: human contact is more immediately toxic for many ecosystems than are radioactive materials. The DOE wildlife reserve/sacrifice zone dual structure seems to argue, however, that nuclear materials can be kept in place and that the border between preserve and wasteland can be effectively patrolled over millennia. This logic is trumped most convincingly at the Hanford Reservation in Washington State, which produced plutonium for the U.S. arsenal from 1945 to 1992 and is now recognized as the most seriously polluted site in the United States. The DOE has recently devoted 89,000 acres of Hanford's 540 square miles to preserving the long-billed curlew, Hoover's desert parsley, and Columbia yellow cress (DOE, PNNL 1999). However, mulberry trees on the Hanford Reservation have been showing increasing amounts of strontium-90 over the past decade (Lavelle 2000), and the Russian thistle plant has recently created a new kind of environmental hazard: the radioactive tumbleweed (Associated Press 2001). The Russian thistle shoots its roots down twenty feet into the earth, sucking strontium-90 and cesium into its system from contaminated areas. The head of the plant eventually breaks off to become a windblown radiation source. Hanford now spends millions of dollars each year managing this form of contamination and has crews armed with pitchforks patrolling the reservation in trucks to wrangle the radioactive weeds. This inability to enforce the distinction between wilderness and wasteland was further dramatized at Hanford in 1998, when fruit flies landed in liquid radioactive material and carried contamination far and wide over the next weeks, requiring nothing less than a $2.5 million DOE cleanup operation (Stang 1998).

Radioactive tumbleweeds, contaminated fruit flies, and toxic alligators—these are all survivals of the Cold War nuclear project, as well as new forms of nuclear nature. Adjacent to each of the DOE wildlife preserves, however, are sites that are not just minimally radioactive according to federal standards, but rather present such profound environmental hazards that they will need to be fenced off and monitored for, in some cases, literally tens of thousands of years. These sites represent Cold War survivals of another kind. Despite the rhetorical and institutional effort to find areas of "purity" within the ecology of the nuclear complex, the broader context involves a massive state-sponsored territorial sacrifice during the Cold War, one that has been wildly productive in specific areas. The U.S. nuclear complex could not have produced seventy thousand nuclear weapons from 1943 to 1992 without favoring industrial production over environmental concerns. Just as the current background radiation rate normalizes the atmospheric effects of above-ground nuclear testing as an aspect of nature, the new wildlife zones offer an image of nature created through nuclear politics and radioactive practices. The wildlife preserve is thus an exception that proves the rule within the U.S. nuclear complex. Despite the new bureaucratic recognition of the ferruginous hawk, the pygmy rabbit, and the larkspur, the division between normal, abnormal, and pathological is being redefined in these nuclear sites, as contaminated nature is recognized to be not only valuable and robust, but to greater or lesser degrees, ever-present. In other words, the experimental projects that produced and now maintain the bomb have collectively turned the entire biosphere into an experimental zone—one in which we all live—producing new mutations, as we shall now see, in both natural and social orders.

ENVIRONMENTAL SENTINELS, OR THE MILITARIZATION
OF THE HONEY BEE

Arturo Escobar argues for a prismatic view of nature, one that "is concerned with finding new ways of weaving together the biophysical, the
cultural, and the technoeconomic for the production of other types of
social nature" (1999: 2). He suggests that we consider the imbrication of
"regimes" of nature, offering a tripartite model of "organic nature" (an
ecological view of the linkages between human and natural forms), "capitalist nature" (involving the objectification, management, and resource
extraction of nature), and "technonature" (including biocultural technologies that reinvent society and nature, such as the new genetics).[14]
Within this scheme, understandings of nature are always positional and
hybrid, requiring an ethnographic framing of physical context, cultural
logic, and global/local forms. The value of Escobar's approach is precisely its openness to new configurations of nature and society and its
attention to local detail; his political ecology is one that is in motion,
subject to continuing historical transformation but still capable of recognizing multiplicity. Pursuing this kind of a political ecology through a
theory of mutation focuses critical attention on the *multigenerational*
outcomes of specific fusions of nature and culture, of environment and
technology, of the global and the local. Mutation is a logic of generational reproduction that both privileges the multiplicity that is at the center of Escobar's useful formulation of a political ecology and
acknowledges environmental effects, but it is also one that requires a
critical stance toward each instantiation of the mutant form—as evolution, as degeneration, or as noise.

In the previous section, we saw how the Cold War U.S. nuclear project produced new forms of radioactive nature, now paradoxically
marked for federal conservation as valued "survivals" of industrial
nuclear America. Only possible because of the massive state-sponsored
ecological sacrifices of the Cold War nuclear complex, these newly recognized zones of biodiversity are not untouched by the nuclear state.
Indeed, many sites contain radioactive signatures that could change the
biological structure of plants and animals over time, making the deep
future of the radioactive wildlife preserve (as a natural and socially valued space) an open question. The radioactive future of the Cold War
nuclear complex is already mutating in the post–Cold War period, producing a complex mobilization of future generations, technoscience, and
state institutions. The DOE has not only offered up zones of conservation to future generations but also acknowledged that as many as 109
sites within the nuclear complex are too contaminated to remediate

effectively. The challenge of what do to with these radioactive sites over decades, centuries, and in some cases, millennia, is now articulated through a new discourse of environmental surveillance and control known as "long-term stewardship." On its homepage, the DOE defines this project in the following manner:

> The Long-Term Stewardship Program will maintain and continuously improve protection of public health, safety, and the environment at a site or portion of a site assigned to DOE for such purposes. This mission includes providing sustained human and environmental well-being through the mitigation of residual risks and the conservation of the site's natural, ecological, and cultural resources. Mission activities will include vigilantly maintaining "post-cleanup" controls on residual hazards; sustaining and maintaining engineered controls, infrastructure, and institutional controls; seeking to avoid or minimize the creation of additional "post-cleanup" long-term stewardship liabilities during current and future site operations; enabling the best land use and resource conservation within the constraints of current and future contamination; and periodic re-evaluation of priorities and strategies in response to changes in knowledge, science, technology, site conditions, or regional setting. The Long-Term Stewardship Program will coordinate activities to identify and promote additional research and development efforts needed to ensure this protection and to incorporate new science and technology developments that result in increased protection of human health and the environment and lower costs.[15]

Sustained human and environmental well-being through the mitigation of risk. The Long-Term Stewardship Program approaches the radioactive and chemical legacies of Cold War nuclear production as a bureaucratic, as well as technoscientific, problem. Promising an increasingly intimate interaction with contaminated sites, the Long-Term Stewardship Program hopes to minimize future environmental effects by systematically deploying as yet undeveloped technologies (see Figure 7.10; also DOE, 1999f, 2001). Through constant surveillance, the Long-Term Stewardship Program naturalizes the environmental problems of the Cold War by orchestrating institutions, technoscientific projects, and communities around managing contaminated ecologies and industrial sites for an indefinite future. This is a utopian program that imagines perfect management of Cold War nuclear waste and contaminated sites for millennia—despite the prior half century of environmental neglect.

Creating "sustained human and environmental well-being" in a post-nuclear environment, however, requires a complex new form of governmentality. For Foucault (1991), governmentality is the focus of the state on policing its population to improve the health and well-being of its citizens. In long-term stewardship, the logic of national security is

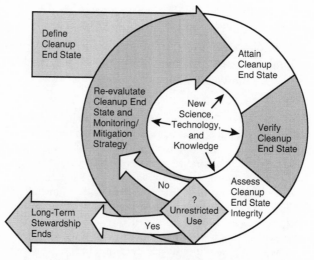

Inside the diagram:
- Define Cleanup End State
- Attain Cleanup End State
- Re-evalutate Cleanup End State and Monitoring/ Mitigation Strategy
- New Science, Technology, and Knowledge
- Verify Cleanup End State
- No
- ? Unrestricted Use
- Assess Cleanup End State Integrity
- Long-Term Stewardship Ends
- Yes

7.10. DOE Long-Term Stewardship Program diagram. (Redrawn from the Long-term Stewardship Web site, U.S. Department of Energy)

inverted, as the threat of foreign arsenals and armies is replaced by an internal discourse of contamination and territorial colonization.[16] In this context, governance means protecting citizens from the industrial effects of the nuclear security state, thus redrawing the lines between policing and welfare. However, it is not clear how "environmental well-being" can or will be defined. The DOE cannot return ecosystems to a prein-dustrial, prenuclear state. Rather, "cleanup" here means meeting U.S. regulatory standards, which are dependent on expected land use.[17] The hope of the Long-Term Stewardship Program is that, through surveil-lance and applying cutting-edge science to the environmental legacy of the Cold War, a kind of ecological stasis can be achieved in the near term, as science improves over time to solve the problems posed by radioactive contamination and waste. However, in recognizing that some sites are too damaged to treat effectively, the program also reveals that the Cold War maintains a powerful claim on a deep future. With budget projec-tions currently made out only to the year 2070, the DOE estimates that the program will require $100 million *per year* simply to maintain the 109 long-term stewardship sites, which it must do for an indefinite future (DOE 2001: 108).

If the wildlife zone is one new form of nuclear nature, the long-term stewardship site is another, with an equally deep claim on future genera-tions. Indeed, in orienting scientists, technologies, and communities around long-term stewardship sites, the DOE is also creating long-term stewardship communities, producing entirely new ecosocial orders. To make this point, we do not have to look thousands or even hundreds of years into the future. One long-term stewardship site in Los Alamos is known as Area G, which has been the laboratory's primary nuclear waste site since 1957. Area G is a hundred-acre facility located on Mesita del Buey, one of the finger-like mesas that make up the Pajarito Plateau. Low-level radioactive waste (consisting mostly of objects contaminated during laboratory operations), as well as significant quantities of plutonium-239 and uranium-238 from nuclear weapons research, is stored in five hundred foot-long pits and in deep shafts. While inventories have been carefully documented since 1988, few records were kept for the 1957–71 period, and poor records for the 1971–88 period. The incomplete knowledge of what is in Area G is important because just to the east of the site is the town of White Rock (population 6,800), while immediately north is San Ildefonso Pueblo territory. Pueblo members collect plants and hunt game in the shadow of Area G, as well as maintain shrines and sacred sites in the area. A recent laboratory "performance assessment" concludes that Area G will be completely full by 2044, initiating a new kind of territorial project:

> Active institutional control will continue for a period of 100 years (between 2047 and 2146). During institutional control, site access will be controlled, environmental monitoring will be performed, and closure cap integrity will be maintained. After the institutional-control period, it is assumed the site will be maintained by the DOE or its equivalent for as-yet undefined industrial uses. This industrial-use period is assumed to prevail for the 900 years remaining in the compliance period (between 2147 and 3046). (Hollis 1997:10)

The 900 years remaining in the compliance period (between 2147 and 3046). Evaluating the exposure risks to future populations along a variety of intrusion scenarios, the report confirms that the Manhattan Project inaugurated a new ecological regime on the Pajarito Plateau, one that is now intimately involved with negotiating the 24,000-year half-life of plutonium and other nuclear materials (see Rothman 1992; Graf 1994). Currently evaluating risk only on a thousand-year time frame, Area G is nonetheless one instantiation of a larger Cold War nuclear legacy that the discourse of long-term stewardship rhetorically seeks to contain using rational technoscientific measures.

The Area G Performance Assessment concludes, "The ability to contain radioactivity locally depends largely on nature, while the ability to prevent intrusion depends solely on man." It therefore assumes from the start that "current natural conditions will prevail" and "a government entity will maintain the site and control access to it" for the next thousand years (Hollis 1997: 16). Both nature and the state are, for the sake of the study, assumed to be stable entities across the next millennium, even as the evidence of the past fifty years shows a dramatic change in both. Indeed, more subtle changes are already shaping the nuclear future of the Pajarito Plateau, offering a new state of nature, more mutant than stable. Plumes of tritium contamination as well as chemical residues from high explosives are already leaking from Area G, demonstrating that the geology of the Pajarito Plateau is more permeable than previously assumed.[18] Traces of tritium found in wells drilled around LANL have also raised concerns about the mechanisms of transport through the geological tuft and the long-range safety of the regional aquifer.[19] Even as the performance assessment assumes a forever-vigilant state agency to watch over a stable ecosystem at Area G, environmental surveillance is revealing a more mobile ecological formation. Indeed, surveillance itself has become the basis for new kinds of nature.

Consider the role now played by the Italian honeybee (*Apis mellifera*) at Area G. As a creature that flies over a wide area foraging for pollen and nectar in flowers and then returns to a fixed location (the hive) to produce honey, the honeybee is a natural environmental surveyor. Los Alamos scientists have demonstrated that the honeybee is particularly sensitive to tritium, a radioactive substance used in nuclear weapons to enhance the size of the explosion that is notoriously difficult to contain. Deploying the honeybee as an environmental tool since the late 1970s, scientists have documented increasing tritium contamination rates at Area G through the 1990s (see Figure 7.11; Fresquez, Armstrong, and Pratt 1997). This instrumentalization of the honeybee takes more than one form at Los Alamos, but in the context of Area G, it reveals a profound transformation in ecological regimes. Neighboring Pueblo communities identify mesa tops as areas of particular cultural importance, containing shrines and sacred sites that participate in a different conception of nature. Pueblo cosmology has traditionally worked, not to deploy nature as a technoscientific object, but to integrate Pueblo members into the local ecology (see A. Ortiz 1969). Within eastern Pueblo cosmologies, the bee plays a crucial role in pollinating plants and is both a symbol and an agent of life itself; consequently, pollen figures prominently in ceremonies of purification and seasonal renewal. The Manhattan Project replaces this ecological regime with one that focuses on the technoscientific deployment of nature (first, by transforming nuclear energy into a bomb and then by mobilizing the bee as an environmental monitor). The value of the bee, in this new context, is no

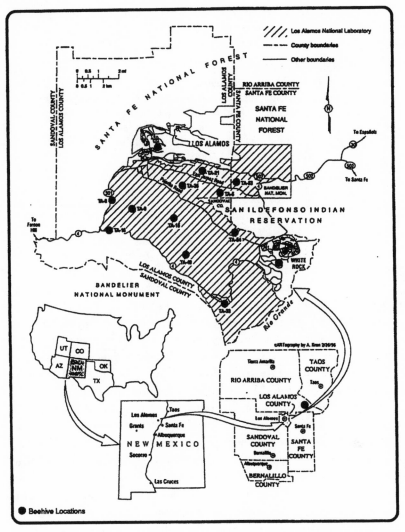

7.11. Location of beehives within LANL. (Courtesy of Los Alamos National Laboratory)

longer as a life-giving entity but as a toxic being, marking the transformation of the plateau from a wild space of nature to a new kind of mutant ecology.

Within this ecology, the bee becomes an agent of the national security state. The militarization of the bee is an expansive project, linking "environmental surveillance" at Los Alamos with a broader Department of Defense (DOD) concern with "controlled biological systems" research. As the Defense Advanced Research Projects Agency (DARPA) describes this project on its homepage:

> The principal objective of the program is to utilize biological organisms for real-time collection of information in the environment. Applications of interest include controlling the distribution of biological systems for real-time monitoring of individual or populations of organisms (e.g., swarms, hives, dens, schools) to seek out and collect information in the environment (air, land, or water) about agents of harm including chemical or biological weapons and unexploded ordnance ... To accomplish this objective, the program will seek to monitor and utilize the sensory signals (e.g., chemical, visual, thermal, acoustic, other) and sensorimotor behavior employed by biological organisms to forage and reproduce in their environment.[20]

To utilize biological organisms for real-time collection of information. DOD research on controlled biological systems currently takes the form of three novel deployments of nature: (1) vivisystems, the use of insects (bees and moths) and other animals as "environmental sentinels" (currently used for tracking chemical weapons, explosives, and radioactive materials in the environment); (2) hybrid biosystems, an effort to create cyborg bugs and animals for surveillance or, as the project puts it, to "integrate living and nonliving components for novel device applications"; and (3) biomimetics, building mechanical devices that mimic the abilities or structures of living beings, particularly insects.[21] Combining insects and nanotechnology promises a whole new kind of cyborg creature, remote-controlled and deployable for surveillance in the literal form of the fly on the wall. The controlled biological systems concept is an instrumentalization of life using state-of-the-art technology, making it a genealogical descendent of the biological testing programs conducted during above-ground nuclear testing. The deployment of the pig in the 1950s was also a "real-time collection of information" through biological organisms, exploring the impact of the exploding bomb rather than the environmental effects of nuclear production. In post–Cold War Los Alamos one can find work on vivisystems—environmental sentinels in the form of tritium-sniffing bees—and also the biomimetic project of engineering robots with insect-like abilities. Figure 7.12 is an illustration of the new robot insects—an artificial dragonfly and butterfly—designed at Los Alamos, part of a wider project to think about the social uses of "mechanical" life forms (see Shroyer 1998: 159). The militarization of the honeybee is, therefore, only one aspect of the new "state of nature" on the Pajarito Plateau put in motion by the Manhattan Project.

7.12. Robot bugs designed at LANL. (Courtesy of Los Alamos National Laboratory)

While specific animal forms are being deployed—and reinvented—to shape environmental politics in post–Cold War Los Alamos, a more subtle aspect of the Manhattan Project has been to transform regional human populations into radiation monitors. Activist groups spent much of the 1990s pushing for environmental impact studies and increased regulation of the laboratory, helping to produce a cross-cultural regional dialogue about the environmental consequences of nuclear weapons research at Los Alamos. Concurrently, LANL scientists, Pueblo representatives, as well as officials from the Bureau of Indian Affairs, each began conducting independent tests of air, water, soil, plants, and animals in the region, not only to define the level of risk to Pueblo citizens living adjacent to the laboratory but also to confirm the accuracy of LANL science.[22] The Pueblos of Jemez, Cochiti, Santa Clara, and San Ildefonso have begun training new generations of youth as environmental scientists to prepare them to take over responsibility for monitoring the environmental effects of the laboratory. Thus, by the end of the 1990s, communities throughout the region—LANL scientists, Los Alamos community members, Native Americans, Nuevomexicanos, and antinuclear activists—all claimed the title of "environmentalist," maintaining deeply felt, if asymmetrical, investments in the Pajarito Plateau. However, while each of these populations is committed to preserving the regional ecology, their cultural understandings of that ecology are construed on radically different terms.

Life within northern New Mexico's nuclear economy is not simply a political or imaginative project. As New Mexicans began to take an increasingly public interest in LANL's environmental standing in the 1990s, many also played the unwitting role of environmental test subjects throughout the Cold War. New Mexicans did so at two levels: first, as workers at the laboratory who were monitored for radiation exposures on the job, and second, as regional populations who (often unwittingly) participated in the Los Alamos Tissue Analysis Program, an effort started in the 1950s to track radiation exposure via tissue sampling. In the late 1990s, relatives of 407 individuals who had tissue samples taken during autopsies in Los Alamos and regional hospitals brought a class-action lawsuit against the laboratory.[23] The multimillion-dollar settlement acknowledged that informed consent was not received from family members during these autopsies. Workers in the laboratory as well as residents of northern New Mexico—similar to the bees—have thus been part of a larger environmental monitoring project for decades, but, in this case, their own bodies have been placed in the role of "environmental sentinel." In this sense, tracking radionuclides through the biosphere and specific bodies in northern New Mexico has become an expanding project for all concerned. The medical knowledge produced by these efforts, however, remains partial and controversial. The fourfold elevated presence of thyroid cancer in Los Alamos discovered in the 1990s might simply be an effect, for example, of the intensity of the screening regime in Los Alamos hospitals (Athas 1996). Nevertheless, while the long-term health effects of nuclear production at Los Alamos remain controversial at the level of technoscience, there is no doubt of the effect they have had on social imaginations in northern New Mexico. Illnesses throughout the region are attributed to the laboratory, revealing another important aspect of the reinvention of nature since 1945—proliferating cross-cultural experiences of the nuclear uncanny.

THE SOCIAL LOGICS OF MUTATION

While interviewing Los Alamos employees who believed their health had been damaged on the job, I was told repeatedly about a videotape reported to document hazardous work conditions at Area G. For these workers, the tape held the promise of standing as evidence in future legal proceedings, a means of making visible to the outside world the everyday practices that were usually shielded by gates, security, and the power of the nation-state. A former Area G worker, who was concerned about his health and did not believe in the veracity of the cumulative radiation badge measurements recorded in his Los Alamos medical file, invited me to view the videotape in his home. As I watched, I was confronted with a complex textual record of mutation. The tape was originally made by Los Alamos personnel to document efforts to consolidate space at Area G for the accruing nuclear waste from laboratory operations. The banality of worker job descriptions is soon ruptured, however, when a tractor accidentally punctures a partially buried barrel of nuclear waste. The narrative then shifts from recording the formal statements of workers during the handling of the ruptured barrel to informal moments with the work crew playing to the camera. Eventually, the multiracial workforce splits along racial lines, as the Anglo program managers don anticontamination gear to test the drum for radionuclides, while the Nuevomexicano and Pueblo workers remain in normal work clothes. The manual labor of digging up and moving barrels of radioactive waste takes place underneath the deep blue New Mexican sky with a ferocious wind that completely covers workers in dust from the site. My host claimed that the dust from the waste site might well have contaminated workers, and then explained to me how easily the radiation monitors could be turned off at Area G to allow such exposures to go unrecorded.

The videotape reveals the difficult work conditions and physical labor needed to move drums of nuclear waste, but the novel presence of the camera also becomes central to the recording: the workers not only practice describing their jobs prior to formal taping and then deal with the accident, while being taped, but they also mug for the camera. Midway through the video, my host interrupts to tell me that he knows what happened to Karen Silkwood, the Kerr-McGee whistleblower who died mysteriously in a car crash in 1974. Her organs were sent to Los Alamos for analysis as part of the tissue registry program but were then mysteriously lost. He tells me that her organs were placed in a laboratory refrigerator, which subsequently failed, and was then dumped at Area G, packed full of the damaged organs of U.S. nuclear workers. Area G becomes, in his presentation, not merely an ongoing health threat to current workers but also literally a grave, a site where the human evidence of radiation exposures is buried as industrial waste. He hopes that the videotape can help reveal this fact, documenting for an outside world the ongoing biological sacrifice of nuclear workers. Twenty minutes into the videotape, the scene shifts to the office spaces at Area G, where the camera operator discovers and then plays with the mirror function on the video camera to produce a series of special effects. For the next twenty minutes of tape, he entertains his fellow workers—by giving them a third eye, or merging their foreheads into giant mutant forms, or giving them tails, while laughing hysterically at the visual results. The videotape that begins with the serious work of nuclear waste disposal, in other words, shifts to a literal discourse of mutation, one that visually transforms each Area G worker into a monstrous being. The Area G workers I spoke with focused more on the official acts documented in the first half of the videotape, than on the cultural logics and fears revealed in the second half. But the videotape records not only the everyday practices at Area G, the brute work of moving nuclear waste around and the precariousness of containment, but also a surreal form of nuclear play that displays workers not as potential mutants but as present ones—linked by tails, misshaped heads, and multiple eyes.

The Area G videotape ends on an equally jarring note, as it cuts from the play of mutation at the nuclear waste site to a garage somewhere in the northern Rio Grande Valley, where a Nuevomexicano relative of the camera operator (who has taken the camera home) stands stiffly and without emotion in the center of the screen, playing ranchero music on an accordion. This eruption of the non-nuclear everyday into the narrative of Area G is a reminder of the multiple cultural worlds informing life in northern New Mexico that are linked both formally and informally to the nuclear project at Los Alamos. The Area G videotape reveals the radical transformation of the region into a nuclear economy. It documents the burying of nuclear waste on the plateau, permanently transforming the ecology of that space. It also documents the mobilization of whole communities that are now devoted simply to monitoring and working with the nuclear waste produced by America's national security regime, and ultimately, it demonstrates the fears of mutation that permeate workers' psyches, underscoring the psychosocial effects of living within a nuclear ecology. These forces are not static, but rather highly mobile, making it impossible to discuss the regional effects of the Manhattan Project without taking into account how material realities fuse with sociocultural logics and nuclear fear.

A political ecology of the bomb that investigates the interaction between regimes of nature reveals the American nuclear project to have been ecologically transformative and multigenerationally productive: it has reinvented the biosphere as a nuclear space, transformed entire populations of plants, animals, insects, and people into "environmental sentinels," and embedded the logics of mutation within both ecologies and cosmologies. The giant cinematic ants of 1954 have, in other words, been replaced now by far more subtle and serious forms of life defined by the ambiguities and dangers of inhabiting specific radioactive spaces, mutant ecologies that now present an ever-evolving biosocial, political, and ethnographic terrain. The Manhattan Project is, from this local perspective, no longer adequately explained as a nature-culture hybrid, or a national security project, or a technoscientific achievement. Rather, the atomic bomb project is now a multigenerational mutation, an increasingly productive set of institutions, logics, and practices, linking new kinds of nature with anxious social formations. After the Cold War, New Mexicans across race, class, and employment lines confront a past and a future that are no longer contained and purified by the rhetorical power of nuclear deterrence but rather informed by the details of life within specific mutant ecologies that are mobile, productive, and highly unpredictable. In this light, northern New Mexicans are indeed nuclear "survivors," but the question remains, survivors of which nuclear trauma?

8 Epilogue
The Nuclear Borderlands

A weapon has been developed that is potentially destructive beyond the wildest nightmares of the imagination; a weapon so ideally suited to sudden unannounced attack that a country's major cities might be destroyed overnight by an ostensibly friendly power. This weapon has been created not by the devilish inspiration of some warped genius but by the arduous labor of thousands of normal men and women working for the safety of their country.
—Henry De Wolf Smyth, *Atomic Energy for Military Purpose* (1947)

Terror attaches to new knowledge. It has an unmooring quality.
—J. Robert Oppenheimer, "Tradition and Discovery" (1960)

The post–Cold War period ended after September 11, 2001, with the formal conversion of the United States to a counterterrorism state. Americans who once thought the end of the Cold War had fundamentally transformed their relationship to the bomb were, after the terrorist strikes on September 11, once again witness to an escalating discourse of nuclear terror: the airwaves were filled with stories of vulnerability, of unsecured ports through which a terrorist nuclear device could be smuggled, of unprotected nuclear power plants open to suicide attacks by airplane, of radiological dirty bombs, which might contaminate major U.S. cities, rendering them uninhabitable. A newly formed Department of Homeland Security (DHS) soon launched the first civil defense campaign in more than a generation, seemingly designed more to maintain nuclear fear than reduce it. The Ready.Gov campaign officially advised citizens to stockpile potassium iodide pills to deal with potential radioactive poisoning, while doing their best to avoid contact with an exploding nuclear device (see Figure 8.1). Meanwhile, a new Homeland Security Advisory System kept Americans at a state of "elevated" to "high" risk of terrorist attack, institutionalizing a new kind of official terror, buttressed by frequent speculations from the DHS and FBI about possibly imminent catastrophic attacks. By the

BE INFORMED
NUCLEAR BLAST

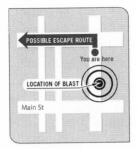

1. Take cover immediately, below ground if possible, though any shield or shelter will help protect you from the immediate effects of the blast and the pressure wave.

2. Consider if you can get out of the area;

3. Or if it would be better to go inside a building and follow your plan to "shelter-in-place".

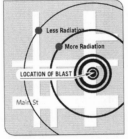

4. **Shielding**: If you have a thick shield between yourself and the radioactive materials more of the radiation will be absorbed, and you will be exposed to less.

5. **Distance**: The farther away from the blast and the fallout the lower your exposure.

6. **Time**: Minimize time spent exposed will also reduce your risk.

8.1. Department of Homeland Security, 2003 Civil Defense Instructions. (*Source*: Ready.Gov Website, Department of Homeland Security)

fall of 2004, when asked in their first debate to identify the single greatest threat to the national security of the United States, both presidential candidates agreed it was the atomic bomb: Senator Kerry put it in the context of "nuclear proliferation," while President Bush stated the greatest danger to the United States was nuclear weapons "in the hands of a terrorist enemy."[1]

In the new century, nuclear insecurity once again formally linked the foreign and the domestic under the sign of apocalyptic nuclear risk, creating a political space in which anything seemed possible. National Security Advisor Condoleeza Rice, for example, made a case for war with Iraq simply by stating that "we don't want the smoking gun to be a mushroom cloud."[2] In doing so, she mobilized the threat of an imaginary Iraqi nuclear arsenal to enable the most radical foreign policy decision in modern American history: a "preventative" war, which involved invading another country to eliminate a nuclear threat before it actually existed.[3] In a few short years, nuclear fear writ large was politically mobilized into an enormously productive force in the United States, enabling a reconfiguration of U.S. military affairs (embracing covert action on a global scale), a massive bureaucratic reorganization of federal institutions (the Department of Homeland Security), a reconfiguration of civil liberties and domestic policing laws (the U.S.A. Patriot Act), and an entirely new concept of war (preemption). All of these projects were pursued in the name of a "war" on "terror," which was energized by an explicit nuclear discourse after the September 11 attacks on Washington, D.C., and New York. The post–Cold War period (1991–2001), thus, concluded with the official transformation of the United States from a countercommunist to a counterterrorist state, a conversion that would not have been possible in its speed, scale, or lack of debate without a discourse of nuclear terror.

Given the scale of this transformation, it is difficult now to remember a time, only a few years ago, when it was difficult to focus American public attention on the bomb. Looking back on when I started researching this book in the mid-1990s, public reactions to nuclear weapons from the early post–Cold War moment now appear quite strange. Outside of New Mexico, a description of this book project, for example, often produced puzzled looks from U.S. citizens, and statements that suggested for many Americans the bomb had already become a thing of the past, of historical interest but not an ongoing political concern. A common response was surprise that Los Alamos National Laboratory (LANL) was "still" involved in nuclear weapons work, and/or "shock" that the United States remained committed to the bomb after the demise of the Soviet Union. This immediate psychological effort to declare the bomb history in the wake of the Cold War is as remarkable as the feverish nuclear discourses following the decidedly non-nuclear September 11 attacks, and is part of the same structural logic: these psychosocial strategies reveal the American cultural tradition of approaching the bomb either as a banal object, not worthy of attention, or as a hysterical threat, requiring a total mobilization of the imagination. This banal/apocalyptic dual structure works to deny the U.S. commitment to the bomb by either cloaking it in a normative everyday space or by displacing attention onto solely external nuclear threats. In both instances, the internal politics and effects of the U.S. nuclear arsenal are erased, even as the core relevance of U.S. nuclear weapons to everyday American life is powerfully revealed by a bomb that is either all too absent or all too present.

But as our opening statements underscore, while nuclear weapons have always been embedded within a discourse of terror, the source of that terror has not always been solely derived from the foreign bomb. Published in 1947, the Smyth Report stands as the first state history of the Manhattan Project. Subtitled "The Official Report on the Development of the Atomic Bomb under the Auspices of the United States Government, 1940–1945," it provided the first public technical description of the engineering success of the Manhattan Project and the effects of the exploding bomb. Describing the first achievement of American big science as a weapon "destructive beyond the wildest nightmares of the imagination," the report struggles to transform the technological achievement of an atomic bomb into a purely productive national accomplishment. Built not by "warped geniuses" but by the "thousands of normal men and women working for the safety of their country," an apocalyptic sensibility challenges American national identity here by blurring the distinction between an enemy-other and the American worker. For what does it say about "thousands of normal men and women" that they are capable of producing a weapon so terrifying it is beyond the "wildest nightmares of the imagination," one that is perfectly suited for a sneak attack on friend and foe alike? Since 1945, this ambiguity about the status of the U.S. bomb (and what it says about American society) has been readily displaced onto an external other, whose nuclear ambitions are marked as "devilish," "warped," or simply "evil" while the U.S. bomb has been officially emplotted as a noble and necessary enterprise. After 1945, however, "security" becomes an increasingly difficult term to define under the weight of the accumulating environmental effects of the nuclear test program and an escalating nuclear arms race. Importantly, the Smyth Report documents that nuclear terror was already installed in the center of the American nation-building project *before* the Cold War began, making the nuclear future always a complex negotiation of the anxieties and ambiguities within American military technoscientific self-fashioning.

Indeed, the post–Cold War period revealed that the United States remains committed to the bomb on its own terms, making deterrence a side benefit. Between the twentieth century's Soviet nuclear threat and the twenty-first century's "war on terror," came a decade in which the United States faced no explicit nuclear enemy yet undertook a massive reinvestment in the bomb. The expectations for nuclear disarmament and test bans that started the post–Cold War period were quickly transformed into an aggressive global U.S. military posture supported by a newly reconfigured, state-of-the-art nuclear complex committed to maintaining the bomb for the foreseeable future. By the end of the 1990s, nuclear weapons budgets exceeded those of the Cold War at the national laboratories.[4] Concurrently, the United States began rejecting or withdrawing from international arms control agreements for the first time in modern American history.[5] The post–Cold War U.S. nuclear hedge, the decision to stop nuclear testing while simultaneously reinvesting in nuclear weapons, established at the level of national policy a contradiction that is now embedded in both international relations as well as the laboratory science of nuclear weapons work. This contradiction will have unforeseen consequences over the long term, not only in international affairs where the lost opportunities of the 1990s already haunt nuclear nonproliferation efforts, but also in terms of how nuclear weapons are conceptualized within the nuclear complex itself. In Los Alamos, the post–Cold War experimental regime has transformed weapons scientists into technoaesthetic guardians of machines and computer simulations whose contemporary use value—though highly fetishized—is at best unclear. Outside the nuclear laboratory, the U.S. bomb continues to transform everyday life, not only in terms of local ecologies and cosmologies, but also in the form of U.S. political institutions that are ever more secretive and paranoid, increasingly "hypersecure" in their effort to protect the bomb. Nuclear fear not only energizes the national fetish, it is once again a remarkably powerful political and cultural resource, used to mobilize people, logics, institutions, and international relations through an apocalyptic sensibility that is simultaneously inchoate and easily directed.

Perhaps this is another way of describing the "unmooring" quality that J. Robert Oppenheimer attributed to the bomb in one of his final essays. Stating "terror attaches to new knowledge," he struggled throughout his post–Los Alamos career to advocate scientific research while negotiating the global effects of the escalating nuclear arms race. Already in 1946, he put the social challenge of the Manhattan Project this way:

> We have made a thing, a most terrible weapon, that altered abruptly and profoundly the nature of the world. We have made a thing that by all the standards of the world we grew up in is an evil thing. And by doing so, by our participation in making it possible, we have raised again the question of whether science is good for men, of whether it is good to learn about the world, to try to understand it, to try to control it, to help give to the world

of men increased insight, increased power . . . Because we are scientists we must say an unalterable yes to these questions: it is our faith and our commitment, seldom made explicitly, even more seldom challenged, that knowledge is a good in itself, knowledge and such power as must come with it. (Oppenheimer 1946: 7)

By all the standards of the world we grew up in.   Here, Oppenheimer directly confronts the "terror" of new knowledge, implying that the role of scientists in a nuclear age is now to engage intellectually the social effects of scientific research as well as the pleasures of technoscientific inquiry. The focus of the scientist, he suggests, can no longer be simply the experimental laboratory. For, Los Alamos weapons scientists, as we have seen, transformed the entire world into a biosocial experimental space. The Manhattan Project was not simply a technoscientific success; it was an act of world-making, whose implications and effects far exceed what Los Alamos scientists could possibly have imagined. That the world we now live in is no longer capable of imagining a prenuclear United States is another marker of the bomb's ultimate effect as a multigenerational social mutation.

This book has been a study of the internal effects of the U.S. nuclear arsenal on U.S. citizens, one that resists the longstanding American tradition of limiting nuclear politics to the realm of international relations. It is an effort to engage the terms of the nuclear revolution in northern New Mexico, focusing not only on the communities that produced the bomb but also on those who have lived for more than a half century within a plutonium economy that has dramatically reshaped the terms of their everyday lives. It has been a study of the "unmooring" effects of the U.S. bomb, looking at how different domains of everyday New Mexican life—technoscientific, cultural, environmental, psychosocial, and philosophical—have been transformed by the long-term effects of the Manhattan Project. Yet, it has also documented a vast diversity within northern New Mexico on precisely the terms, languages, knowledges, and effects of the Manhattan Project. The diversity in experiences of U.S. citizenship, as well as of the nuclear economy, in northern New Mexico challenges the terms of a U.S. "national security" discourse, which assumes a stable and homogeneous national subject. As an ethnographic study of the long-terms effects of the bomb in New Mexico, this book demonstrates that security is both a more flexible and specific discourse than the concept of "national security" allows. Support for the bomb links economics, technoscience, and nationalism, even as the terror of the bomb has proliferated to include concerns about species integrity, cultural reproduction, technoscientific progress, and the terms of democratic order. The complexity of these issues and the diverse local perspectives on them provides a partial map of the broader effects of the nuclear revolution in the United States, a technological achievement that is not only the basis for United States "superpower status" but that has also installed deep contradictions at the center of American democratic process. The psychosocial effects of the bomb remain largely unexamined in the United States, allowing a strange slippage today between the nuclear terror of the Cold War and the new "war on terror."

Many Americans, for example, were gripped by an experience of the nuclear uncanny following the September 11 terrorist strikes, intuitively understanding the attacks on New York and Washington, D.C., through a nationalized notion of violence developed during the Cold War nuclear standoff. One of the most powerful effects of the bomb, I believe, has been to nationalize a sense of apocalyptic violence in the United States, unifying the nation through images of its own end. The cultural effects of the Cold War nuclear standoff—the decades of life situated within the thirty-minute temporal frame of a nuclear war that may have always already started—has produced a new kind of psychic intimacy with mass violence. The sheer number of times Americans have experienced the destruction of New York City in Hollywood films (e.g., in *When Worlds Collide* [1951], *Fail Safe* [1963], *The Planet of the Apes* [1968], *Escape from New York* [1981], *Independence Day* [1996], *Deep Impact* [1998], *Armageddon* [1998]), in civil defense scenarios (from the 1950s, 1960s, 1980s, and 2000s), and in U.S. political discourse set the psychosocial stage for the attacks on the World Trade Center, blurring how citizens interpreted the event by making them so strangely familiar. Amy Kaplan (2003) has argued that the scripting of the World Trade Center site in New York as "ground zero" reveals a series of repressed discourses about U.S. militarism and nuclear nationalism. Tracing the etymology of "ground zero" from its first appearance in 1946, as the site of a nuclear explosion, to its more general usage today as a place where things simply "start over," she asks why the "ground zero" reference in New York is discursively tied not to the atomic bombings of Hiroshima and Nagasaki, where civilians were also targeted, but to the Japanese military attack on the U.S. naval base at Pearl Harbor:

> The term Ground Zero both evokes and eclipses the prior historical reference, using it as a yardstick of terror—to claim that this was just like the horrific experiences of a nuclear bomb—while at the same time consigning the prior reference to historical amnesia. I believe Ground Zero relies on a historical analogy that cannot be acknowledged because to do so would be to trouble the very binary oppositions and exceptionalist narrative erected on the ground—between before and after, between being "with us" or "with the terrorists," between the "American way of life" and the "axis of

evil." Instead, the use of Ground Zero today implies that only terrorists could inflict such a level of untold suffering on a civilian population. (84)

Kaplan points here to an implicit nuclear context informing how many Americans experienced and now remember the violence on September 11, 2001. One strand of U.S. Cold War culture rehearsed the possibility of regenerating the nation through nuclear violence, of returning to a frontier state where the United States could be built again out of the ashes. The violence on September 11, 2001, has been mobilized in a similar project, revealing an effort to regenerate the nation through victimization, displaced memory, and amnesia. Similar in form to local reactions to the Cerro Grande fire in northern New Mexico, a decidedly non-nuclear event becomes one in the cultural imagination, allowing not only the repressed past to return but also a glimpse into the scale of the nuclear imaginary in the United States. However, the claim that "everything changed" with September 11 is also a project to eliminate memory of the Cold War, to cut off the security state from its past, enabling nuclear nationalism to be unhindered by its own history. Nuclear terror here is revealed to be a highly mobile experience, linking a notion of extreme violence with victimization and a desire to repress the historical fact that the United States remains the only country to have used nuclear weapons in war.

In the early twenty-first century, the United States remains the nation-state most thoroughly colonized by the bomb, maintaining not only the largest investment in nuclear weapons but also the most nuclear-terrorized national-culture. For, as we have recently witnessed, anything can be done in the name of countering nuclear terror. The normalization of the U.S. nuclear economy since 1945 has thus come with a high social cost. Within the nuclear complex, a common nonmilitary logic for maintaining a state-of-the-art nuclear arsenal is what some humorously call the "Tang" argument: I collected many versions of this perspective which, in essence, states that if a nation-state goes to the moon, the technological challenge of that project has many unanticipated benefits for its citizens, including the development of an artificial orange drink. Proponents of this view argue that the bomb, at any given time, may be a politically, militarily, or even ethically ambiguous project but that its infrastructural effects on society are not. The Cold War pursuit of the bomb produced a vast amount of knowledge in engineering, chemistry, computing, as well as earth and space sciences that are now incorporated into everyday technologies. The post–Cold War pursuit of Science Based Stockpile Stewardship (SBSS) similarly promises to expand the frontiers of knowledge, allowing the possibility of technological advances in supercomputing, in the understanding of how materials behave in extreme conditions, and perhaps, in the production of nuclear energy. And indeed, a powerful argument can be made that since 1945, the United States has largely built its core institutions—military-industrial-academic-political—via the bomb. But this argument only focuses on the technological benefits of a more than $5.8 trillion investment in nuclear weapons since 1940 (Schwartz 1998), not on the projects that might otherwise have been funded, and not on the other long-term effects of nuclear nationalism.

As this book has argued, a full accounting of the Manhattan Project is a more complicated affair, and must take into account not only technoscience but also the cumulative social, environmental, and political effects of radioactive nation-building. Perhaps most importantly, the bomb has produced a split between national security, which makes a claim on all citizens through a shared sense of belonging, and state security—the project to manage internally the nuclear economy, its systems of patronage, and its structures of secrecy. Today, for example, there is more knowledge that is classified than is not, more knowledge that is produced and locked up in the military industrial state than is offered by all non-military academic literatures. Peter Galison (2004: 2) has suggested that the classified universe of knowledge may now be five to ten times larger than the open library, noting that while there "are 500,000 college professors in the United States" over "four million people hold clearances." Produced in the name of citizens who have no access to this knowledge, the classified universe is not simply a means of protecting the nation-state from the spread of dangerous military information; secrecy is a means of socially regulating American society. The concept of a "state secret" was not invented during the Manhattan Project, but the state structures that were established to build the bomb have evolved into a unprecedented and massive infrastructure in the United States—so prominent in fact, that its sheer scale renders the security state largely invisible to its citizens who walk everyday in its infrastructure, rely on its technoscientific products, and unknowingly carry traces of its toxic effects in their bodies.

So how should we now define the experimental scope of the Manhattan Project? The standard histories of the Manhattan Project locate it between 1940 and 1945, beginning with the state program to develop a new kind of superweapon and ending with the achievement of the atomic bomb on July 16, 1945, and its military use three weeks later in Hiroshima and Nagasaki. But the Manhattan Project put in motion a revolution in American society, creating the concept of the nuclear superpower, making technoscience one of the key U.S. national projects of the twentieth century, installing a new system of secrecy within American democracy, and beginning a new kind of nation-building built on nuclear fear. Consequently, the Manhattan Project is now best thought of as a multigenerational social mutation, one that has not only transformed the earth's surface into a biosocial experiment, but that has also provided the core structures for organizing both American society and the international order. In the twentieth century, the United States did not just build the bomb; it built itself through the bomb. The sheer scale of the techno-scientific infrastructure, the institutional collaborations, the economic investment, and the environmental effects of that ongoing project now link every citizen directly to the Manhattan Project, marking them as national subjects, as members of a military-industrial economy, as residents of the United States, and as biological beings. For Los Alamos weapons scientists, the experimental laboratory has always ultimately been the world itself, as the bomb has been mobilized to produce a new kind of international order through nuclear science, even as trace elements of weapons science have been distributed globally through bodies and biosphere. The Manhattan Project is, consequently, a total experiment, one that not only mobilized the total resources of the nation-state but whose success has transformed our concepts of nature, security, power, and citizenship, as well as the terms of everyday life. These effects are global, but are especially visible within communities like those in northern New Mexico self-consciously working within the plutonium economy.

Defetishizing the U.S. bomb is thus a powerful and necessary way of engaging the terms of the world in which we live, as well as of interrogating the kind of nation-state that will dominate world politics in the coming decades. This requires breaking the cycles of banality and terror that block discussion of the U.S. bomb by culturally displacing it into either a normalized past or an apocalyptic future. Given the multimillennial longevity of plutonium, there may be no practical end to the Manhattan Project, but attending to the political, psychosocial, and environmental effects of the bomb may still offer us an alternative way of living in the nuclear borderlands.

NOTES

CHAPTER 1: THE ENLIGHTENED EARTH

1. While the first chain reaction was achieved in Chicago in 1942 (technically launching the nuclear age), the atomic bomb (designed and tested in New Mexico) was the first nuclear technology to enter popular consciousness in the United States. After 1945, Los Alamos was widely recognized as the world leader in the development of nuclear technologies.

2. On the history of the Manhattan Project, see Rhodes (1986); on the history of the Trinity test, see Szasz (1984), Lansing (1965), and Kunetka (1979). For technical histories of the Trinity test, see Hawkins (1983) and Hoddeson et al. (1993); for a hyperbolic account of the Trinity explosion by the only journalist allowed to witness the test, see Laurence (1946).

3. Indeed, the "unthinkability" of the nuclear age has been a growth literature; as a follow-up to his programmatic 1960 book *On Thermonuclear War* (Princeton: Princeton University Press), nuclear strategist Herman Kahn wrote *Thinking About the Unthinkable* (New York: Horizon Press) in 1962, and *Thinking about the Unthinkable in the 1980s* (New York: Simon and Schuster) in 1984. Among many other offerings in this, and counterdiscursive, veins, see Brian Easlea's *Fathering The Unthinkable: Masculinity, Scientists, and the Arms Race* (London: Pluto Press, 1983), and Jeff Smith's *Unthinking the Unthinkable: Nuclear Weapons and Western Culture* (Bloomington: Indiana University Press, 1989). Few Cold War conversations about nuclear war are without at least a nod to its "unthinkability." For example, the first governmental text to describe for the public what a nuclear war might be like (entitled *The Effects of Nuclear War*) begins with a disclaimer stating that "the mind recoils from the effort to foresee the details of such a calamity." Its first finding is that "the effects of a nuclear war that cannot be calculated are at least as important as those for which calculations are attempted. Moreover, even these limited calculations are subject to very large uncertainties" (OTA 1979: 3). The report then goes on to describe in minute detail a nuclear war under several different scenarios, imagining the effects on bodies, the environment, the economy, and the global political situation. We might, thus, think about the evocation of the "unthinkability" of nuclear war as a call to discourse, an opening up of a psychosocial space in which other kinds of national-cultural work (besides nuclear war planning) are undertaken.

4. Here we see a prohibition on thought that produces a proliferation of discourse similar to what Michel Foucault revealed in his analysis of Victorian sexuality (1978). This is particularly evidenced in the new languages of the nuclear age, produced despite the bomb's "unthinkability." See Cohn (1987) for an analysis of how the technostrategic language of "defense

intellectuals" allows them to abstract and distance themselves from the visceral effects of (nuclear) war, preventing them from articulating the position of nuclear victims. See also Aubrey (1982) as well as Hilgartner, Bell, and O'Connor (1982) on the technical language of the nuclear complex.

5. As William Chaloupka (1992: 8) explains it: "nuclear opponents implicitly admit that nuclear war is a representation, then put that image in a rhetorical context that evokes (represents) the most profound absence possible. The nuke implies a prospect for such thorough annihilation that it is 'unspeakable,' an image of future negation so total as to illuminate a sort of new, negative totality on which to base political action."

6. For Benjamin, the smile that people use in crowds to signify that they do not want to be engaged characterizes this new sensory/social order (e.g., see Benjamin 1976: 133–34). Susan Buck-Morss notes that for Benjamin the smile that deflects social contact is but one example of a series of new reflexes that work as "mimetic shock absorbers," cushioning consciousness from tactile sensation in an age of industrial shock (1992: 17–18).

7. Benjamin is widely celebrated for his reading of how mechanical reproduction broke through the aura of the original work of art, allowing a new kind of mass media which, he thought, could have revolutionary potential (1969b). Buck-Morss (1992) directly engages Benjamin's artwork essay, assessing both its revolutionary potential and its concern with how technology can be used to promote fascism. She states that Benjamin's ultimate project is to claim for art the power to "undo the alienation of the corporeal sensorium, to restore the instinctual power of the human bodily senses for the sake of humanity's self-preservation, and to do this not by avoiding the new technologies, but by passing through them" (1992: 5).

8. On the attempt by nuclear scientists on the Manhattan Project to control the use of the atomic bomb, see Rhodes (1986), Boyer (1994), and Alperovitz (1995).

9. Buck-Morss traces the intellectual history of the term *aesthetics*, noting its inversion from the Greek word *aisthisis*, meaning sensory perception of the world, to its modern reference as something to do with art (i.e., something that is separate from the tactile borders of the body). She recovers this original meaning of aesthetics as a form of cognition, one that examines how the surfaces of the body engage the world. She names this "aesthetic system of sense-consciousness, decentered from the classical subject, wherein external sense-perceptions come together with the internal images of memory and anticipation, the 'synaesthetic system'" (1992: 13). In other words, the synaesthetic system is that which combines "physical sensation, motor reaction, and psychical meaning" in the experience of being in the world. She calls the psychic process whereby a sensory experience of the world is blocked in order to protect the sensorium from trauma the *anaesthetic* and traces how this new kind of sensorium developed in the late nineteenth and early twentieth centuries in Europe.

10. See Byrnes et al. (1955). See also, ACHRE (1996: 291–93).

11. In a previous flashblindness experiment at the Nevada Test Site in

1952 several participants suffered serious eye damage. As the ACHRE describes it:

> Twelve subjects witnessed the detonation from a darkened trailer about sixteen kilometers from the point of detonation. Each of the human "observers" placed his face in a hood; half wore protective goggles, while the other half had both eyes exposed. A fraction of a second before the explosion, a shutter opened, exposing the left eye to the flash. Two subjects incurred retinal burns at which point the project for that test series was terminated. (1996: 292)

In 1951, during the Desert Rock I test of Operation Buster-Jangle, "subjects orbited at an altitude of 15,000ft in an airforce C-54 approximately 9 miles from the atomic detonation. The test subjects were exposed to three detonations after which changes in their visual acuity were measured" (ACHRE 1996: 292). The ACHRE notes that participants were possibly exposed to ionizing radiation during these experiments, although this was not acknowledged in the final reports of the test program (ibid.).

12. See Kuran (1999) for film footage, as well as Weisgall (1994) for a history of Operation Crossroads. The countdown from the first Crossroads explosion was broadcast by radio throughout the world, enabling almost everyone to experience the bomb in real time (Weisgall 1994: 184). The mistargeting of the first bomb left reporters, and hence most of their readers and listeners, with the impression that the bomb was not as destructive as it had been reported to be. This diminished public awareness of the second shot, Baker, which performed as expected and had severe regional radiological effects in the form of fallout. In 1995 dollars, Operation Crossroads cost $575 million, not including future payments to those dislocated or injured by fallout in the tests (Schwartz 1998). A total of twenty-three nuclear explosions were ultimately conducted at Bikini Island.

13. Operation Crossroads was followed by over one hundred nuclear explosions in the South Pacific. In 1954, the United States detonated a hydrogen bomb at Enewetak Atoll that proved to be three times larger than anticipated—fifteen megatons (i.e., the equivalent of fifteen million tons of TNT or 750 Hiroshima bombs). The fallout from Bravo covered an area of fifty-thousand square miles with "serious to lethal levels of radioactivity" (Weisgall 1994: 305). For the effects of fallout on the lives of the Bikini Islanders, see Weisgall (1980) and Kiste (1974). On the continuing effects of military testing in the South Pacific, see Weingartner (1991) and Barker (2000).

14. On the theory and history of the phantasmagoria, see Buck-Morss (1991, 1992) and Castle (1988).

15. Project Star Gate was started in 1972 in response to rumors that Soviet psychics were being used to spy on American military bases from afar (see "Scientists at Odds Over CIA Psychic Experiments," *San Francisco Chronicle*, November 28, 1995). These experiments used 1,200 American psychics to "remotely view" Soviet military bases, and are reportedly only one of a number of U.S. intelligence projects involving psychics over the past thirty years.

16. From this perspective the threat of nuclear war is simply a more abstract form of a kind of national-cultural mobilizing through political demonizing that has a long history in the United States; see Campbell (1992), Rogin (1987), and Hofstadter (1965). For an analysis of how this tactic has been used in the post–Cold War period, see Klare (1995).

17. For analysis of conspiracy theory in the post–Cold War United States, see F. Cohen (1996), Dean (2002), and Knight (2002).

18. This involves 928 detonations at the Nevada Test Site, 5 at The Nellis Air Force Range, 3 in New Mexico, 2 in rural Nevada, 2 in Mississippi, and 2 in Colorado. The United States also detonated 3 bombs, including one of the largest ones, in Amchitka, Alaska, 3 in The South Atlantic Ocean, and a total of 106 in the South Pacific (at Enewetak, Bikini, Johnston, and Christmas islands [DOE 2000a].

19. It is estimated that cleanup of the Cold War nuclear complex will cost between $250 and $500 billion. However, a number of sites like Hanford and the Nevada Test Site are too contaminated to ever reclaim effectively. Nonetheless, they will require a major engineering effort to stabilize the long-term threats they pose to the environment. See DOE (1995a, 1995b), and also Schwartz (1998).

20. At the end of the 1990s, the United States spent about $36 billion annually on maintaining and deploying nuclear weapons (Schwartz 1998).

21. This is part of a new program for maintaining the viability of the nuclear arsenal without underground nuclear testing. Prior to the 1992 test moratorium, if weapons scientists had any questions about the reliability of a weapon, they could pull one out of the stockpile and detonate it at the Nevada Test Site. Today, a new infrastructure of modern technologies is under construction at the three nuclear weapons laboratories to test weapons without actually detonating them. This involves building new supercomputers to simulate nuclear explosions in virtual reality, as well as new laser and imaging facilities to examine every aspect of a weapon's implosion system. This new type of weapons management, SSBS, represents a significant new phase in the evolution of the U.S. nuclear complex. SSBS is expected to cost well over $70 billion between 1995 and 2010 to implement.

22. When President Clinton signed a Comprehensive Test Ban Treaty in 1996, a clause was added to the treaty declaring the U.S. nuclear arsenal to be of "supreme national interest." This means that if confidence is lost in the viability of the nuclear arsenal (as determined by the directors of the U.S. national laboratories), the United States has reserved the right to begin nuclear testing again at any time.

23. The Soviet nuclear arsenal peaked at 45,000 in 1986 but between 1949, when they detonated their first bomb, and 1976, the Soviets were always significantly outnumbered by U.S. forces. In the 1950s, for example, at the height of the Cold War nuclear fear, the U.S. nuclear arsenal outnumbered the Soviet arsenal by more than ten to one (see Norris and Arkin 1993).

24. On the theory of a nuclear winter effect, see Sagan (1983) and Turco et al. (1983); also Solomon and Marston (1986). Former CIA director Admiral Stansfield Turner (1997) presents a devastating critique of U.S. nuclear war

planning during the Cold War. Reviewing the Single Integrated Operational Plan (SIOP), which is the nuclear war targeting plan for a battle with the Soviet Union, Turner found that very small targets, bridges, for example, that could be easily destroyed with conventional weapons were targeted with nuclear weapons. He argues that the SIOP by the 1970s had become a one-million-page operational plan involving over 27,000 nuclear weapons that no single person in government understood completely. Nevertheless, Turner was presented with arguments to increase the size of the nuclear arsenal. Asking why any nation would need such an arsenal, he writes: "It would take 55 billion aircraft bombs, each bomb containing 500 pounds of TNT, to unleash as much energy as 32,500 nuclear warheads. To put this in perspective, each state in the union could be carpeted with 1 billion bombs with 5 billion to spare—something quite beyond imagination" (1997: 9).

25. The United States detonated a total of 107 weapons in the South Pacific and at the Nevada Test Site during this period. Atmospheric fall-out from these tests was a significant factor in the United States, as noted in the recent National Cancer Institute study of iodine-131 contamination (1997). In one three-week period in May 1962, for example, the United States detonated seventeen bombs in three different parts of the world by four different means (over the Pacific Ocean, at Christmas Island in the South Pacific, at the Nevada Test Site, and by rocket, torpedo, airdrop, and underground burial); see DOE (2000a). This was a remarkable expenditure, given that the average nuclear test at the Nevada Test Site in the mid-1980s, with the infrastructure for testing already built, was well over $1 million a shot.

26. See OTA (1989) for a description of the technoscience of underground testing and OTA (1988) on the seismic monitoring of nuclear weapons treaties. For a history of early Cold War efforts by the United States to monitor the globe for nuclear explosions, see Ziegler and Jacobson (1995).

23. The National Cancer Institute's ten-thousand-page report is available on the World Wide Web at http://rex.nci.nih.gov/massmedia/Fallout/contents.html.

28. New social formations include those of atomic veterans, uranium miners, indigenous victims of nuclear testing, as well as the peace and antinuclear movements; see Makhjani and Schwartz (1998), Gallagher (1993), Lifton (1991), Kuletz (1998), and Petryna (2002).

29. In the 1950s, fear of radioactive fallout produced an American popular culture obsessed with fears of genetic mutation. See Boyer (1994), Weart (1988), Caufield (1989), and Winkler (1993) on the cultural effects of fallout; see Hacker (1994), Miller (1986), and Fradkin (1989) for histories of this era of nuclear testing and its health effects.

30. The global sweep of atmospheric fallout led RAND Corporation scientists, in a Project Sunshine study, to conclude:

First, we fear that the concept of uniform worldwide contamination has little meaning and that the necessary assumptions for such a calculation are unrealistically simple. The contamination undoubtedly will occur unevenly—in "blobs" over large areas—mainly because of large differences in localized fallout concentrations. Nuclear detonations occurring on a worldwide scale and possible with a long term "atmospheric storage" may smooth out the distribution somewhat. Secondly, differences in eating habits, disease, and environmental natural strontium content of soil will render certain populations more vulnerable to the contaminant than others. We believe the strontium ratio model to be applicable to problems of localized fallout, ethnic, and environmental differences, but the number of parameters still unknown prohibit such a calculation at the present time. We are thus forced to submit, for the present, an idealized calculation on a worldwide scale. (1953: 5)

Thus, the RAND Corporation concluded in 1953 that it was impossible to estimate accurately the global risk from atmospheric nuclear explosions, and proposed a massive biological testing project—marked by location, ethnicity, and diet—to produce a global portrait of human exposure to strontium-90.

31. This quotation is from a transcript of the 1953 meeting on Project Sunshine declassified for the President's Advisory Committee on Human Radiation Experiments (1996: 402–7).

32. The Partial Test Ban Treaty was signed by the United States, the Soviet Union, and Great Britain on August 5, 1963; it prohibited nuclear testing in the atmosphere, under water, and in outer space. Over one hundred nations eventually signed the treaty with the exception of China and France, which continued atmospheric testing. See Cantelon, Hewlett, and Williams (1991: 185).

33. On the biological effects of radiation, see Schull (1995), Solomon and Marston (1986), IPPNW and IEER (1991). On the psychosocial effects of radiation exposure, see Edelstein (1988), Vyner (1988), Beck (1992), Lifton (1991), Gallager (1993), and Petryna (2002).

CHAPTER 2: NUCLEAR TECHNOAESTHETICS

1. This is not to say that weapons scientists have not actively participated in U.S. nuclear policy debates; see Herken (1992), York (1995), and Broad (1992). Weapons scientists have also been instrumental in designing technologies for verifying nuclear treaties, and for improving the command and control of nuclear weapons for safety purposes.

2. In Los Alamos, the post–Cold War period began September 30, 1992, with the implementation of the Hatfield-Exon Amendment, which initiated a nine-month moratorium on U.S. underground nuclear testing (signed by President George H. Bush and then extended by President Bill Clinton).

3. Galison (1997) argues that laboratory knowledge is produced out of the intersection of conceptual theories and questions, specific machines and instrumentation, and experiment designs. Each of these attributes of laboratory practice has a historical and ethnographic reality that can be studied as part of the expert process of producing scientific knowledge.

4. My argument builds on Susan Buck-Morss's (1992) suggestive rereading of Walter Benjamin's (1969b) analysis of the cultural effects of mechanical reproduction. Buck-Morss argues that while technology can extend human senses in radical new ways, it also opens the human sensorium up to new

kinds of trauma. Industrial modernity, in her view, demands therefore not only a constant production of new technological forms, but also a continual reconfiguration of human sensory experience to negotiate the shock of a technologically mediated world. In my reading of the Los Alamos nuclear program, technoaesthetics are aesthetics delivered through machines, constituting a specific fusion of appearance and utility.

5. See Traweek (1988) for an important discussion of the role of corridor talk in the professional development of high-energy physicists, and Gusterson (1996a, 1996b) for ethnographic analysis of the training program and acculturation of a new recruit into the world of Cold War weapons science at LLNL.

6. For classic theoretical discussions of knowledge production within the cultural spaces of nonmilitary laboratory work, see Knorr-Centina (1999), Galison (1997), Galison and Hevly (1992), Latour (1987), Nader (1996), and Pickering (1992). For discussions of Cold War military science, see MacKenzie (1990), Edwards (1996), and Gusterson (1996a).

7. The "central axiom" of U.S. nuclear weapons science within the laboratory, as Gusterson has shown in his study of LLNL (1996a: 53–59), is that nuclear weapons are built so that they will never be used as weapons. By deterring potential adversaries from launching an attack against the United States, most weapons scientists believe that nuclear weapons prevented World War III, and thus are vital to maintaining global order.

8. Indeed, the advancing speed of nuclear war became such a problem during the Cuban Missile Crisis that the United States and Soviet Union set up a direct telecommunications link—the hot line—in 1964 explicitly to slow down the war machine, to reintroduce a human manager to the logics of nuclear war (Virilio 1986); see Edwards (1996) for an analysis of the "closed world" of Cold War science; and see Freedman (1981) for an overview of how changes in nuclear weapons systems were linked to U.S. nuclear policy toward the Soviet Union.

9. See Medalia (1994: 22); and the Commission on Maintaining United States Nuclear Weapons Expertise (1999).

10. A 1995 report for the DOE, led by Motorola Chairman Paul Galvin, recommended that the nuclear complex be consolidated at LANL. LLNL, because it was responsible for only four weapons in the ongoing U.S. stockpile, would be, under this recommendation, tasked with other national research priorities. Livermore representatives fought the Galvin Report, and were successful in arguing that nuclear weapons design work is proprietary, that moving responsibility for a Livermore warhead to Los Alamos might compromise the U.S. arsenal. Five years later, as part of a reorganization of the weapons complex, the DOE moved responsibility for the W-80 warhead from Los Alamos to Livermore. This act broke one of the principal logics of the Cold War nuclear complex (that pitted Los Alamos and Livermore against one another as competitors), leading one Los Alamos weapons designer to quit in protest. In my conversations with Los Alamos scientists at the time, many thought the move of the W-80 to Livermore would mean that Los Alamos would ultimately take over responsibility for the entire nuclear arsenal, as the

recommendations of the Galvin Report could now be acted on in light of a successful transfer of warhead responsibilities; see Secretary of Energy Advisory Board (1995). See John Fleck, "LANL Manager Steps Down in Dispute," *Albuquerque Journal North*, July 24, 1999.

11. See Rosenthal (1990) for analysis of the Cold War weapons program at Los Alamos; Gusterson (1996a) for an ethnography of LLNL weapons program at the end of the Cold War; see Bailey (1995) and Shroyer (1998) for accounts of the post–Cold War evolution in weapons science at LANL. See McNamara (2001) for a detailed analysis of information management within the post–Cold War weapons program at Los Alamos.

12. On the concept of the sublime, see Kant (1986), as well as Burke's (1993) rather different formation; for critical analysis of technologies and the sublime, see Nye (1994) and Klein (1993); for discussions of a "nuclear sublime," see Gusterson (1999a), Ferguson (1984), and R. Wilson (1991); see also Canaday (2000) for a discussion of religious imagery during the Manhattan Project.

13. Ted Taylor: from *Change of Heart*, chapter 2. Autobiography posted online at http://www.tbtaylor.com/chapt2.htm (accessed March 3, 2001)

14. For historical analysis of radiation exposures to U.S. military personnel during above-ground nuclear testing, see Ball (1986), Miller (1986), and Hacker (1994). For broader discussions of the health effects of nuclear testing, see Gallager (1993); Kuletz (1998); ACHRE (1996); Makhijani, Hu, and Yih (1995); and Makhijani and Schwartz (1998).

15. See FCDA (1955) and DOD (1955); see also McEnaney (2000: 54), who argues that Operation Cue was a "public relations morality play" designed to shift responsibility from the nuclear state to the individual citizen for civil defense. See Ott (1999) and Oakes (1994) for discussion of civil defense during the 1950s.

16. The nonclassified record of this experimental project is *The Effects of Nuclear Weapons* (edited by Samuel Glasstone and Philip Dolan) first published in 1950 with major revisions in 1957, 1962, and 1977. It documents how a nuclear explosion conducted at high altitude, in the air, on land, and underwater will affect buildings, equipment, machines, plants, animals, and people.

17. For critical analysis of American popular culture during the era of above-ground nuclear testing (1945–63), see Boyer (1994); Franklin (1988); Henrikson (1997); Evans (1998); Weart (1988); and Shapiro (2002). For analysis of the antinuclear movement during this period, see Wittner's three-volume history (1993, 1997, and 2003), as well as Titus (1986) and Wang (1999).

18. From 1945 to 1952, Los Alamos scientists conducted all U.S. nuclear test detonations. After the creation of Lawrence Livermore Laboratory in 1952, tests were eventually divided evenly between the two weapons programs, which were fierce competitors throughout the Cold War. See Gusterson (1996a: 24).

19. The United States did not conduct nuclear detonations in 1947, 1949, or 1950, or during the test moratorium of October 1959 to September 1961. Out-

side of these periods, the U.S. test program was active from 1945 to 1992, conducting as few as one experimental test in 1945 (Trinity) and as many as 96 in 1962. During the 348-month period of the underground testing regime (October 1963–September 1992) the United States conducted 717 detonations (695 U.S. plus 22 joint U.S./U.K. tests) for an average of 2 tests per month. By the last decade of the Cold War, the United States was conducting between 11 and 18 tests per year; see DOE (2000a).

20. The 40-year progression from the Fat Man implosion design, which weighed 10,000 pounds and detonated with a force of 21 kilotons, to Los Alamos's state-of-the-art W-88 warhead, which weighs about 450 pounds and can produce a 475-kiloton explosion, is a significant engineering accomplishment. The W-88 is less than 1/22 the size of Fat Man while more than 30 times as powerful.

21. Effects tests continued throughout the underground test regime but were limited in scale and devoted mostly to "hardening" parts from other military machines (nose cones, satellite parts, communication systems) against blast and radiation effects; see OTA (1989).

22. This includes 2,051 nuclear tests (see NRDC 1998) and the Hiroshima and Nagasaki bombings. Most estimates of the total explosive power detonated during World War II place it in the neighborhood of three megatons. If accurate, this means that just one of America's larger thermonuclear devices carries as much destructive power as used during the entirety of World War II.

23. Gusterson (1996a: 138) quotes Livermore weapons scientists, who said of underground testing: "It's not like you're watching the old atmospheric test. I mean it's pretty benign really. You can see a shock wave ripple through the earth. It's a couple thousand feet under the ground. Nevertheless you see a ripple, and under the ground there's still a fireball and that material gets molten." While the sensory experience of the underground test might not be very dramatic, the effort to understand the detonation itself focuses scientists on some of the most complicated physical processes achievable.

24. Underground testing did not achieve a total containment of the bomb, however, as periodically nuclear tests vented radioactivity into the atmosphere, creating fallout clouds that threatened test site workers and neighboring communities. Because of work at the Nevada Test Site, the United States is the most nuclear-bombed country on earth. See Gallager (1993) and Kuletz (1998) for analysis of the effects of testing on the environment and on neighboring communities.

25. President Nixon signed the Threshold Test Ban Treaty in 1974. However, the Senate did not ratify it until 1990, as it was formally linked to other arms control agreements negotiated during the 1980s. The United States and Soviet Union, however, did not test over 150 kilotons after the mid-1970s; see DOE (2000a).

26. The United States conducted only one full-scale test of a missile and nuclear warhead during the Cold War. In May 1962, a Polaris A-1 missile was launched from the USS *Ethan Allan* in the Pacific as part of Operation Dominic; see Commission on Maintaining United States Nuclear Weapons

Expertise (1999). See also MacKenzie (1990: 342–45) for a discussion of the technological and political assumptions informing intercontinental missile targeting accuracy; he points out that, despite never having undergone a full-scale test during the Cold War (as to do so could have been interpreted as an act of war), the United States assumed its intercontinental missiles were accurate to within a few yards of their target. This assumption allowed "counterforce" targeting, in which U.S. weapons were targeted on Soviet weapons, enabling a major escalation in the arms race.

27. There is a debate in the United States over what constitutes a "new" nuclear design. Within the national laboratories a new nuclear design is one that involves a new physics package and that has entered into the seven-step production cycle for military deployment. Critics of the nuclear program tend to define a new nuclear weapon as any change in the military use of a nuclear device. In the 1990s, for example, Los Alamos scientists changed the casing of the B-61 bomb to give it a greater "earth penetrating" ability. For weapons scientists this change did not constitute a "new" design, but for many in the disarmament movement this modification demonstrated that even under a Comprehensive Test Ban Treaty the United States is committed to finding new uses for nuclear weapons. See Mello (1997), as well as Paine and McKinzie (1998a).

28. President Bill Clinton signed the Comprehensive Test Ban Treaty in 1996. The U.S. Senate voted down the treaty in 1999, although the terms of the treaty remain in effect. The directors of the Los Alamos and Lawrence Livermore National Laboratories can challenge the test ban at any time SBSS produces "uncertainty" in their minds about the military performance of the U.S. nuclear arsenal. In addition to the question of the reliability of nuclear arsenal, the Comprehensive Test Ban Treaty debate in the Senate focused on the verification of foreign nuclear tests and raised a series of questions about whether or not the United States could detect deeply buried low-yield explosions. NAS (2002) investigated these concerns and concluded that a Comprehensive Test Ban Treaty could be verified. The Comprehensive Test Ban Treaty remains at the controversial center of alternative policy views about the role of nuclear weapons in constituting U.S. military power.

29. The Stockpile Stewardship and Management Program consists of four major projects: (1) DARHT at LANL (which produces three-dimensional X-ray images of imploding primaries); (2) the National Ignition Facility at LLNL (which will be the world's most powerful laser research center, able to simulate the energy regimes of an exploding thermonuclear weapon); (3) Subcritical Testing at the Nevada Test Site (explosive testing on plutonium and uranium that does not produce a nuclear yield; and (4) the Accelerated Strategic Computing Initiative (a major investment in supercomputing, designed to model the results of SBSS and previous nuclear test data; see DOE (1998c, 1999e) for a program overview. For assessments of the stockpile stewardship program, see Gusterson (2001); Lichterman and Cabasso (1998); Zerriffi and Makhijani (1996); as well as Paine and McKinzie (1998a, 1998b).

30. During the Cold War the U.S. national laboratories averaged $3.7 billion per year for the design and testing program. The first budgets for SBSS

were \$4.5 billion per year, which by 2003 had risen to \$6.5 billion a year. Thus, the fifteen-year project of SBSS is likely to cost well over \$70 billion. See Schwartz (1998) for an accounting of the entire U.S. nuclear project from 1940 to 1996; he estimates that the United States spent \$5.8 trillion on the nuclear production complex, weapons delivery systems, and environmental management.

31. For analysis of bodily metaphors within weapons science, see Cohn (1987); Gusterson (1996a: 101–30); Chaloupka (1992); Keller (1992); Scarry (1985); and Easlea (1983).

32. From 1945 to 1992, the United States built seventy thousand nuclear weapons, relying on new design work to maintain the viability of the stockpile. Aging has thus not been a major concern of U.S. nuclear planners until the post–Cold War era. Some nuclear components change over time—tritium has a half-life of 12.5 years, and plutonium decay produces a helium element that could potentially change the symmetry of a nuclear weapon trigger over many decades of storage. Other changes, such as cracks and distortions, can occur in non-nuclear components over time. How these aging issues change the ability of any specific nuclear device to produce a nuclear explosion remains controversial; see Johnson, et al. (1995), as well as Zerriffi and Makhijani (1996).

33. Indeed, the multiple yield function of a modern Los Alamos weapon allows for at least three modes of detonation involving: just the primary, a "boosted" primary for greater yield, or the coupled primary and secondary for a thermonuclear explosion; see Garwin and Charpak (2001: 62–65).

34. See McNamara (2001) for a nuanced ethnographic discussion of the LANL archiving project.

35. Between 1993 and 1996, LANL hired 115 scientists into the weapons programs, while losing over 400. See Commission on Maintaining United States Nuclear Expertise (1999: 8); see also Medalia (1994: 27).

36. The effort to construct a mathematical model of a nuclear weapon has been a core project at Los Alamos since the early Manhattan Project. The first "computers" were, in fact, rooms filled with the wives of Los Alamos scientists who did the mammoth calculations for the first atomic bombs by hand. The U.S. nuclear weapons program subsequently drove the development of supercomputing throughout the Cold War, also relying on state-of-the-art supercomputing to recruit scientists to the national laboratories; see MacKenzie (1996) and Galison (1996).

37. ASCI has formal alliances with five universities: the California Institute of Technology, Stanford University, the University of Chicago, the University of Illinois-Urbana-Champaign, and the University of Utah. For a programmatic overview of the Academic Strategic Alliance program, see its World Wide Web homepage at http://www.llnl.gov/asci/alliances/. See also McKinzie, Cochran, and Paine (1998).

38. MacKenzie and Spinardi (1996) have argued that, over time, the tacit knowledge inherent in the Cold War nuclear production complex could be forgotten, allowing the "uninvention" of nuclear weapons. Certainly the ability to reproduce highly miniaturized nuclear weapons, optimized with multi-

ple yield capabilities and loaded with safety and security measures, presents a substantial engineering challenge; elements of this production cycle represent a kind of "folk culture." SBSS is directly aimed at capturing and preserving that folk culture, and a recent article by weapons scientist Stephen Younger (2000) argues that the United States could deploy new nuclear weapons based on the bomb design used over Hiroshima without nuclear testing. Thus, the long-term absence of underground nuclear testing will more likely influence the complexity of future nuclear weapon designs rather than the ability to create a nuclear explosion.

CHAPTER 3: ECONATIONALISMS

1. The "LANL 2000: The Role of the National Laboratory in the 21st Century" conference was held in Glorieta, New Mexico, in 1993. Herman Agoyo's speech as well as several other activists' comments are reprinted in a special issue of *Race, Poverty and the Environment* (spring–summer 1995) devoted to nuclear issues.

2. On Pueblo stories of emergence, see A. Ortiz (1969), Parsons (1994), Benedict (1981), Bunzel (1992: 545–609), Stirling (1942), Sando (1982: 4), and R. Gutierrez (1991: 3–36).

3. For example, a social disagreement within San Juan Pueblo in the early twentieth century resulted in a lapse of nearly ten years in one of the most important pilgrimages in the yearly ritual cycle because, as Curtis notes, "they could not approach the gods with offerings while their hearts were divided" (1970: 9).

4. Alfonso Ortiz summarizes the relationship this way: "Among human beings the primary causal factors are mental and psychological states; if these are harmonious, the supernaturals will dispense what is asked and expected of them. If they are not, untoward consequences will follow just as quickly, because within this relentlessly connected universal whole the part can effect the whole, just as like can come from like. Men, animals, plants and spirits are intertransposable in a seemingly unbroken chain of being" (1972: 143).

5. See A. Ortiz (1969), as well as (1972), (1977), (1979), and (1994).

6. See A. Ortiz (1977). In this regard to speak the name of a place is to evoke not simply its existence but the story of how it came to be known to the people, thus placing it within the larger story of the tribe's movement through space. On Pueblo concepts of landscape and storytelling, see Silko (1996a); cf. Basso (1996).

7. See A. Ortiz (1977), (1979), and (1994). See also Jill Sweet (1989) on Pueblo practices of burlesquing outsiders.

8. For the Tewa, the northern mountain is San Antonio Peak, the west is Tsikumu (or Obsidian Covered Mountain) to the north of Los Alamos, the south is Sandia Mountain, and the eastern mountain is Lake Peak in the Sangre De Cristos (Hewett and Dutton 1945: 34; see also A. Ortiz 1969).

9. For the northeastern Pueblo nations that directly border contemporary Los Alamos—Santa Clara, San Ildefonso, Cochiti, and Jemez—the greater

Pajarito Plateau has immediate cultural and historical significance. Frijoles Canyon (now part of Bandelier National Monument) is the ancestral land of Cochiti Pueblo, a place where they lived after their emergence and before the Spanish arrived in the region (see Benedict 1981: 185–86; also Lange 1959: 228). Santa Clara identifies Puye ruins, twenty miles north of LANL, as one of their own places of emergence (Hewett and Dutton 1945: 49; Whitman 1947). San Ildefonso Pueblo identifies the central Pajarito Plateau—and the area now occupied by the laboratory—as ancestral land, with major ruins at Otowi and Tsirege (ibid.; Harrington 1916: 278).

10. Quoted in Biddle Duke, "LANL Results Challenged: Contamination Test Inaccurate, Pueblo Charges," *Santa Fe New Mexican*, October 22, 1992.

11. Quoted in John Fleck, "Indians Want Los Alamos Lab to Offer Jobs, Protect Nature," *Albuquerque Journal*, November 20, 1992; and in Mark Oswald, "Pueblo Leaders Want UC Regents to Hold Lab Pact Hearing in N.M.," *Santa Fe New Mexican*, October 20, 1992. The coalition letter sent to the University of California regents asking for hearings in New Mexico and an environmental impact study of LANL was signed by the members of the Eight Northern Pueblo Indian Council as well as eighteen NGOs in New Mexico.

12. The four Accord Pueblos now have the opportunity to influence the standards used in Los Alamos, regulating the quality of the air and water that move off the plateau and onto Pueblo lands. In 1995, several of the Accord Pueblos were contemplating using the standards set by Isleta Pueblo in the early 1990s. Officials at Isleta Pueblo set water standards that were higher than those mandated by the U.S. Environmental Protection Agency, handing Albuquerque (which is immediately upstream from Isleta and home to Sandia National Laboratory) an unexpected, multimillion-dollar regulatory mandate (LANL 1995a).

13. Prior to this agreement the tribes refused to recognize state authority over them, preferring to deal on a nation-to-nation basis with Washington, D.C. The resulting ambiguity, however, also meant that federal and state governments could play off each other in the courts, leaving the terms of tribal sovereignty to be negotiated on an issue-by-issue basis.

14. William Graf (1994) concluded that 10 percent of the plutonium in Cochiti Lake was from runoff from laboratory operations; the rest he attributed to atmospheric fallout. However, better methods of analysis at LANL in the late 1990s demonstrated that more like half is from laboratory operations, documenting a greater regional environmental impact than previously recognized.

15. The Tewa Study, conducted by the Soil Conservation Service (1939), concluded that San Ildefonso Pueblo did not have enough farmland to feed its citizens in the 1930s, and tracks the turn to pottery-making as a new industry at the Pueblo.

16. See Grinde and Johansen (1995), Eichstaedt (1994), Silko (1996b), Churchhill (1997), and Kuletz (1998).

17. Florence Hawley (1948) also notes that Pueblo veterans returning from World War II had a difficult time adjusting both to traditional Pueblo

life and to the limited opportunity mainstream American life now offered. See Wyaco (1998) for an autobiographical history of how these issues played out at Zuni; and Wadia (1957) for a study of postwar assimilation patterns at Tesuque Pueblo.

18. Indeed, the Los Alamos domestic economy may have had as much effect on the Pueblo, particularly as women from the valley now participated in a cash economy and had steady opportunities to work in Los Alamos homes. Another important economic factor for the Pueblos remains the impact increased traffic to Los Alamos (and through Pueblo lands) has on the art trade. See Social Conservation Service (1939), Dietz (1989), and Rothman (1992).

19. Reacting to Pueblo protests, LANL stopped referring to the criticality research laboratories as "kivas" in 2001. See, Jennifer McKee, "Lab Bunkers No Longer Called Kivas," *Albuquerque Journal*, January 4, 2001.

20. Thus, some of the sites around contemporary Los Alamos were probably rarely visited and only by a few members of each Pueblo who were ritually prepared to visit the mountains (see A. Ortiz 1979: 278). It might consequently be difficult for some Pueblos to reproduce the cultural knowledge of the sites on what is now LANL territory that existed prior to 1943.

21. The longstanding ethnographic discourse on Pueblo secrecy has argued: (1) that secrecy is a means of compartmentalizing Pueblo culture from outside influences, creating a protected interior core of Pueblo knowledge that is insulated from missionaries, colonial interests, anthropologists, and the invasively curious (see Dozier 1961); and (2) that secrecy is a means of allocating social and political power within Pueblo societies, structuring the divisions not only between "insider" and "outsider" but also between status groups—political factions, clans, men and women, old and young (Brandt 1977). While these rationales get at the political import of secrecy reiterating Simmel's [1906] insight that the wish to be socially invisible works most profoundly to control internal membership, regulating those who carry secrets through everyday practices of silence and by instilling a personal commitment to a social hierarchy of who knows what and why) these insights still do not evaluate the tactile effects of secrecy, of why even after a secret is made public it is nevertheless vigorously protected in New Mexico. Thus, Pueblo secrecy involves an issue of cultural "privacy" as well as concealment; see Bok (1983).

22. See, for example, the May 1979 special issue of *The Progressive* that details efforts by the U.S. government to suppress an article by Howard Morland (1979) on how to build a nuclear weapon—an article that drew solely upon previously published sources.

23. Transcribed from a videotape of the LANL 2000 conference, made available to me by Concerned Citizens for Nuclear Safety, one of the co-sponsors of the event.

24. The Advisory Committee was established by President Clinton in 1994 following a series in the *Albuquerque Tribune* by Eileen Welsome detailing Cold War plutonium experiments conducted on unknowing citizens by members of the U.S. nuclear complex. Its purview grew to encompass a wide

range of Cold War nuclear projects with potentially adverse and covert effects on the American population (see ACHRE 1996).

25. From the transcript of the January 30, 1995 hearing of the ACHRE in Santa Fe, New Mexico. See also ACHRE (1996: 329–33).

26. LANL scientists have concluded that if one relied on the Los Alamos Canyon garden for a year's worth of produce, it would constitute 74 percent of a year's maximum recommended dose of radiation for all sources (Fresquez et al. 1997). When other environmental sources are added to the mix, living off of Los Alamos Canyon produce would provide a statistically significant increased probability of cancer.

27. For example, see Silko (1996b) for a discussion of the social and cosmological effects of uranium mining at Laguna Pueblo—effects symbolized by the sudden appearance of a gigantic stone stake in the landscape near the uranium mine. Her novel *Ceremony* (1977) also explores the unique psychosocial consequences of the nuclear age for Pueblo people at Laguna.

28. Quoted from a transcript of a meeting at San Ildefonso Pueblo: DOE-LANL Site Wide Environmental Impact Statement: Meeting on LANL Use and Transfer with the Los Alamos Pueblo Project, December 12, 1994.

29. Pueblo nations in New Mexico have contributed (in numbers greater than the national average) to the U.S. military since World War II. Many of the political leaders of the northern Pueblo are U.S. veterans and support the basic military mission of the laboratory. Many Pueblo citizens are therefore more immediately concerned about the environmental contamination and religious desecration resulting from nuclear weapons work on the plateau than about the politics of nuclear weapons.

30. The contesting nature of these regimes is illustrated by the fact that in the 1990s as Pueblo leaders regained the right to revisit cultural sites closed off behind the U.S. nuclear fence during the Cold War, they were required to submit to laboratory security measures. To visit ruins and cultural sites that had been tended for generations prior to the Manhattan Project, Pueblo leaders needed to sign in with LANL security teams and be accompanied by an escort at all times. The Accord Pueblos were also relying heavily on those citizens who also work at the laboratory and maintain U.S. national security clearances to access politics of access and control of sites. Thus, Pueblo access to sites within laboratory boundaries is still mediated by official U.S. logics. The screening process and escort must affect Pueblo engagements with those places as the location and meaning of certain sites, as well as the rituals performed on such sites, remain Pueblo state secrets.

31. Ruins are important points of connection to ancestors, places that physically identify the people's path from emergence to their current sites. Alfonso Ortiz states (1969: 20): "Souls belonging to a larger category of spirits and man-associated objects called *xayeh*, which also includes fossilized bone, sea shells, tools, weapons, and other objects rescued from ruins; in essence, all objects which have been used by people are endowed with sacredness because they are associated with the souls and with the sacred past." Ruins can also be dangerous, as Pueblo people traditionally buried the dead close to the village; disturbing those sites thus disturbs the spirits at rest

there. Parsons (1929: 62–63) records Tewa beliefs in the 1920s that a number of mysterious deaths at San Ildefonso were caused by tribal members' participation in archaeological work at Puye. Disturbing ancestral remains is inherently dangerous, and complicated by the fact that some Pueblo peoples (e.g., the Hopi; see Dongoske 1996) have repatriation rituals while some do not (e.g., the Zuni; see Ferguson, Anyon, and Ladd 1996). Thus, while archaeologists are now required by federal law to contact tribes concerning the disposition of discovered and archived ancestral remains, not all groups have a means of containing the power of those remains, creating difficult and often heart-wrenching problems for tribal members. The silence with which some indigenous nations meet such requests can be less an index of a lack of concern, than a register of the spiritual danger ancestral remains evoke; for example, see Sheper-Hughes (1987) on secrecy and silence, and see Simmons (1974) for an analysis of Pueblo witchcraft beliefs.

32. As of 1993, however, Area G was near to capacity and an enormous facility: it included 33 pits (some measuring 600 feet by 100 feet by 65 feet deep), 220 shafts (each 2 to 4 feet in diameter by 65 feet deep), 4 trenches (filled with 400 cement casks carrying a total of at least 7,200 grams of plutonium-238), as well as 3 storage pads and 3 storage domes (holding up to 16,000 barrels of waste ultimately headed for the WIPP in Carlsbad, New Mexico)—with more nuclear waste coming in every day.

33. See Fresquez, Vold, and Narano Jr. (1996), and Fresquez, Armstrong, and Pratt (1997).

34. Tritium is a material that flows as fast as water and thus is used as a tracer element in environmental monitoring; while the current tritium levels pose no immediate health risk, they may signal that more dangerous materials are working their way through the mountain, and may pose a danger in future years. See Stephen Shankland, "Tritium Found in Aquifer Test Wells," *Los Alamos Monitor*, February 24, 1995.

35. See Hanson (1998), Stoffle and Evans (1988), and Kuletz (1998). By 1995, two hundred indigenous communities in the United States had been approached by corporations interested in locating waste facilities of one kind or another on tribal land, and of the fourteen county, state, and tribal governments actively considering Monitored Retrievable Storage for nuclear waste, eleven were indigenous (Goldtooth 1995). See also Gedicks (1993), Churchill (1997), and Weaver (1996) for analysis of contemporary environmental assaults on indigenous territories in North America.

36. See Zack Van Eyck, "Nuclear Waste on Indian Land?" *Santa Fe New Mexican*, March 25, 1994, A-1.

37. In the post–Cold War era, this has taken on a new international dimension, as the initial outlines of a transnational Native American nuclear waste storage economy were beginning to take shape in New Mexico in 1995. The Mescalaro Apache Nation was simultaneously pursuing negotiations with two dozen nuclear energy corporations to open up an MRS on tribal lands and discussing permanent storage for U.S. nuclear waste with a coalition of Cree nations from northern Canada. The North American Free Trade Agreement (NAFTA) explicitly marked radioactive waste as a nontariff item, paving the

way for this kind of transnational indigenous nuclear waste infrastructure (Hanson 1998). The Mescalaro plan was ultimately put on hold after a bitter, internal struggle on the Mescalaro reservation (which, as point of fact, is located between two prominent U.S. nuclear sites: the White Sands Missile Range, where the first atomic device was detonated, and the WIPP, the first planned repository for U.S. military nuclear waste in southern New Mexico).

38. Canes are symbols of Pueblo authority in New Mexico (and are held by the legitimate political leaders); they are also signifiers of international respect. Canes were given to Pueblo governors by Spanish and Mexican governments as well as by American Presidents Abraham Lincoln and Richard Nixon. See Dailey (1994) for a history of the canes, and see Pandey (1977) for an examination of the symbolic power of the canes as emblems of Pueblo political authority.

39. Pojoaque was paid $27,000 in 1959 for land access for U.S. Highway 84/285, a road that bifurcates their land and that remains the major thoroughfare from Santa Fe to Española and to Los Alamos.

CHAPTER 4: RADIOACTIVE NATION-BUILDING IN NORTHERN NEW MEXICO

1. On the ecological foundation of the Pueblo revolt, see Grinde and Johansen (1995: 57–78) and R. Gutierrez (1991: 130–40).

2. In January 1995, LANL employed 5,486 residents of Los Alamos County, 2,345 residents of Rio Arriba County, and 1,878 residents of Santa Fe County. These three counties provide 90 percent of the LANL workforce. A few hundred additional employees commute from Taos and Albuquerque. These statistics are drawn from the LANL Community Relations Office, "Data Profile, January 1995" information sheet.

3. As R. Gutierrez (1991) notes, Nuevomexicano Catholicism places special emphasis on the corporal suffering of Christ, and a particular cultural focus on the body. See Weigle (1976) on Penitente ritual forms; on Nuevomexicano folk traditions, see Rodriguez (1996) and Briggs (1988).

4. In 1888, for example, Charles Lummis held a group of Penitentes at San Mateo at gunpoint to photograph their self-mortifications (Weigle 1976: 172). Similarly, Cordova (1973: 47) reports that in the early twentieth century, Anglo fascination with the Penitentes led frequently to disruptions at Holy Week ceremonies at Abiquiu; he notes times when visitors surrounded the Morada (a Penitente meeting house) with their automobile headlights turned on, and other occasions on which outsiders disrupted processions to take photographs. Thus, following a tactic used by the Pueblos to maintain religious privacy, the Penitentes concealed their practices from outside gazes during the American territorial period, a tradition that continues to this day.

5. The Santuario de Chimayo was founded by Bernardo Abeyta, who reportedly discovered a crucifix buried in the field where the shine is now located. He took the crucifix home with him only to discover it had miraculously returned to the field the next day. This miraculous event occurred sev-

eral times, leading to the construction of the Santuario; see Usner (1995: 86–93).

6. See Rosenthal (1990: 149–59) for a discussion of Catholic views toward nuclear weapons work in New Mexico; for a similar discussion around LLNL, see Gusterson (1996a: 60–67); and at the Pantex plant, see Mojtabai (1986).

7. The near collapse of village economies in the northern Rio Grande valley left little money for schools or basic services, leaving Nuevomexicano families, as a whole in 1934, with the highest birth and death rates in the United States, with an average of less than six acres under cultivation per family, and with only 13 percent of students finishing high school (Forrest 1989: 11–12). Suzanne Forrest argues (1989: 17): "If there is one single factor responsible for the transformation of a once proud, independent, and self-sufficient people to abject poverty and dependence, it is the inexorable seizure of wealth and power that accompanies the superimposition of a technologically and economically dominant culture upon a preindustrial civilization. What happened in New Mexico was, in microcosm, what happened throughout the Third World in the nineteenth and twentieth century. The process began shortly after United States annexation in 1848 and accelerated rapidly after the arrival of the railroad in the 1870s." See also Sanchez (1967), Rosenbaum (1981), Briggs and Van Ness (1987), Pulido (1996), and Gomez (2000).

8. More specifically, *The State of New Mexico v. Aamodt*, which began in 1965, is still trying to sort out water rights in the north-central Rio Grande valley, involving claims from Santa Fe to San Ildefonso to communities north of Española.

9. The mayordomo distributes the water within the ditch system, organizes the spring cleaning of the acequia, and settles any disputes about water allocation. See Crawford (1988) for an excellent account of a year-long cycle of acequia management, as well as numerous insights into the contemporary cross-cultural politics of farming and life in the northern Rio Grande valley. See Simmons (1972) and Rivera (1998) for historical analyses of the acequia system.

10. See, A. Ortiz (1969: 112–17) on Pueblo irrigation and participation in the acequia system. See also Ford (1992) on Pueblo ecology and irrigation systems.

11. See Graf (1994) for an analysis of plutonium deposits in the Rio Grande from LANL activities.

12. This is evidenced by new efforts to preserve cultural memory in the 1990s, a new Colonial Spanish Cultural Center and Museum in Santa Fe, and new publications like *La Herencia del Norte: Our Past, Our Present, Our Future*, a Santa Fe quarterly begun in 1994 to maintain Nuevomexicano culture and history.

13. Within what is now Los Alamos County are three former land grants— The Juan Tafoya Grant, the Rito de los Frijoles Grant, and the Ramon Vigil Grant. See Ebright (1994: 225–48) for a legal history of the Ramon Vigil Grant. See Rothman (1992) for an extended discussion of the development

of the Pajarito Plateau. See also Chambers (1974) for a history of the Ramon Vigil Grant and the early days of the Manhattan Project.

14. Nuevomexicanos maintained ranching and farming interests on the plateau through this period, even as specific tracts changed hands. Rothman (1992: 15) explains:

> Like many other land grants, the Vigil Grant functioned as common property. Although it was originally a private land grant, the way in which the *pobladores* used the grant turned it into an informal community grant. Many of the people in the Pojoaque and Española valleys were blood relatives of the owners of the grant; many more were related by marriage. As elsewhere in the Rio Arriba region, a visible sense of interdependence dominated interaction between people in the valley and those on the plateau. Despite frequent arguments among members of the extended group that used the grant, an informal social compact dictated that unused land belonged to any member of the extended community who needed it.

15. In the late 1990s, the laboratory, allowed the descendents of the Pajarito Plateau homesteaders access to the ruins of family homes; see Foxx and Tierney (1999). This process mirrors the post–Cold War program to allow members of neighboring Pueblos access to culturally important sites within laboratory boundaries.

16. On the Treaty of Guadalupe Hidalgo, see Castillo (1990); on land grant litigation and history in New Mexico, see Westphall (1983), Briggs and Van Ness (1987), and Ebright (1994). For studies of land management practices and environmental justice in northern New Mexico, see Pulido (1996) and deBuyes (1985).

17. See "Tijerina Citizen's Arrest Attempt Unsuccessful," *Santa Fe New Mexican*, June 8, 1969.

18. Throughout the northern Rio Grande valley conflicts over development in the 1990s often broke down over racial lines. For example, struggles were waged in villages over whether or not to pave access roads. In several cases, longtime Nuevomexicano residents wanted to pave the roads, while Anglo immigrants did not. This references the life choice that brings many Anglos to New Mexico, one that involves an escape from cities and an embrace of a semirural existence. Concurrently, village communities north of Santa Fe were experiencing problems gaining land rights to expand village cemeteries. In this case, conflicts over land (particularly with the U.S. Forest Service) involved the seemingly basic right to bury residents of the village in the local church cemetery with their families, underscoring a sense that locals were being displaced from important centers of cultural meaning. For a detailed analysis of the development of Santa Fe, see C. Wilson (1997).

19. See Matt Mygatt, "Turner Close to Making Deal to Buy Vermejo Park Ranch," *Santa Fe New Mexican*, June 20, 1996.

20. William deBuys has argued that National Forests in New Mexico are the most contested in the United States; of the Carson National Forest, he

writes: "Twenty-two percent of the Carson and Santa Fe National Forests consists of patented Spanish and Mexican land grants, and a large additional acreage includes grants that Hispanos claimed but U.S. courts never confirmed. The unconfirmed claims were incorporated into the National Forest System along with other portions of the public domain, while the patented grants were obtained through outright purchase ... No other National Forests in the United States are plagued with as unhappy a historical legacy as those of northern New Mexico and none exist in as complex a cultural environment" (1985: 257).

21. See Antonio DeVargas, "Enviro-hypocrisy Threatens Northern Villages," *Santa Fe New Mexican*, December 12, 1995.

22. In 1998, during the four hundredth anniversary of the settling of the northern Rio Grande valley, for example, an equestrian statue of Don Juan Oñate was vandalized at the Oñate Cultural Center outside of Española. The right foot of the bronze statue was hacked off, reenacting how Oñate punished members of Acoma Pueblo who revolted against Spanish rule in 1599.

23. In local memory, Nuevomexicanos fought the American army as it entered New Mexico in 1847. Several versions of the following narrative, as told to me, can be found in the northern Rio Grande valley:

When they say that the Mexican War was won without a shot being fired, that's not true, you know. There was a big battle, the battle of Embudo here, where there were about 700 local people that set themselves up to fight against Stephen Price in '47. They were fighting with very crude weapons that they had, mostly handmade. Probably most of them were farming implements, the Americans with their howitzers, you know they killed a lot of people here. So when they say it was a bloodless conquest it's a bunch of lies. A lot of people gave their lives. They had battles in Santa Cruz, in Embudo, in Taos, in Mora.

See Usner (1995: 74–75) for another version of this story, as told in Chimayo. Similarly, in northern New Mexico, Don Juan de Vargas is remembered as having achieved a peaceful reconquest of New Mexico in 1693; however, the actual events included a three-day siege of Santa Fe, after which seventy Pueblo warriors were executed and four hundred Pueblo women and children were distributed among the colonists as slaves (see R. Gutierrez 1991: 145).

24. Signs of the reconquest permeate local structures in Santa Fe. Outside of the Santa Fe Fiesta, for example, the conflict between Spanish conquistadors and the Pueblos is symbolically reenacted every time the De Vargas Junior High School Conquerors meet the Santa Fe Indian School Running Braves for a basketball game. See McWilliams (1948: 35–46) for a discussion of the Spanish "fantasy heritage," evoked by former Mexican citizens as a means of negotiating racism in the United States; see also Anaya and Lomeli (1989) for the Chicano response to the mythology of pure Spanish bloodlines in New Mexico; also R. Gutierrez (1991) for a discussion of the complex racial and blood categories used in the Spanish colonial period in New Mexico.

25. For a firsthand account of the DOE ten thousand-year communications study, see Benford (1999); for a broad assessment of the politics surrounding the WIPP project, see McCutcheon (2002).

The only sites under consideration are the WIPP facility near Carlsbad, New Mexico (which opened in 1999 to hold military nuclear waste), and the Yucca Mountain Project, located on the Nevada Test Site, which is still undergoing environmental review (and is designed to receive both military and commercial nuclear waste).

26. On the evolution of the Chicano movement in the Southwest, see Acuna (1988), Barrera (1979, 1988), and J. Chavez (1984). On the specific claims in northern New Mexico, see Nostrand (1992), and R. Ortiz (1980). On Manifest Destiny, see Stephanson (1995); on the Treaty of Guadalupe Hidaldo, see Castillo (1990).

27. On the 1960s land grant movement, see Garner (1970), Nabokov (1969), Gonzalez (1969), and Tijerina (1978).

28. See Ben Neary, "Congress Won't Pass Land Grant Bills This Year," *Santa Fe New Mexican*, October 4, 1998.

29. In his study, "Communication Measures to Bridge Ten Millennia," Thomas Sebeok argues that new cultural forms need to be developed expressly to maintain knowledge of the millennial dangers of nuclear waste. He argues:

> Information [should] be launched and artificially passed on into the short-term and long-term future with the supplementary aid of folkoristic devices, in particular a combination of an artificially created and nurtured ritual and legend ... The legend and ritual, as now envisaged, would be tantamount to laying a "false trail," meaning that the uninitiated will be steered away from the hazardous site for reasons other than the scientific knowledge of the possibility of radiation and its implication; essentially, the reason would be accumulated superstition to shun a certain area permanently. A ritual annually renewed can be foreseen with the legend retold year by year (with, presumably, slight variations). The actual "truth" would be entrusted exclusively to—what we might call for dramatic emphasis—an "atomic priesthood," that is, a commission of knowledgeable physicists, experts in radiation sickness, anthropologists, linguists, psychologists, semioticians, and whatever additional expertise may be called for now and in the future. Membership in the "priesthood" would be self-selective over time. (1984: 24)

Thus, Sebeok also assumes that institutional control over present-day nuclear sites cannot be maintained over the millennia and suggests that an entirely new kind of cultural project be undertaken, a "nuclear priesthood" created simply to care for and maintain knowledge about the radioactive legacies of the Cold War.

30. By 1994, per capita income in Los Alamos County was $29,762, while in neighboring Rio Arriba County it was $11,731 (DOE 1998b: 4–164). In 1994, out of 476 individuals in the top three layers of management at LANL (identified as group leaders, associate managers, and top management) a total

of thirty-one were identified as "Hispanic" by laboratory employment figures (two of sixty-eight at the management or associate management level). In contrast, at the next lower, and largest overall, level of management, those identified as supervisors, "Hispanics" made up nearly 24 percent of that job class, fueling Nuevomexicano concerns about a glass ceiling (LANL 1995d: F1–F10). When publicly confronted with these statistics, LANL representatives argued that the problem was not a glass ceiling but the educational requirements necessary for those doing "world-class science." They discussed LANL's commitment to affirmative action and educational outreach efforts in the valley, and said that while the laboratory recruits from a national pool, the number of "Hispanics" completing doctoral degrees in science in the United States is much smaller than the percentage of Nuevomexicanos in northern New Mexico. And indeed, excluding the support staff, of those enjoying the highest-paying jobs at the laboratory (scientists and mid- to upper level managers) 80 percent had at least a master's degree, and most had doctorates. But this explanation merely revealed another regional disparity and returned the debate about Nuevomexicano economic standing to a question of institutional bias—this time concerning school funding in the northern Rio Grande valley.

31. In 1994, a U.S. General Accounting Office Report also concluded that Native American and Hispanic employees at Sandia and Los Alamos National Laboratories lost their security clearances at a statistically higher rate than Anglos or other minorities, and called for greater attention to race and ethnicity issues in the management of security clearances. See GAO (1994).

32. Los Alamos schools were opened to students from the valley in the early 1980s: see Rothman (1992: 277–28). Nevertheless, profound differences in educational structures remain. In 1994, the average salary for a teacher in Los Alamos was $38,624; in Española it was $26,099. Los Alamos had 481 high school students in advanced placement classes while Pojoaque had 35 and Española 22. In Los Alamos, 87.5 percent of high school graduates applied to college, while less than half that number did in Española or Pojoaque. See David Roybal, "DOE Funds Give Los Alamos Schools Unfair Advantage," *Santa Fe New Mexican*, May 26, 1995.

33. Reprinted in *Los Alamos Independent Press*, June 7, 1996, 17.

34. See Ray Rivera, "In Newest Settlement, Laid-off LANL Workers Get $2.8 Million," *The New Mexican*, May 16, 1998. See also Charmian Schaller, "UC Settles RIF-related Labor Case for $625K," *Los Alamos Monitor*, May 13, 1998.

CHAPTER 5: BACKTALKING TO THE NATIONAL FETISH

1. See Stephen T. Shankland, "Seven Seek Entry to Lab Facilities, Saying U.S. is Disarming Too Slowly," *Los Alamos Monitor*, March 27, 1998.

2. This quotation is drawn from the LASG press release dated March 23, 1998, entitled "Citizen Verification Team to Hold UNSCOM-style Inspection at Los Alamos National Lab," available on the World Wide Web at http://www.lasg.org/news/cvt.htm.

3. See Los Alamos Study Group, "Billboards," available on the World Wide Web at http://www.lasg.org/billbord.html.

4. For discussion and analysis of antinuclear protests at Lawrence Livermore, see Gusterson (1996a); at the Nevada Test Site, see Solnit (1994); and at Los Alamos, see Rosenthal (1990). For a comparative history of antinuclear movements worldwide, see Wittner (1993, 1997, 2003) and Nelkin and Pollak (1981). For historical analyses of specific antinuclear groups in the United States, see Krasniewicz (1992) and Katz (1986).

5. Daubert and Moran (1985), for example, in their global, comparative study of antinuclear protest, found evidence of only three protests in New Mexico between 1977 and 1983: one concerning the WIPP facility (involving 150 people), one on the anniversary of the bombing of Hiroshima in Los Alamos (involving twenty people), and a third, sparked by the deployment of the MX missile at the Kirtland airbase in Albuquerque, involving two hundred people; see also Nelkin and Pollak (1981).

6. The following statistics are drawn from two major studies of American attitudes toward nuclear weapons: the first, by the Public Agenda Foundation took place at the height of the Reagan-era Cold War in 1984 (Yankelovich, Kingston, and Garvey 1984); the second, by the Henry L. Stimson Center (1998), is the most recent study of post–Cold War attitudes; see also Jenkins-Smith, Barke, and Harron (1995).

7. In the Henry L. Stimpson Center study (1998), Russia was no longer considered by most Americans to be a significant threat to the United States despite its enormous Cold War nuclear arsenal, and terrorism was felt to be the greatest single threat to U.S. security.

8. See U.S. Office of Technology Assessment (1991) and DOE (1995a, 1995b, 1996, 2000b).

9. See ACHRE (1996), as well as the special issue of *Los Alamos Science* (1995, Number 23) devoted to exploring LANL's historical role in the human radiation experiments.

10. In the spring of 1998, India and Pakistan both detonated nuclear devices, becoming the first new nuclear powers of the post–Cold War period.

11. See Mary Riseley and Karin Salzman, "Nuclear Weapons on Trial," *Santa Fe Reporter*, November 29, 1995. In 1996, the World Court in the Hague did rule that a first-strike use of nuclear weapons was against international law; however, judges left room in their decision for a "defensive" use of nuclear weapons; see Burroughs (1997).

12. For analysis of the *Enola Gay* controversy, see Harwit (1996) and Linenthal and Engelhardt (1996). For the complete text of the proposed exhibit, see Nobile (1995), and for analysis of cultural logic informing American reactions to the bombing of Hiroshima, see Lifton and Markusen (1995).

13. For narrative analysis of the Bradbury Science Museum, and the early engagements with Santa Fe activists, see Taylor (1996a, 1996b).

14. See Patrick Armijo, "Groups Vie for Lab Display Space," *Albuquerque Journal*, June 7, 1995.

15. The charges were eventually dropped after the LASG sued, and LANL agreed to pay the LASG members' legal fees. See Caroline Spaeth, "Charges

against Bradbury Leafleters Dropped Thursday," *Los Alamos Monitor*, September 9, 1997; and also Caroline Spaeth, "Study Group Will Continue to Leaflet Bradbury Science Museum," *Los Alamos Monitor*, July 22, 1998.

16. See Gusterson (1996a: 131–64) for a detailed discussion of the importance of underground nuclear testing within the culture of weapons scientists at Livermore, as well as the consequences of the test ban.

17. The Galvin Commission Task Force was doubly notable because among its participants was Daniel Kerlinsky, the president of the New Mexico chapter of Physicians for Social Responsibility. His participation on the task force marks perhaps the first time a U.S. peace activist has been given a U.S. security clearance to review the scope and execution of the U.S. nuclear complex.

18. See Stephen T. Shankland, "LANL Responsible for Five Nuclear Weapons Systems," *Los Alamos Monitor* (special insert: "Lab in Transition"), March 1, 1998. LLNL is responsible for the remaining three weapons systems—The W62, W87, and B83; see DOE (1999e).

19. LANL produced its first plutonium pit since the late 1940s in March 1998. See Ian Hoffman, "LANL Celebrates Plutonium Pit Production," *Albuquerque Journal*, March 20, 1998.

20. Former Secretary of Energy Hazel O'Leary has in fact become a key witness in whistleblower suits against the DOE. She has stated publicly that a number of DOE facilities maintain a hostile attitude toward whistleblowers, noting in particular the removal of security clearances for those that publicize problems within the nuclear complex. See Peter Eisler, "Whistleblowers Getting Back at DOE," *USA Today*, May 21, 1998.

21. The Natural Resources Defense Council, for example, has described the SBSS program as an "End Run" around the Comprehensive Test Ban Treaty. They conclude, Paine and McKinzie (1998a):

In place of a relatively straightforward strategy for maintaining stockpile confidence, such as periodic remanufacture of proven warheads to test-certified specifications, the Administration is offering a complex (and expensive) tale of elaborate new modeling capabilities to "predict" the degradation in nuclear performance of "aging" warheads—warheads whose service lives have been deliberately "extended" until a new generation of weapons "designers" can develop and certify replacement warheads, using 3-D codes not yet written and massive new experimental facilities not yet built.

The *End Run* report is available on the World Wide Web at http://www.igc.apc.org/nrdc/nrdcpro/endrun/erinx.html. See also Zerriffi and Machijani (1996).

22. And indeed, the headlines in Los Alamos the day after Clinton announced support for the Comprehensive Test Ban Treaty read "Labs Get Funding from CTBT Deal"; see Stephen T. Shankland, "Labs get Funding from CTBT Deal," *Los Alamos Monitor*, September 23, 1997.

23. See Stephen T. Shankland, 'Supercomputers Are Picking Up Where Nuclear Tests Left Off," *Los Alamos Monitor* (special insert: "Lab in Transition"), March 1, 1998.

24. See Stephen T. Shankland "New Director Leads Lab into New Future," *Los Alamos Monitor* (special insert: "Lab in Transition"), March 1, 1998.

25. Santa Fe activists, for example, cited articles on nuclear weapon reliability issues written by J. Carson Mark, who was a senior weapons scientist at LANL from the Manhattan Project through the early 1970s. Mark (1990) argues that the most serious reliability issues evoked by laboratory and DOE officials come from a series of weapons that were added to the U.S. stockpile during the test moratorium of the late 1950s, which were not subjected to the full range of predeployment tests. He concludes that reliability discussions often do not represent the true status of the modern U.S. nuclear arsenal and are a politicized means of maintaining the nuclear status quo. Santa Fe activists also gained access in 1995 to a declassified summary of a Sandia National Laboratory "Stockpile Life Study" (1993), which documented a total of 257 problems in the entire history of the U.S. stockpile (involving seventy thousand weapons since 1945) that might affect safety or reliability issues. A similar joint study by LANL, LLNL, and Sandia weapons scientists in 1995, however, found 370 problems affecting safety or reliability issues in the U.S. stockpile as well as 2,400 recorded defects in nuclear weapons (see Johnson et al. 1995). Antinuclear activists argue that this "tri-lab" study exaggerates the number of problems with the U.S. stockpile, notably by including weapons systems that are not in the post–Cold War stockpile. They also criticize the report for exaggerating the scale of the problems found, noting that some major findings would merely diminish the size of the nuclear detonation produced by a particular weapon, not render it useless from a military point of view. See also Zerriffi and Machijani (1996).

26. Through litigation with the DOE, the Natural Resource Defense Council got access to a copy of the post–Cold War nuclear planning document, Stockpile Stewardship Plan, the so-called Green Book (see DOE 1998a). The Green Book details U.S. commitments to maintaining the full range of nuclear weapons expertise in design and testing, and plans to move the nuclear weapons certification process increasingly into a computer-based testing regime. It also states that new design work will be ongoing, a necessary part of the program to maintain nuclear weapons expertise.

27. LANL produces about one thousand fifty-five-gallon drums of transuranic waste each year destined for the WIPP. In the late 1990s, LANL had over forty thousand drums stacked in temporary dome enclosures on the Pajarito Plateau awaiting the opening of the WIPP facility. See Charmian Schaller, "40,000 Drums at Lab Await Shipment to WIPP," *Los Alamos Monitor*, January 31, 1999.

CHAPTER 6: LIE DETECTORS

1. On the espionage activities of Klaus Fuchs, see Williams (1987), and on Theodore Hall, see Albright and Kunstel (1997). Rumors of a third Soviet agent, code-named Perseus, were resurrected in the 1990s by publication of

Pavel Antolievich Sudoplatov's *Special Tasks: The Memoirs of an Unwanted Witness, a Soviet Spymaster* (Boston: Little, Brown, 1994). Sudoplatov was involved in Soviet espionage activities within the United States during and after World War II, and claims in his autobiography that a number of key Manhattan Project personnel including Erico Fermi, Neils Bohr, and J. Robert Oppenheimer passed secrets to the Soviet Union. While *Special Tasks* was largely rejected in the United States as propaganda, Sudoplatov's book did raise old questions about whether a third agent, or possibly a team of Soviet agents, using the code-name Perseus, was active in Los Alamos during the Manhattan Project. Indeed, the hunt for Perseus continues to make its way through Manhattan Project luminaries. In his 1999 autobiography *"Every Man Should Try": Adventures of a Public Interest Activist* (New York: Public Affairs Press), Jeremy Stone accused Philip Morrison of being Perseus. Morrison has publicly rejected the accusation; see Linda Rothstein, "Nuclear Secrets: The Perseus Papers," *Bulletin of the Atomic Scientists* 55(4) (1999): 17–19. For a broader analysis of the role of espionage in the spread of nuclear technologies immediately following World War II, see Rhodes (1995).

2. For residents of Los Alamos, the espionage allegations were the start of the most difficult period in the history of their technoscientific community, which culminated in May 2000, when a prescribed burn by the U.S. Forest Service got out of control and burned nearly fifty thousand acres in the Los Alamos area, destroying hundreds of homes and shutting down the laboratory for several weeks. For an overview of the summer events of 1999, which included not only the institutional fallout from the security scandal but also the largest single antinuclear protest in Los Alamos history, see Gusterson (1999b).

3. The Rudman Report (PFIAB 1999) was commissioned by President Clinton as a reply to a report by the Select Committee of the U.S. House of Representatives on U.S. National Security—also known as the Cox Report—which concluded that China had received U.S. nuclear weapons design information from Los Alamos. The unclassified version of the Cox Report, however, provided little data to back up its conclusions and has been strongly criticized; see May (1999). See also GAO (1999b) for a summary of the longstanding concerns about security within the DOE and the national laboratories, and see also LANL (1999a: xiii) for a mission statement that defines the post–Cold War mission of the laboratory as "enhancing global security."

4. The U.S. Court of Appeals for the Tenth Circuit in February 2000 supported the District Court's decision to deny Wen Ho Lee bail, agreeing that Lee "presents a clear and present danger to the United States" and that "no combination of conditions of release would reasonably assure the safety of the community or the nation" (see *United States v. Wen Ho Lee, decided without published opinion*, 208 F.3d 228 [10th Cir. Feb. 29, 2000]).

5. Lee eventually told his story in a book, co-written with Helen Zia (2001), entitled *My Country Versus Me*. The best journalistic account of the legal case and its broader national security politics is Stober and Hoffman (2001).

6. On U.S. secrecy during the Cold War, see Moynihan (1998) and Shils (1996); for analysis of the scope of secrecy within the nuclear complex, see Burr, Blanton, and Schwartz (1998); and for Cold War secrecy practices

among weapons scientists at LLNL, see Gusterson (1996a: 68–100). For a broad analysis of the social impacts of secrecy, see Bok (1983), and on the concept of the public secret, see Taussig (1999).

7. On U.S. satellite surveillance programs, see Richelson (1999). For analysis of the seismic monitoring systems for underground nuclear detonations, see OTA (1988).

8. The bomb that destroyed Hiroshima in 1945 weighed 8,900 pounds and produced an atomic yield of 15 kilotons. By the mid-1980s, the W-88 warhead designed at Los Alamos weighed less than 400 pounds and could produce a yield of 475 kilotons; see Hansen (1988: 121).

9. Indeed, while U.S. officials accused Wen Ho Lee of disrupting the global balance of power, they consistently failed to mention how that balance of power was constituted. In 1999, the United States had deployed some 7,000 nuclear weapons around the world (with nearly 4,000 in storage that could be quickly reassembled) and a vast array of delivery systems, while China's nuclear arsenal consisted of roughly 400 weapons and less than 25 intercontinental missiles (see NRDC 2000). This means that just one of the 11 deployed U.S. Trident submarines was more powerful than the entire Chinese nuclear arsenal (as a Trident submarine can carry 24 missiles, each missile packed with 8 of the W-88, 475-kiloton warheads). A single Trident submarine, therefore, is capable of destroying a total of 196 separate nuclear targets/cities in under 30 minutes; see Mello (2000).

10. Another measure of the size of the official trade in secrets in the United States is the number of people waiting for security clearances. Over nine hundred thousand would-be government employees were waiting for clearances in 2000, and the backlog was such that the average top secret security clearance took 306 days to investigate. See Walter Pincus, "900,000 People Awaiting Pentagon Security Clearances," *Washington Post*, April 22, 2000.

11. On the political use of secrecy within the U.S. security state, see Welsome (1999), Schwartz (1998), and Moynihan (1998).

12. The National Cancer Institute, for example, estimates that tens of thousands of U.S. citizens have developed thyroid cancer as a result of fallout from atmospheric testing at the Nevada Test Site. The National Cancer Institute's ten thousand-page report is available on the World Wide Web at http://rex.nci.nih.gov/massmedia/Fallout/contents.html. See also IPPNW and IEER (1991).

13. The U.S. Congress passed the Energy Employee's Occupational Illness Compensation Act of 2000 on January 11, 2001, which offers a $150,000 lump sum payment plus health care coverage to workers at 317 sites within the U.S. nuclear complex, who contracted beryllium disease or cancer on the job. Heirs to nuclear workers who have already died as a result of on the job health problems will also be able to apply for the $150,000 payment. The total bill for the program could reach as high as $2 billion over the next ten years. See President Bill Clinton, Executive Order of December 7, 2000, available on the World Wide Web at http://www.tis.eh.doe.gov/benefits/announce/20001207eo.html.

14. The Lee case led to a substantial revision in how nuclear weapons information is classified, including the proposed addition of three new

Sigmas. See "Sigma Category Definition" posted on the Federation of American Scientists' Web site at www.fas.org/sgp/othergov/doe/sigmas.html.

15. For example, while the computer codes were represented in Wen Ho Lee's bail hearing as the foundation of U.S. national security, two months earlier at the Senate hearings over U.S. ratification of the Comprehensive Test Ban Treaty, the "unreliability" of the codes was repeatedly evoked as a means to defeat ratification of the treaty. Moreover, the DOE changed the security classification of the nuclear weapons computer codes after they discovered Lee had downloaded them. Previously, they were not classified as "secret" or "confidential" but under the "protect as restricted data," or PARD, category, a lower classification. While penalties still exist for mishandling PARD information, the security protocols are significantly less stringent than for "classified" or "secret" data. See Broad (2000).

16. In 1999, for example, LANL maintained a computer system running at one teraflop (i.e., capable of running one trillion operations per second), and had a hundred-teraflop system already in planning (LANL 1999a).

17. Critics of the DOE's SBSS program argue that it relies on facilities that are equally useful for designing new nuclear weapons (as maintaining aging ones) and thus question the ultimate goal of the SBSS concept. They point out that DOE has already begun "modifications" on existing nuclear weapons so that they could be used for new missions, and see a next-generation nuclear complex ultimately producing a new generation of nuclear weapons (see Mello 2000).

18. Indeed, a loose generational gap divides LANL weapons scientists on the question of the value of the computer codes without a complementary regime of nuclear testing. Several scientists who established their expertise during the Cold War resisted making decisions about the U.S. nuclear arsenal based solely on the codes, arguing that there can be no certainty without underground tests. On the other hand, a new, post–Cold War generation of weapons scientists, who were hired into a more virtual U.S. nuclear design environment, expressed more confidence that a computer-based stockpile program would be successful in maintaining U.S. nuclear weapons.

19. See MacKenzie with Spinardi (1996) for an analysis of the "tacit" knowledge—that is, the everyday cultural experience not codified in blueprints or computer codes—involved in building nuclear weapons. They suggest that tacit knowledge is so important to building a nuclear weapon that it might be possible to "uninvent" or to forget culturally how to build nuclear weapons within a few generations simply by ending nuclear production.

20. In 1987, for example, there were a total of 89 foreign national employees at LANL, a number that grew to 456 by 1999. The number of LANL scientists born in China grew from 0 in 1987 to 97 in 1999 and constituted the single largest foreign national group at the laboratory (followed by Germany, 49; India, 42; Canada, 36; the United Kingdom, 28; and Russia, 24). See LANL Fellows (1999).

21. As head of the counterintelligence office at LANL, Robert Vrooman was in charge of the investigation into the "walk in" documents. He was

also one of three LANL officials disciplined by Secretary of Energy Bill Richardson for their handling of the Wen Ho Lee investigation. In response to his censure, Vrooman stated:

> I have worked on this case since June 23, 1995. I know that there is not one shred of evidence that the information that the Intelligence Community identifies as having been stolen by the Chinese came from Wen Ho Lee, Los Alamos National Laboratory, the Department of Energy complex or from a DOE office. The information known to have been obtained by the Chinese was available in documentary form on many classified documents distributed to hundreds of locations through the US government and contractor complex . . . Dr. Lee was identified by the Department of Energy's Office of Counterintelligence as the prime suspect based on an, at best, cursory investigation at only two facilities, Los Alamos and Lawrence Livermore National Laboratory. The details of this investigation are still classified, but it can be said at this time that Mr. Lee's ethnicity was a major factor. (1999)

See also Vernon Loeb, "Ex-Spy Catcher Looks for Medal, Not Scorn," *Washington Post*, December 20, 1999.

22. See Vernon Loeb and Walter Pincus, "New Leads Found in Spy Probe," *Washington Post*, November 19, 1999; and John Soloman, "FBI's Focus Changing," Associated Press, December 13, 1999.

23. Asian American organizations had held rallies on Lee's behalf in New Mexico, California, and Washington, D.C., in 2000.

24. A precedent exists in New Mexico for this kind of covert interpretation of language. During World War II, Navajo Codetalkers were deployed throughout the Pacific Theater as a means of ensuring secret communication. Using coded *Dine* words, the Codetalkers successfully provided classified communication between frontline troops and military command and control. The Japanese never broke the code. The existence of the Navajo Codetalkers remained a state secret for over forty years in the United States.

25. In response to the espionage allegations, LANL had a week-long standdown of all of its computer systems in April 1999 to search for security breaches, and another two-day stand-down the following June to address "security" at the laboratory. The DOE then conducted a systemwide standdown of its facilities to address the racial profiling issue on April 20, 2000.

26. See DOE (1995a, 1995b, 1996, 1997, 2000b). See also IPPNW and IEER (1991).

27. For an analysis of recruitment practices within the U.S. nuclear weapons programs at LLNL, see Gusterson (1996a: 38–67).

28. Steven Aftergood, in his email list *Security News* on February 6, 2001, reports that "at least one civilian was prosecuted under the Atomic Energy Act in 1965" and "one military officer was court-martialed under the Act in 1959"; see http://www.fas.org/sgp/index.html. Thus, Wen Ho Lee is perhaps the third person charged under the Atomic Energy Act.

29. The accuracy of polygraph tests has been wildly disputed, from studies claiming a less than one percent false positive rate, to those showing that

more than 20 percent of those tested were falsely accused of lying. The Office of Technology Assessment, a congressional research group, concluded that a trustworthy measurement of the accuracy of polygraph testing was ultimately impossible because:

> the polygraph test is, in reality, a very complex process that is much more than the instrument. Although the instrument is essentially the same for all applications, the types of individuals tested, training of the examiner, purpose of the test, and types of questions asked, among other factors, can differ substantially. A polygraph test requires that the examiner infer deception or truthfulness based on a comparison of the person's physiological responses to various questions. (1983: 2)

Weapons scientists responded immediately to the ambiguity built into the polygraph tests, refusing to allow someone else to simply "infer" deception or truthfulness. Scientists at LLNL labeled the proposed polygraph testing a "witch hunt" worthy of the McCarthy era, and at Los Alamos, one scientist described the polygraph rules as "Orwellian" for demanding that scientists sign a paper agreeing that the test was "voluntary" when their jobs would clearly be at stake for not taking the test. Some suggested that this discrepancy alone would cause them to fail the test, giving investigators the excuse to invade all aspects of their lives. Over 70 percent of the members of X division, which is the core division for nuclear weapons design work at Los Alamos, signed a petition protesting the proposed rule.

30. An unclassified version of the interview is available at wenholee.org/transcript4868.htm.

31. At a laboratory meeting to explain the process of polygraph testing in the summer of 1999, for example, a DOE counterintelligence officer described how the machine reads physiological changes in the body to specific questions, concluding that polygraphs are "a snapshot of your emotions when asked a question. That's all this is. It's not a witch-hunting thing. We're looking for the great majority of people to pass the test." This suggestion that the polygraphs were not a witch hunt but were also not perfectly accurate did little to comfort LANL scientists, who soon thereafter protested vociferously at DOE hearings on the polygraph proposal. See *LANL Newsbulletin*, September 10, 1999; and also DOE (1999d).

32. The accusations against former CIA director John Deutch were similar to those against Wen Ho Lee, but the cases were handled very differently. The disparity between the hard line taken against Lee and the latitude give Deutch (who was never jailed and was ultimately pardoned by President Clinton) has been evoked by supporters of Lee as an illustration of both a double standard and the role of race within the Lee investigation. Deutch was not the subject of a criminal investigation until comparisons were made in the national media with the accusations against Lee. While Lee was incarcerated for 278 days while waiting for trial, Deutch never spent a day in jail. While he was negotiating the final step in a plea agreement, consisting of a $5,000 fine and no jail time, President Clinton

granted Deutch an executive pardon. See James Risen, "CIA Inquiry of its Ex-Director was Stalled at Top, Report Says," *New York Times*, February 1, 2000; and Bill Miller and Walter Pincus, "Deutch Had Signed Plea Agreement, Sources Say," *Washington Post*, January 24, 2001, A13; see also Steven Mufson, "State Department Transfers Security Duties After Criticism Over Vanished Laptop," *Washington Post*, April 25, 2000.

33. President George W. Bush, Speech to a Joint Session of Congress, September 20, 2001 (transcript available at http://www.whitehouse.gov/news/releases/2001/09/20010920-8.html).

34. In his remarks to the Republican Governors Association on October 25, 2001, Vice President Dick Cheney stated: "Homeland security is not a temporary measure just to meet one crisis. Many of the steps we have now been forced to take will become permanent in American life. They represent an understanding of the world as it is, and dangers we must guard against perhaps for decades to come. I think of it as the new normalcy" (transcript available at http://www.whitehouse.gov/vicepresident/news-speeches/speeches/vp20011025.html).

35. See Executive Order 13233, "Further Implementation of the Presidential Records Act" (available at http://www.fas.org/irp/offdocs/eo/eo-13233.htm), and President Bush's November 13 Military Order on tribunals (available at http://www.fas.org/sgp/news/2001/11/bush111301.html).

36. In his FOIA Memorandum of October 12, 2001, Attorney General Ashcroft wrote: "When you carefully consider FOIA requests and decide to withhold records, in whole or in part, you can be assured that the Department of Justice will defend your decisions unless they lack a sound legal basis or present an unwarranted risk of adverse impact on the ability of other agencies to protect other important records" (available at http://www.usdoj.gov/oip/foiapost/2001foiapost19.htm); the text of the PATRIOT Act can be found at http://www.fas.org/asmp/resources/billlaws.html.

37. See Hearing of the Senate Judiciary Committee, Subject: The Department of Justice and Terrorism (Chaired by Senator Patrick Leahy [D-VT]) Witness: Attorney General John Ashcroft, November 6, 2001 (transcript available at http://www.nytimes.com/library/politics/011207ashcroft-text.html).

38. For a White House overview of the new terrorist warning system, see http://www.whitehouse.gov/news/releases/2002/03/20020312-5.html.

39. See President George W. Bush, 2002 State of the Union address (transcript available at whitehouse.gov/news/releases/2002/01/20020129-11.html).

40. Excerpts of the 2002 Nuclear Policy Review can be found at http://www.globalsecurity.org/wmd/library/policy/dod/npr.htm. See Nolan (1999) for an analysis of how the 1994 Nuclear Posture Review was derailed by competing political interests in Washington, who were ultimately unable to do anything but reaffirm the Cold War nuclear status quo they set out to fundamentally reform. See Klare (1995) on the invention and deployment of the "rogue" state concept at the end of the Cold War.

CHAPTER 7: MUTANT ECOLOGIES

1. See "Cerro Grande . . . Facing the Flames," *Los Alamos Monitor*, Special Section, June 18, 2000; LANL, "A Great Laboratory Comes Back," *Dateline: Los Alamos*, Summer 2000; Alvarez and Arends (2000); Concerned Citizens For Nuclear Safety and the Nuclear Policy Project, "Fire, Water, and the Aftermath: A Public Forum on the May 2000 Cerro Grande Fire and its Effects on the Rio Grande/Bravo Watershed," transcript, July 8, 2000.

2. The atmospheric monitoring stations established by LANL in northern New Mexico in the 1990s under pressure from concerned citizens registered radiation levels twenty to thirty times normal during the fire. Los Alamos scientists judge these rates to be within expectations for a forest fire (Fresquez, Velasquez, and Naranjo Jr. 2000).

3. The reaction to the fire was surprising given that the region experienced major fires in 1954, 1977, 1986, and 1998.

4. The United States heavily censored postbombing images of Hiroshima and Nagasaki. See Braw (1997); Goldstein, Wenger, and Dillon (1997); and Lifton and Mitchell (1995). Fear of radioactive contamination from the Bravo test created panic throughout the Pacific, leading U.S. officials to send radiation monitors in full protective gear to fish markets in the United States armed with Geiger counters to ensure the safety of the food supply.

5. For critical analysis of atomic popular culture during the era of aboveground nuclear testing (1945–63), see Boyer (1994), Franklin (1988), Henrikson (1997), Evans (1998), Weart (1988), and Shapiro (2002).

6. Radiation standards also assume a kind of universal national subject. The cultural diversity of northern New Mexico, which includes quite distinct land use, as well as access to health care, challenges such a formation; see Basso (1996); A. Ortiz (1969); Briggs and Van Ness (1987).

7. On the concept of the risk society, see Beck (1992). For work on nuclear risk societies, see Kultez (1998); Petryna (2002); Lifton (1991); Gerber (2002); Gusterson (1996a); Fusco and Caris (2001); Lindee (1994); ACHRE (1996); Welsome (1999); Makjihani, Hu, and Yi (1995); Gallager (1993); Dalton et al. (1999); and Peluso and Watts (2000).

8. A recent study by the GAO on radiation standards, for example, concluded, "U.S. regulatory standards to protect the public from the potential health risks of nuclear radiation lack a conclusively verified scientific basis, according to a consensus of recognized scientists" (GAO 2000: 4). For a history of radiation standards, see Walker (1999) and Schull (1995); for analysis of human radiation experiments, see ACHRE (1996). For studies of toxic discourse, see Beck (1992); Buell (1998); Davis (1993, 1998); Edelstein (1988); Fortun (2001); Peluso and Watts (2001); and Vyner (1988).

9. While the same could be said of many industrial pollutants, and certainly there has been no pristine state of nature since the advent of agriculture and animal husbandry, the global nuclear economy does represent something new. For the first time, the effects of industrial transformation are both worldwide

and nationalized through a discourse of state security. The result is that each nuclear effect speaks not only to state security but also to experiences of national belonging or alienation. As Jean and John Comaroff have noted in their study of "alien-nation" in South Africa (2000: 36), the deployment of nature is often used "as alibi, as a fertile allegory for rendering some people and objects strange, thereby to authenticate the limits of the ('nature') order of things; also to interpolate within it new social and political distinctions." In this case, the effects of a nuclear economy are simultaneously material, social, ecological, and political—state-sponsored and embedded in everyday life. See Raffles (2002) for a remarkable discussion of the linked social and ecological forces involved in the production of Amazonia.

10. Latour (1993), for example, argues that scientific discourse has traditionally relied on a purification process whereby nature is ideologically reproduced as external to human intervention, making the act of scientific research inseparable from its authorizing mechanisms. On the value of the cyborg to contemporary social theory, see Haraway (1991), Downey and Dumit (1997), and Gray (1995).

11. On the radiological effects of the Chernobyl accident on people and the environments, see Fusco and Caris (2001); Petryna (2002); Stephens (2002); and Theroux (2001).

12. In addition to marking the effects of the exploding bomb on the body of the pig, Operation Plumbbob included a series of experiments for controlling atmospheric fallout: Shot Rainier, for example, was the first contained U.S. underground detonation (enabling the U.S. underground test regime of 1963–92). While containing fallout was an experimental concern for the test series, the immediate project behind each nuclear detonation (or "shot") was to increase U.S. nuclear-war fighting capabilities.

13. Operation Plumbbob also involved a series of experiments to "harden" the human body against the effects of the exploding bomb. Flash-blindness experiments were conducted, in which volunteers tested a new high-speed electromechanical shutter on goggles (in hopes of protecting Air Force pilots who would be fighting a nuclear war). Concerned that troops would panic at the first sight of a nuclear explosion, the Department of Defense also ran an experiment designed to test how soldiers would respond to seeing an atomic blast for the first time. During Shot Galileo, one hundred soldiers were exposed to the exploding bomb, and then asked to perform certain drills, such as assembling and disassembling their rifles, to test response times (U.S. Defense Nuclear Agency 1981b: 21).

14. For related work in the anthropology of science, see Gusterson (1996a); Haraway (1997); Helmreich (2000); Latour (1988); Martin (1994), Petryna (2002); Rabinow (1996, 1999); and Redfield (2000).

15. See the DOE's Long-Term Stewardship Program mission statement at http://lts.apps.em.doe.gov/mission.asp, accessed October 15, 2003.

16. For ethnographic investigations into the aftermath of environmental disaster, see Petryna (2002), Kuletz (1998), and Fortun (2001).

17. For analysis of environmental laws and the U.S. military complex, see Dycus (1996) and Ehrlich and Birks (1990). For recent efforts to incorporate

environmental concern into the definition of national security, see Dalby (2002); see Shrader-Frechette (2002) for an analysis of the environmental justice movement in the United States.

18. For analysis of Area G environmental contamination, see Hollis (1997) and DOE (1995a, 1995b, 2001).

19. For information about plutonium and tritium contamination from nuclear research at Los Alamos, see Graf (1994) and LANL (1994, 1995b).

20. See the DARPA "Controlled Biosystems" Web site at http://www.darpa.mil/dso/thrust/biosci/cbs/objectiv.html (accessed October 15, 2003).

21. See DARPA (2003). See also Revkin (2002); Stone (1999a, 1999b); and the U.S. Army Center for Environmental Health Research "Environmental Sentinels" homepage at http://usacehr.detrick.army.mil/envsen2.html (accessed October 15, 2003).

22. Within the first year of cooperative agreements signed between four neighboring Pueblo Nations and LANL in 1992, environmental testing at the laboratory markedly increased: in 1993 LANL scientists collected 11,500 environmental samples and subjected them to 215,000 tests for contaminants—an increase of approximately 40 percent in samples and 70 percent in tests from the previous year (LANL 1995b).

23. For information and legal briefs related to the Class Action settlement on the Los Alamos Tissue Analysis Program, see: http://www.kelleysettlement.com/ (accessed October 15, 2003).

CHAPTER 8: EPILOGUE

1. See the transcript for the first presidential debate of the 2004 campaign, which took place at the University of Florida on September 30, at http://www.debates.org/pages/trans2004a.html (accessed October 15, 2004).

2. National Security Advisor Condoleeza Rice first made this argument on the *CNN Late Edition* television show on September 8, 2002. President Bush repeated it a month later in a Cincinnati, Ohio speech devoted to making the case that Saddam Hussein represented a profound threat to the United States. Evoking the September 11 attacks, he said, "Knowing these realities, America must not ignore the threat gathering against us. Facing clear evidence of peril, we cannot wait for the final proof—the smoking gun—that could come in the form of a mushroom cloud." The transcript of this speech is available at http://archives.cnn.com/2002/ALLPOLITICS/10/07/bush.transcript/ (accessed October 15, 2004).

3. See Cirincione et al. (2004), for a careful analysis of all the prewar U.S. intelligence assessments of the Iraq weapons of mass destruction program.

4. See Paine (2004) for an economic and political analysis of the U.S. nuclear program since 1995. He notes that annual funding for nuclear weapons science during the Cold War averaged $4.2 billion. In the post–Cold War period, funding for the bomb reached a low of $3.4 billion in 1995, then under the evolving SBSS program, grew to $5.19 billion in 2001 and $6.5 billion in 2004 (Paine 2004: 2).

5. In December 2001, President Bush withdrew the United States from the 1972 Antiballistic Missile Treaty, in order to pursue an expansive missile defense program. The single nuclear arms treaty the Bush administration signed—the 2002 Moscow Treaty—seemed to promise quick reductions in the size of the U.S. and Russian nuclear arsenals. However, reading the fine print on the treaty reveals it to be a sham agreement, no more than a public relations stunt that does damage to the idea of arms control. The Natural Resources Defense Council has provided a careful reading of the "Orwellian" terms of the Moscow Treaty, which is worth quoting at length for what it says about the power of the national fetish (available on-line at http://www.nrdc.org/nuclear/atreaty02.asp; accessed October 15, 2004):

> Bush's treaty reportedly only limits the number of nuclear warheads mounted on operational missiles and bombers 10 years from now, and only for *one day*—December 31, 2012. Before and after that date, the number of deliverable nuclear warheads could exceed the treaty's maximum "limit" of 2,200 "operational" warheads. Both countries would be free to keep thousands of "reserve" warheads in storage, which could be remounted on delivery systems within weeks or months. The treaty's lower limit of 1,700 warheads is entirely voluntary. It appears to have been added solely to permit the Bush White House to claim that its arms control initiative is bolder than the 2,000- to 2,500-warhead range that Presidents Clinton and Yeltsin agreed to at Helsinki in 1997 for the proposed START III treaty. The treaty imposes no additional limits on either side's nuclear forces, and does not require the destruction of a single nuclear warhead, missile, silo, bomber or submarine. Moreover, the treaty does nothing to constrain or eliminate large stockpiles of *nonstrategic*, or tactical, nuclear weapons deliverable by shorter-range systems, such as cruise missiles, battlefield missiles, artillery, torpedoes and tactical aircraft. Russia has more than 8,000 tactical nuclear weapons, many at poorly secured military bases . . . While attempting to take credit for "liquidating" the legacy of the Cold War, President Bush is in fact ensuring that through 2012 the United States will retain more deployed strategic nuclear warheads than it had in 1956. That arsenal would have the explosive yield equivalent of 42,000 Hiroshima bombs.

REFERENCES

Acuna, Rodolfo
    1988   *Occupied America: A History of Chicanos*. New York: HarperCollins.

Adler, Allan Robert
    1994   "Public Access to Nuclear Energy and Weapons Information." In David O'Very, Christopher Paine, and Dan W. Reicher (eds.). *Controlling the Atom in the 21st Century*. Pp. 73–105. Boulder: Westview Press.

Advisory Committee on Human Radiation Experiments (ACHRE)
    1996   *The Human Radiation Experiments: Final Report of the President's Advisory Committee*. New York: Oxford University Press.

Aftergood, Steven
    1999   "Wrongheaded Protection: Declassification Threatened by Chinese Espionage Scandal." *Bulletin of the Atomic Scientists* 55(4): 6.

Agnew, Harold
    1983   "Vintage Agnew." *Los Alamos Science* 7: 71.

Agoyo, Herman
    1995   "Who Here Will Begin This Story?" *Race, Poverty, and the Environment* 5(3–4): 37–38.

Agoyo, Herman, and Lynnwood Brown (eds.)
    1987   *When Cultures Meet: Remembering San Gabriel Del Yunge Oweenge*. Santa Fe: Sunstone Press.

Albright, Joseph, and Marcia Kunstel
    1997   *Bombshell: The Secret Story of America's Unknown Atomic Spy Conspiracy*. New York: Times Books.

Almaguer, Tomas
    1994   *Racial Faultlines: The Historical Origins of White Supremacy in California*. Berkeley: University of California Press.

Alperovitz, Gar
    1995   *The Decision to Use the Atomic Bomb and the Architecture of an American Myth*. London: HarperCollins.

Alvarez, R., and J. Arends
    2000   *Fire, Earth and Water: An Assessment of the Environmental, Safety and Health Impacts of the Cerro Grande Fire on Los Alamos National Laboratory, a Department of Energy Facility*. Santa Fe: Concerned Citizens for Nuclear Safety. Accessed at http://www.nuclearactive.org/docs/fire4.html.

Anaya, Rudolfo A., and Francisco Lomeli (eds.)
    1989   *Aztlan: Essay on the Chicano Homeland*. Albuquerque: Academia/ El Norte Publications.

Anderson, Benedict
  1996 "Introduction." In Gopal Balakrishnan (ed.). *Mapping the Nation.* Pp. 1–16. London: Verso.
  1992 "The New World Disorder." *New Left Review* 193(May–June): 3–13.
  1991 *Imagined Communities: Reflections on the Origin and Spread of Nationalism.* Rev. ed. New York: Verso.
Arellano, Juan Estevan
  1997 "La Querencia: La Raza Bioregionalism." *New Mexico Historical Review* 72(1): 31–38.
Arkin, William M., and Richard W. Fieldhouse
  1985 *Nuclear Battlefields: Global Links in the Arms Race.* Cambridge: Ballinger Publishing Company.
Associated Press
  2001 "Getting Rid of Radioactive Weeds." May 4.
  1999 "Biological Bounty at Former Nuclear Bomb Factory." June 24.
Athas, William F.
  1996 *Investigation of Excess Thyroid Cancer Incidence in Los Alamos County.* Santa Fe: New Mexico Department of Health.
Aubrey, Crispin (ed.)
  1982 *Nukespeak: The Media and the Bomb.* London: Comedia.
Baca, Jimmy Santiago
  1986 "Choices." In *Black Mesa Poems.* Pp. 60-61. New York: A New Directions Book.
Bailey, Janet
  1995 *The Good Servant: Making Peace with the Bomb at Los Alamos.* New York: Simon and Schuster.
Balakrishnan, Gopal (ed.)
  1996 *Mapping the Nation.* London: Verso.
Baldridge, W. Scott, Lawrence W. Braile, Michael C. Fehler, and Frederico A. Moreno
  1997 "Science and Sociology Butt Heads in Tomography Experiment in Sacred Mountains." *EOS, Transactions, American Geophysical Union* 78(39): 417–28.
Ball, Howard
  1986 *Justice Downwind: America's Atomic Test Program in the 1950s.* Oxford: Oxford University Press.
Barker, Holly
  2000 *Bravo for the Marshallese: Regaining Control in a Post-Nuclear, Post-Colonial Age.* Boston: Wadsworth Publishing.
Barrera, Mario
  1988 *Beyond Aztlan: Ethnic Autonomy in Comparative Perspective.* Notre Dame: University of Notre Dame Press.
  1979 *Race and Class in the Southwest: A Theory of Racial Inequality.* Notre Dame: University of Notre Dame Press.
Basso, Keith H.
  1996 *Wisdom Sits in Places: Landscape and Language Among the Western Apache.* Albuquerque: University of New Mexico Press.

Beck, Ulrich
  1992   *Risk Society: Towards a New Modernity*. London: Sage.
Benedict, Ruth
  1981 [1931]   *Tales of the Cochiti Indians*. Albuquerque: University of
    New Mexico Press.
Benford, Gregory
  1999   *Deep Time: How Humanity Communicates Across Millennia*.
    New York: Avon Books.
Benjamin, Walter
  1976   *Charles Baudelaire: A Lyric Poet in the Era of High Capitalism*.
    London: Verso.
  1969a   "Theses on the Philosophy of History." In *Illuminations*.
    Pp. 253–64. New York: Schocken.
  1969b   "The Work of Art in the Age of Mechanical Reproduction." In
    Illuminations. Pp. 217–51. New York: Schocken.
Bodine, John J.
  1968   "A Tri-ethnic Trap: The Spanish American in Taos." In June
    Helm (ed.). Spanish-speaking People in the United States. *Pro-
    ceedings of the 1968 Annual Meetings of the American Ethnolog-
    ical Society*. Pp. 145–53. Seattle: American Ethnological Society.
Bok, Sissela
  1983   *Secrets: On the Ethics of Concealment and Revelation*.
    New York: Vintage Books.
Borneman, John
  1995   "American Anthropology as Foreign Policy." *American Anthro-
    pologist* 97(4): 663–72.
  1992   *Belonging in the Two Berlins: Kin, State, Nation*. Cambridge:
    Cambridge University Press.
Boyarin, Jonathan
  1992   *Storm from Paradise: The Politics of Jewish Memory*. Minneapo-
    lis: University of Minnesota Press.
Boyer, Paul
  1994   *By the Bomb's Early Light: American Thought and Culture at
    the Dawn of the Atomic Age*. Chapel Hill: University of North
    Carolina Press.
Bradbury, Norris
  1980   "Los Alamos: The First 25 Years." In Lawrence Badash, Joseph
    O. Hirschfelder, and Herbert P. Broida (eds.). *Reminiscences of
    Los Alamos 1943–1945*. Pp. 161–75. Boston: D. Reidel Publish-
    ing Company.
Bradley, David
  1948   *No Place to Hide*. Boston: Little, Brown and Company.
Brandt, Elizabeth
  1977   "The Role of Secrecy in a Pueblo Society." In Thomas C.
    Blackburn (ed.). *Flowers of the Wind: Papers on Ritual, Myth,
    and Symbolism in California and the Southwest*. Pp. 11–28.
    Socorro, N.M.: Ballina Press.

Braw, Monica
  1997   *The Atomic Bomb Suppressed: American Censorship in Occupied Japan.* Armonk N.Y.: M. E. Sharpe.
Briggs, Charles L.
  1988   *Competence in Performance: The Creativity of Tradition in Mexicano Verbal Art.* Philadelphia: University of Pennsylvania Press.
Briggs, Charles L., and John R. Van Ness (eds.)
  1987   *Land, Water and Culture: New Perspectives on Hispanic Land Grants.* Albuquerque: University of New Mexico Press.
British American Security Information Council (BASIC)
  1998   *Nuclear Futures: Proliferation of Weapons of Mass Destruction and U.S. Nuclear Strategy.* BASIC Research Report 98.2. Available on the World Wide Web at http://www.basicint. org/nfuture2.pdf.
Broad, William J.
  2000   "Files in Question in Los Alamos Case Were Reclassified." *New York Times*, April 15.
  1999   "Spies versus Sweat: The Debate over China's Nuclear Advance." *New York Times*, September 7.
  1992   *Teller's War: The Top Secret Story Behind the Star Wars Deception.* New York: Simon and Schuster.
Brode, Bernice
  1960   "Los Alamos and the Indians." *Los Alamos Scientific Laboratory Community News.* August 25: 5–7.
Brown, F. Lee, and Helen M. Ingram
  1987   *Water and Poverty in the Southwest.* Tucson: University of Arizona Press.
Buck-Morss, Susan
  1992   "Aesthetics and Anaesthetics: Walter Benjamin's Artwork Essay Reconsidered." *October* 62 (Fall): 3–42.
  1991   *The Dialectics of Seeing: Walter Benjamin and the Arcades Project.* Cambridge, Mass.: MIT Press.
Buell, Lawrence
  1998   "Toxic Discourse." *Critical Inquiry* 24(3): 639–65.
Bulletin of the Atomic Scientists
  2001   "Defense: When Money Is No Object." *Bulletin of the Atomic Scientists* 57(5): 36–37.
Bunzel, Ruth L.
  1992 [1932]   *Zuni Ceremonialism: Three Studies.* Albuquerque: University of New Mexico Press.
Burke, Edmund
  1993   "A Philosophical Enquiry into the Origin of Our Ideas of the Sublime and Beautiful." In Ian Harris (ed.). *Pre-Revolutionary Writings.* Pp. 63–77. Cambridge: Cambridge University Press.
Burr, William, Thomas S. Blanton, and Stephen I. Schwartz
  1998   "The Costs and Consequences of Nuclear Secrecy." In Stephen I. Schwartz (ed.). *Atomic Audit: The Costs and Consequences of*

U.S. Nuclear Weapons Since 1940. Pp. 433–83. Washington, D.C.: Brookings Institution Press.

Burroughs, John
    1997   *The (Il)legality of Threat or Use of Nuclear Weapons: A Guide to the Historic Opinion by the International Court of Justice.* International Association of Lawyers Against Nuclear Arms. Piscataway, N.J.: Transaction.

Byrnes, Victor A., D. V. L. Brown, H. W. Rose, and Paul Cibis
    1955   *Ocular Effects of Thermal Radiation From Atomic Detonation Flashblindness and Chorioretinal Burns.* Operation Upshot-Knothole. Project 4.5. U.S. Army, November 30.

Campbell, David
    1993   *Politics Without Principle: Sovereignty, Ethics, and the Narratives of the Gulf War.* Boulder: Lynne Rienner Publishers.
    1992   *Writing Security: United States Foreign Policy and the Politics of Identity.* Minneapolis: University of Minnesota Press.

Canaday, John
    2000   *The Nuclear Muse: Literature, Physics and the First Atomic Bombs.* Madison: University of Wisconsin Press.

Cantelon, Philip L., Richard G. Hewlett, and Robert C. Williams (eds.)
    1991   *The American Atom: A Documentary History of Nuclear Policies From the Discovery of Fission to the Present.* 2d ed. Philadelphia: University of Pennsylvania Press.

Carter, Paul
    1988   *The Road to Botany Bay: An Exploration of Landscape and History.* New York: Alfred A. Knopf.

Castillo, Richard Griswold del
    1990   *The Treaty of Guadalupe Hidalgo: A Legacy of Conflict.* Norman: University of Oklahoma Press.

Castle, Terry
    1988   "Phantasmagoria: Spectral Technology and the Metaphorics of Modern Reverie." *Critical Inquiry* 15(1): 26–61.

Caufield, Catherine
    1989   *Multiple Exposures: Chronicles of the Radiation Age.* Chicago: University of Chicago Press.

Chaloupka, William
    1992   *Knowing Nukes: The Politics and Culture of the Atom.* Minneapolis: University of Minnesota Press.

Chambers, Marjorie Bell
    1974   "Technically Sweet Los Alamos: The Development of a Federally Sponsored Scientific Community." Ph.D. dissertation, Department of History, University of New Mexico.

Chatterjee, Partha
    1993   *The Nation and Its Fragments: Colonial and Postcolonial Histories.* Princeton: Princeton University Press.

Chavez, Fray Angelico
   1975   *La Conquistadora: The Autobiography of an Ancient Statue.*
          Santa Fe: The Sunstone Press.
Chavez, John R.
   1984   *The Lost Land: The Chicano Image of the Southwest.*
          Albuquerque: University of New Mexico Press.
Church, Peggy Pond
   1959   *The House at Otowi Bridge: The Story of Edith Warner and Los
          Alamos.* Albuquerque: University of New Mexico Press.
Churchill, Ward
   1997   "Cold War Impacts on Native North America: The Political
          Economy of Radioactive Colonialism." In *A Little Matter of
          Genocide: Holocaust and Denial in the Americas 1492 to the
          Present.* Pp. 289–362. San Francisco: City Lights Books.
Cirincione, Joseph, Jessica T. Mathews, George Perkovich, with Alex Orton
   2004   *WMD in Iraq: Evidence and Implications.* Washington, D.C.:
          Carnegie Endowment for International Peace.
Clemmer, Richard O.
   1984   "Effects of the Energy Economy on Pueblo Peoples." In Joseph
          G. Jorgensen (ed.). *Native Americans and Energy Development II.*
          Pp. 79–115. Boston: Anthropology Resource Center and Seventh
          Generational Fund.
Cohen, Felix S.
   1986 [1942]   *Handbook of Federal Indian Law.* Albuquerque: Five
          Rings Press.
Cohen, Jeffrey Jerome
   1996   "Preface: In a Time of Monsters." In Jeffrey Cohen (ed.).
          Monster Theory: Reading Culture. Pp. vii-xviii. Minneapolis:
          University of Minnesota Press.
Cohn, Carol
   1987   "Sex and Death in the Rational World of Defense Intellectuals."
          Signs 12(4): 687–718.
Comaroff, Jean, and John L. Comaroff
   2000   "Naturing the Nation: Aliens, Apocalypse, and the Postcolonial
          State." *HAGAR: International Social Science Review* 1(1): 7–40.
Commission on Maintaining United States Nuclear Weapons Expertise
   1999   Report to Congress and the Secretary of Energy. Washington,
          D.C.: Commission on Maintaining United States Nuclear
          Weapons Expertise.
Cordova, G. Benito
   1994   "Descansos: New Mexico's Highway Markers to Heaven." *La
          Herencia del Norte* (Summer Issue): 17–19.
   1973   *Abiquiu and Don Cacahuate: A Folk History of a New Mexican
          Village.* Los Cerrillos: San Marco Press.
Courtright, W. Clarence
   1963   *TA-10 Bayo Canyon Cleanup* (LAMS-2945). Los Alamos: Los
          Alamos Scientific Laboratory.

Cousins, Norman
1945   *Modern Man is Obsolete*. New York: Viking.
Craig, Campbell
1988   *Destroying the Village: Eisenhower and Thermonuclear War.*
        New York: Columbia University Press.
Crawford, Stanley
1988   *Mayordomo: Chronicle of an Acequia in Northern*
        New Mexico. Albuquerque: University of New Mexico
        Press.
Curtis, Edward S.
1970 [1926]   *The North American Indian*. Vol. 17. New York: Johnson
        Reprint Corporation.
Dailey, Martha LaCroix
1994   "Symbolism and Significance of the Lincoln Canes for the Pueb-
        los of New Mexico." *New Mexico Historical Review* 69(2):
        127–44.
Dalby, Simon
2002   *Environmental Security*. Minneapolis: University of Minnesota
        Press.
Dalton, Russell J., Paula Garb, Nicholas P. Lovrich, John C. Pierce, and
John M. Whiteley
1999   *Critical Masses: Citizens, Nuclear Weapons Production, and*
        Environmental Destruction in the United States and Russia.
        Cambridge, Mass.: MIT Press.
Dao, James
2002   "Bush Sees Big Rise in Military Budget for Next 5 Years." *New*
        York Times, February 2.
Daubert, Victoria L., and Sue Ellen Moran
1985   *Origins, Goals, and Tactics of the U.S. Anti-nuclear Protest*
        Movement. A RAND Note (N-2192-SL). Santa Monica: RAND
        Corporation.
Davis, Mike
1998   *Ecologies of Fear: Los Angeles and the Imagination of Disaster.*
        New York: Vintage Books.
1993   "Dead West: Ecocide in Marlboro Country." *New Left Review*
        200 (July–August): 49–73.
Dawson, Jane I.
1996   *Eco-nationalism: Anti-nuclear Activism and National Identity in*
        Russia, Lithuania, and Ukraine. Durham: Duke University
        Press.
Dean, Jodi
2002   *Publicity's Secret: How Technoculture Capitalizes on*
        Democracy. Ithaca: Cornell University Press.
deBuys, William
1985   *Enchantment and Exploitation: The Life and Hard Times of*
        a New Mexico Mountain Range. Albuquerque: University of
        New Mexico Press.

Defense Advanced Research Projects Agency (DARPA)
    2003   *Controlled Biosystems*. Electronic document, available at
            http://www.darpa.mil/dso/thrust/biosci/cbs/objectiv.html
            (accessed October 15, 2003).
Department of Health and Human Services, Centers for Disease Control
and Prevention, and the National Cancer Institute
    2001   *A Feasibility Study of the Health Consequences to the American
            Population From Nuclear Weapons Test Conducted by the
            United States and Other Nations*. Washington, D.C.: U.S. Gov-
            ernment Printing Office.
Derrida, Jacques
    1984   "No Apocalypse, Not Now (Full Speed Ahead, Seven Missiles,
            Seven Missives)." *Diacritics* 20: 20–31.
DeWitt, Hugh
    1984   "Labs Drive the Arms Race." *Bulletin of the Atomic Scientists*
            40(9): 40–42.
Dietz, Chris
    1989   "The Impact of Los Alamos National Laboratory on Northern
            New Mexico." M.A. thesis, Department of Behavioral Sciences,
            New Mexico Highland University.
Dolar, Mladen
    1991   "'I Shall Be with You On Your Wedding-Night': Lacan and the
            Uncanny." *October* 58: 5–23.
Dongoske, Kurt E.
    1996   "The Native American Graves Protection and Repatriation
            Act: A New Beginning, Not the End, for Osteological Analysis—
            A Hopi Perspective." *American Indian Quarterly* 20(2):
            287–96.
Douglas, Gordon (dir.)
    1954   *Them!* 92-min. feature film. Los Angles: Warner Brothers.
Douglass, William Boone
    1915   "Notes on the Shrines of the Tewa and Other Pueblo Indians
            of New Mexico." Pp. 344–78. *Proceedings of the Nineteenth
            International Congress of Americanists*. Washington, D.C.:
            International Congress of Americanists.
Downey, Gary Lee, and Joseph Dumit (eds.)
    1997   *Cyborgs and Citadels: Anthropology Interventions in Emerging
            Sciences and Technologies*. Santa Fe, N.M.: School of American
            Research.
Dozier, Edward P.
    1970   *The Pueblo Indians of North America*. Prospect Heights, Ill.:
            Waveland Press.
    1961   "Rio Grande Pueblos." In Edward Spicer (ed.). *Perspectives in
            American Indian Culture Change*. Pp. 94–186. Chicago:
            University of Chicago Press.
Drinnon, Richard
    1980   *Facing West: The Metaphysics of Indian Hating and Empire
            Building*. New York: Schocken Books.

Dubrova, Yuri E., Rakhmet I. Bersimbaev, Leila B. Djansugurova,
   Maira K. Tankimanova, Zaure Mamyrbaeva, Riitta Mustonen,
   Carita Lindholm, Maj Hulten, and Sisko Salomaa
   1996   "Human Minisatellite Mutation Rate after the Chernobyl
           Accident." *Nature* 380(1037): 683–86.
   2002   "Nuclear Weapons Tests and Human Germline Mutation Rate."
           Science 295 (5557): 1037.
DuMars, Charles T., Marilyn O'Leary, and Albert E. Utton
   1984   *Pueblo Indian Water Rights: Struggle for a Precious Resource.*
           Tucson: University of Arizona Press.
Dummer, J. E., J. D. Taschner, and C. C. Courtright
   1997   *The Bayo Canyon/Radioactive Lanthanum (RaLa) Program*
           (LA-13044–H.) Los Alamos: Los Alamos National Laboratory.
Dunmire, William W., and Gail D. Tierney
   1995   *Wild Plants of the Pueblo Province: Exploring Ancient and
           Enduring Uses.* Santa Fe: Museum of New Mexico Press.
Dycus, Stephen
   1996   *National Defense and the Environment.* Hanover, N.H.:
           University Press of New England.
Easlea, Brian
   1983   *Fathering the Unthinkable: Masculinity, Scientists and the
           Nuclear Arms Race.* London: Pluto Press.
Ebright, Malcolm
   1994   *Land Grants and Lawsuits in Northern New Mexico.*
           Albuquerque: University of New Mexico Press.
Edelstein, Michael R.
   1988   *Contaminated Communities: The Social and Psychological Impacts
           of Residential Toxic Exposure.* Boulder: Westview Press.
Edwards, Paul N.
   1996   *The Closed World: Computers and the Politics of Discourse in
           Cold War America.* Cambridge, Mass.: MIT Press.
Ehrlich, Anne H., and John W. Birks (eds.)
   1990   *Hidden Dangers: Environmental Consequences of Preparing for
           War.* San Francisco: Sierra Club Books.
Eichstaedt, Peter H.
   1994   *If You Poison Us: Uranium and Native Americans.* Santa Fe:
           Red Crane Books.
Else, Jon
   1980   *The Day After Trinity: J. Robert Oppenheimer and the
           Atomic Bomb.* Film, on CD-ROM. New York: The Voyager
           Company.
Engelhardt, Tom
   1995   *The End of Victory Culture: Cold War America and the Disillu-
           sioning of a Generation.* New York: Basic Books.
Erickson, Jon D., Duane Chapman, and Ronald E. Johnny
   1994   "Monitored Retrievable Storage of Spent Nuclear Fuel in Indian
           Country: Liability, Sovereignty, and Socioeconomics." *American
           Indian Law Review* 19(1): 73–103.

Escobar, Arturo
    1999   "After Nature: Steps to an Antiessentialist Political Ecology."
            Current Anthropology 40(1): 1–30.

Etzold, Thomas H., and John Lewis Gaddis (eds.)
    1978   *Containment: Documents on American Policy and Strategy,*
            1945–1950. New York: Columbia University Press.

Evans, Joyce A.
    1998   *Celluloid Mushroom Clouds: Hollywood and the Atomic Bomb.*
            Boulder: Westview Press.

Federal Bureau of Investigation (FBI)
    1999   Interview with Dr. Wen Ho Lee, March 7, 1999. Transcript
            available on the World Wide Web at http://wenholee.org/
            transcript4868.htm.

Federal Civil Defense Administration (FCDA)
    1955   *Cue for Survival.* Washington, D.C.: U.S. Government Printing
            Office.

Ferenbaugh, Roger W., Thomas E. Buhl, Alan K. Stoker, and Wayne
   R. Hansen
    1982   *Environmental Analysis of the Bayo Canyon (TA-10) Site, Los
            Alamos, New Mexico* (LA-9252-MS). Los Alamos: Los Alamos
            National Laboratory.

Ferguson, Frances
    1984   "The Nuclear Sublime." *Diacritics* 20 (Summer): 4–9.

Ferguson, T. J., Roger Anyon, and Edmund J. Ladd
    1996   "Repatriation at the Pueblo of Zuni: Diverse Solutions to
            Complex Problems." *American Indian Quarterly* 20(2):
            251–73.

FitzGerald, Francis
    2000   *Way Out There in the Blue: Ronald Reagan, Star Wars, and the
            End of the Cold War.* New York: Simon and Schuster.

Ford, Richard I.
    1992 [1968]   *An Ecological Analysis Involving the Population of
            San Juan Pueblo, New Mexico.* New York: Garland
            Publishing.

Forrest, Suzanne
    1989   *The Preservation of the Village: New Mexico's Hispanics and the
            New Deal.* Albuquerque: University of New Mexico Press.

Fortun, Kim
    2001   *Advocacy After Bhopal: Environmentalism, Disaster, New
            Global Orders.* Chicago: University of Chicago Press.

Foucault, Michel
    1991   "Governmentality." In Graham Burchell, Colin Gordon,
            and Peter Miller (eds.) *The Foucault Effect: Studies in
            Governmentality.* Pp. 87–104. Chicago: University of Chicago
            Press.
    1978   *The History of Sexuality, Volume One: An Introduction.*
            New York: Vintage Books.

Foxx, Taralence S., and Gail D. Tierney
  1999 *Historical Botany of the Romero Cabin: A Family Homestead on the Pajarito Plateau* (LA-13644–H). Los Alamos: Los Alamos National Laboratory.
Fradkin, Philip L.
  1989 *Fallout: An American Nuclear Tragedy*. Tucson: University of Arizona Press.
Franklin, Bruce H.
  1988 *War Stars: The Superweapon and the American Imagination*. Oxford: Oxford University Press.
Freedman, Lawrence
  1981 *The Evolution of Nuclear Strategy*. New York: St. Martin's Press.
Fresquez, P. R., D. R. Armstrong, M. A. Mullen, and L. Naranjo Jr.
  1997 *Radionuclide Concentrations in Pinto Beans, Sweet Corn, and Zucchini Squash Grown in Los Alamos Canyon at Los Alamos National Laboratory* (LA-13304MS). Los Alamos: Los Alamos National Laboratory.
Fresquez, P. R., D. R. Armstrong, and L. H. Pratt
  1997 *Tritium Concentrations in Bees and Honey at Los Alamos National Laboratory: 1979–1996* (LA-13202-MS). Los Alamos: Los Alamos National Laboratory.
Fresquez, P. R., T. S. Foxx, and L. Naranjo Jr.
  1995 *Strontium Concentrations in Chamisa (Chrysothamnus nauseosus) Shrub Plants Growing in a Former Liquid Waste Disposal Area in Bayo Canyon* (LA-13050 MS). Los Alamos: Los Alamos National Laboratory.
Fresquez, P. R., W. R. Velasquez, L. Naranjo Jr.
  2000 *Effects of the Cerro Grande Fire (Smoke and Fallout Ash) on Soil Chemical Properties Within and Around Los Alamos National Laboratory*. Los Alamos: Los Alamos National Laboratory.
Fresquez, P. R., E. L. Vold, and L. Naranjo Jr.
  1996 *Radionuclide Concentrations in/on Vegetation at Radioactive-Waste Disposal Area G during the 1995 Growing Season* (LA-13124–PR). Los Alamos: Los Alamos National Laboratory.
Freud, Sigmund
  1919 "The Uncanny." In *The Standard Edition of the Complete Psychological Works of Sigmund Freud*. Translated by James Strachey. Volume 17: 219–54. London: The Hogarth Press and the Institute of Psychoanalysis.
Furman, Necas Stewart
  1990 *Sandia National Laboratories: The Postwar Decade*. Albuquerque: University of New Mexico Press.
Fusco, Paul, and Magdalena Caris
  2001 *Chernobyl Legacy*. Millbrook, N.Y.: de.MO.

Galison, Peter
  2004   "Removing Knowledge." *Critical Inquiry*. Available at
         http://www.uchicago.edu/research/jnl-crit-inq/features/
         artsstatements/arts.galison.htm (accessed October 15,
         2004).
  1997   *Image and Logics: A Material Culture of Microphysics*. Chicago:
         University of Chicago Press.
  1996   "Computer Simulations and the Trading Zone." In Peter Galison
         and David J. Stump (eds.). *The Disunity of Science: Boundaries,
         Context and Power*. Pp. 118–57. Stanford: Stanford University
         Press.
Galison, Peter, and Bruce Hevly
  1992   *Big Science: The Growth of Large-Scale Research*. Stanford:
         Stanford University Press.
Gallager, Carole
  1993   *American Ground Zero: The Secret Nuclear War*. Cambridge,
         Mass.: MIT Press.
Garb, Paula, and Galina Komarova
  2001   "Victims of 'Friendly Fire' at Russia's Nuclear Weapons Sites." In
         Nancy Lee Peluso and Michael Watts (eds.). *Violent Environments*.
         Pp. 287–302. Ithaca: Cornell University Press.
Gardner, Richard
  1970   *Grito!: Reies Tijerina and The New Mexico Land Grant War of
         1967*. New York: Harper Colophon Books.
Garwin, Richard L., and Georges Charpak
  2001   *Megawatts and Megatons: A Turning Point in the Nuclear Age?*
         New York: Alfred A. Knopf.
Gedicks, Al
  1993   *The New Resource Wars: Native and Environmental Struggles
         Against Multinational Corporations*. Boston: South End Press.
Gerber, Michele Stenehjem
  2002   *On the Home Front: The Cold War Legacy of the Hanford
         Nuclear Site*. Lincoln: University of Nebraska Press.
Glasstone, Samuel, and Philip J. Dolan (eds.)
  1977   *The Effects of Nuclear Weapons*. 3d ed. Washington, D.C.:
         U.S. Department of Defense and U.S. Department of
         Energy.
Gluckman, Max
  1963   "Gossip and Scandal." *Current Anthropology* 4(3): 307–16.
Goldstein, Donald, J. Michael Wenger, and Katherine V. Dillon
  1997   *Rain of Ruin: A Photographic History of Hiroshima and
         Nagasaki*. New York: Brasseys.
Goldtooth, Tom B. K.
  1995   "Indigenous Nations: Summary of Sovereignty and Its Implica-
         tions for Environmental Protection." In Bunyun Bryant (ed.).
         Environmental Justice: Issues, Policies, and Solutions.
         Pp. 138–48. Washington, D.C.: Island Press.

Gomez, Laura E.
  2000   "Race, Colonialism, and Criminal Law: Mexican and the
          American Criminal Justice System in Territorial New Mexico."
          Law and Society Review 34(4): 1129–1202.

Gonzalez, Nancie L.
  1969   *The Spanish-American of New Mexico: A Heritage of Pride.*
          Albuquerque: University of New Mexico Press.

Graf, William L.
  1994   *Plutonium and the Rio Grande: Environmental Change and
          Contamination in the Nuclear Age.* New York: Oxford Univer-
          sity Press.

Gray, Chris Hables (ed.)
  1995   *The Cyborg Handbook.* New York: Routledge.

Griffith, James
  1992   *Beliefs and Holy Places: A Spiritual Geography of the Pimeria
          Alta.* Tucson: University of Arizona Press.

Grimes, Ronald L.
  1976   *Symbol and Conquest: Public Ritual and Drama in Santa Fe.*
          Albuquerque: University of New Mexico Press.

Grinde, Donald A., Jr., and Bruce E. Johansen
  1995   *Ecocide of Native America: Environmental Destruction of
          Indian Lands and Peoples.* Santa Fe: Clear Light Books.

Gusterson, Hugh
  2001   "The Virtual Nuclear Weapons Laboratory in the New World
          Order." *American Ethnologist* 28(2): 417–37.
  1999a   "(Anti)nuclear Pilgrims." *Anthropologiska Studier* (62–63):
          61–66.
  1999b   "Los Alamos: Summer Under Siege." *Bulletin of the Atomic
          Scientists* 55(6): 36–41.
  1996a   *Nuclear Rites: A Weapons Laboratory at the End of the Cold
          War.* Berkeley: University of California Press.
  1996b   "Nuclear Weapons Testing: Scientific Experiment as Political
          Ritual." In Laura Nader (ed.). *Naked Science: Anthropological
          Inquiry and Boundaries, Power, and Knowledge.* Pp. 131–47.
          New York: Routledge.
  1991   "Nuclear War, the Gulf War, and the Disappearing Body."
          Journal of Urban and Cultural Studies 2(1): 45–55.

Gutierrez, Joe
  1999   "The Hispano Homesteaders." *Beyond the Bomb: A New
          Agenda for Peace and Justice Conference.* August 8, Albu-
          querque, N.M.

Gutierrez, Ramon A.
  1995   "El Santuario de Chimayo: A Syncretic Shrine in New
          Mexico." In Ramon A. Gutierrez and Genevieve Fabre (eds.).
          *Feasts and Celebrations in North American Ethnic Com-
          munities.* Pp. 71–86. Albuquerque: University of New Mexico
          Press.

1991   *When Jesus Came, The Corn Mothers Went Away: Marriage,
        Sexuality, and Power in New Mexico, 1500–1846.* Stanford:
        Stanford University Press.

Hacker, Barton C.
    1994   *Elements of Controversy: The Atomic Energy Commission
            and Radiation Safety in Nuclear Weapons Testing 1947–1974.*
            Berkeley: University of California Press.
    1987   *The Dragon's Tail: Radiation Safety in the Manhattan Project,
            1942–1946.* Berkeley: University of California Press.

Hales, Peter Bacon
    1997   *Atomic Spaces: Living on the Manhattan Project.* Urbana:
            University of Illinois Press.

Handler, Richard
    1988   *Nationalism and the Politics of Culture in Quebec.* Madison:
            University of Wisconsin Press.

Hansen, Chuck
    1988   *U.S. Nuclear Weapons: The Secret History.* Arlington: Aerofax.

Hanson, Randel D.
    1998   "From Environmental Bads to Economic Goods: Marketing
            Nuclear Waste to American Indians." Ph.D. dissertation, Depart-
            ment of American Studies, University of Minnesota.

Haraway, Donna
    1997   *ModestWitness@SecondMillennium.Femal Man_Meets
            OncoMouse:* Feminism and Technoscience. *New York:
            Routledge.*
    1991   *Simians, Cyborgs and Women: The Reinvention of Nature.* New
            York: Routledge.

Harrington, John Peabody
    1916   *The Ethnogeography of the Tewa Indians.* Bureau of American
            Ethnology, 29th Annual Report. Washington, D.C.: U.S. Govern-
            ment Printing Office.

Harwit, Martin D.
    1996   *An Exhibit Denied: Lobbying the History of the Enola Gay.*
            New York: Copernicus.

Hawkins, David
    1983 [1946]   *Project Y: The Los Alamos Story.* Los Angeles: Tomash
            Publishers.

Hawley, Florence
    1948   *Some Factors in the Indian Problem in New Mexico.* Albu-
            querque: Division of Research, Department of Government,
            University of New Mexico.

Hecht, Gabrielle
    1998   *The Radiance of France.* Cambridge, Mass.: MIT Press.

Hecker, Sig
    1995   "Reflections on Hiroshima and Nagasaki." *Los Alamos National
            Laboratory Newsbulletin.* August 4.
    1993   "Los Alamos Beginning the Second Fifty Years." *Los Alamos
            Science* 21: 218–26.

Hecker, Sig, and Joe Martz
  2000   "Aging of Plutonium and its Alloys." *Los Alamos Science* 26:
          238–43.
Helmreich, Stefan
  2000   *Silicon Second Nature: Culturing Artificial Life in a Digital
          World.* Berkeley: University of California Press.
Henderson, Junius, and John Peabody Harrington
  1914   *Ethnozoology of the Tewa Indians.* Bureau of American
          Ethnology, Bulletin 56. Washington, D.C.: U.S. Government
          Printing Office.
Henriksen, Margot A.
  1997   *Dr. Strangelove's America: Society and Culture in the Atomic
          Age.* Berkeley: University of California Press.
Herken, Gregg
  2002   *Brotherhood of the Bomb.* New York: Henry Holt.
  1992   *Cardinal Choices: Presidential Science Advising from the
          Atomic Bomb to SDI.* Oxford: Oxford University Press.
Hewett, Edgar L., and Bertha P. Dutton
  1945   *The Pueblo Indian World: Studies on the Natural History of
          the Rio Grande Valley in Relation to Pueblo Indian Culture.*
          Albuquerque: University of New Mexico Press.
Hilgartner, Stephen, Richard Bell, and Rory O'Connor
  1982   *Nukespeak: The Selling of Nuclear Technology in America.*
          New York: Penguin.
Hoddeson, Lillian, Paul W. Henriksen, Roger A. Meade, and Catherine
  Westfall
  1993   *Critical Assembly: A Technical History of Los Alamos During the
          Oppenheimer Years, 1943–1945.* New York: Cambridge Univer-
          sity Press.
Hoffman, Ian
  1999a   "Love with Foreigners Must Be Reported." *Albuquerque
          Journal*, September 1.
  1999b   "National Labs Look Beyond Tomorrow." *Albuquerque
          Journal*, September 19.
Hofstadter, Richard
  1965   *The Paranoid Style in American Politics and Other Essays.*
          New York: Alfred A. Knopf.
Hollis, Diana
  1997   *Performance Assessment and Composite Analysis for Los
          Alamos National Laboratory Material Disposal Area G.* Los
          Alamos: Los Alamos National Laboratory.
Holscher, Mark
  1999   "Statement by Suspect's Lawyer: He Assisted FBI." *New York
          Times*, May 8.
Hopkins, John C.
  2000   Nuclear Stockpile Stewardship. Electronic document at
          http://www.sumnerassociates.com/stockpile.html (accessed
          September 1, 2003).

Hora, Stephen C., Detlof von Winterfeldt, and Kathleen M. Trauth (eds.)
　　1991　*Expert Judgment on Inadvertent Human Intrusion into the
　　　　　Waste Isolation Pilot Plant* (SAND90-3063/UC-721). Albu-
　　　　　querque: Sandia National Laboratories.
Horsman, Reginald
　　1981　*Race and Manifest Destiny: The Origins of American
　　　　　Racial Anglo-Saxonism.* Cambridge, Mass.: Harvard University
　　　　　Press.
Howerton, Walter, Jr.
　　1996　"Histories Ghosts." *Santa Fe Reporter.* January 31: 14–19.
Huxley, Aldous
　　1946 [1932]　*Brave New World.* New York: Harper and Row.
Inkret, Bill, and Guthrie Miller (eds.)
　　1995　"On the Front Lines: Plutonium Workers Past and Present Share
　　　　　Their Experiences." *Los Alamos Science* 23: 125–73.
International Physicians for the Prevention of Nuclear War and the Insti-
　　tute for Energy and Environmental Research (IPPNW and IEER)
　　1991　*Radioactive Heaven and Earth: The Health and Environmental
　　　　　Effects of Nuclear Weapons Testing In, On, and Above the
　　　　　Earth.* New York: Apex Press.
Ivy, Marilyn
　　1995　*Discourses of the Vanishing: Modernity, Phantasm, Japan.*
　　　　　Chicago: University of Chicago Press.
Jaimes, M. Annette (ed.)
　　1992　*The State of Native America: Genocide, Colonization and
　　　　　Resistance.* Boston: South End Press.
Jenkins-Smith, Hank C., Richard P. Barke, and Kerry G. Herron
　　1995　*Public Perspectives on Nuclear Weapons in the Post-Cold
　　　　　War Environment.* Albuquerque: The Institute for Public Policy,
　　　　　University of New Mexico.
Johnson, Kent, Joseph Keller, Carl Ekdahl, Richard Krajcik, Luis Salazar,
　　Earl Keely, and Robert Paulsen
　　1995　*Stockpile Surveillance: Past and Future.* Washington, D.C.: U.S.
　　　　　Department of Energy.
Kant, Immanuel
　　1986　"Analytic of the Sublime." In Ernst Behler (ed.). *Philosophical
　　　　　Writings.* Pp. 201–23. New York: Continuum.
　　1952 [1790]　*The Critique of Judgement.* Oxford: Clarendon Press.
Kaplan, Amy
　　2003　"Homeland Insecurities: Reflection on Language and Space."
　　　　　Radical History Review 85 (Winter): 82–93.
Kaplan, Amy, and Donald E. Pease (eds.)
　　1993　*Cultures of United States Imperialism.* Durham: Duke University
　　　　　Press.
Katz, Milton S.
　　1986　*Ban the Bomb: A History of SANE, the Committee for a Sane
　　　　　Nuclear Policy, 1957–1985.* New York: Greenwood Press.

Kay, Elizabeth
1987   *Chimayo Valley Traditions*. Santa Fe: Ancient City Press.
Keller, Evelyn Fox
1992   "From Secrets of Life to Secrets of Death." In *Secrets of Life:
        Essays on Language, Gender and Science*. Pp. 39–55. New York:
        Routledge.
Kiste, Robert C.
1974   *The Bikinians: A Study in Forced Migration*. Menlo Park, Calif.:
        Cummings Publishing Company.
Klare, Michael
1995   *Rogue States and Nuclear Outlaws: America's Search for a New
        Foreign Policy*. New York: Hill and Wang.
Klein, Richard
1993   *Cigarettes are Sublime*. Durham: Duke University Press.
Knight, Peter (ed.)
2002   *Conspiracy Nation: The Politics of Paranoia in Postwar
        America*. New York: New York University Press.
KNME-TV (Albuquerque) and the Institute of American Indian Arts
1992   *Surviving Columbus: The Story of the Pueblo People*. Film,
        directed by Diane Reyna; written by Larry Walsh; produced by
        Edmund Ladd. Distributed by PBS Video.
Knorr-Centina, Karin
1999   *Epistemic Cultures: How the Sciences Make Knowledge*.
        Cambridge, Mass.: Harvard University Press.
Koselleck, Reinhart
1985   "The Historical-Political Semantics of Asymmetric Counter-
        concepts." In *Futures Past: On the Semantics of Historical Time*.
        Pp. 159–97. Cambridge, Mass.: MIT Press.
Krasniewicz, Louise
1992   *Nuclear Summer: The Clash of Communities at the Seneca
        Women's Peace Encampment*. Ithaca: Cornell University
        Press.
Kuletz, Valerie
1998   *The Tainted Desert: Environmental and Social Ruin in the
        American West*. New York: Routledge.
Kunetka, James W.
1979   *City of Fire: Los Alamos and the Atomic Age,
        1943–1945*. Albuquerque: University of New Mexico
        Press.
Kuran, Peter (prod. and dir.)
1999   *Trinity and Beyond: The Atomic Bomb Movie*. 120-min. film.
        Thousand Oaks, Calif.: Goldhil DVD.
Lange, Charles H.
1959   *Cochiti: A New Mexico Pueblo, Past and Present*. Austin:
        University of Texas Press.
Lansing, Lamont
1965   *Day of Trinity*. New York: Atheneum.

Laski, Vera
    1958   *Seeking Life. Memoirs of the American Folklore Society.* Vol. 50.
            Philadelphia: American Folklore Society.
Latour, Bruno
    1996   *Aramis of the Love of Technology.* Cambridge, Mass.: Harvard
            University Press.
    1993   *We Have Never Been Modern.* Cambridge, Mass.: Harvard
            University Press.
    1988   *The Pasteurization of France.* Cambridge, Mass.: Harvard
            University Press.
    1987   *Science in Action.* Cambridge, Mass.: Harvard University Press.
Laurence, William L.
    1946   *Dawn Over Zero: The Story of the Atomic Bomb.* New York:
            Alfred A. Knopf.
Lavelle, Pat
    2000   *Facing Reality at Hanford.* Seattle: Government Accountability
            Project.
Lawrence Livermore National Laboratory (LLNL)
    2000   "A New World of Seeing." *Science and Technology Review*
            (October): 4–12.
Lee, Wen Ho (with Helen Zia)
    2001   *My Country Versus Me.* New York: Hyperion.
Lichterman, Andrew, and Jacqeline Cabasso
    1998   *A Faustian Bargain: Why "Stockpile Stewardship" is Fundamen-
            tally Incompatible with the Process of Nuclear Disarmament.*
            Oakland: Western States Legal Foundation.
Lifton, Robert
    1991   *Death in Life: Survivors of Hiroshima.* Chapel Hill: University of
            North Carolina Press.
Lifton, Robert Jay, and Greg Mitchell
    1995   *Hiroshima in America: A Half Century of Denial.* New York:
            Avon Books.
Limerick, Patricia Nelson
    1987   *The Legacy of Conquest: The Unbroken Past of the American
            West.* New York: W. W. Norton and Company.
Lindee, M. Susan
    1994   *Suffering Made Real: American Science and Survivors at
            Hiroshima.* Chicago: University of Chicago Press.
Linenthal, Edward T., and Tom Engelhardt (eds.)
    1996   *History Wars: The Enola Gay and Other Battles for the
            American Past.* New York: Metropolitan Books.
Loeb, Vernon, and Walter Pincus
    1999   "New Leads Found in Spy Probe." *Washington Post,*
            November 19.
Los Alamos National Laboratory (LANL)
    2001   "DARHT Working to Fill the Test Ban Gap." *Dateline: Los
            Alamos* (January): 8–11.
    2000   "Detonators." *Weapons Insider* 7(1): 4–5.

1999a   *Institutional Plan: FY 2000–FY 2005* (LADP-99-151). Los Alamos: Los Alamos National Laboratory.

1999b   *International Collaborations at Los Alamos National Laboratory.* Los Alamos: Los Alamos National Laboratory.

1997a   "TITANS." *Weapons Insider* 4(2): 3.

1997b   *Performance Assessment and Composite Analysis for Los Alamos National Laboratory Material Disposal Area G* (LA-UR-97-85). Los Alamos: Los Alamos National Laboratory.

1996a   *Russian American Collaborations to Reduce the Nuclear Danger.* Special Issue of *Los Alamos Science.* Vol. 24. Los Alamos: Los Alamos National Laboratory.

1996b   "Program News." *Weapons Insider* 3(8): 2.

1995a   Executive Meeting on Laboratory and Pueblo Cooperative Agreements, December 14, 1995. Los Alamos: Los Alamos National Laboratory.

1995b   *Environmental Surveillance at Los Alamos During 1993* (LA-12973-ENV). Los Alamos: Los Alamos National Laboratory.

1995c   *Institutional Plan: FY 1996–FY 2001.* Los Alamos: Los Alamos National Laboratory.

1995d   Affirmative Action Program, Calendar Year 1995. Los Alamos: Los Alamos National Laboratory.

1994a   *Institutional Plan, FY 1995–FY 2000: Science Serving Society.* Los Alamos: Los Alamos National Laboratory.

1994b   *Environmental Surveillance at Los Alamos during 1992* (LA-12764-ENV). Los Alamos: Los Alamos National Laboratory.

1993   "Taking on the Future: Harold Agnew and Los Alamos Scientists Discuss the Potential of the Laboratory." *Los Alamos Science* 21: 4–30.

1986   *Native American Task Force Report.* Los Alamos: Los Alamos National Laboratory.

1988   *The Los Alamos Nuclear Test Program: Field Test Operations* (LALP-88-21). Los Alamos: Los Alamos National Laboratory.

Los Alamos National Laboratory Fellows

1999   *Report on Foreign National Involvement at Los Alamos National Laboratory.* Los Alamos: Los Alamos National Laboratory.

Lutz, Catherine

2001   *Homefront: A Military City and the American 20th Century.* Boston: Beacon Press.

MacKenzie, Donald

1996   "Nuclear Weapons Laboratories and the Development of Supercomputing." In *Knowing Machines: Essay on Technical Change.* Pp. 99–130. Cambridge, Mass.: MIT Press.

1990   *Inventing Accuracy: A Historical Sociology of Nuclear Missile Guidance.* Cambridge, Mass.: MIT Press.

MacKenzie, Donald, with Graham Spinardi

1996   "Tacit Knowledge and the Uninvention of Nuclear Weapons." In Donald MacKenzie. *Knowing Machines: Essays on Technical Change.* Pp. 215–60. Cambridge, Mass.: MIT Press.

Mahoney, Martin C., and Arthur M. Michalek
    1998   "Cancer Control Research Among American Indians and
            Alaska Natives: A Paradigm for Research Needs in the Next
            Millennium." *American Indian Culture and Research Journal*
            22(3): 155–69.
Makhijani, Arjun, Howard Hu, and Katherine Yih (eds.)
    1995   *Nuclear Wastelands: A Global Guide to Nuclear Weapons Pro-
            duction and Its Health and Environmental Effects.* Cambridge,
            Mass.: MIT Press.
Makhijani, Arjun, and Stephen I. Schwartz
    1998   "Victims of the Bomb." In Stephen I. Schwartz (ed.). *Atomic
            Audit: The Costs and Consequences of U.S. Nuclear Weapons
            Since 1940.* Pp. 395–431. Washington, D.C.: Brookings Institu-
            tion Press.
Makhijani, Arjun, Stephen I. Schwartz, and William J. Weida
    1998   "Nuclear Waste Management and Environmental Remediation."
            In Stephen I. Schwartz (ed.). *Atomic Audit: The Costs and Con-
            sequences of U.S. Nuclear Weapons Since 1940.* Pp. 353–93.
            Washington, D.C.: Brookings Institution Press.
Mark, J. Carson
    1990   "Do We Need Nuclear Testing?" *Arms Control Today*
            November: 12–17.
Martin, Emily
    1994   *Flexible Bodies: Tracking Immunity in American Culture,
            from the Days of Polio to the Age of AIDS.* Boston: Beacon
            Press.
Marx, Karl
    1967 [1887]   *Capital: A Critique of Political Economy. Volume One:
            The Process of Capitalist Production.* Edited by Frederick
            Engels. New York: International Publishers.
Maschke, George W.
    1999   *The Lying Game: National Security and the Test of Espionage
            and Sabotage.* Available on the World Wide Web at http://
            www.fas.org/sgp/othergov/polygraph/maschke.html.
Mauss, Marcel
    1990 [1925]   *The Gift: The Form and Reason for Exchange in Archaic
            Societies.* New York: W. W. Norton.
May, M. M. (ed.)
    1999   *The Cox Committee Report: An Assessment.* Palo Alto: Stanford
            University Center for International Security and Cooperation.
McClintock, Anne
    1995   *Imperial Leather: Race, Gender and Sexuality in the Colonial
            Contest.* New York: Routledge.
McCutcheon, Chuck
    2002   *Nuclear Reactions: The Politics of Opening a Radioactive
            Waste Disposal Site.* Albuquerque: University of New Mexico
            Press.

McEnaney, Laura
  2000   *Civil Defense Begins at Home: Militarization Meets Everyday Life in the Fifties*. Princeton: Princeton University Press.
McKinzie, M. G., T. B. Cochran, and C. E. Paine
  1998   *Explosive Alliances: Nuclear Weapons Simulation Research at American Universities*. Washington, D.C.: National Resources Defense Council.
McNamara, Laura Agnes
  2001   "Ways of Knowing about Weapons: The Cold War's End at the Los Alamos National Laboratory." Ph.D. dissertation, Department of Anthropology, University of New Mexico.
McPhee, John
  1974   *The Curve of Binding Energy*. New York: Farrar, Straus and Giroux.
McWilliams, Carey
  1948   *North From Mexico: The Spanish Speaking People of the United States*. New York: Greenwood Press.
Medalia, Jonathan E.
  1998   *Nuclear Weapons Production Capability Issues* (98-519-F). Washington, D.C.: Congressional Research Service, Library of Congress.
  1994   *Nuclear Weapons Stockpile Stewardship: The Role of Livermore and Los Alamos National Laboratories* (94-418-F). Washington, D.C.: Congressional Research Service, Library of Congress.
Mello, Greg
  2000   "That Old Designing Fever." *Bulletin of the Atomic Scientists* 56(1): 51–57.
  1997   "New Bomb, No Mission." *Bulletin of the Atomic Scientists* 53(3): 28–32.
Merk, Frederick
  1963   *Manifest Destiny and Mission in American History*. New York: Vintage Books.
Miller, Richard L.
  1986   *Under the Cloud: The Decades of Nuclear Testing*. New York: The Free Press.
Mitchell, Timothy
  1988   *Colonizing Egypt*. Berkeley: University of California Press.
Mojtabai, A. G.
  1986   *Blessed Assurance: At Home with the Bomb in Amarillo, Texas*. Albuquerque: University of New Mexico Press.
Morland, Howard
  1979   "The H-Bomb Secret: To Know How Is to Ask Why." *The Progressive* (November): 14–23.
Mortensem, Jeannette
  1983   "Critical Assemblies." *LANL Newsbulletin* 3(15): 7–8.

Moynihan, Daniel Patrick
    1998   *Secrecy.* New Haven: Yale University Press.
Nabokov, Peter
    1969   *Tijerina and the Courthouse Raid.* Berkeley: The Ramparts
            Press.
Nadel, Alan
    1995   *Containment Culture: American Narratives, Postmodernism, and
            the Atomic Age.* Durham: Duke University Press.
Nader, Laura (ed.)
    1996   *Naked Science: Anthropological Inquiry into Boundaries, Power
            and Knowledge.* New York: Routledge.
Naranjo, Tessie
    1992   "Social Change and Pottery-Making at Santa Clara Pueblo."
            Ph.D. dissertation, Department of Sociology, University of New
            Mexico.
Naranjo, Tito, and Rina Swentzell
    1989   "Healing Spaces in the Tewa Pueblo World." *American Indian
            Culture and Research Journal* 13(3): 257–65.
Nash, Gerald D.
    1985   *The American West Transformed: The Impact of the Second
            World War.* Lincoln: University of Nebraska Press.
National Academy of Sciences (NAS)
    2002   *Technical Issues Related to the Comprehensive Test Ban Treaty.*
            Washington, D.C.: National Academy Press.
National Cancer Institute (NCI)
    1997   *Interim Report on Iodine-131 Contamination From Above
            Ground Nuclear Testing at the Nevada Test Site.* Available on
            the World Wide Web at http://rex.nci.nih.gov/massmedia/
            Fallout/contents.html.
National Economic Council (NEC)
    2000   Interagency Working group with the National Economic Coun-
            cil. *The Link Between Exposure to Occupational Hazards and
            Illnesses In the Department of Energy Contractor Workforce.*
            Available on the World Wide Web at http://www.tis.eh.doe/
            benefits/nec/necreport1.pdf.
National Nuclear Security Administration (NNSA)
    2002   "NNSA Laboratories Each Complete First 3D Simulation
            of a Complete Nuclear Weapons Explosion." *NNSA News*
            March 7, 2002. Washington, D.C.: U.S. Department of
            Energy.
Natural Resources Defense Council (NRDC)
    2000   "NRDC Nuclear Notebook: Global Nuclear Stockpiles,
            1945–2000." *Bulletin of the Atomic Scientists* 56(2): 79.
    1998   "NRDC Nuclear Notebook: Known Nuclear Tests Worldwide,
            1945–1998." *Bulletin of the Atomic Scientists.* Electronic
            document, available at http://www.thebulletin.org/issues/
            nukenotes/nd98nukenote.html (accessed September 1, 2003).

Nelkin, Dorothy, and Michael Pollak
  1981 *The Atom Besieged: Antinuclear Movements in France and Germany*. Cambridge, Mass.: MIT Press.
Nietchman, Bernard, and William Le Bon
  1987 "Nuclear Weapons States and Fourth World Nations." *Cultural Survival Quarterly* 11(4): 5–7.
Nobile, Philip (ed.)
  1995 *Judgment at the Smithsonian*. New York: Marlowe and Company.
Nolan, Janne E.
  1999 *An Elusive Consensus: Nuclear Weapons and American Security After the Cold War*. Washington, D.C.: Brookings Institution Press.
Norris, Robert S., and William M. Arkin
  1997 "NRDC Nuclear Notebook: Where the Bombs Are, 1997." *Bulletin of the Atomic Scientists* 53(5): 62.
  1993 "Nuclear Notebook: Estimated Nuclear Stockpiles 1945–1993." *Bulletin of Atomic Scientists* 49(10): 57.
Nostrand, Richard L.
  1992 *The Hispano Homeland*. Norman: University of Oklahoma Press.
Nye, David E.
  1994 *American Technological Sublime*. Cambridge, Mass.: MIT Press.
Oakes, Guy
  1994 *The Imaginary War: Civil Defense and American Cold War Culture*. Oxford: Oxford University Press.
Office of Technology Assessment (OTA) (Congress of the United States)
  1991 *Complex Cleanup: The Environmental Legacy of Nuclear Weapons Production* (OTA-0-484). Washington, D.C.: U.S. Government Printing Office.
  1989 *The Containment of Underground Nuclear Explosions* (OTA-ISC-414). Washington, D.C.: U.S. Government Printing Office.
  1988 *Seismic Verification of Nuclear Testing Treaties* (OTA-ISC-361). Washington, D.C.: U.S. Government Printing Office.
  1983 *Scientific Validity of Polygraph Testing: A Research Review and Evaluation*. Washington, D.C.: U.S. Government Printing Office.
  1979 *The Effects of Nuclear War* (OTA-NS-89). Washington, D.C.: U.S. Government Printing Office.
O'Neill, Kevin
  1998 "Building the Bomb." In Stephen I. Schwartz (ed.). *Atomic Audit: The Costs and Consequences of U.S. Nuclear Weapons Since 1940*. Pp. 33–104. Washington, D.C.: Brookings Institution Press.
Oppenheimer, J. Robert
  1984 [1960] "Tradition and Discovery." In N. Metropolis, Gian-Carlo Rota, and David Sharp (eds.). *Uncommon Sense*. Boston: Birkhauser.

1946   "Atomic Weapons." *Proceedings of the American Philosophical Society* 90(1): 7–10.

Ortiz, Alfonso

1994   "The Dynamics of Pueblo Cultural Survival." In Raymond J. Demallie and Alfonso Ortiz (eds.). *North American Indian Anthropology: Essays on Society Culture*. Pp. 296–306. Norman: University of Oklahoma Press.

1979   "San Juan Pueblo." In Alfonso Ortiz (ed.). *Handbook of North American Indians: Southwest*. Vol. 9, pp. 278–95. Washington, D.C.: Smithsonian Institution Press.

1977   "Some Concerns Central to the Writing of 'Indian' History." *The Indian Historian* (Winter): 17–22.

1976   "A Conversation with Alfonso Ortiz." *La Confluencia* 1(2): 32–39.

1972   "Ritual Drama and the Pueblo World View." In Alfonso Ortiz (ed.). *New Perspectives on the Pueblos*. Pp. 135–61. Santa Fe: School of American Research Press.

1969   *The Tewa World: Space, Time, Being, and Becoming in a Pueblo Society*. Chicago: University of Chicago Press.

Ortiz, Alfonso (ed.)

1972   *New Perspectives on the Pueblos*. Santa Fe: School of American Research Press.

Ortiz, Roxanne Dunbar

1980   *Roots of Resistance: Land Tenure in New Mexico, 1680–1980*. Los Angeles: Chicano Studies Research Center and American Indian Studies Center at the University of California, Los Angeles.

Ott, Thomas (writer, prod, and dir.)

1999   *Race for the Superbomb*. 2 hrs. Film PBS: The American Experience Series.

Otway, Harry

1991   "Altered Political Control: The Free State of Chihuahua." In Stephen C. Hora, Detlof von Winterfeldt, and Kathleen M. Trauth (eds.). *Expert Judgment on Inadvertent Human Intrusion into the Waste Isolation Pilot Plant: Appendix D: Southwest Team Report* (SAND90 3063/UC-721). Pp. 31–35. Albuquerque: Sandia National Laboratories.

Paine, Christopher E.

2004   *Weaponeers of Waste: A Critical Look at the Bush Administration Energy Department's Nuclear Weapons Complex and the First Decade of Science-Based Stockpile Stewardship*. New York: National Resources Defense Council.

Paine, Christopher E., and Matthew G. McKinzie

1998a   *End Run: The U.S. Government's Plan for Designing Nuclear Weapons and Simulating Nuclear Explosions under the Comprehensive Test Ban Treaty*. Washington, D.C.: Natural Resources Defense Council.

1998b   "Does the U.S. Science-Based Stockpile Stewardship Program pose a Proliferation Threat?" *Science and Global Security* 7: 151–93.

Pandey, Triloki Nath
  1977   "Images of Power in a Southwestern Pueblo." In Raymond
          D. Fogelson and Richard N. Adams (eds.). *The Anthropology
          of Power: Ethnographic Studies From Asia, Oceania, and the
          New World*. Pp. 195–215. New York: Academic Press.
Parsons, Elsie Clews
  1996 [1939]   *Pueblo Indian Religion*. Lincoln: University of Nebraska
          Press.
  1994 [1926]   *Tewa Tales*. Tucson: University of Arizona Press.
  1929   *The Social Organization of the Tewa of New Mexico. Memoirs
          of the American Anthropological Association, Number 36*.
          Menasha, Wis.: The American Anthropological
          Association.
Pauling, Linus
  1963   Nobel Peace Prize speech. Available on the World Wide web at
          http://www.nobel.se/peace/laureates/1962/pauling-lecture. html
          (accessed September 1, 2003).
Paxton, Hugh C.
  1981   *Thirty-Five Years at Pajarito Canyon Site* (LA-77121-H).
          Los Alamos: Los Alamos National Laboratory.
Pearce, Roy Harvey
  1965   *Savagism and Civilization: A Study of the Indian and the
          American Mind*. Baltimore: Johns Hopkins Press.
Peluso, Nancy Lee, and Michael Watts (eds.)
  2001   *Violent Environments*. Ithaca: Cornell University Press.
Peña, Devon G.
  1997   *The Terror of the Machine: Technology, Work, Gender,
          and Ecology on the U.S.-Mexico Border*. Austin: CMAS Books.
Petryna, Adriana
  2002   *Life Exposed: Biological Citizens after Chernobyl*. Princeton:
          Princeton University Press.
Pickering, Andrew (ed.)
  1992   *Science as Practice and Culture*. Chicago: University of Chicago
          Press.
Pincus, Walter
  2000   "Lee: Tapes Went in Trash." *Washington Post*, December 1.
President's Foreign Intelligence Advisory Board (PFIAB, or "The Rudman
          Report")
  1999   *Science at its Best, Security at its Worst: A Report on Security
          Problems at the U.S. Department of Energy*. Washington, D.C.:
          U.S. Government Printing Office.
Pulido, Laura
  1996   *Environmentalism and Economic Justice: Two Chicano
          Struggles in the Southwest*. Tucson: University of Arizona
          Press.
Rabinow, Paul
  1999   *French DNA: Trouble in Purgatory*. Chicago: University of
          Chicago Press.

1996   "Artificiality and Enlightenment: From Sociobiology to
        Biosociality." In *Essays on the Anthropology of Reason.*
        Pp. 91–111. Princeton: Princeton University Press.
Raffles, Hugh
    2002   *In Amazonia: A Natural History.* Princeton: Princeton University
            Press.
RAND Corporation
    1953   *Worldwide Effects of Atomic Weapons: Project Sunshine.* Santa
            Monica: RAND Corporation.
Redfield, Peter
    2000   *Space in the Tropics: From Convicts to Rockets in French
            Guiana.* Berkeley: University of California Press.
Revkin, Andre C.
    2002   "Bees Learning Smell of Bomb With Backing From Pentagon."
            New York Times, May 12.
Rhodes, Richard
    1995   *Dark Sun: The Making of the Hydrogen Bomb.* New York:
            Simon and Schuster.
    1986   *The Making of the Atomic Bomb.* New York: Simon and Schuster.
Richards, Thomas
    1993   *The Imperial Archive: Knowledge and the Fantasy of Empire.*
            London: Verso.
Richelson, Jeffrey T.
    2001   *The Wizards of Langley: Inside the CIA's Directorate of Science
            and Technology.* Boulder: Westview Press.
    1999   *America's Space Sentinels: Dsp Satellites and National Security.*
            Kansas City: University of Kansas Press.
Risen, James, and Jeff Gerth
    1999   "China Stole Nuclear Secrets from Los Alamos, U.S. Officials
            Say." *New York Times*, March 6.
Risen, James, and David Johnston
    1999   "U.S. Will Broaden Investigation of China Nuclear Secrets Case.
            New York Times, September 23.
Rivera, Jose A.
    1998   *Acequia Culture: Water, Land and Community in the Southwest.*
            Albuquerque: University of New Mexico Press.
Rodriguez, Sylvia
    1996   *The Matachines Dance: Ritual Symbolics and Interethnic Rela-
            tions in the Upper Rio Grande Valley.* Albuquerque: University
            of New Mexico Press.
    1987   "Land, Water, and Ethnic Identity in Taos." In Charles L. Briggs,
            and John R. Van Ness (eds.). *Land, Water, and Culture:
            New Perspectives on Hispanic Land Grants.* Pp. 313–403.
            Albuquerque: University of New Mexico Press.
    1986   "The Hispano Homeland Debate." Working Paper Series
            No. 17. Stanford: Stanford Center for Chicano Research.
Rogers, Margaret Anne
    1977   *History and Environmental Setting of LASL Near-Surface Land*

Disposal Facilities for Radioactive Wastes (Areas A, B, C, D, E, F, G, and T) (LA-6848 MS, Vol. 1). Los Alamos: Los Alamos Scientific Laboratory.

Rogin, Michael
　1987　*Ronald Reagan, The Movie, and Other Episodes in Political Demonology*. Berkeley: University of California Press.

Romero, Hilario
　1995　"Los Alamos, D.C.: Growing Up Under a Cloud of Secrecy." *Race, Poverty and the Environment* 5 (3–4): 9–10.

Rosenbaum, Robert J.
　1981　*Mexicano Resistance in the Southwest: The Sacred Right of Self-Preservation*. Austin: University of Texas Press.

Rosenthal, Debra
　1990　*At the Heart of the Bomb: The Dangerous Allure of Weapons Work*. New York: Addison Wesley Publishing.

Rothman, Hal K.
　1992　*On Rims and Ridges: The Los Alamos Area Since 1880*. Lincoln: University of Nebraska Press.

Rudnick, Lois Palken
　1996　*Utopian Vistas: The Mabel Dodge Luhan House and the American Counterculture*. Albuquerque: University of New Mexico Press.

Russell, Edmund
　2001　*War and Nature: Fighting Humans and Insects with Chemicals From World War 1 to Silent Spring*. Cambridge: Cambridge University Press.

Sagan, Carl
　1983　"Nuclear War and Climatic Catastrophe: Some Policy Implications." *Foreign Affairs* 62(2): 257–92.

Sahlins, Peter
　1989　*Boundaries: The Making of France and Spain in the Pyrenees*. Berkeley: University of California Press.

Sanchez, George I.
　1967 [1940]　*Forgotten People: A Study of New Mexicans*. Albuquerque: Calvin Horn Publisher.

Sandia National Laboratory
　1993　*Stockpile Life Study*. Albuquerque: Sandia National Laboratory.

Sando, Joe S.
　1998　*Pueblo Profiles: Cultural Identity through Centuries of Change*. Santa Fe: Clear Light Publishers.
　1992　*Pueblo Nations: Eight Centuries of Pueblo Indian History*. Santa Fe: Clear Light Publishers.
　1982　*Nee Hemish: A History of Jemez Pueblo*. Albuquerque: University of New Mexico Press.

Scarry, Elaine
　1985　*The Body in Pain: The Making and Unmaking of the World*. New York: Oxford University Press.

Schell, Jonathan
　1982　*The Fate of the Earth*. New York: Knopf.

Scheper-Hughes, Nancy
    1987   "The Best of Two Worlds, The Worst of Two Worlds: Reflections on Culture and Field Work Among the Rural Irish and Pueblo Indians." *Comparative Studies in Society and History* 29(1): 56–75.

Schull, William J.
    1995   *Effects of Atomic Radiation: A Half-Century of Studies From Hiroshima and Nagasaki.* New York: Wiley-Liss.

Schwartz, Stephen (ed.)
    1998   *Atomic Audit: The Costs and Consequences of U.S. Nuclear Weapons Since 1940.* Washington, D.C.: Brookings Institution Press.

Sebeok, Thomas A.
    1984   *Communication Measures to Bridge Ten Millennia: Technical Report.* Columbus: Office of Nuclear Waste Isolation.

Secretary of Energy Advisory Board
    1995   *Alternative Futures for the Department of Energy National Laboratories.* Washington, D.C.: U.S. Department of Energy.

Select Committee, U.S. House of Representatives (also known as "The Cox Report")
    1999   *Report of the Select Committee on U.S. National Security and Military/Commercial Concerns with the People's Republic of China.* Washington, D.C.: U.S. Government Printing Office.

Shaner, Marja H., and Louis Naranjo Jr.
    1995   *Partnering with Pueblos: Involving American Indians in Environmental Restoration Activities at Los Alamos National Laboratory, New Mexico* (LA UR-95-376). Los Alamos: Los Alamos National Laboratory.

Shapin, Steven
    1994   *A Social History of Truth: Civility and Science in Seventeenth-Century England.* Chicago: University of Chicago Press.

Shapiro, Jerome F.
    2002   *Atomic Bomb Cinema.* New York: Routledge.

Shils, Edward A.
    1996   *The Torment of Secrecy: The Background and Consequences of American Security Policies.* Chicago: Elephant Paperbacks.

Shrader-Frechette, Kristin
    2002   *Environmental Justice: Creating Equality, Reclaiming Democracy.* Oxford: Oxford University Press.

Shroyer, Jo Ann
    1998   *Secret Mesa: Inside Los Alamos National Laboratory.* New York: John Wiley and Sons, Inc.

Shutes, Jeanne, and Jill Mellick
    1996   *The Worlds of P'otsunu: Geronima Cruz Montoya of San Juan Pueblo.* Albuquerque: University of New Mexico Press.

Siegel, James
    1997   *Fetish, Recognition, Revolution.* Princeton: Princeton University Press.

Silko, Leslie Marmon
  1996a   "Interior and Exterior Landscapes: The Pueblo Migration
            Stories." In *Yellow Woman and a Beauty of the Spirit: Essays on
            Native American Life Today*. Pp. 25–47. New York: Simon and
            Schuster.
  1996b   "Fifth World: The Return of Ma ah shra true ee, the Giant
            Serpent." In *Yellow Woman and a Beauty of the Spirit: Essays
            on Native American Life Today*. Pp. 124–34. New York: Simon
            and Schuster.
  1977   *Ceremony*. New York: Viking Press.
Simmel, Georg
  1906   "The Sociology of Secrecy and of Secret Societies." *American
            Journal of Sociology* 11(4): 441–98.
Simmons, Marc
  1974   *Witchcraft in the Southwest: Spanish and Indian Supernatural-
            ism on the Rio Grande*. Lincoln: University of Nebraska Press.
  1972   "Spanish Irrigation Practices in New Mexico." *New Mexico
            Historical Review* 47(2): 135–50.
Slotkin, Richard
  1992   *Gunfighter Nation: The Myth of the Frontier in Twentieth-
            Century America*. New York: Harper Perennial.
Smith, Jas Mercer
  1995   "The SBSS Challenge." *Weapons Insider* 2(4): 1–4.
Smyth, Henry DeWolf
  1947   *Atomic Energy for Military Purposes: The Official Report on
            the Development of the Atomic Bomb under the Auspices of the
            United States Government, 1940–1945*. Princeton: Princeton
            University Press.
Soil Conservation Service
  1939   *Tewa Basin Study*. Volume One: *The Indian Pueblos*.
            Albuquerque: Soil Conservation Service, Region Eight,
            Division of Economic Surveys.
Solnit, Rebecca
  1994   *Savage Dreams: A Journey into the Hidden Wars of the
            American West*. San Francisco: Sierra Club Books.
Solomon, Fredric, and Robert Q. Marston (eds.)
  1986   *The Medical Implications of Nuclear War*. Washington, D.C.:
            National Academy Press.
SouthWest Organizing Project
  1993   *Report on the Interfaith Hearing on Toxic Poisoning in Com-
            munities of Color*. Albuquerque: SouthWest Organizing Project.
Spicer, Edward
  1962   *Cycles of Conquest: The Impact of Spain, Mexico, and the
            United States on the Indians of the Southwest, 1533–1960*.
            Tucson: Arizona University Press.
Stang, John
  1998   "Tainted Tumbleweeds Concern Hanford." *Tri-city Herald*.
            December 27.

Steele, Thomas J., and Rowena A. Rivera
  1985 *Penitente Self-Government: Brotherhoods and Councils,*
        1797–1947. Santa Fe: Ancient City Press.
Steen, Charlie R.
  1977 *Pajarito Plateau Archaeological Survey and Excavations*
        (LASL-77-4). Los Alamos: Los Alamos Scientific Laboratory.
Stein, Gertrude
  1947 "Reflections on the Atomic Bomb." *Yale Poetry Review* 7: 3–4.
Stephanson, Anders
  1995 *Manifest Destiny: American Expansion and the Empire of Right.*
        New York: Hill and Wang.
Stephens, Sharon
  2002 "Bounding Uncertainty: The Post-Chernobyl Culture of
        Radiation Protection Experts." In Susanna M. Hoffman and
        Anthony Oliver-Smith (eds.). *Catastrophe and Culture: The*
        Anthropology of Disaster. Pp. 91–111. Santa Fe: School of
        American Research.
Stewart, Kathleen
  1996 *A Space on the Side of the Road: Cultural Poetics in an "Other"*
        America. Princeton: Princeton University Press.
Henry L. Stimson Center
  1998 *Public Attitudes on Nuclear Weapons: An Opportunity for*
        Leadership. Washington, D.C.: Henry L. Stimson Center. Avail-
        able on the World Wide Web at http://www.stimson.org/ policy.
Stirling, Matthew W.
  1942 *Origin Myth of Acoma and Other Records.* Bureau of American
        Ethnology, Bulletin 135. Washington, D.C.: U.S. Government
        Printing Office.
Stober, Dan
  2000 "How FBI Wiretap Launched Spy Case." *San Jose Mercury*
        News, April 13.
  1999 "Nuclear Secrets: Steal This!" *Bulletin of the Atomic Scientists*
        55(4): 14–16.
Stober, Dan, and Ian Hoffman
  2001 *A Convenient Spy: Wen Ho Lee and the Politics of Nuclear*
        Espionage. New York: Simon and Schuster.
Stoffle, Richard W., and Michael J. Evans
  1988 "American Indians and Nuclear Waste Storage: The Debate at
        Yucca Mountain, Nevada." *Policy Studies Journal* 16(4): 751–67.
Stone, Paul
  1999a "Research Buzzing about Possible Use of Bees to Detect Land
         Mines." *American Forces Press Service* (July): 1. Available at
         http://www.dod.gov/news/Jul1999/n07281999_9907281.
         html (accessed October 15, 2003).
  1999b "Creature Feature Possible Defense Applications." *American*
         Forces Press Service (July): 1. Available at http://www.dod.
         gov/specials/bees/creatures.html (accessed October 15, 2003).

Suina, Joseph
   1999   "From Crossbows and Arrows to the Atomic Bomb." *Director's Colloquium Series*, Los Alamos National Laboratory, June 15.
Sweet, Jill D.
   1989   "Burlesquing 'The Other' in Pueblo Performance." *Annals of Tourism Research* 16: 62–75.
Swentzell, Rina Naranjo
   1982   "A Comparison of Basic Incompatibilities Between European/American Educational Philosophies and Traditional Pueblo World-view and Value System." Ph.D. dissertation, Department of American Studies, University of New Mexico.
Szasz, Ferenc Morton
   1984   *The Day The Sun Rose Twice: The Story of the Trinity Site Nuclear Explosion, July 16, 1945*. Albuquerque: University of New Mexico Press.
Taussig, Michael
   1999   *Defacement: Public Secrecy and the Labor of the Negative*. Stanford: Stanford University Press.
Taylor, Bryan C.
   1996a   "Revis(it)ing Nuclear History: Narrative Conflict at the Bradbury Science Museum." *Studies in Cultures, Organizations, and Societies* 1: 1–27.
   1996b   "Make Bomb, Save World: Reflections on Dialogic Nuclear Ethnography." *Journal of Contemporary Ethnography* 25(1): 120–43.
Taylor, Theodore B.
   2001   *Change of Heart*. Available on the World Wide Web at http://www.tbtaylor.com (accessed March 3, 2001).
Teller, Edward
   1993   "The Laboratory of the Atomic Age." *Los Alamos Science* 21: 32–37.
Theroux, Marcel
   2001   "Chernobyl: Alive in the Dead Zone." *Travel and Leisure*, May 2001. Available at http://webcenter.travel.travelandleisure.netscape.com (accessed July 10, 2004).
Tijerina, Reies Lopez
   1978   *Mi Lucha Por La Tierra*. Mexico City: Fondo De Cultura Economica.
Titus, A. Constandina
   1986   *Bombs in the Backyard: Atomic Testing and American Politics*. Las Vegas: University of Nevada Press.
Traweek, Sharon
   1988   *Beamtimes and Lifetimes: The World of High Energy Physicists*. Cambridge, Mass.: Harvard University Press.
Turco, R. P., O. B. Toon, T. P. Ackerman, J. B. Pollack, and C. Sagan
   1983   "Nuclear Winter: Global Consequences of Multiple Nuclear Explosions." *Science* 222: 1283–92.

Turner, Stansfield
  1997   *Caging the Nuclear Genie: An American Challenge of Global
           Security*. Boulder: Westview Press.
Udall, Stewart L.
  1994   *The Myths of August: A Personal Exploration of Our Tragic
           Cold War Affair with the Atom*. New York: Pantheon Books.
U.S. Atomic Energy Commission (AEC)
  1971   *In the Matter of J. Robert Oppenheimer: Transcripts of a Hear-
           ing before the Personnel Security Board and Texts of Principal
           Documents and Letters*. Cambridge, Mass.: MIT Press.
U.S. Defense Nuclear Agency (DNA)
  1981a   *Plumbbob Series 1957*. Washington, D.C.: U.S. Government
           Printing Office.
  1981b   *Shot Priscilla: A Test of the Plumbbob Series*. Washington,
           D.C.: U.S. Government Printing Office.
  1981c   *Shot Galileo: A Test of the Plumbbob Series*. Washington,
           D.C.: U.S. Government Printing Office.
U.S. Department of Defense (DOD)
  1994   *Nuclear Posture Review*. Washington, D.C.: U.S. Department
           of Defense.
  1957   *Operation Plumbbob: Military Effects Studies*. 31 min. film.
           Washington, D.C.: U.S. Department of Defense.
  1955   *Shot Apple 2: A Test of the TEAPOT Series*. Washington, D.C.:
           Defense Nuclear Agency.
U.S. Department of Energy (DOE)
  2003   Long-Term Stewardship Program mission statement. Available
           at http://lts.apps.em.doe.gov/mission.asp (accessed October 15,
           2003).
  2001   *Long-Term Stewardship Study*. Washington, D.C.: U.S. Govern-
           ment Printing Office.
  2000a   *United States Nuclear Tests: July 1945 through September
           1992* (DOE/NV-209, Rev. 15). Washington, D.C.: U.S. Govern-
           ment Printing Office.
  2000b   *Final Report: Task Force against Racial Profiling*. Available
           on the World Wide Web at http://home.doe.gov/news/docs/
           rprofilerpt.pdf (no longer publicly available as of September 11,
           2001).
  2000c   *Paths to Closure: Status Report*. Available on the World
           Wide Web at http://www.em.doe.gov/closure/fy2000/
           statusrpt.html.
  1999a   *"Drawing Back the Curtain of Secrecy": Restricted Data
           Declassification Decisions, 1946 to the Present* (RDD-5).
           Washington, D.C.: U.S. Government Printing Office.
  1999b   "DOE Definition of 'Close and Continuing' Contact with Sensi-
           tive Country Foreign Nationals." Los Alamos: Los Alamos
           National Laboratory.
  1999c   "Polygraph Examination Regulation: Final Rule." *Federal
           Register* 64(242): 70961–80.

1999d   Public Hearing at Los Alamos National Laboratory concerning
        Polygraph Examination Regulations. Transcript available
        on the World Wide Web at http://home.doe.gov/news/
        9–17hear.pdf. (no longer publicly available as of
        September 11, 2001).

1999e   *Stockpile Stewardship Plan: Executive Overview, Fiscal Year
        2000.* Washington, D.C.: DOE Office of Defense Programs.

1999f   *From Cleanup to Stewardship* (DOE/EM-0466). Washington,
        D.C.: U.S. Government Printing Office.

1998a   *Stockpile Stewardship Plan: Second Annual Update (FY 1999).*
        Washington, D.C.: DOE Office of Defense Programs.

1998b   *Draft Site-Wide Environmental Impact Statement for Contin-
        ued Operation of the Los Alamos National Laboratory* (DOE/
        EIS-0238). Albuquerque: U.S. Department of Energy.

1997   *Linking Legacies: Connecting the Cold War Nuclear Weapons
        Production Processes to Their Environmental Consequences*
        (DOE/EM-0319). Washington, D.C.: DOE Office of Environ-
        mental Management.

1996   *Taking Stock: A Look at the Opportunities and Challenges
        Posed by Inventories from the Cold War Era* (DOE/EM-0275).
        Washington, D.C.: DOE Office of Environmental Management.

1995a   *Estimating the Cold War Mortgage* (DOE/EM-0232).
        Washington, D.C.: DOE Office of Environmental Management.

1995b   *Closing the Circle on the Splitting of the Atom.* Washington,
        D.C.: DOE Office of Environmental Management.

1995c   *Dual Axis Radiographic Hydrodynamic Test Facility: Final
        Environmental Impact Statement,* 3 vol. (DOE/EIS-0228). Los
        Alamos: U.S. Department of Energy.

1995d   *Alternative Futures for the Department of Energy National
        Laboratories.* Washington, D.C.: U.S. Department of Energy.

1984   *Nuclear Weapons Planning and Acquisitions.* Albuquerque:
        DOE Albuquerque Operations Office.

U.S. Department of Energy, Idaho National Engineering and Environmen-
    tal Laboratory (DOE, INEEL)
1999   "Energy Department, Bureau of Land Management Create
        Sagebrush Steppe Reserve." *News Release,* July 19: 1–2.

U.S. Department of Energy, Los Alamos Area Office (DOE, LAAO)
1999   "Richardson Announces 1,000 Acres at Los Alamos
        National Laboratory to Protect Wildlife." *News Release,*
        October 30: 1–2.

U.S. Department of Energy, Pacific Northwest National Laboratory (DOE,
        PNNL)
1999   "Ecology Reserve: A Haven for Plants and Animals." *Back-
        grounders,* August: 1–2.

U.S. Department of Energy, Savannah River Operation Office (DOE, SROO)
1999   "Department of Energy Teams With State on Dedication and
        Management of 10,000 Acre Crackerneck Wildlife Management
        Area and Ecological Reserve." *News Release,* June 24: 1.

U.S. Government Accounting Office (GAO)

2000   *Radiation Standards: Scientific Basis Inconclusive, and EPA and NRC Disagreement Continues* (GAO/RCED-00-152). Washington, D.C.: U.S. Government Printing Office.

1999a   *Nuclear Weapons: Government Needs to Improve Oversight of $5 Billion Strategic Computing Initiative* (GAO: RCED-99-195). Washington, D.C.: U.S. Government Printing Office.

1999b   *Key Factors Underlying Security Problems at DOE Facilities* (GAO/T-RCED-99-159). Washington, D.C.: U.S. Government Printing Office.

1998   *Defense Spending and Employment: Information Limitations Impede Thorough Assessments* (GAO/NSIAD-98-57). Washington, D.C.: U.S. General Accounting Office.

1994   "Managing DOE: Further Review Needed of Suspensions of Security Clearances for Minority Employees" (GAO/RCED-195-45) (Washington, D.C.: U.S. General Accounting Office, December).

United States of America v. Wen Ho Lee

2000   Order and Judgment. United States Court of Appeals for the Tenth Circuit. (February 29, 2000).

1999a   Indictment. Albuquerque: United States District Court for the District of New Mexico (December 19, 1999).

1999b   Transcript of Proceeding (Bail Hearing). Albuquerque: United States District Court of the District of New Mexico (December 27, 1999).

Usner, Don J.

1995   *Sabino's Map: Life in Chimayo's Old Plaza*. Santa Fe: Museum of New Mexico Press.

Virilio, Paul

1989   *War and Cinema: The Logistics of Perception*. London: Verso.

1986   *Speed and Politics: An Essay on Dromology*. New York: Semiotext(e).

Vrooman, Robert

1999   "Here Is the Complete Text of Robert Vrooman's Statement." *Los Alamos Monitor*, August 19.

Vyner, Henry M.

1988   *Invisible Trauma: The Psychosocial Effects of Invisible Environmental Contaminants*. Lexington, Mass.: Lexington Books.

Wadia, Maneck Sorabji

1957   "Tesuque: A Community Study in Acculturation." Ph.D. dissertation, Indiana University.

Walker, J. Samuel

1999   *Permissible Dose: A History of Radiation Protection in the Twentieth Century*. Berkeley: University of California Press.

Wang, Jessica

1999   *American Science in an Age of Anxiety: Scientists, Anticommunism and the Cold War*. Chapel Hill: University of North Carolina Press.

Weart, Spencer R.
  1988   *Nuclear Fear: A History of Images.* Cambridge, Mass.: Harvard University Press.
Weaver, Jace (ed.)
  1996   *Defending Mother Earth: Native American Perspectives on Environmental Justice.* Maryknoll, N.Y.: Orbis Books.
Weigle, Marta
  1989   "From Desert to Disney World: The Santa Fe Railway and the Fred Harvey Company Display the Indian Southwest." *Journal of Anthropological Research* 45(1): 115–37.
  1976   *Brothers of Light, Brothers of Blood: The Penitentes of the Southwest.* Santa Fe: Ancient City Press.
Weigle, Marta (ed.)
  1975   *Hispanic Villages of Northern New Mexico: A Reprint of the Volume II of the1935 Tewa Basin Study with Supplementary Materials.* Santa Fe: The Lightning Tree.
Weigle, Marta, and Peter White
  1988   *The Lore of New Mexico.* Albuquerque: University of New Mexico Press.
Weingartner, Erich
  1991   *The Pacific: Nuclear Testing and Minorities. A Minority Right Group Report.* London: Minority Rights Group.
Weisgall, Jonathan M.
  1994   *Operation Crossroads: The Atomic Tests at Bikini Atoll.* Annapolis: Naval Institute Press.
  1980   "The Nuclear Nomads of Bikini." *Foreign Policy* 39: 74–98.
Welsome, Eileen
  1999   *The Plutonium Files: America's Secret Medical Experiments in the Cold War.* New York: The Dial Press.
Westphall, Victor
  1983   *Mercedes Reales: Hispanic Land Grants of the Upper Rio Grande Region.* Albuquerque: University of New Mexico Press.
Weunberg, Robert A.
  1998   *One Renegade Cell: How Cancer Begins.* New York: Basic Books.
Whitman, William
  1947   *The Pueblo Indians of San Ildefonso: A Changing Culture.* New York: Columbia University Press.
Williams, Jerry L. (ed.)
  1986   *New Mexico in Maps.* Albuquerque: University of New Mexico Press.
Williams, Robert Chadwell
  1987   *Klaus Fuchs, Atom Spy.* Cambridge, Mass.: Harvard University Press.
Wilson, Chris
  1997   *The Myth of Santa Fe: Creating a Modern Regional Tradition.* Albuquerque: University of New Mexico Press.

Wilson, Rob
 1991 *American Sublime: The Genealogy of a Poetic Genre*. Madison:
   University of Wisconsin Press.
Winkler, Allan M.
 1993 *Life Under A Cloud: American Anxiety About the Atom*.
   Oxford: Oxford University Press.
Wittner, Lawrence S.
 2003 *Toward Abolition: A History of the World Nuclear Disarmament
   Movement 1971 to the Present*. Stanford: Stanford University
   Press.
 1997 *Resisting The Bomb: A History of the World Nuclear Disarma-
   ment Movement 1954–1970*. Stanford: Stanford University Press.
 1993 *One World of None: A History of the World Nuclear Disarmament
   Movement through 1953*. Stanford: Stanford University
   Press.
Wolff, Walter P.
 1984 *A Typical Los Alamos National Laboratory Underground
   Nuclear Test*. Los Alamos: Los Alamos National Laboratory.
Wolfson, Richard
 1991 *Nuclear Choices: A Citizen's Guide to Nuclear Technology*.
   Cambridge, Mass.: MIT Press.
Wyaco, Virgil
 1998 *A Zuni Life: A Pueblo Indian in Two Worlds*. Albuquerque:
   University of New Mexico Press.
Yankelovich, Daniel, Robert Kingston, and Gerald Garvey (eds.)
 1984 *Voter Options on Nuclear Arms Policy: A Briefing Book for the
   1984 Elections*. New York: The Public Agenda Foundation.
Yoneyama, Lisa
 1999 *Hiroshima Traces: Time, Space, and The Dialectics of Memory*.
   Berkeley: University of California Press.
York, Herbert
 1995 "Comprehensive Test-Ban Negotiations." In *Arms and the Physi-
   cist*. Pp. 161–200. Woodbury, N.Y.: American Institute of
   Physics Press.
 1970 *Race to Oblivion: A Participant's View of the Arms Race*.
   New York: Simon and Schuster.
Young, Robert J. C.
 1995 *Colonial Desire: Hybridity in Theory, Culture and Race*.
   New York: Routledge.
Younger, Stephen
 2000 *Nuclear Weapons in the Twenty-First Century*. Los Alamos: Los
   Alamos National Laboratory.
 1999 "Security Immersion Talk." Los Alamos National Laboratory,
   June 21.
Zerriffi, Hisham, and Arjun Makhijani
 1996 *The Nuclear Safety Smokescreen: Warhead Safety and Reliabil-
   ity and the Science Based Stockpile Stewardship Program*.

Washington, D.C.: Institute for Energy and Environmental Research.

Ziegler, Charles, and David Jacobson

1995   *Spying Without Spies: Origins of America's Secret Nuclear Surveillance System.* London: Praeger.

INDEX